This Is a Classic

Literatures, Cultures, Translation

Literatures, Cultures, Translation presents books that engage central issues in translation studies such as history, politics, and gender in and of literary translation, as well as books that open new avenues for study. Volumes in the series follow two main strands of inquiry: one strand brings a wider context to translation through an interdisciplinary interrogation, while the other hones in on the history and politics of the translation of seminal works in literary and intellectual history.

Series Editors

Brian James Baer, Kent State University, USA
Michelle Woods, the State University of New York, New Paltz, USA

Editorial Board

Paul Bandia, Professeur titulaire, Concordia University, Canada, and Senior Fellow, the W.E.B. Du Bois Institute for African American Research, Harvard University, USA
Susan Bassnett, Professor of Comparative Literature, Warwick University, UK.
Leo Tak-hung Chan, Guangxi University, Hong Kong, China
Michael Cronin, Dublin City University, Republic of Ireland
Edwin Gentzler, University of Massachusetts Amherst, USA
Carol Maier, Kent State University, USA
Denise Merkle, Moncton University, Canada
Michaela Wolf, University of Graz, Austria

Volumes in the Series

Translation and the Making of Modern Russian Literature
Brian James Baer

Interpreting in Nazi Concentration Camps
Edited by Michaela Wolf

Exorcising Translation: Towards an Intercivilizational Turn
Douglas Robinson

Literary Translation and the Making of Originals
Karen Emmerich

The Translator on Stage
Geraldine Brodie

Transgender, Translation, Translingual Address
Douglas Robinson

Western Theory in East Asian Contexts: Translation and Translingual Writing
Leo Tak-hung Chan

The Translator's Visibility: Scenes from Contemporary Latin American Fiction
Heather Cleary

The Relocation of Culture: Translations, Migrations, Borders
Simona Bertacco and Nicoletta Vallorani

The Art of Translation in Light of Bakhtin's Re-accentuation
Edited by Slav Gratchev and Margarita Marinova

Migration and Mutation: New Perspectives on the Sonnet in Translation
Edited by Carole Birkan-Berz, Oriane Monthéard, and Erin Cunningham

This Is a Classic: Translators on Making Writers Global
Edited by Regina Galasso

*Language Smugglers: Postlingual Literatures and Translation
within the Canadian Context*
Arianne Des Rochers (forthcoming)

This Is a Classic

Translators on Making Writers Global

Edited by
Regina Galasso

BLOOMSBURY ACADEMIC
NEW YORK • LONDON • OXFORD • NEW DELHI • SYDNEY

BLOOMSBURY ACADEMIC

Bloomsbury Publishing Inc
1385 Broadway, New York, NY 10018, USA
50 Bedford Square, London, WC1B 3DP, UK

BLOOMSBURY, BLOOMSBURY ACADEMIC and the Diana logo are
trademarks of Bloomsbury Publishing Plc

First published in the United States of America 2023

Copyright © Regina Galasso, 2023
Each chapter © Contributors, 2023

Cover design: Eleanor Rose
Cover image © Regina Galasso

All rights reserved. No part of this publication may be reproduced or transmitted in any form or by any means, electronic or mechanical, including photocopying, recording, or any information storage or retrieval system, without prior permission in writing from the publishers.

Bloomsbury Publishing Inc does not have any control over, or responsibility for, any third-party websites referred to or in this book. All internet addresses given in this book were correct at the time of going to press. The author and publisher regret any inconvenience caused if addresses have changed or sites have ceased to exist, but can accept no responsibility for any such changes.

Whilst every effort has been made to locate copyright holders the publishers would be grateful to hear from any person(s) not here acknowledged.

Library of Congress Cataloging-in-Publication Data
Names: Galasso, Regina, editor.
Title: This is a classic : translators on making writers global /
edited by Regina Galasso.
Description: New York: Bloomsbury Academic, 2023. | Series: Literatures, cultures, translation | Includes bibliographical references and index. |
Summary: "Translators reflect on what it means to translate literary classics and canonical texts from a variety of languages into English"–
Provided by publisher.
Identifiers: LCCN 2022031288 (print) | LCCN 2022031289 (ebook) |
ISBN 9781501376917 (hardback) | ISBN 9781501376900 (paperback) |
ISBN 9781501376924 (epub) | ISBN 9781501376931 (pdf) |
ISBN 9781501376948 (ebook other)
Subjects: LCSH: Canon (Literature)–Translations into English–History and criticism. |
Translating and interpreting. | LCGFT: Essays.
Classification: LCC PR131 .T45 2023 (print) | LCC PR131 (ebook) |
DDC 418/.04–dc23/eng/20220921
LC record available at https://lccn.loc.gov/2022031288
LC ebook record available at https://lccn.loc.gov/2022031289

ISBN: HB: 978-1-5013-7691-7
PB: 978-1-5013-7690-0
ePDF: 978-1-5013-7693-1
eBook: 978-1-5013-7692-4

Typeset by Deanta Global Publishing Services, Chennai, India
Printed and bound in Great Britain

To find out more about our authors and books visit www.bloomsbury.com
and sign up for our newsletters.

Contents

Introduction: Literary Classics through Translation
    Regina Galasso   1

Prologue: The Translator's Agency and the Literary Classic Abroad: Emily Dickinson's Voyage to Brazilliput
    Adalberto Müller   25

1. Chinese Classics: The Commentarial Tradition
    Sabina Knight with Kidder Smith   39

2. Happy Hour Homer: On Translating and Performing the *Iliad* Live in a Bar
    Lynn Kozak   51

3. Today in the Temple of Language: Translating Dante
    Mary Jo Bang   59

4. True Confessions of a Literary Translator
    Arvind Krishna Mehrotra   69

5. What Is a Classic? The Case of Esperanto
    Humphrey Tonkin   79

6. The Russian Canon in Retranslation
    Marian Schwartz   101

7. Translating Yiddish Classics: Redefining Tradition in Modern Yiddish Literature through the Prism of Kadya Molodowsky
    Chantal Ringuet   111

8. Víctor Català's *A Film (3,000 meters):* Translating a Catalan Classic
    Peter Bush   125

9. Translation as Storytelling
    Susan Bernofsky   137

10. In Terror and Pandemic: Translating García Lorca's *Poet in New York*
    Mark Statman   147

11. Stopping at the Surface: Translating Clarice Lispector's *The Besieged City* and *A Breath of Life*
    Johnny Lorenz   157

12	Tanizaki's *The Key* in Translation: Will You Still Need Me, Will You Still Read Me, When I'm (Over) Sixty-Four?	
	Anna Zielinska-Elliott	167
13	An Essay on Nichita Stănescu: The Classic and the Personal in Translation	
	Sean Cotter	179
14	From Arabic to English, What Is a Classic?	
	Michelle Hartman	193
15	Translating a Classic into the Future: *Tómas Jónsson—Bestseller*	
	Lytton Smith	203
16	*Love, Anger, Madness* Making a Classic: Amplifying Marie Vieux-Chauvet's Haitian Trilogy	
	Carolyn Shread	215
17	What Besides Words?: Translating Bilge Karasu's *A Long Day's Evening*	
	Aron Aji	237
18	Nonsense in a Given Direction: Translating the Timelessness of Marguerite Duras	
	Emma Ramadan	249
19	"Sentence" as Lifeline: Translating David Albahari's Novels	
	Ellen Elias-Bursać	257

Epilogue: Matching Socks in the Dark; or How to Translate from Languages You Don't Know
    Ilan Stavans   267
A Translation Experiment: Kleptomaniac Classic: *Ramona*
    Esther Allen and Sean Cotter   273

Notes on Contributors   309
Index   315

Introduction

Literary Classics through Translation

Regina Galasso

In the Classroom

Thursday, March 12, 2020, was the last day I met with my students in person before Covid-19 shut things down. The course was "Hispanic New York." We were studying "Vuelta de paseo" from *Poeta en Nueva York* (1940) by Federico García Lorca (1898–1936). The language of *Poeta en Nueva York* is simple, but the combinations of words can distance the reader from the text. Colleagues who teach Lorca talk about generating more enthusiasm for Lorca's work among students. I recommend they read multiple translations of a single Lorca poem to lead students to engage more actively with the text. This activity is not reserved for students and professors; anyone can read Lorca through translation.

On that day, March 12, 2020, my students and I were reading Lorca's "Vuelta de paseo" in addition to three published English translations by Ben Belitt, Greg Simon and Steven F. White, and Pablo Medina and Mark Statman (published in 1955, 1998 [revised in 2013], and 2008, respectively). Lorca's short poem presents a confined space with an overwhelming verticality that arises from a defined base filled with life-deficient little figures. "[A]rquitectura extrahumana y ritmo furioso. Geometría y angustia" are the words Lorca used to describe the two elements the traveler experiences in the big city (qtd. in Díez de Revenga 41). Dinitia Smith, presenting Lorca in English translation, uses the words "[e]xtrahuman architecture, its furious rhythm, its geometry and anguish" (Smith n.p.). I reminded my students that this poem opens *Poeta en Nueva York*, a collection of poems written mostly in 1929 by a young Lorca in New York. But now, what stood out was not the poem's presentation of the city space, but the suddenness of being struck by something new and big; the poem's first and last lines are "Asesinado por el cielo" and "¡Asesinado por el cielo!," respectively. In the English translations, these lines are "Heaven-murdered one" (qtd. in Smith), "Cut down by the sky" (Simon and White 7), and "Murdered by the sky" (Medina and Statman

5). We lingered in a discussion about the poet encountering something never experienced before with no way out.

It was our best class of the semester. I don't know if it's because we sensed this would be our last day together in anticipation of the official university news that we wouldn't return to campus after the upcoming spring break, or if it's because of something in Lorca's work. Regardless, the strength and established durability of Lorca's poem, the existence of multiple translations, and the inspiration from the previous translators all cleared and sharpened our critical eyes.

About nine months later, to end a full fall semester of teaching and learning remotely, I asked the students in my introductory translation course to translate "Vuelta de paseo." I didn't share existing translations of the poem with them, as I wanted their translations to be fresh. Among the twenty-something students in the class, several of them translated "asesinado por el cielo" as "killed by the sky." None of the previous translators of the published translations of "Vuelta de paseo" had made this choice—"Murdered by the sky" (Medina and Statman 5), "Cut down by the sky" (Simon and White 7), and "Heaven-murdered one" (Belitt qtd. in Smith n.p.), yes, but never "Killed." My students are confident about their developing language and translation skills, but I needed to go to Google Translate to see if it was spitting out "killed" for "asesinado," in case that would explain why many students chose this word. No. Google Translate, at least on my computer, on the day I searched, offered "murdered." When these students from fall 2020 translated this poem, Covid-19 had been part of their lives for about nine months. And by this time, many of them had a loved one who had suffered from the virus. I never asked if any of them knew someone who was killed by the virus. My students also felt a dramatic loss because they had to suddenly give up how they were living. If the virus didn't literally kill a loved one, it killed their way of life, and they were dealing with it. "Killed by the sky" is a fitting late 2020 translation of Lorca's poem, written almost a century earlier.

I open with this anecdote to illustrate what the considerations of literary classics through translation offers in the physical or remote classroom and beyond. While we read texts in translation, that experience is enriched if we read them through the lens of translation—tuning into the possibilities of the *in*. Reading texts with an awareness of translation enlightens and enriches our experiences. And because literary classics often invite further translations, we can understand our times and make the text and the time our own through translation. This volume presents what there is to learn about literary classics through translation.

My students provided further inspiration for this book. I teach a literary translation workshop for students working on combinations of Catalan,

English, Portuguese, and Spanish. In the introduction to her translation project, one of my students, who asked to remain anonymous, wrote: "In my translation, I tried to emphasize the fact that the text is still accessible in the twenty-first century, much like Shakespeare's works, if it can be understood as something other than a 'classic,' a descriptor that makes it difficult for contemporary readers to find it welcoming and worth reading." First, I was thrilled by the student's efforts to make her translation accessible to contemporary readers. Then, I was amused by her definition of a classic: "A descriptor that makes it difficult for contemporary readers to find it welcoming and worth reading." Some students are turned off by the term "classic." I wondered what classics they are reading, how these classics are presented to them, and what translation's role is in their selection of which version of a given literary classic they read.

Another student gave me some answers. Chatting before class one day, she told me she was reading Gustave Flaubert's *Madame Bovary* (1856) for another class—a French class. She was reading it in English with the professor's permission. She didn't like it very much. She didn't know which English translation she was reading other than "the one available for free on the internet," and her professor didn't care which English translation it was. I didn't know which English translation of *Madame Bovary* she was reading, but I suspected it wasn't the 2011 Lydia Davis translation, published by Penguin. Soon after, we discovered she was reading the Eleanor Marx-Aveling translation from 1886. I gave her a copy of Davis's translation and recommended she try reading this one if her professor didn't mind. Not long after, she reported that she was having a greatly improved experience with *Madame Bovary*. She was enjoying it. She wanted to read it. This doesn't mean that Davis's translation is better than Marx-Aveling's. It all depends on what the reader is looking for. For this student, a more contemporary translation as an introduction to this literary classic was more suitable for the moment. It's possible that Davis's translation will spark such an interest in *Madame Bovary* that this young reader will one day read another English translation of Flaubert's novel. She may return to Marx-Aveling's translation. Literary classics in translation have the potential to lead readers to more translations.

My student's experience is not uncommon. I've heard of other university students reading a book in English, in translation, with no care for which translation they read. What's more, sometimes the word "translation" is never used. Sometimes there is no differentiation between books in English and books in translation (Grossman, *Why* 27). In *Why Translation Matters* (2010), Edith Grossman discusses how English departments declare "a monopoly on the teaching of what they choose to call world literature or humanities, putting together lists of readings that include a large number of works in translation" (27). The consequences of such a move mean that "in the process foreign-language departments and their teachers of literature, the ones with real expertise in the works studied, are effectively snubbed" (27). These texts don't belong in any single university department, but the cultures in which translated texts originate and circulate should be acknowledged, as their move to English does not mean they've abandoned their "foreign-language" origins. The presentation of texts in translation should benefit from a variety of multilingual and multicultural angles.

My students have also taught me that some literary classics are such a part of the literary landscape that we forget that they ever needed a translator if their language of origin is one we cannot read. Bright students, literature majors, find out in my class that *Don Quixote* was first written in Spanish, as their first exposure to the book was in English. They are initially surprised that a work so grand was first born in another language. They report that they had never thought about it and that no educator had yet presented the book, or any book, as a translation. Even in casual conversations I am reminded that some highly educated and cultured regular readers of literature haven't yet dedicated time to thinking about the fact that when they read a book by Haruki Murakami, for example, in English, they're reading words selected by a translator.

Another student reported that in his high school English class, he and his classmates read the English translation *Chronicle of a Death Foretold* by Gregory Rabassa (1922–2016) of Gabriel García Márquez's *Crónica de una muerte anunciada*. The translator's name was never mentioned in the classroom. He, as the only Spanish-speaker in the class, was asked to also read García Márquez's short story and talk about the differences with the class. While there was acknowledgment that *Chronicle of a Death Foretold* was first written in Spanish, the broad task of addressing the differences in the two versions gives the bilingual student not only more work but an introduction to translation without guidance; this task overlooks the remarkable complexities of translation. Translation makes everything different. Lawrence Venuti reminds us of that with the title of his book, *Translation Changes Everything: Theory and Practice* (2013). Translation not only changes everything, but, during and through that change, translation also challenges everything. Translation challenges the translator's knowledge, creativity, and own experiences and decisions.

The treatment of translations in US classrooms isn't news to translators based in the United States or those translating into English. However, the flurry of the abovementioned examples came to me in a short period of time and led to the compilation of this collection for my students, my colleagues, and readers of literature, especially for those developing their sense of translation. If literary classics—literary texts that attract notable attention either because they're on a course reading list or because they're part of an individual's must-read list—can be recognized as translations and cared for as translations, these practices might carry over into other choices about reading that would favor a stronger culture of and increased support for translation.

This Is a Classic

This Is a Classic: Translators on Making Writers Global continues the work of literary translators, educators, scholars, and others who have initiated shifts in the treatment of literary classics in translation and translated literature in general. In doing so, this volume doesn't offer a single definition of a literary classic. Instead, it departs from the idea that classics are classics because a stakeholder—writer, translator, agent, publisher, professor, publication, influential reader—uses the four short words "this is a classic" to describe a literary text.

These four words in relation to a given book elicit a range of responses: from shame that we have never read or finished reading the book, to increased pressure to read it and the desire to reread it, to doubt that it is a classic, and disagreement because we don't like this label and know that because that book achieved such a status might mean that another one didn't. In some cases, we know details of a literary classic without ever having read it, or we only saw the movie, if there is one. The poet, essayist, and author Elisa Gabbert in her *Paris Review* column "Mess With a Classic" "revisits canonical works of literature and addresses the anxiety of confronting the art of the past (and the past in general)" (n.p.). While Gabbert brings attention to literary classics in popular discourse and settings, recognizing feelings and experiences as readers, she mostly focuses on US classics, occasionally mentioning an international classic, with no engagement with translation's role in giving the English-language audience access to those classics.

Dismissing translation and translators from a discussion about a literary classic suggests that a work that is a classic in one language will remain a classic in translation and vice versa. In other words, it promotes the idea that translation or translators have no role in the existence of literary classics. Failure to acknowledge a work as a translation ignores translators' contributions to making writers global. Without translators, writers would only be available to readers who read the language in which they write, and readers could only read books in the languages they know. Literature would not have the ability to move around the globe.

Goethe's 1827 term *Weltliteratur*, which began to circulate in 1835, after the poet's death, has been used to refer to literary works that travel. David Damrosch in *What Is World Literature?* (2003) "take[s] world literature to encompass all literary works that circulate beyond their cultural origin, either in translation, or in their original language.... In its most expansive sense, world literature could include any work that has ever reached beyond its home base" (4). With a "huge corpus of works" (4), Damrosch clarifies that there is not a single set canon (5) of world literature, nor is there a "single way of reading [that] can be appropriate to all texts, or even to any one text at all times" (5). Variability as a "leading characteristic of world literature" (281) manifests itself in several ways, including the expectation that "different readers will be obsessed with different constellations of texts" (Damrosch 281).

An alternative subtitle to this volume could be "Translators on the Making of World Literature." Despite the openness and variability associated with world literature as presented by Damrosch, I've opted to emphasize the participation of translators in the literary ecosystem. Writers need translators, in most cases, if their writing is to go beyond its origin. Publishers need translators. Readers need translators. Global presents a perspective while world literature has the potential to indicate a landing pad. In North America, world literature was long defined "as an established canon of European masterpieces" ("What Is World Literature?"). What is more, as Edith Grossman notes in the earlier quote, there is debate over where world literature belongs in university departments. The title of Damrosch's recent book *Comparing the Literatures: Literary Studies in a Global Age* (2022) excludes world literature. "Translators on Making Writers Global" attempts to invite readers and their curiosities about literary classics in translation, and to communicate that their destination is open.

This volume magnifies translation's role in the making of literary classics and presents translators' expertise and insight on how classics get defined according to language pairs and contexts. Each chapter is authored by a literary translator, contributing to existing efforts to recognize translators. The social media campaign #NametheTranslator, started with the help of Helen Wang, responds to reviewers' and marketers' tendency to omit the name of the translator, only mentioning the original author of a given work. The emergence of translator studies, a scholarly effort to humanize translation studies, "does not seek to supplant translation studies but wants to use the personal perspectives of translators to confirm, correct or revitalize our current understanding of translation and translators" (22) as emphasized by Klaus Kaindl in his introduction to *Literary Translator Studies* (2021). Esther Allen and Susan Bernofsky's edited volume *In Translation: Translators on Their Work and What It Means* (2013), which includes perspectives on translation by translators, is a solid contribution to Literary Translator Studies.

In addition to its contribution to translator studies, *This Is a Classic* expands the bibliography of scholarship on the links of translation and literary classics. *Translation and the Classic: Identity as Change in the History of Culture* (2008), edited by Alexandra Lianeri and Vanda Zajko, appeals principally to classicists while also reaching non-specialist readers with chapters focused on what a classic is, how texts become classics, and translation's role in determining a classic. Among the theoretical pieces is Lawrence Venuti's "Translation, Interpretation, Canon Formation," which addresses the classics' relationship to canonicity. Edith Hall and Henry Stead further connect the classics to canon formation in the first part, "Canons, Media, and Genres," of their co-authored *A People's History of Classics: Class and Greco-Roman Antiquity in Britain and Ireland, 1689 to 1939* (2020). In its entirety, their nearly 700-page book zooms in on a select region to explore working-class engagements with classical sources from Greece and Rome. Continuing in the line of how texts in translation impact culture, *Key Cultural Texts in Translation* (2018), edited by Kirsten Malmkjær, Adriana Serban, and Fransiska Louwagie, presents a range of studies on a variety of languages, cultures, and media. Outstanding examples of monographs that address translation's role in the making of authors and national canons are Michelle Woods's *KafKa Translated: How Translators Have Shaped Our Reading of Kafka* (2013) and Brian James Baer's *Translation and the Making of Modern Russian Literature* (2015). Baer and Woods further support scholarship that places translation in a wider context and highlights the translation roots of seminal works as the series editors of Literatures, Cultures, Translation, to which *This Is a Classic* belongs. Also part of the book series is Karen Emmerich's *Literary Translation and the Making of Originals* (2017), which examines some of the key topics addressed in this volume, including translation's relationship with national and international canons, and how marketplace culture impacts translation and translators.

Different from these publications, *This Is a Classic* prioritizes the translator-centered approach to provide greater access to translators' knowledge, skills, creativity, and relationships with the texts they translate from, the authors whose works they translate, and the translations they make. This volume's presentation of the range of translators, languages, and time periods covering classical to modern classics, while opening avenues for the consideration of future classics, aims to not only be a resource for scholars, students, and translators but also a type of reference book for anyone who wants to read themselves around the globe with this book as a guide and companion.

Why Do It Again

What leads translators to translate a literary classic, especially one that has been translated over and over again? Laurie Patton made the 251st translation of the Sanskrit classic *The Bhagavad Gita*, published by Penguin Classics in 2008. In a 2020 conversation, "Untranslating the Classics," Patton responds to the question "why do that?" by sharing that there is no intellectual reason, but there are generational ones. For instance, she wanted to introduce "one" over the gendered pronoun "him," to focus on the poetic simplicity that was not present in other existing English translations, and to use concrete language. Most translators would agree with Patton that new translations are initiated by translators to "give the world a very small alternative to the many other wonderful translations that [are] out there" ("Untranslating").

There's no single answer to the question *why translate literary classics?* The translators of this volume agree that we shouldn't look for a definitive translation of a classic, nor should we think of a subsequent translation as a substitution; a translation is an alternative, as Patton states. Pablo Medina and Mark Statman didn't translate Lorca's *Poeta en Nueva York* in its entirety into English because they wanted to replace, correct, or compete with Simon and White's, Belitt's, or Rolfe Humphries's translations. In fact, when I interviewed Statman for *Translation Review* in 2015, he commented that there were not enough translations of *Poeta en Nueva York* (Galasso 3). Instead, their translation was motivated by the need to translate this collection of poetry for themselves, for a wounded New York, and for the time in which the translation was created and published.

Nor did Edith Grossman think that her translation of *Don Quijote* would replace any of the existing twenty-something English translations of Cervantes's work, ranging from the early seventeenth century to the early twenty-first century. Grossman claims that, before she started translating *Don Quijote*, she had only read one English translation, that of Samuel Putman from 1949 (Conversation). As primarily a translator of contemporary Latin American literature, Grossman was surprised when a publisher first approached her to make the translation he wanted to publish. Publishers initiate a new translation of a classic for a variety of reasons, ranging from the expiration of a copyright to the desire to join the list of publishers having their own translation of a literary classic.

Beowulf, a poem with "many translations out there, enough that you could read one a day for a month and not repeat" (Headley x), was recently translated by Maria Dahvana Headley, "a novelist, interested in rendering the story continuously and clearly, while also creating a text that feels as bloody and juicy as [she] think[s] it ought to feel" (Headley xvi). In her introduction to *Beowulf*, a "new translation," as stated on the book's cover, she invites her audience to read other translations: "It is both pleasurable and desirable to read more than one translation of this poem, because when it comes to translating *Beowulf*, there is no sacred clarity. What the translated text says is a matter of study, interpretation, and poetic leaps of faith. Every translator translates this poem differently. That is part of its glory" (xv). A new translation offers an additional seat at the "the banquet table[s]" (Headley xv) of existing translations with the potential to transform the dynamics of all the relationships at the entire table.

When multiple translations of a literary classic exist, readers often wonder about the role of the existing translations in the making of more translations? Grossman says that "despite the dynasty of [*Don Quixote*] translations, [she] really doesn't know anything about it" (Conversation). Grossman, when she started the translation, even made a deliberate decision not to look at anyone else's English translation of *Don Quijote* in order to determine what the voice should be in her own translation. Headley shares in her introduction to her translation that she consulted other English translations throughout the making of her translation of *Beowulf*. Marta Rebón, a translator of several Russian literary classics into Catalan and Spanish, consults the available versions in the languages she knows, a reminder that translators, although moving a text from one language to another one, jump to other languages as resources along the way (qtd. in Gascón n.p.). Javier Calvo's response to the frequent question of how to translate a word or phrase, "No hay reglas, solamente casos," is helpful to keep in mind regarding other questions about translation (9). Calvo says that there aren't rules, just the circumstances that guide translators when they translate a given text. *Literary Retranslation in Context* (2017), edited by Susanne M. Cadera and Andrew Samuel Walsh, examines retranslations and the corresponding historical, cultural, and social contexts with a focus on ideology, censorship, and reception in the case of peninsular Spanish.

Even if translators wish to remain alone with the literary classics they translate, the world that surrounds a literary classic is hard to ignore. Grossman confesses that she felt terror and huge excitement to take on the *Don Quijote* translation project (Conversation). Murakami, when he was in his late thirties, told people that he was waiting until he turned sixty to translate F. Scott Fitzgerald's *The Great Gatsby* (169), the book that has meant the most to him (172). He thought that by sixty his "skill would have improved to the point where [he] could do the job properly" (169). Eventually, he couldn't wait until he was sixty and gave in three years ahead of schedule. He was translating a work he had "long dreamed of putting [his] hand to" (170), a project that would be "a heavy undertaking" (173). Despite the planning and excitement associated with the translation of a classic, a new translation is still not set up to blow other translations out of the water. New translations are meant to "refresh" literary classics, "wash them anew" (Murakami 170).

On Retranslation

Some scholars have understood the multiplicity of translations of literary classics by engaging with the contested term "retranslation." Scholars have posited different definitions as to what constitutes a retranslation. Koskinen and Paloposki suggest it's chronological: "retranslation (as a product) denotes a second or later translation of a single source text into the same target language" (294). They also see retranslation as a process "that occurs over a period of time, but in practice, simultaneous or near-simultaneous translations also exist, making it sometimes hard or impossible to classify one as the first translation and the other as a second translation" (Koskinen and Paloposki 294). Other scholars suggest different ontologies. For Lawrence Venuti some texts carry an inherent retranslatability because of hermeneutic ambiguities or possibilities ("Retranslations" 96–7). Others argue that indirect or relay translations, when a text gets translated into one language from the translation of the same text into another language, are retranslations. Retranslation can also be used to refer to the same text translated into the same language but for different markets, such as the case with the British and the US markets, for example.

While "retranslations help texts achieve the status of a classic, and the status of a classic often promotes further retranslations" (Koskinen and Paloposki 295), retranslation should not be understood as an early requirement for a literary classic. In their contributions to this volume, Sean Cotter and Michelle Hartman note that some languages have a paucity of retranslated literary works in English. Time will tell how many translations are made of a single text. The more space readers and the market make for literature in translation, the more translations we'll have in circulation. It is also necessary to acknowledge that the quantity or success of retranslations of literary classics is not indicative of the literary work's status as a classic in the language it was translated from, such as the case of *A Thousand and One Nights* in Arabic, as Hartman addresses in this volume.

Vitor Alevato do Amaral highlights that the widespread notion of retranslation relies on one text going into the same language. In "Broadening the Notion of Retranslation" (2019), he argues to reverse this by encouraging efforts to allow "retranslations to breathe outside the domain of a single language" (244) and to open considerations of retranslation to multilingual practices. In so doing, Alevato do Amaral points out that from an early stage, although it "has been smothered by the quasi-totality of the approaches on the subject" (244), Antoine Berman promoted a broad idea of retranslation as one that happens not only in the space of "the receiving language/culture, but in other languages/cultures" (Berman qtd. in Alevato do Amaral 244). Some translators consult several translations of a given work into several languages as they create their own translations. Sometimes awareness that a work has already been translated without actually seeing or studying the translation is enough to impact a subsequent translation. For Berman, "every translation made after the first translation of a work is therefore a retranslation" (Berman quoted in Alevato do Amaral 245). Alevato do Amaral promotes an expanded understanding of retranslation so that it is not seen as a single bridge from one language to another, but rather as an act that "attract[s] the complex (aesthetic, cultural, historical, linguistic, philosophical, etc.) translation issues" (246).

Additional scholarly efforts to broaden the scope of retranslation include not limiting translation to linguistic source texts, but expanding the field of retranslation to its multimodal dimensions, as explored in a 2020 special issue of *The Translator* edited by Özlem Berk Albachten and Sehnaz Tahir Gürçaglar called *Retranslation, Multidisciplinarity, and Multimodality*. This shift in retranslation studies moves beyond the written work or the printed book, while "foray[ing] into the realms of other disciplines that also offer critical frameworks for the study of the works in question" (Berk Albachten and Tahir Gürçaglar 2).

When Larissa Kyzer introduced the conversation between Laurie Patton, Gopal Sukhu, and Vivek Narayanan titled "Untranslating the Classics," she not only used the term "retranslations" to discuss foundational texts in translation, but she also presented an alternative term, "untranslations," to define these translations as "daring interpretations and creative works in their own right, pushing both reader and translator to look at familiar canonical works with new eyes." A new translation of a literary classic reminds us that familiar titles and texts were once groundbreaking. A new translation makes a literary classic inviting and worth reading once again. All works, as long as they continue to be read, will need to be translated again. In the making, reading, or study of those translations, the "potentially polyglot and intertextual" nature of translation should not be overlooked (Alevato 246). "Retranslation remains a translation, and consequently conveys all problems related to the act of translating," according to Yves Chevrel (12; qtd in Alevato 246). Furthermore, Edwin Gentzler pushes for new horizons for scholarship and ideas about translation. In the final paragraph of *Translation and Rewriting in the Age of Post-Translation Studies* (2017), he says: "translation is one of the most revolutionary acts: bringing across an idea or form from another culture and offering the possibility to *change* people's lives. Because translations themselves are metaphoric, multilingual, and multisensory, so too must translation studies include multisensory forms of analysis" (230).

Translation and Innovation

For some readers, the classics might be seen as an inflexible category. The classics should not be excluded as tools to foster greater inclusion. Through translation or translational acts, the classics can be for everyone. Translators can choose to translate a literary classic because none of the existing translators represent their reading of the book, or because no existing translation allows them to teach the book the way they want to teach it. When I lead short translation activities in the classroom involving a selection from a classic, my students with a solid background in literature feel a strong sense that they can make the classics their own through translation. These activities are also a reminder that the classics are tools for developing writers.

The classics provide a foundation from which writers and translators practice writing in and experimenting with a language. In this volume, Humphrey Tonkin writes about the importance of translating Shakespeare into Esperanto for the establishment and growth of the language. Shakespeare's work gave Esperanto the literary texts through which the language could develop and gain visibility. In 2002, in a radio studio in Barcelona, Ilan Stavans was told by a member of the Real Academia Española that Spanglish, as a language, wouldn't be taken seriously until it produced a novel like *Don Quijote* (Stavans, "In Defense of Spanglish"). After the radio conversation, the editor-in-chief of the literary supplement of Barcelona's *La vanguardia* called Stavans asking him to translate Chapter One, Part One of *Don Quijote* into Spanglish, "the verbal encounter between Anglo and Hispano civilizations" (Stavans, *Spanglish: The Making of a New American Language* 5). He did so, and his translation was first published in *La vanguardia* on July 3, 2002, provoking a "global controversy" (Stavans, "In Defense of Spanglish"). Stavans considered his translation of *Don Quijote* an experiment, but not all readers appreciated the activity and harshly criticized it (Kunz 234). Stavans reported:

"I received death threats from the United States, Spain, Mexico, Colombia, and Argentina. But I was also showered with endless applause" ("In Defense of Spanglish"). Stavans went on to create a graphic novel adaptation of *Don Quijote*, illustrated by Roberto Weil, and continues to translate literary classics into Spanglish. *El Little Príncipe*, his Spanglish translation of Antoine de Saint-Exupéry's *The Little Prince* (1943), was published in 2016, and *Alicia's Adventuras en Wonderlandia*, his Spanglish translation of Lewis Carroll's *Alice's Adventures in Wonderland*, was published in 2021. Like Spanglish, the use of a gender-neutral Spanish in literature elicits various opinions. Ethos Traductora, a publisher in Buenos Aires, published *El principito*, a gender-neutral Spanish translation of *The Little Prince* by Julia Bucci in 2018.

The classics are a vehicle for artistic and literary innovation. Sometimes the publication of a literary classic in translation attracts innovation in other areas beyond the textual and linguistic. For example, in the early 1940s the Illustrated Modern Library was created to provide previously issued Modern Library titles with "original new illustrations," targeting book collectors with a restricted budget (Satterfield 160). According to Jay Satterfield, author of *The World's Best Books: Taste, Culture, and the Modern Library* (2002), these books were meant to be artistic showpieces not "for reading, but as books 'created so that the booklover of modest means may acquire beautifully illustrated and designed books of enduring worth for his library'" (160). The Illustrated Modern Library had the goal of linking "America's foremost living artists" with the "world's great literature" ("Illustrated"). In 1946, the Illustrated Modern Library published the Peter Motteux (1663–1718) English translation *The First Part of the Life and Achievements of the Renowned Don Quixote de la Mancha* and commissioned Salvador Dalí (1904–89) to provide the illustrations. Among the several illustrations of *Don Quixote* that Dalí produced throughout his life, his first are those included in this edition.[1] It is thanks to the publication of a literary classic in translation the publisher's initiative to make beautiful books more affordable that Dalí shared his own interpretations of the work.

Organization and Contributions

David Karashima, in his book *Who We're Reading When We're Reading Murakami* (2020), says "[w]hile Murakami's books have now been published in

---

[1] The Fundación Gala-Salvador Dalí confirms that these *DQ* illustrations were the first by Dalí (Jutge).

more than fifty languages and have sold millions of copies globally, it is easy to forget that the works that a great many of his readers—devotees, fans, critics, and detractors alike—have come to know are also creations of translators, editors, and publishers around the world" (3). In *Kafka Translated: How Translators Have Shaped Our Reading of Kafka* (2013), Michelle Woods points out:

> [w]e read Kafka in translation. Not only, as we might imagine, in a linguistic form of translation, but also in a network of translation: a translation of the man, Franz Kafka, into an icon, a critical translation of his works into various schools of theory, a commercial translation of the man and his work, and popular—screen translations—of his work and himself. (3)

Both Woods and Karashima advocate for more acknowledgment of translation and translators on a text's global impact. Sharing a similar intention, *This Is a Classic* illuminates the overlooked networks that contribute to the making of literary classics through the voices of multiple translators, without whom writers would have a difficult time reaching a global audience. They share their perspectives on what it means to translate an established, becoming, or future literary classic, while considering what the term "classic" means to each translator based on the translator's language pair, experience, knowledge, and creativity. The translators in this volume were brought together because of connections, relationships, availability, and timing. In no way does this collection pretend to be an exhaustive collection of translators of literary classics working today in Anglophone circuits. I hope readers will focus on what is gained with this collection of chapters and not on what is missing, and continue the conversation beyond the covers of this book.

That being said, this volume presents the work of some of today's most accomplished literary translators who translate classics into English or who work closely with translation in the US context. The chapters are organized in chronological order according to the publication date of the main text of each chapter and do not need to be read in any particular order. The languages featured include Chinese, Japanese, ancient Greek, Italian, Hindi, Sanskrit, Russian, Yiddish, Catalan, German, Spanish, Portuguese, Romanian, Arabic, Icelandic, French, Turkish, French, and Serbian. The collection's longer chapters not only allow more space for discussion of some of the lesser-known languages but also highlight the scholarly depth of literary translation. The chapters that discuss moving out of English or among another language pair are purposely included as a reminder to readers that translators of different language pairs share with and learn from each other. Translators, regardless of their working languages, are a resource for one another.

This volume answers many questions about translation and translators and generates more. If this volume convinces readers to get their hands on multiple translations of literary classics, or to read the words of translators of the classics, then it might lead readers to wonder what US literary classics look like in translation. What can we learn about US literature from the translators of US literature? What can we learn about the translations of the works of Walt Whitman, Edgar Allen Poe, Emily Dickinson, William Faulkner, F. Scott Fitzgerald, Toni Morrison, Julia Alvarez, Nella Larsen, and Sylvia Plath, for example, from the translators who make them available to new readers who cannot yet or prefer not to access English? *This Is a Classic* highlights the processes, challenges, solutions, and conditions involved in the scholarly and creative work of literary translation with the goal of providing readers with a greater appreciation of how literary classics are shaped by translation. Readers are encouraged to apply the insights shared here to other existing and future literary classics.

As I write about literary classics just over a mile away from the Homestead and the Evergreens, two historic houses belonging to the Emily Dickinson Museum, I cannot ignore the local literary roots. Therefore, I invited Adalberto Müller, who translated Dickinson's complete poems into Brazilian Portuguese, to open this volume. "The Translator's Agency and the Literary Classic Abroad: Emily Dickinson's Voyage to Brazilliput" weaves together professional, creative, and personal experiences to present some of the specifics of Müller's approach to translating Dickinson, translation's impact on a literary classic, and a literary classic's reliance on translation to reach new realms of the creation and experience of literature.

Following Müller's prologue, Sabina Knight interviews Kidder Smith in "Chinese Classics: The Commentarial Tradition." Knight and Smith introduce key aspects about Chinese classical classics that apply to more contemporary literary classics. They indicate that the commentaries themselves have acquired classical status and that classical texts were seldom the work of a single author. They present solutions brought to translation to explain the context of a remote epoch and address how translators go beyond the words they're translating to offer supplemental text to readers.

Chapter 2 focuses on the ancient Greek poem the *Iliad*, which saw at least eight new English-language translations in the first two decades of the twenty-first century. In "Happy Hour Homer: On Translating and Performing the *Iliad* Live in a Bar," Lynn Kozak traces their process to find a way to perform the entire *Iliad*, which spanned twenty-nine weeks. Kozak notes that performing a text while translating it adds a new dimension because the performer needs to embody the views of the text.

In Chapter 3, "Today in the Temple of Language: Translating Dante," Mary Jo Bang highlights that the classics are never alone. Classics like the ones she translated, *Inferno* and *Purgatorio*, attract communities of readers, ask what of the past is present today, and consider how those distant times look with a contemporary background. One of the goals of Bang's translations is to lure new readers not only to Dante's *Inferno* and *Purgatorio* but also to translations other than her own.

In Chapter 4, "True Confessions of a Literary Translator," Arvind Krishna Mehrotra shares the experiences that led to the 2012 publication of his translations of the poems of Kabir, the fifteenth-century Indian poet, as *Songs of Kabir*. He recalls encountering the unknowns that arise during the translation of a literary classic and speaks to the benefits for poets of "translating blind" (69) since they can trust their instinct as they would with the creation of their own poetry.

In Chapter 5, "What Is a Classic? The Case of Esperanto," Humphrey Tonkin uses Esperanto, a constructed language for international use, to illustrate what translation means to a language. He covers translations of Shakespeare into Esperanto, explores how literary classics from other languages can become assimilated into Esperanto through translation, and discusses the possibilities of a "classic" originally composed in Esperanto. It was an achievement not only to have classics of world literature in Esperanto but also to have the translations be classics of Esperanto style. For Tonkin, Esperanto is a *translated* culture, "in which everyone is in some sense a translator, mediating between his or her native idiom and the practice of international community" (96).

In Chapter 6, Marian Schwartz presents Russian classics and their role in sustaining and making Russian literature known to an English-reading audience. She notes that in the twenty-first century there have been four new translations of Leo Tolstoy's *Anna Karenina*, evidence of the deep tradition of retranslation into English in the context of Russian literature. Schwartz discusses the literary translator Constance Clara GarNett and how her translations of Russian classics "set off an Anglophone love affair with Russian literature" (102), noting that a first translation of a work can be the one that eases readers into a work that is not only foreign but also perhaps demanding in terms of style and ideas. For Schwartz retranslations uncover "overlooked treasures" (108) within literary works, providing, along the way, the opportunity to interact with past and present scholars and translators.

Chantal Ringuet, in "Translating Yiddish Classics: Redefining Tradition in Modern Yiddish Literature through the Prism of Kadya Molodowsky," argues that classics take on different definitions in the context of translation, raising a series of questions that include how non-dominant and minor literatures make their way into translations in dominant and major languages. Ringuet reclaims the foundational concept of the Yiddish classic for women writers within an international frame, as illustrated by the work of Kadya Molodowsky (1894–1975). She focuses on her poem "Froyen-lider" or "Women-Poems" to exemplify the tensions of tradition and modernity as well as contact with words that carry deep emotional and historical depth. Ringuet questions how translating the classics of Yiddish literature raises specific issues pertaining to what works deserve to be classics of modern Yiddish literature.

In "Víctor Catalá's *A Film (3,000 meters)*: Translating a Catalan Classic," Peter Bush introduces Catalan language and publishing history under Francisco Franco and during the first years after his death in 1975. Then he focuses on *A Film (3,000 meters)*, an entertaining, experimental novel, first published in 1921 by Víctor Català, the pseudonym of Caterina Albert, the leading Catalan woman writer of the first half of the last century. Bush calls *A Film* "a very different kind of 'classic'" and confesses that presenting this classic to an English-speaking audience for the first time is a responsibility. Bush highlights how writers of literary classics are reintroduced through translation in collaboration with publishers and cultural institutions.

In Chapter 9, Susan Bernofsky, the translator of several literary classics from German, brings the discussion back to retranslations, noting that retranslation for her happens because she has a story to tell about the book that hasn't yet been told and needs telling. In "Translation as Storytelling," Bernofsky provides examples from her translations of Hermann Hesse's *Siddhartha*, Franz Kafka's *The Metamorphosis*, and Thomas Mann's *The Magic Mountain*, underlining what she wants to highlight in her translations and shows the reader how she does that in the language of her translations. Bernofsky provides a translation journey of a word from *The Magic Mountain* and reveals how her solution was found not in looking at the earlier translations but by focusing on the multilingual setting of the novel.

In Chapter 10, "In Terror and Pandemic: Translating García Lorca's *Poet in New York*," Mark Statman offers the context that inspired his collaborative translation with Pablo Medina of Lorca's collection of poetry—the attacks of September 11, 2001, on the World Trade Center. The two New York poets and devoted readers of Lorca wanted a literary response to this tragic event to show the city as it was after 9/11. Not only did Lorca's poetry help them do that, but it also provided a bridge to the city's past during another time of grief. On literary classics, Statman shares that they "endure because they represent the best part of what we hope our civilization endures" (154). Statman's chapter exhibits a deep understanding of how the journey of the poet, Lorca, can be his own journey as the poet Statman.

In Chapter 11, Johnny Lorenz, English translator of two of the Brazilian writer Clarice Lispector's novels, demonstrates that translators of literary classics, especially when responsible for presenting a text for the first time to an audience of a given language, can teach their audiences how to read the text and better understand the literature in general of a given author. In "Stopping at the Surface: Translating Clarice Lispector's *The Besieged City* and *A Breath of Life*," Lorenz concentrates on Lispector's use of syntax and more specifically on the surface of her writing. In defense of translators, especially working with the expectations of an English-reading audience, he states that badly written sentences are not always the translator's mistakes; sometimes, something in the original indicates the purpose of this badly written sentence as a tactic of the author. These aspects remind us to be open to art and allow ourselves to experience the complexities of it.

Anna Zielinska-Elliot's contribution to this volume steps away from translation into English and focuses on her translation of a 1956 controversial novel by Junichirō Tanizaki from Japanese to Polish. In "Tanizaki's *The Key* in Translation: Will You Still Need Me? Will You Still Read Me, When I'm (Over) Sixty-Four?," Zielinska-Elliot relates the publication and translation history of *The Key* (*Kagi*), a modern classic of Japanese literature translated into over twenty languages. While working on her 2019 translation of the novel, Zielinska-Elliot looked to other translations for clues, as well as to the archives of Harold Strauss, editor-in-chief at Knopf, who initiated the English translation by Howard Hibbert, in which she found comments on the translation. Zielinska-Elliott's review of the extant translations into English and other languages informed her translation. As she translated, she found passages and phrases missing in the English translation. When faced with the challenge of translating a classic, Zielinska-Elliot asks how do translators preserve innovation.

In Chapter 13, "An Essay on Nichita Stănescu: the Classic and the Personal in Translation," Sean Cotter discusses the terms "classic" versus "canonical," as well as the role of retranslations to define a classic. He argues for the classic function of certain texts to be determined on a micro-scale, on the scale of a single person. Combining literary history and personal anecdotes, Cotter highlights the elevated status of poetry in Romania and Stănescu's four-line canonical poem "Poem." Since translation, however, is required for the poem to become a classic, he discusses his own experience with English translations of this poem making it the most translated work of Romanian literature in history. Cotter's contribution encourages leaving space for the comfort, importance, and existence of the personal classic.

In Chapter 14, "From Arabic to English, What is a Classic?," Michelle Hartman introduces the numerous factors surrounding the presentation of

Arabic literary classics in English translation. She covers a range of topics, including the different definitions of what makes a work literary and the disproportionate power involved with making, reviewing, and teaching translations. She proposes ways of considering what makes a classic that involve women's writing, geographical regions, and genre.

In Chapter 15, Lytton Smith focuses on Guðbergur Bergsson's 1966 *Tómas Jónsson Metsölubók*, which he translated from the Icelandic as *Tómas Jónsson—Bestseller*. Smith advocates for the book's greatness and discusses the translation world that surrounds it. For Smith, *Tómas Jónsson—Bestseller* contributes to understandings of what makes a literary classic, arguing that it is less about whether a translation can be a classic than about what we've misunderstood about classics and the classic's role in a future understanding of the literary work.

In Chapter 16, "*Love, Anger, Madness* Making a Classic: Amplifying Marie Vieux-Chauvet's Haitian Trilogy," Carolyn Shread presents the numerous factors that contribute to a classic and how a classic can survive in the face of discrimination and other factors. Not only does Shread offer a detailed exploration of Vieux Chauvet's work, but she also gives an overview of the linguistic history of French and Haitian Creole, and the role of English translation in responding to a long history of colonization and exile. Shread highlights readers' and translators' roles in cultivating the life and survival of a classic.

In Chapter 17, "What Besides Words?: Translating Bilge Karasu's *A Long Day's Evening*," Aron Aji offers an intimate view of the decisions he made while translating the work of one of the most inventive prose writers of Turkey. Karasu's multilingual profile guided some of Aji's choices. Also in his translation, Aji had to grapple with Karasu's unconventional syntax. Aji strove to narrow the gap between experience and expression in his translation.

Emma Ramadan, in "Nonsense in a Given Direction: Translating the Timelessness of Marguerite Duras," writes about the conditions for introducing a classic from one language into another. While Marguerite Duras is a household name in France and has been translated by multiple translators into multiple languages, the timing and mood have to be right to introduce a translation to its audience. Ramadan worked with Olivia Baes on the translation of *Me & Other Writing* (2019), a more complicated work by Duras. Ramadan identifies what about Duras's language that has made her a classic name in France and abroad, and how she and Baes entered that language to write like Duras.

What is to be gained by sticking with an author through the years? In Chapter 19, "'Sentence' as Lifeline: Translating David Albahari's Novels," Ellen Elias-Bursać discusses her translations of war-story novels from the Serbian by David Albahari. She translated two collections of Albahari's short stories and five of his fifteen novels, the most recent being *Checkpoint*, which came out thirty years after their collaboration began. Elias-Bursać's contribution presents an appreciation for the writer's work that has emerged from a rare, decades-long relationship between writer and translator that has allowed her to identify the development of themes in Albahari's work.

While the contributions to this volume are from translator-scholars who have expansive knowledge about their languages, there are instances when translators take on translating from languages unknown to them. In the epilogue, "Matching Socks in the Dark; or How to Translate from Languages You Don't Know," Ilan Stavans invites the reader to experience the questions a translator asks himself. The results reveal that translation is about intimacy with a language, understanding a text, and the resulting impact of the language of the translation. Familiar metaphors for translation include tapestries, veils, and repaired vases; Stavans offers the image of matching socks in the dark to talk about translation.

There are multiple ways of defining what a classic is, what it can be, and what we can do with it. My students have shared that a literary classic, more than any other literary text, is a text they can make their own through translation. As a classic offers the opportunity to experiment with literature, *This Is a Classic* ends with an opportunity to read a literary classic through translation. Esther Allen and Sean Cotter offer a translation experiment in which they interact with *Ramona* (1884) by Helen Hunt Jackson and its Spanish translation *Ramona, novela americana* (1915) by José Martí. In addition to offering their own translations of passages, Allen and Cotter contextualize the project: the backstory of the novel, Martí's translation, connections between Jackson and Martí, and a glimpse into the decisions they make to guide their translations. Their experiment brings together how a literary classic can move through translation to generate new understandings for new audiences while uncovering the translation roots of literary history.

In *Why Read the Classics?* (1991), Italo Calvino opens by listing fourteen definitions of the classics that either begin with "The classics are . . .," "A classic is . . .," or "'Your' classic is . . ." (7). For Calvino, classics share characteristics with other classics, are singular works with an exceptional feature that earns them the label of a classic, and are open to personal preferences. In closing, I give a translator the last word. I invite readers to create their own constellations of classics based on Calvino's words, translated into English by Martin McLaughlin:

> All that can be done is for each of us to invent our own ideal library of our classics; and I would say that one half of it should consist of books we

have read and that meant something for us, and the other half of books which we intend to read and which we suppose might mean something to us. We should also leave a section of empty spaces for surprises and chance discoveries.

Works Cited

Alevato do Amaral, Vitor. "Broadening the Notion of Retranslation." *Cadernos de Tradução*, vol. 39, no. 1, January 2019, pp. 239–59.

Allen, Esther and Susan Bernofsky, eds. *In Translation: Translators on Their Work and What It Means.* Columbia UP, 2013.

Baer, Brian. *Translation and the Making of Modern Russian Literature.* Bloomsbury, 2015.

Belitt, Ben, trans. *Poet in New York.* By Federico García Lorca. Grove, 1955.

Berk Albachten, Özlem and Sehnaz Tahir Gürçaglar. "Retranslation and Multimodality: Introduction." *The Translator.* Special issue: *Retranslation, Multidisciplinarity and Multimodality*, vol. 26, no. 1.

Bucci, Julia, trans. *El principito.* By Antoine de Saint-Exupéry. Ill. Malena Gagliesi. Ethos Traductora, 2019.

Cadera, Susanne M. and Andrew Samuel Walsh, eds. *Literary Retranslation in Context.* Peter Lang, 2017.

Calvino, Italo. *Why Read the Classics?* Trans. Martin McLaughlin. Mariner Books, 1999.

Calvo, Javier. *El fantasma en el libro: La vida en un mundo de traducciones.* Seix Barral, 2016.

Damrosch, David. *Comparing the Literatures: Literary Studies in a Global Age.* Princeton UP, 2022.

Damrosch, David. *What Is World Literature?* Princeton UP, 2003.

Davis, Lydia, trans. *Madame Bovary.* By Gustave Flaubert. Penguin, 2011.

Díez de Revenga, Francisco Javier. "García Lorca: Geometría y angustia: de 'Poeta en Nueva York.'" *Monteagudo*, vol. 58, 1977, pp. 41–7, digitum.um .es/digitum/bitstream/10201/15085/1/05%20vol58%20Garcia%20Lorca.% 20Geometria%20y%20angustia%20de%20Poeta%20en%20Nueva%20York. pdf.

Emmerich, Karen. *Literary Translation and the Making of Originals.* Bloomsbury, 2017.

Gabbert, Elsa. "Mess With a Classic." *The Paris Review*, theparisreview.org/blog/ columns/mess-with-a-classic/.

Galasso, Regina. "An Interview with Mark Statman." *Translation Review*, March 2015, pp. 1–14.

Gascón, Daniel. "Una buena traducción debe causar en el lector la impresión que el lector pretendía producir. Entrevista a Marta Rebón." *Letras Libres*, vol. 16, February 2016, letraslibres.com/revista-espana/una-buena-traducci on-debe-causar-en-el-lector-la-impresion-que-el-autor-pretendia-producir -entrevista-a-marta-rebon/.

Gentzler, Edwin. *Translation and Rewriting in the Age of Post-Translation Studies*. Routledge, 2017.

Grossman, Edith. Conversation with Eduardo Lago. New York, February 5, 2009.

Grossman, Edith. *Why Translation Matters*. Yale UP, 2010.

Hall, Edith and Henry Stead, eds. *A People's History of Classics: Class and Greco-Roman Antiquity in Britain and Ireland, 1689 to 1939*. Oxford UP, 2020.

Headley, Maria Dahvana. "Introduction." *Beowulf: A New Translation*. FSG, 2020, pp. i–xxxiv.

"Illustrated Modern Library. The Modern Library." Advertisement. *Publishers' Weekly*, vol. 144, August 14, 1943, pp. 452–3.

Jutge, Cristina. Re: Dalí y El Quijote. E-mail to Regina Galasso. November 17, 2004.

Kaindl, Klaus. "(Literary) Translator Studies: Shaping the Field." *Literary Translator Studies*. Eds. Klaus Kaindl, Waltraub Kolb, and Daniela Schlager. John Benjamins Publishing Company, 2021, pp. 1–38.

Karashima, David. *Who We're Reading When We're Reading Murakami*. Soft Skull Press, 2020.

Koskinen, Kaisa and Outi Paloposki. "Retranslation." *Handbook of Translation Studies*. Vol. 1. Eds. Yves Gambier and Luc van Doorslaer. John Benjamins Publishing Company, 2010, pp. 294–7.

Kunz, Marco. "'In un placate de La Mancha of which nombre no quiero remembrearme': *Don Quijote* en *Spanglish* y los desafíos de la traducción bilingüe." vol. 4, 2005, pp. 231–42.

Kyzer, Larissa. "Untranslating the Classics." *Translating the Future*, 2020, www.centerforthehumanities.org/programming/retranslating-the-classics.

Lianeri, Alexandra and Vanda Zajko. *Translation and the Classic: Identity as Change in the History of Culture*. Oxford UP, 2008.

Malmkjær, Kirsten, Adriana Serban, and Fransiska Louwagie, eds. *Key Cultural Texts in Translation*. John Benjamins, 2018.

Medina, Pablo and Mark Statman. "Introduction." *Poet in New York*. By Federico García Lorca. Grove Press, 2007.

Murakami, Haruki. "As Translator, as Novelist: The Translator's Afterword." Trans. Ted Goossen. *In Translation: Translators on Their Work and What It Means*. Eds. Esther Allen and Susan Bernosky. Columbia UP, 2013, pp. 169–82.

Narayanan, Vivek. "Untranslating the Classics." With Laurie Patton and Gopal Sukhu. *Translating the Future*, 2020, www.centerforthehumanities.org/programming/retranslating-the-classics.

Patton, Laurie, trans. *The Bhagavad Gita*. Anonymous. Edited and with introduction by Laurie Patton. Penguin Classics, 2008.

Patton, Laurie. "Untranslating the Classics." With Vivek Narayana and Gopal Sukhu. www.centerforthehumanities.org/programming/retranslating-the-classics.

Rabassa, Gregory, trans. *Chronicle of a Death Foretold*. By Gabriel García Márquez. Penguin Books, 1996.
Satterfield, Jay. *The World's Best Books: Taste, Culture, and the Modern Library*. UP Massachusetts, 2002.
Simon, Greg and Steven F. White, trans. *Poet in New York*. Ed. and intro. Christopher Maurer. Farrar, Straus and Giroux, 2018.
Smith, Dinitia. "Poetic Love Affair with New York; For García Lorca, the City Was a Spiritual Metaphor." *New York Times*, July 4, 2000, www.nytimes.com /2000/07/04/books/poetic-love-affair-with-new-york-for-garcia-lorca-city -was-spiritual-metaphor.html.
Stavans, Ilan. Adaptation of *Don Quijote*. By Miguel de Cervantes. Illustrated by Roberto Weil. Penn State University Press, 2018.
Stavans, Ilan, trans. *Alicia's Adventuras en Wonderlandia*. By Lewis Carroll. *Alice's Adventures in Wonderland*. Evertype, 2021.
Stavans, Ilan, trans. *El Little Príncipe*. Edition Tintenfass, 2016.
Stavans, Ilan. "In Defense of Spanglish: Low-Bred Languages, the Class Struggle, and Why Amherst College Teaches Spanglish." *The Common Reader: A Journal of the Essay*, October 1, 2014.
Stavans, Ilan. *Spanglish: The Making of a New American Language*. Harper Collins, 2003.
"Untranslating the Classics." With Vivek Narayanan, Laurie Patton, and Gopal Sukhu. *Translating the Future*, 2020, www.centerforthehumanities.org/ programming/retranslating-the-classics.
Venuti, Lawrence. "Retranslations: The Creation of Value." *Bucknell Review*, vol. 47, no. 1, January 2003, go.gale.com/ps/i.do?id=GALE%7CA123082667 &sid=googleScholar&v=2.1&it=r&linkaccess=abs&issn=00072869&p=LitR C&sw=w&userGroupName=camb27002.
Venuti, Lawrence. *Translation Changes Everything: Theory and Practice*. Taylor & Francis Group, 2013.
Venuti, Lawrence. "Translation, Interpretation, Canon Formation." *Translation and the Classic: Identity as Change in the History of Culture*. Eds. Alexandra Lianeri and Vanda Zajko. Oxford UP, 2008, pp. 27–51.
"What Is World Literature? By David Damrosch." *Princeton University Press*, February 23, 2022, https://press.princeton.edu/books/paperback /9780691049861/what-is-world-literature.
Woods, Michelle. *Kafka Translated: How Translators Have Shaped Our Reading of Kafka*. Bloomsbury, 2013.

Prologue

The Translator's Agency and the Literary Classic Abroad: Emily Dickinson's Voyage to Brazilliput

Adalberto Müller

Presenting the Actor Representing the Author

Having experienced the everyday life of actors during many years, and having tried myself to be a filmmaker, I learned skills that would be helpful for my translation of Emily Dickinson's 1,800 poems into Brazilian Portuguese—a work of seven long years.[1] To be more specific, I worked with Konstantin Stanislavski's idea of acting based on "emotional memory." In a nutshell, Stanislavski believed that in order to interpret a role, an actor or actress should find in his/her own affective memory features that could meet a character's personality, creating a double-bind performance: the actor/actress presents himself while he or she represents the character. This situation is obviously paradoxical, but this paradox could also help to understand the relationship between the translator and the author. Based on Stanislavski's method, I created for my own sake a situation in which the translator becomes an actor and an author at the same time.

I had already been translating Dickinson for three years[2] when I started asking myself things like "who am I, who is Me, this person translating a literary classic of the English language, this female American poet from two centuries ago, writing in a language I know only the basics? Wherefore?" This is where the Russian emigrated stage director Stanislavski became my guide. And that was in 2016, right after I left the Emily Dickinson Museum, the Homestead, after a second visit. I understood back then that I had to define this I if I really wanted to represent and present her. It doesn't mean that I would dress like her or drink like her (she loved Spanish sherry and

---

[1] Emily Dickinson, *Poesia Completa*, vol. 1, vol 2. It's a bilingual two-volume edition that mostly follows Emily Dickinson: *Poems as She Preserved Them*, edited by Cristanne Miller.
[2] Dickinson was already one of the more translated authors in Portuguese when I started translating with her, although her works were never completely published in Portuguese. On her translations to Spanish and Portuguese, see Adalberto Müller, *Dickinson Latina: Imaginary Geography*.

rum, by the way, and I prefer Kentucky Bourbon). But I did take for granted the gender issues while reading and translating her poems and these issues would also define my work at its final stage.

I Am the Border: An Excerpt from an Autopsyfiction

So, who is Me, the "Brazilian" translator of Emily Dickinson? Actually, I am not only Brazilian.

I am the border.

If we look at writing as a form of breaking walls, I'd like to introduce myself as Adalberto Tapir-*Mborevi*, the cyborg-gardener. It is not easy to translate this though. You can't translate a translation, if translating means bringing something from one bank to the other, as in German: *Übersetzen*. This *myself* dwells "in Possibility," as Emily Dickinson's poetry-*nẽẽpoty*[3] says. How can we translate the translator's task? What you cannot translate, you'd better *trans-tale*. Ambiguity belongs to borders. I am a streaming matter.

Multiplicity is my dam-nation.

From one side, I am the sitting cyborg, whose extensions are connected to keyboards, screens, and wires and therefore to the invisible and omnipresent web-*ñanduti* where image skins flow as rapidly as falling stars. From the other side, I am the running animal-*memby* moving blindly to survive amid the remnants of an old forest that is burning and disappearing into smoke carried away by the wind. Both of these are lecturing inside me on losses and gains, about choosing or not choosing sides. I often feel like Herman von Keyserling's "technisierter Wilder" (I translate: wired Wild). Except: *Ich bin kein Kannibale*! (I don't eat meat!) My real father is the tapir-*mborevi*. The tapir-*mborevi* is a big fat animal that only eats plants and grass, and intersperses seeds through the forest by defecating it. Gross, isn't it? Better to consider him a gardener. A gleaner. I am a gleaner like the *mborevi*. Gleaning one seed here, putting it there. Plucking one branch here, planting it there, smelling the rich soils that are so wet! We, the tapir-*mborevi*, are truly gardeners of the forest and savannas!

I live to translate the cyborg into the tapir, and the tapir into the cyborg. It's not that complicated when you live on the border and understand it. Just like when you live on the bank of a river. The banks are where you meet

---

[3] "Poetry" (literally, blossoming-language) in Guarani, the third language spoken at the border of Brazil and Paraguay. I'm using some words in Guarani here. Don't worry! The words are always preceded from their "translations," as in: "tapir-*mborevi*." Hyphenating words is a way of writing in *GuaranEnglish*.

the flow. The banks are also where you lose limits. In the whirlpools. But you might find illuminations in small whirlpools once you're floating on the surface of the bigger rivers. The Paraguay, the river-sea, I'm still floating over there like a small lost canoe!

But let's get to the facts. Suppose I am Nowhere Man:

> Nowhere Man came from a faraway place in Latin-America right in between the Pacific and the Atlantic, where the savanna keeps the springs of clear waters. He was born in 1966 on the border between Brazil and Paraguay in a place where two small cities meet: Ponta Porã (Brazil) and Pedro Juan Caballero (Paraguay). Three languages are spoken there: Portuguese, Spanish, and Guarani, and translation is an everyday practice. He was raised when violent military dictatorships were ruling on both sides. The traces of the violence from the military dictatorship and from other forms of violence belong to his own experience and to his deep memory. His Native American ancestors have been killed by the weapons and diseases of white Europeans since 1500. They were also massacred (together with the priests) in the Jesuit reductions, where a form of "benign colonialism" was being introduced. After that came the Triple Alliance War (1864–70)—also backed by white Europeans. He still remembers this in his deep memory. The young Paraguayans striving for survival after being raped by African-Brazilian soldiers, who were freed from slavery if they fought brutally for the Empire. How many were born out of this genocide, carrying the human stain within themselves from generation to generation? He, the Paraguayan-He, He knows it, although it's not *easy to say*. Who wants to know this? Besides, who wants to know if thousands upon thousands of his relatives are being killed right now in the rainforest and the grasslands, the tapir-*mborevi* brothers, the makaw-*guaka* sisters, the jaguar-*jaguarete* great-uncles?[4]

After the Great War, others came who also left marks and scars. His Paraguayan grandfather, Antonio Saldívar, had a scar from the Chaco War. Oil companies, as you know, promoted this. Ninety-thousand people were killed. His white European grandmother's radio was confiscated by Vargas's police in 1943 because she was "German," and all Germans were considered to be Nazis when Vargas broke with the axis of evil. Then there was Morígino in Paraguay, who fought a war against the "communists" backed by Perón, and an uncle of His was put in prison by Stroessner (how do you spell it?). There are so many wounds and scars on his face.

---

[4] "Jaguar" is a Tupi-Guarani word that comes from *jaguara*. A *jaguarete* is a big jaguar.

When I tell it, I translate it, and translation is a matter of stitch and suture, something I will talk about later on. My Austrian-Bavarian grandparents were also fleeing the famine—the war led for centuries against my poor brother, my ill sister, my abandoned nephew, and my tortured uncle. The work of suture is unending. Is it an enormous, cracked border line? Furthermore, my mother was Paraguayan and my great grandmother was native Amerindian. They also crossed borders as *Auswanderer*, immigrants. They fled the war and the famine. My relatives-*mborevi* are fleeing the fire now in the Pantanal and the Chaco. Поэты—жиды!, wrote Marina Tzvetaeva ("Poets are Jews!"). And Paul Celan rewrote it, translating it to: все поэты жиды. All poets are aus-Wandering Jews. I wander, therefore I am.

Back to the Recent Past

My affair with Dickinson began in 2013.

In early April of that year I was completing the fourth month of a sabbatical year at Yale University, researching the history of Orson Welles's unfinished adaptation of *Don Quijote*. Thanks to the advice of Dudley Andrew, I went to work in several archives in the United States and Europe in order to try to mend the broken pieces of a vast film production puzzle.[5] While traveling from Yale to Harvard via Springfield, Massachusetts, I decided to take a detour in order to visit Amherst, Emily Dickinson's hometown. As a curious reader of her poems and as anyone who read the basics about her, I always felt enticed by the mystery surrounding that reclusive lady-in-white who wrote hundreds of unpublished and enigmatic poems, and never traveled farther than Washington, D.C. The image I had of Dickinson was of her being the antipode of Orson Welles, a cosmopolitan globetrotter who embraced the taste for grandeur and extravagance. However, as Orson Welles, somehow she also seemed to me to be a foreigner in her own country, or someone who never really felt at ease in a land where everybody is supposed to be a winner in life and have their names engraved on some wall of fame—or else to die in the gutter of oblivion.

I was reading *Moby-Dick* at that time because Welles also worked on a "phantom adaptation" of Melville's book for years. I think this book represents Americans' drive toward disaster—a disaster for themselves and for our World as it was before the Anthropocene. It is possible to find many features of American culture in Melville's book. Ahab's monomania, the

---

[5] My research was published as a book in Brazil and as an article in the United States titled Adalberto Müller, "Orson Welles, Author of Don Quixote, Reconsidered," *Cinema Journal*, vol. 56, no. 1, 2016, pp. 43–62.

multiracial issues and tensions inside the Pequod, the capitalist-protestant drive, the transnational enterprise of American trading (always followed by militarism and war), mysticism, alienation, fetishism, the need to voyage to the Outer space ("I am tormented with an everlasting itch for things remote") combined with the domestic vision of the Other as an enemy, the enemy within, with his assault weapons, the everlasting remains of the Native American's massacre and the anxiety of the Civil War, *Star-Trek* and *Alien* embryos, Hollywood and the Bible, fundamentalism, Shakespeare and Bob Dylan, pity, sarcasm, irony, transcendence, nature, gigantism, selfishness, and last but not least, Trumpism! It's not by chance that Melville died poor and unknown in New York City! People like Melville, Dickinson, Welles, they just don't fit to the idea Americans usually have of themselves. And maybe the real White Whale is deep inside one's bones. Who knows?

As any first visitor to Amherst and Dickinson's Homestead, I experienced déjà vu. Despite the cars running on the asphalt of Main Street, you really feel something historic about that place, when you know Dickinson's poems. Every small detail of that old New England wooden house and its garden seems to be related with the images you have in mind after reading her writings. Then you see and touch printed copies of her small booklets (the fascicles, as they are now called), you see the furniture, the stove, you look through her windows, and you gasp remembering the line: "I could not see to see" (F591, M270). You feel the ambience, something that flutters in between the past and the present.

When I came back to my room, I was reading some cheap anthology of her poems that I found in a second-hand book store before traveling, and I decided to translate a few of them. One was "A Little Madness in the Spring" (F1356, M686), which was written on the small blackboard displayed in the Museum's driveway. The other one was "Yesterday Is History" (F1290, M570):[6]

---

[6] I quote Dickinson's poems following the pattern among Dickinson's scholarship: the first line in quotes is followed by the numbers of the two main edition of her poems (R. W. Franklin [F], 1998, and C. Miller [M], 2016). This is one of the eighteen hundred poems I've been translating since that cold April day in Amherst. Two years after that visit, I decided to quit my previous research project on film and literature, and dedicate myself fully to Dickinson's exquisite poems. In July 2015, in Paris, I was presenting a paper at the meeting of the Emily Dickinson International Society, where I met Cristanne Miller and two important translators of her work: Claire Malroux and Gunhild Kübler. The three of them (as well the meetings of EDIS) would be decisive for my future work as a translator of Dickinson's complete poems, for reasons I would only understand two years later, when I decided to follow Miller's edition of *Poems as She Preserved Them*. While working on my own translation since them, I always kept in mind the delicateness of Madame Malroux's translations and a sage advice of Frau Kübler ("always care for the last line!"), who was also never afraid to care for the rhymes in her own translation.

Yesterday is History,
'Tis so far away –
Yesterday is Poetry –
'tis Philosophy –
Yesterday is mystery –
Where it is Today
While we shrewdly speculate   [we] sage. shrewd investigate
Flutter both away

Ontem é História
É tão distante –
Ontem é Poesia – é Filosofia –
Ontem é mistério –
Onde é que o Hoje mora
Enquanto a gente especula   [a gente] investiga . [especula] sagaz
Ambos deram o fora

History, philosophy, mystery, poetry. These are essential terms to define translation as well. First of all, because every translation is produced within the framework of an historical time and is marked by it, in the same sense that Marx states that labor and society relations, as well as economic categories, "bear the traces of history" (82). What escapes that time, and perhaps remains beyond it, is the mystery of poetry.

Stitch and Suture

As for the philosophy of my Dickinson translation, I developed a double-bind conceptual framework, which I named stitch and suture. On one hand, the stitching task forces the translator to adopt an "editorial" position that gives coherence and harmony to each piece and to the set of poems. Besides following Cristanne Miller's edition, I had to read the manuscripts, other editions, the critical debate, and several translations into the languages I know better (Portuguese, French, Spanish, and German). By stitching, the translator plays an active role in the editorial choices in order to create textual stability to a translated edition (considering that a bilingual edition contains the original).

On the other hand, the suturing process accepts the instability of the work, including ellipsis, variants, alternatives, erasures, interpretative disagreements, and provokes the translator to search for an always elusive subject (or meaning) that flickers in the discursive chain and is unattainable by its own nature.[7] Moreover, if the stitching process takes into account the context and the co-text of a poem in order to (re)construct meaning from the manifest content of the work, suturing operates at the level of its latent content, considering that the ellipsis, alternatives, variants, suppressions, and other features create a regime of indeterminacy that the translator should accept and play with. Working under the regime of suture means to accept that something is always "lost in translation," because you have to accept a text in its regime of *undecidability* or "mystery," as Dickinson's poem defines it.

This philosophy led to some choices that go beyond the "meaning" of each individual poem. For example, I opted for a type of verse and rhyme in Portuguese that could come closer to the use of the common meter in Dickinson's poems. In 2018, during a sabbatical year in Buffalo, where I was finishing the translation of Dickinson, I attended the Unitarian Universalist Church and was able to follow closely the living energy of the common meter in the Protestant hymnal. But I always kept in mind that although Dickinson uses the hymn prosody, she constantly subverts the logics of puritanism related to American Protestantism, as she does in a poem from around 1879, "Forbidden Fruit a Flavor Has" (F1482; M615):

Forbidden Fruit a flavor has
That lawful Orchards mocks –
How luscious lies within the Pod
The Pea that Duty locks –

O sabor do Fruto Proibido
O Pomar da lei alicia –
Dentro da Vagem do Dever
A Ervilha é uma delícia –

There's some taste for the "forbidden fruit" in the translator's work, and it's not by chance that he is accused of infidelity or treason. In most of my translations, I have chosen to alternate verses of eight syllables with ones of six syllables, caring as much as possible to not erase essential words for the poem's meaning. At the same time, I kept a rhyme that is almost "slant," due to the change of the accent position in a homogenous ending (*alicIa:* entice/*delÍcia*: delicious).

---

[7] I was familiar with Jean-Pierre Oudart's use of Jacques Lacan's psychoanalytical concept of suture, which I reframed for my own translation theory. See Jean-Pierre Oudart, "Cinema and Suture."

It is up to the translator to observe that, in the *passage* across English and Portuguese, not only words, but rhythm also changes, which requires taking for granted the huge differences between the systems of versification of the English language and the Portuguese language, which have a distinct history and tradition. Contrarily to the versification in English poetry, which is accentual-syllabic, the Portuguese language uses the syllabic system. Thus, the preference, in translation, fell on the verses of six and eight syllables, sometimes alternated or replaced by the verses of five and seven called *redondilhas*, a very popular form of verse. Although being closer to Dickinson's common meter, the use of *redondilhas* only would result in cutting several words in each poem, due to the polysyllabic feature of most Portuguese words.

It is possible to discuss at great length rhythm and metrical issues, but it is also clear that the worth of a verse cannot be fully determined with objective arguments. One fact, however, cannot be denied: the translation quoted earlier is composed of measured lines, lines which, if not identical to, pursue equivalences with the original, insofar as the prosody of the two languages is different. What interests me is that this line sounds like a verse in a poem, and that a set of verses from the poem and the poems between them follow a certain logic of prosody and rhythm, and are coherent with each other in aesthetic terms. When one thinks of this not in 10, 20, or 200, but in 1,800 poems, then one can have the dimension of the translator's task of my Dickinson project. For it is one thing to translate a number of selected poems (to make an "anthology," which means how to choose the best flowers in a garden, or the flowers to choose) according to personal aesthetic criteria, which can be good or bad. Another is translating everything, and trying to maintain a balance in the whole. Or rather, as Dickinson would say, "A Weight with the Needles on the pounds—" (F294, M138).

Besides the use of ellipsis, which only accentuates the already elliptical nature of the English language (in contrast to the analytical character of the Portuguese language), a further challenge in translating Dickinson's poetry comes from the very rich vocabulary of English, particularly because while writing in English it is possible to make choices between words of Latin and Anglo-Saxon origin. A trained Dickinson scholar knows to what extent Dickinson was aware of etymology, generally using Latin words to express abstraction and Anglo-Saxon words to express things concrete. That's what happens in "The Mind Lives on the Heart" (F1384, M523) (my italics for Latin words):

The Mind lives on the Heart
Like any *Parasite* –
If that is full of Meat
The Mind is fat –

> But if the Heart omit –
> *Emaciate* the Wit –
> The *Aliment* of it
> So *absolute*.

> A Cabeça mora no Coração
> Como qualquer Parasita –
> Ela até engorda
> Se tiver a sua Marmita –
>
> Mas se o Coração é enxuto –
> Emagrece o Cocuruto –
> Do Engenho o Alimento
> Tão absoluto –

Besides the contrast between abstract and concrete words, the issues of rhythm, the translation has to deal with this baroque profusion of words ending in -rt, -ite, -eat, -at, -it, -it, it, -ute! In this case, the translator very much looks like a juggler having to spin many plates at the same time. Here I preferred to invest in the contrast between a more literary-philosophical vocabulary equivalent to the original (*Alimento, absoluto*) and more popular/family terms like *marmita* (packed lunch) and *cocuruto* (popular word for head). Of course, as I do in many translations, the work with the rhymes and sound effects lead me to shift the terms of the poem and the original syntax ("lives *on* the Heart" becomes "in the Heart" but the "on" is evoked by the following phrase). But I tried to do so without losing sight of the most important words (such as "Wit," a word from the literary and philosophical universe, and "absolute," which can in no way be suppressed). Likewise, I try to keep the syntactical ellipses as the probable conjunction "since" before the last sentence, which could also be replaced by a "being" after "it": "since the Aliment of it is so absolute" or "the Aliment of it being so absolute." Most of all, what is not lost here is this idea that our thoughts feed on the heart (i.e., on life), and when it stops beating (when sensitivity is lost), the thought loses its wit (*engenho*, ingenuity, cleverness).

A similar problem arises when I translate a poem such as "A Weight with Needles on the Pounds—" (F294, M138). Eventually, my translation expands the meaning of a "Weight . . . Needle," because in Portuguese we have "o fiel da balança" which is the equivalent to balance wheel, both as regulation mechanism of a scale or a stabilizing force in a situation of imbalance (e.g., in a political dispute). In analogic scales (or balances), the needle in the display reflects the amount of weight transmitted by the spring mechanism, or wheel. In Portuguese language, however, it happens that the needle is more important semantically than the wheel, therefore we say "fiel da balança" instead of balance wheel. Besides, "fiel" is technically the needle, but it means literally "faithful" (it is etymologically related to fidelity):

> A Weight with Needles on the pounds–
> To push, and pierce, besides–
> That if the Flesh resist the Heft–
> The puncture– coolly tries–
>
> That not a pore be overlooked
> Of all this Compound Frame–
> As manifold for Anguish–
> As Species–be– for name–

> O Fiel da Balança, nos quilos–
> Além disso, aperta e fura–
> Se a Carne resistir ao Peso–
> A punção–Fria tortura–
>
> Não desconsidera um poro
> Dessa Composta Estrutura–
> Tão diversa para a Angústia –
> Como a Espécie – é – para o nome.

As it happens in the story told by this poem, the translator works as the balance wheel working to create accuracy and fairness. But he also works for the balance: he "punctures" the original, and he "cooly" considers the "compound structure" of a poem as "species" for a "name," meaning something unique but similar to other species (or poems) comprised under a name. Considering the original and the translated poem as two "species," he will try to find a "name," something that is beyond and before, at the same time. In order to have fairness and balance, he will have to "push, pierce, and puncture" the original according to the "Heft"—the foreign words used to read and translate the poem. Thus, his work is on to put a "Weight with needles on the pounds." Or maybe become himself the "needle," "o Fiel da balança," which is precisely like that one from the balance described by Paul Valéry:

> Think of a pendulum oscillating between two symmetrical points. Suppose that one of these extremes represents form: the concrete

characteristics of the language, sound, rhythm, accent, tone, movement—
in a word, the Voice in action. Then associate with the other point, the
acnode of the first, all significant values, images and ideas, stimuli of
feeling and memory, virtual impulses and structures of understanding—
in short, everything that makes the content, the meaning of a discourse.
Now observe the effect of poetry on yourselves. You will find that at each
line the meaning produced within you, far from destroying the musical
form communicated to you, recalls it. The living pendulum that has
swung from sound to sense swings back to its felt point of departure, as
though the very sense which is present to your mind can find no other
outlet or expression, no other answer, than the very music which gave it
birth. (Valéry 64)

Like Valéry, I consider that a poem lives beyond the gesture that generated it. It remains alive in the sense that everything that can reproduce, replicate, expand, or transform itself is capable of being part of the intricate dialectic that entangles nature and history altogether. In his essay on the translator's task, Walter Benjamin considered that translation ensures the afterlife (*Nachleben*) of an original work: it lives after (*es lebt nach*) the original. Now, if I want to relate this idea to Dickinson's poem, then I can state that a translation also transforms the "Compound Frame" of the original work, since it lives *on* the original: as a "parasite," one can think, but also in the enlarged sense of symbiosis, which includes commensalism or mutualism.

Translation, Anthropophagy, and Perspectivism

Thinking about afterlife brings me back to my Guarani and animal (tapir-*mborevi*) roots—and the way I consider them to understand myself as a translator of a classic author such as Emily Dickinson.

Since the early 1980s, Brazilian translation scholars and poets have emphasized the relationship of translation and the cultural-literary concept of anthropophagy as developed by avant-garde poet Oswald de Andrade.[8] More recently, Álvaro Faleiros has stressed the kinship of translation and shamanism, based on anthropologists such as Eduardo Viveiros de Castro.

In order to formulate his concept of "Amerindian perspectivism," Eduardo Viveiros de Castro studies the practice of shamanism and anthropophagy as

---

[8] See, for example, E.R. Vieira Filho, *Antropofagia Literária e Literal na sua relação com os Estudos da Tradução*.

related to what he calls "Amerindian perspectivism" and "multinaturalism." In many native Amerindian cosmogonies, the "person" is not defined by their individuality but by the relation they have with other beings or things. To be a "person" means to be someone to somebody (or to something) in a given circumstance and according to a given perspective. Therefore, one can consider that a jaguar drinks human blood in the same way humans drink *cauim* (a beverage made out of manioc) and where humans see a nothing but a bog, our friend the tapir-*mborevi* sees dreams of paradise. Moreover, under certain circumstances of Amerindian life, the body is considered to be nothing but a carcass, whereas the "real person" is actually *living* under the skin of some other animal or spirit. Therefore, shamans operate as diplomats (or translators), establishing communication with different "people" occupying different spaces at the same time. Things being so, natives maintain a complex relationship with nature, as what we consider nature is for them culture. In it, one can take on the identity of a jaguar, just as we assume our gender identity, sometimes beyond nature (or sex, in this case). Moreover, where we see the jungle (trees, exotic animals, plants, and so on), the native sees a place for fulfillment and transformation. For Amerindians, the jungle is both a sacred place (every being is a "perspective," the jungle being composed of thousands of "eyes") and a profane space, as it is where a politics of being different occurs.

Another topic studied by Viveiros de Castro is the ancient ritual of anthropophagy among the Tupinambá (a native people that disappeared more than three centuries ago). Beyond Montaigne's depiction of Brazilian cannibals in his essay "Des Cannibales," anthropology has shown that anthropophagy was part of a complex network of cultural behaviors related to the social and religious function of vengeance. Among the Tupinambá and other peoples, vengeance was structured as a language. More than an arbitrary act of rage, it was socially codified and participated in the cosmogony of war, tradition, and religion. In war (which was more performative, and very far from being as violent as Western wars), some enemies were kept prisoner and became part of the capturer's family, sometimes even marrying and having children with their daughters and wives. However, one day the capturer would have to decide to kill the prisoner in order to achieve vengeance, and after a very long ritual the whole family would eat their body (in very small portions) in order to achieve a kind of Eucharist. As Viveiros de Castro observes, while in Catholicism the faithful eats symbolic meat (and drinks symbolic blood) to be connected (*re-ligare*) with an abstract idea (Jesus, the Spirit, or God) related to some distant future (the Redemption), the Tupinambá would eat real meat and drink real blood to connect with a concrete strength related to the past (the distant origin of their vengeance) in order to actualize memory in the present. Theirs is in fact a materialist religion.

Despite the cruelty of this practice (according to our civilized perspective)—which disappeared in Brazil some three centuries ago—traces of anthropophagy remain and later became a cultural paradigm in Brazilian culture. During the early twentieth century, Oswald de Andrade published an "Anthropophagic manifesto" in which he proposed that modern Brazilian art should learn to better devour European culture in order to accept the native within and become—at the same point—able to be re-devoured by Europeans.

Now, I'd like to finish this chapter by pointing out that as a translator of a foreign author I am first of all The Translator of Myself. When I sign the cover of Emily Dickinson's translation (as Adalberto Müller), I *undercover* the sign-nature of Adalberto-Mborevi, my ancestral tapir-gardener, who intends to rewrite poetry-*nêẽpoty*, to make language grow and flourish using the seeds from Outer gardens, devouring Dickinson's fascicle-poems, leaf-poems, flower poems, transplanting them according to a certain *perspective*. How could the actor become an author, if not by some art of diplomatic shamanism?[9]

In the borders of time, the tapir is the guardian-gardener of this forest of signs, which we call classic literature—or translation—always retranslating itself anthropophagically.

Works Cited

Castro, Eduardo Viveiros. *The Inconstancy of the Indian Soul: The Encounter of Catholics and Cannibals in Sixteenth-century Brazil*. Prickly Paradigm Press, 2011.
Dickinson, Emily. *Poesia Completa*. Editora da UnB /Editora da Unicamp, 2020, 2021.
Dickinson, Emily. *Poems as She Preserved Them*. Ed. Cristanne Miller. Harvard/Belknap Press, 2015.
Faleiros, Álvaro. *Traduções canibais. Uma poética xamânica do traduzir*. Cultura e Barbárie, 2019.

---

[9] For instance, in the translation of one of Dickinson's classic poems, "My Life Had Stood—A Loaded Gun—" (F764, M354), I use the perspective of a famous Brazilian literary character Riobaldo from *Grande Sertão: Veredas*, as if the voice in the translated poem were Riobaldo's, musing about another important character in João Guimarães Rosa's novel.

Marx, Karl. "Auch die ökonomischen Kategorien, die wir früher betrachtet, tragen ihre geschichtliche Spur." *Das Kapital. Kritik der politischen Ökonomie*. Erster Band. Dietzverlag, 1973, Chapter 4: 3.

Müller, Adalberto. "Dickinson Latina: Imaginary Geography." *The Oxford Handbook of Emily Dickinson*. Eds. Cristanne Miller and Karen Sánchez-Eppler. Oxford University Press, 2022, pp. 497–517.

Müller, Adalberto. "Orson Welles, Author of Don Quixote, Reconsidered." *Cinema Journal*, vol. 56, no. 1, 2016, pp. 43–62, doi:10.1353/cj.2016.0053.

Oudart, Jean-Pierre. "Cinema and Suture." *Screen*, vol. 18, no. 4, 1987, pp. 34–47.

Valéry, Paul. "Poetry and Abstract Thought." Trans. Denise Folliot. *The American Poetry Review*, vol. 36, no. 2, March/April 2007, pp. 61–6.

Vieira, E. R. Filho. "Antropofagia Literária e Literal na sua relação com os Estudos da Tradução." *Tradterm*, vol. 33, 2019, pp. 98–122.

1

Chinese Classics

The Commentarial Tradition

Sabina Knight with Kidder Smith

SK: Chinese classics are defined from early times by their place in powerful discussions. When scholars read classical works in Chinese, most of the time they read authoritative commentaries alongside or within them. To read a classic is to read the inner texts in conversation with traditional commentaries.

KS: Yes, Chinese classics are unexceptionally embedded in commentary. There is no stand-alone. The reader thus finds her/himself already in an explicit conversation. All the more so insofar as most commentaries are nearly as old as their originating text. I'm speaking especially of commentaries on the traditional "Confucian canon."

SK: The earliest Chinese novels have commentaries too. In most editions at least one commentary is embedded within the lines of the original text. In the great eighteenth-century novel, *Dream of the Red Chamber*, for example, the interlinear notes are vital to the novel's meanings. The commentaries are also vital to each work's evolution. Unfortunately, translators virtually never render the commentaries into English.

KS: That's right, and it's too bad. For we could say that, in a sense, Chinese classics come with their own translations. Many of these commentaries—especially on the Confucian canon—have classical status themselves and have acquired their own sub-commentaries.

The Art of War

SK: Classical texts are often terse and suggestive, and a reader begs for guidance. Sun Tzu's *Art of War* is a good example. How did you and your translation group make the text comprehensible for Anglophone readers?

KS: In our translation we sought to match the *Sun Tzu*'s difficulty, phrase by phrase. Where the Chinese is compressed or bewildering, our English is as well: as best we can, we recreate the lithic diction of the original. In fact, our English has only 25 percent more words than the Chinese—whereas a translation of the text into modern Chinese is usually two or three times longer. As are most translations into Western languages. Our concision is a measure of our confidence in both the Chinese text and our American reader.

SK: Under the right circumstances, perhaps the text's difficulties can entice readers to discover their own understanding.

KS: But difficulties can also block that process. So we wrote a commentary ourselves, to provide a bit of help. We stuck it at the end of the book, though, after people had had a chance to examine the bare text (which of course is bare only to them).

SK: Did a desire to make the book accessible to educated readers account for your choice to translate it with a group?

KS: We formed the Denma Translation Group to show how the vision of our teacher, Trungpa Rinpoche, manifested through an ancient Chinese text that predated him by 2,000 years. Though our first audience was his Buddhist community, we also had a stealth dharma approach, thinking that this wisdom might be of interest to many. It turns out to be true—we've sold 200,000 copies of the book, and it's been translated into seven languages, including Arabic and Hebrew.

SK: I taught a course on Sun Tzu's *The Art of War* 孫子兵法, and my students read your translation. The cover presents the title as simply *The Art of War*. That title is likely more accurate for a translation aimed at readers unfamiliar with traditional Chinese literary practices. For classical texts were very seldom the work of a single author.

KS: Whether a Master Sun existed is itself uncertain. Even if he did exist and did elaborate this school of thought for managing conflict, the text would still be a palimpsest developed by a number of authors.

SK: In teaching it became clear that the wisdom of the *Sun Tzu* is situation specific. The meaning always depends on the present confrontation.

KS: That's one of the book's central points. In chapter 1 it says, "These are the victories of the military lineage. They cannot be transmitted in advance." That is, you must figure things out right now, right here. We comment, "These victories cannot be set aside for future use. Nor can they be taught. There can be no strategic dogma."

SK: Not dogma, but still principles, no? As you write in your introduction, *The Art of War* offers "a radically new perspective on conflict, whereby one might attain victory without going to battle."

KS: Maybe, but these principles can seldom be made explicit. So, in chapter 4, the text tells us "The battles of the skilled are without extraordinary victory, without reputation for wisdom and without merit for courage." We remark: "The basis of these victories is secret, not apparent to others. Thus one chooses to fight an enemy who is easily defeated—no Rough Riders here, charging up San Juan Hill. And so the skilled general remains invisible to the competition for fame."

The Japanese Zen Master Ikkyū

SK: Let's turn to poetry. You've translated two books of poems, one by one of the two or three most beloved of Chinese poets, the other by a Japanese poet who wrote in Classical Chinese. Can you explain how a Japanese poet came to write in Chinese?

KS: The Japanese Zen master Ikkyū 一休 (1398–1491) wrote extensive poetry in Chinese—this was a common practice in Japan in the fifteenth century.

SK: Most Chinese texts are filled with allusions to other texts. Classical poets not only filled their poems with allusions but often wrote poems in direct response to earlier poems. That response would often be a rewriting of another poem, sometimes a rewriting as simple as rearranging the characters.

KS: Writing Chinese poetry has long been a practice of intense intertextuality. Reading it too, I would add. A single image, conveyed in a particular way, takes the reader back to another time. And then that other time is brought into the present time.

SK: How much does Ikkyū follow in this tradition?

KS: His sampling practices go much further than do those of most other poets. He frequently pulls from the full range of China's cultural history. He draws as well from a wide variety of Buddhist texts, including kōans.

SK: From what I've gathered, Ikkyū never explains these allusions.

KS: He simply assumes a readership as well educated as he. Translators have generally chosen one of two solutions to this richness: some have expanded his line to include as much information as possible, while others have added extensive annotations.

SK: Which approach did you follow?

KS: For this project we developed a new approach. We wondered, what would fifteenth-century readers bring with them to Ikkyū's work? How could we reproduce that knowledge for a twenty-first-century audience? Our solution was to write a brief essay to introduce each poem, identifying Ikkyū's otherwise invisible interlocutors through a mixture of story, translation, history, and lore.

SK: Your approach strikes me as a twenty-first-century version of a traditional Chinese commentary.

KS: That's a generous characterization. I'd add only that these essays are more assemblages than narrative, one piece placed beside another until they create a cloud of knowledge. Here is an example.

> Manjushri is the bodhisattva of wisdom. But what is wisdom?
>
> Buddha's great disciple Ananda accomplished the wisdom of an arhat, someone who has left the red dust of samsara far behind, who is free of desire and hatred. This is rare indeed!
>
> But he didn't even start the next journey, that of those bodhisattvas who will never abandon the sorrow of samsara, always present for others in that hell, who progress along the stages of the path until they reach Manjushri's Great Wisdom and finally Buddhahood.
>
> Nor could he have imagined the next step after that, to take passion itself as wisdom, free within desire, taking passion as his compassionate connection to all appearance, finding wisdom in the dusty street, the sweet potato vender's song, her hand resting on my sleeve.
>
> The *Lankavatara Sutra* tells this story:
>
>> At that time Ananda went begging for food and, following along the streets, passed by some whorehouses. There he met the woman Matangi, who had great skill in sorcery and used the Kapila Brahma mantra to draw him into the whorehouse. She bent forward, fondling him, and was about to destroy the essence of his vows.
>>
>> The Buddha knew how the prostitute's mantra was done, so from the crown of his head he manifested a great light, bejeweled in fearlessness. Within the light appeared a thousand-petaled

jeweled lotus, on which was sitting the transformation form of the Buddha in demon-subduing posture, proclaiming a sacred mantra. He ordered Manjushri to recite a mantra of protection, and the evil mantra was extinguished. Thereupon Ananda and Matangi were carried off to the place of the Buddha. Ananda prostrated and put the Buddha's feet on his head, weeping in compassion.

Manjushri uselessly chanting in the whorehouse dream. Ananda, saved too soon, fleeing from his chance for full emancipation, terrified of his body's wisdom, the sorcerer's play of form, which is Buddha's truer body.

And so this poem:

> An arhat who emerges from dust pushes away Buddhahood.
> Once entering a brothel, I exhibit the Great Wisdom.
> I laugh deeply at Manjushri reciting mantra in the *Lankavatara Sutra*.
> He has lost the whole business of his youthful passion. (Smith, *Having Once Paused* 52–3)

出塵羅漢遠佛地
一入婬坊發大智
深咲文殊唱楞經
失卻少年風流事

One could of course read the poem first and then seek the background stories—this is how it's often done. But that's a bit like beginning a joke by telling the punch line first.

SK: Your approach makes sense. And like most traditional commentaries, it encourages the reader to come away with a specific teaching. It thus follows the didactic tradition of *wenyi zaidao* 文以載道 "Writing conveys the moral Way."

I would just want us not to forget that most Classical Chinese poetry remains open to multiple meanings. To demonstrate, I've re-translated one of the poems in your book. Here is the original, followed by your translation:

題淫坊
美人雲雨愛河深
樓子老禪樓上吟

我有抱持睫吻興
意無火聚捨身心

Ode to the Brothel

Beautiful woman, cloud and rain, love's deep river.
Old Zen Pavilion Monk, up in the pavilion singing.
I have such refined passion for hugging and kissing.
My mind doesn't say: the world is a fire, give up your body.
(Smith, *Having Once Paused* 29)

Here is my translation:

Ode to a Brothel

Beautiful one,
like clouds and rain,
our lovemaking,
like the river's depths.

The master of the pavilion,
an old Zen Monk,
chants upstairs.

My passion
for long lashes,
for kissing with eyes wide open
I've retained.

What the body knows:
the fire that gathers,
I have no intention
to relinquish.

KS: This example, I hope, speaks for itself.

The Chinese Poet Li Bo

SK: In your most recent book, *Li Bo Unkempt*, you translate Li Bo 李白 (a.k.a Li Bai, 702–61), the Tang-dynasty poet whom many consider China's greatest poet.

KS: When Ikkyū invokes a story, it's always very pointed. You know who the actors are, and why. Li Bo is far more complex. His poems are gold seams leading to hermits, unheard music, or to vast interstellar treasuries, the moon. The poems skip out from this lore, embellish it, return, transform it.

SK: So, as with Ikkyū, you provide background in brief accompanying essays.

KS: Yes, but in the case of Li Bo the essays are a kind of Baedeker, where we reveal the dimensions, hues, and gestures of an extraordinary world. We don't know another book of Chinese translation that's as committed to this poetry's full force.

SK: Quite a feat. In the Chinese tradition, Li Bo is called an immortal.

KS: The closest understanding we have in our culture is that he's a realized being.

SK: And your renderings bring out that dimension? Enlightenment.

KS: Well, actually, we do more than that. These poems are magical acts. So we offer multiple ways to realize that magic. The essays are demonstrations, a spell-book, an extension of this irregular knowing.

SK: For me, reading and translating Li Bo is also profoundly intimate.

KS: So intimate that we have to speak indirectly of it, asking questions, dropping hints. Making jokes. The short essays can handle only a certain amount of this intensity. We thus stick the rest in endnotes, camouflaged amidst a minimal scholarly apparatus. There we undo a lot of the more ordinary views we've just established in the essays that accompany the poems.

SK: Such a small part of the translation process entails finding a good English word for a good Chinese word. Instead a translator has to be willing to be pulled out past words.

KS: We're speaking here of poetry, after all.

SK: And you trust your reader will see it this way too?

KS: Perhaps they come along, or perhaps they won't. This is the chance we take. The briefest example, a famous poem of self-definition:

In the mountains, replying to a man of the world

> You ask me why I would lodge at Emerald Mountain.
> I smile and do not reply, my heart at ease in itself.
> Peach blossoms, flowing water, gone out of sight.
> There are other heavens and earths, not human. (Smith and Zhai, *Li Bo Unkempt*, 83)

山中答俗人
問餘何意棲碧山, 笑而不答心自閒
桃花流水窅然去, 別有天地非人間

SK: It might be tempting to see this poem as just a hermit's joy. Or as a nature poem. Or as a state of mind. Whereas of course this poem can be read all three ways at once.

KS: Yes, but beyond that too. Concealed in Li Bo's silence are the vibrant, myriad dimensions of the immortals, as you brought up. Those beings who are beyond the world and yet somehow still of it. Riding the elements, they rise and descend at will; they roam the whole universe, visible and invisible; they live an indeterminable length of time, perhaps as long as Heaven-and-Earth. The poem is thus also a grimoire of the world of form, appearance, transformation, and disappearance.

SK: So your book gives Li Bo a new world of form. It allows him to appear, transform, and disappear?

KS: And how it shall transform, we shall see. Because few Westerners have seen this Li Bo before.

The *I Ching*

SK: You've also translated parts of the *I Ching* (*Yijing* 易經), the *Classic of Change*. There are few books as cryptic, or as powerful. Presenting it was one of my greatest challenges in *Chinese Literature: A Very Short Introduction*. How would you situate it?

KS: Early in the first millennium BCE, a tradition of divination practices coalesced around sixty-four six-line figures, each of them made up of solid and broken lines, such as ䷄. Each hexagram acquired a name. (This one's called *xu* 需, "attending" or "waiting.") And early on each acquired a text, consonant with its name, and six more texts, one for each line. For example, in this case the hexagram text says that "It will be advantageous to ford the great river." And each of the six line-texts elaborates on this situation, showing the subject waiting to cross, with various auspicious or baleful outcomes.

SK: What do we do with this prophecy? How does the classical tradition recuperate it as something useful to governance, ritual, and self-cultivation, its usual concerns?

KS: Already by the sixth century BCE scholars were interpreting the hexagrams as the confluence of various natural phenomena— water, fire, heaven, earth, and so on. And by the third century BCE the hexagram and line texts had also acquired more rationalized explanations, applying their advice to the conduct of a gentleman.

This, of course, was insufficient. So hundreds of commentaries were written over the next 2,000 years, to rectify this delirious uncertainty.

SK: What does a poor translator do?

KS: Well, Richard John Lynn has a simple and useful solution. He translates the text as the great third-century CE commentator Wang Bi has understood it. It is clear enough, consistent enough, accessible enough.

SK: I note your use of the word "enough."

KS: We're talking about provisional meanings here, not definitive. But that is surely good enough.

SK: Perhaps the moral is that we are ourselves embedded in the tradition of commentaries.

KS: In my own work with the *I Ching* I have either asked how the text was used, or I've investigated the formal qualities that make it so difficult to understand. For example, diviners of the sixth and fifth centuries BCE encountered the same kind of uncertainties that you or I might—does "Great River" mean the Hudson? Any aqueous barrier? And so on.

SK: In the great Confucian revival of the eleventh century CE, scholars paid special attention to the *I Ching*. Its mutability was a perfect foil for their own innovations.

KS: But they took it in wildly different directions, either insisting it was an instruction book of moral conduct, or a blueprint of cosmic time and forces, or a tool to learn the fundamental nature of mind.

SK: Somewhat separately, I'm fascinated by how the textuality of the text allows, even insists upon these possibilities.

KS: But this question is an issue of literary theory, not really of translation.

SK: The *I Ching* might be a good candidate for Roland Barthes's assertion that a text is like an onion—only layers and layers, peeled away, until nothing is left.

KS: But I enjoy smelling all those layers along the way, and the Nothing that is left seems to me quite potent.

Lao Tzu/Laozi 老子 and His Book

SK: To end perhaps we could touch on the *Laozi*, the most translated of all the Chinese classics and the second-most translated in world literature, after the Christian *Bible*.

KS: Yes, we should talk about this guy. I won't touch it, myself. But I can show you why, and maybe you'd like to enter the fray.

SK: Shall we start with the first line of the *Daode jing* 道德經, the *Classic of the Way and Its Power*? It's diabolically hard to translate, since it's all puns: *Dao* means a road, the Way, to speak, to lead:

> 道可道非常道，名可名非常名
>
> The Way that can be spoken of is not the eternal Way,
> Names that can be named are not eternal names.

KS: I'd prefer not to pin down the keywords:

> Dao that can be Dao'ed is not a long-lasting Dao,
> names that can be named are not long-lasting names.

And for a breathtaking version of these lines, there's the magisterial Peter Boodberg (1957),

> Lodehead lodehead-brooking: no forewonted lodehead;
> Namecall namecall-brooking: no forewonted namecall. (618)

SK: The next two sentences are hardly less cryptic:

> 無名天地之始，有名萬物之母
> Without names is the beginning of Sky and Earth.
> Having names is the mother of the ten-thousand things.

KS: Again, I'd prefer something leaving more space:

> "Non-Having" names the pregnancy of Heaven and Earth,
> "Having" names the mother of the ten-thousand things.

For Laozi discerns the Nothing that is rife with all possibility and the Something that gives it birth as all appearance.

SK: Put another way, perhaps we could say that before Laozi there were no things, and afterwards plenty. Before him was only a silent unified realm, and after him the brokenness of language's divisions.

KS: I would add that before him was only a (silent) (silence), and after him the whole of appearance. And yes, in the same breath, he is thus the inventor of language, naming names. Right at the start, then, Laozi tells us that his lineage is based in the esoteric, in a non-evident knowledge of how the world works.

SK: Even a materialist is forced to accept the inadequacy of language.

KS: Others are welcome to go further into his wisdom: wonder-workers, diviners, spirit mediums, life-extenders, herbalists, healers, immortals, martial artists, militarists, all these have based themselves in his writing.

SK: Poets, too. For in poetry wordful activity exceeds the word.

KS: You can even use those teachings as the basis for a theocratic state. More than one Emperor was fully awed, writing their own commentaries. We still feel that awe. So it's up to us.

And then . . .

SK: When we pick up a Chinese classic, we are invited into a commentarial tradition, into a conversation that's been going on a very long time. It's not only a dialogue between us and the classic. It's an explicit textual conference. Perhaps we do this whenever we read, whatever we read, in whatever language, no?

KS: It's the basic intertextual situation. The Chinese are just more up front about it, and willing to name the first layer of our second-tier interlocutors.

SK: Can a translator control this process?

KS: Not really. No police patrol the borders against interlopers who don't respect national boundaries. Sure, we can selectively deselect the conversationalists we find abhorrent, but their ghosts aren't so easily busted—their redolence wafts about for some time.

SK: To use a kinship metaphor, by reading we are marrying into a very large family, some members of which we may find unsavory.

KS: (chuckling) On your metaphor the classic would be the mater-pater familias. They're nominally in charge, but perhaps showing their age a bit.

SK: The idea that the classic is so utterly at the mercy of its commentaries reminds me of Gadamer's interpretive pluralism. Can we let go of the authority we've long abdicated to classics to teach us and face the responsibilities born of our own interpretations?

KS: Yup. The classic never did it alone and won't now. So it's up to us.

Works Cited

Boodberg, Peter. "Philological notes on chapter one of the *Lao Tzu*." *Harvard Journal of Asiatic Studies*, vol. 20, no. 3/4, 1957, pp. 598–618.

Knight, Sabina. *Chinese Literature: A Very Short Introduction*. Oxford UP, 2012.

Lynn, Richard John. *The Classic of Changes: A New Translation of the I Ching as Interpreted by Wang Bi*. Columbia UP, rev. ed., 2004.

Smith, Kidder, Peter K. Bol, Joseph A. Adler, and Don J. Wyatt. *Sung Dynasty Uses of the I Ching*. Princeton UP, 1990.

Smith, Kidder, and the Denma Translation Group. *Sun Tzu: The Art of War*, by Sun Tzu. Shambhala, 2001.

Smith, Kidder, and Sarah Messer. *Having Once Paused: Poems of Zen Master Ikkyu (1394–1481)*. U of Michigan Press, 2015.

Smith, Kidder, and Mike Zhai. *Li Bo Unkempt*. punctum books, 2020.

2

Happy Hour Homer

On Translating and Performing the *Iliad* Live in a Bar

Lynn Kozak

In 2016, the *Daily Beast* published an article entitled, "Translating the *Iliad*? Who Isn't?," rounding up the eight-and-counting new English-language *Iliad* translations that the previous decade had produced with an air of bemused bewilderment. The article came out just as I was finishing up my first book, on the *Iliad*, and looking forward to a project that the book proposed: translating and performing the *Iliad* serially.

*Iliad*s everywhere, but I stormed ahead anyways, for two main reasons. First, despite the abundant *Iliad*s, none of them were translated with performance in mind, and certainly not *through* performance. Second, because I love the *Iliad*—I find its themes of death and loss and the extremes of human behavior constantly compelling. When I started performing shorter bits of the epic in 2016, I found that the only thing I loved more than reading or teaching the *Iliad* was *telling* the *Iliad*. Why tell someone about your favorite story when you can tell the story itself?

The idea of performing the whole *Iliad* became possible because of a discovery I made while performing with Carina de Klerk. In 2014, we did an improvisational show, *Ephemer-illz*, based on ancient Greek lyric poetry, where we would each recite several poems as they thematically fit into our conversation. In the first couple of shows, I tried to translate the poems, and then memorize the translations. It was a disaster. Then for one show I didn't have time to look at the translations, I just translated the poems right before the show, and I found I remembered them. Ancient Greek word order is very different than English, and the very act of translating had seared the poems in my memory, creating a visual pattern where I could see some words and had some clear sense of where things were on the page as I had jumped around translating them. I still can't quite explain it, but that's how it works.

I can't exactly remember the text that I'm translating or the translation, but I can remember the translating, so I can translate.

Armed with this memorization technique, I devised a "serial" *Iliad* schedule that would be simple but intense. I would perform the whole *Iliad*, in order, line-for-line, until I finished it, doing one performance per week. Every week would have a different director. Every week, I would sit down on Tuesday and do a rough translation of a 400-to-600-line chunk of the *Iliad*, with its starting point the previous week's ending point, and its endpoint the director's choice. On Wednesdays I would take that chunk and read a rough English translation aloud (from the Greek) with the director, working through rough patches and thinking about language choices. We would rehearse, in English, from the Greek, Thursday–Sunday, continuing to work on language while incorporating costume choices and blocking, as well as, depending on the week, everything from props to choreography. (One week, at my own request, the very talented Andrew Turner taught me how to wield a lightsabre as I recounted Achilles's battles in the river at the beginning of Book 21.) Monday nights, at 6 p.m., I would perform the chunk live, with no script, at the Bar des Pins, in front of an audience of anywhere between 65 and 120 people. Once I started, some people came every week. It took me twenty-nine weeks to make it through the whole *Iliad*.

So, in a way, by the end of those twenty-nine weeks, I joined the smallish ranks of those who have translated the whole *Iliad* into English (though technically, I dropped 3 to 5 percent of lines every week in my performances so I probably only *performed* about 95 percent of the poem). But I did so through a very unusual approach, not spending years working on meter, or perfecting one section or another, or pouring over scholia and various editions to decide on what lines should stay in. Instead, I raced through a partially improvised performance-based line-for-line translation that I finished in exactly as long as it took me to translate, memorize, and rehearse those passages. No more, no less. No second chances. No time to fret over a missed line or a mistake. Just the relentless pace of the next week, and the fact that no matter what, there would be people at the Bar des Pins at 6 p.m. on Monday, waiting for me to give them a bit more of the *Iliad*.

Approaching an ancient Greek oral epic to translate into spoken English presents several problems right off the bat. First, Homeric epics were composed in dactylic hexameter, a difficult meter to fit in English even for the best poets, but, as I'm not a poet at all, something I abandoned any notion of from the start. Other translators—many, better translators, in fact—have managed to translate Homeric epic into meter. Lattimore tries to emulate the dactylic hexameter of the original; Wilson, like others before her, goes for a more-natural-to-English iambic pentameter line. I just admitted that I'm terrible at meter and moved on. I wanted to tell the audience the *Iliad* for its amazing story, and I knew I could never do that if I tried to do it in meter. But this raised practical questions about how and if the epics' narrative and mnemonic devices, from epithets, to formulaic lines, to extended similes, still work in performance when they no longer fit into or derive from fixed metrics.

Epithets were certainly the first to become very loose in my translations. On the one hand, every week I would notice how epithets shifted and migrated: suddenly, the Achaians, the *Iliad*'s Greek protagonist-army, no longer had great hair, but definitely had nice shinguards. Through such a condensed process of going through and memorizing the whole text, I became more convinced of its paratactic composition: suddenly I could see the seams more where poets or poetic traditions traded off, switched out, faded away or came into vogue, and I could feel my own performative tendencies becoming similarly slippery, under different directors, and through my own preferences. Epithets became the first victims of my taxed memory, becoming fluid since meter didn't clearly dictate which epithet went where. Of course, Hektor, the Trojan commander, had a shiny helmet (translating the adjective κορυθαίολος, which occurs thirty-nine times in the *Iliad*). But maybe he was also horse-taming (ἱππόδαμος, four occurrences). I can't remember which he was where. Mostly, he had a shiny helmet. There were, of course, exceptions. When Andromache, Hektor's wife, goes home after seeing him for the last time, she returns to "the house of man-slaughtering Hektor" (Ἕκτορος ἀνδροφόνοιο, 6.498); when she holds his corpse's head in her hands, again, there, he is "man-slaughtering" (24.724) The *Iliad*'s narrative voice forced these violent epithet-breeches into their domestic intimacy, and so they lingered in my memory, even when other instances fell away.

But what about those nice shinguards? ἐϋκνήμιδες, the first epithet that the *Iliad* applies to the Achaians (1.17) normally translates as "strong-greaved" (Lattimore). The standard Greek-English dictionary (henceforth cited as LSJ) gives "well-equipped with greaves, well-greaved" as its meaning. But what the hell is a greave? You might know, in the context of a suit of armor, that a greave is, well, a shinguard. But most English speakers aren't familiar with that term: Wilson tellingly omits it from her *Odyssey*, opting for more generic "well-armed" or "armed" if she includes it at all. Beyond recognizing the word on the page, in performance, there's the additional issue of how it sounds. With the exact same pronunciation as the much more common "grieve," a casual audience might easily hear "well-grieved" or "strong-grieved" and associate grief with the Achaians—after all, they're fighting a war and many of them are dying. So maybe not greaves. Let's change it up for something clearer, that most everyone would know: shin-guards. But "well-shin-guarded" doesn't exactly roll off the tongue, so time to lose the prefix. And then the context comes in. Here, the priest Chryse comes before the Achaians to beg for his daughter, whom they kidnapped, back. He addresses them as ἐϋκνήμιδες Achaians—and I think that his intention is to flatter, to soften them up so that they might give his daughter back. So that's how I play it, almost grasping for something to praise the Achaians for as I start to beg them: "you Achaians, with your nice shin-guards!" (1.17). But while I translate "nice shinguards" in rehearsal (and throughout the rest of my performances), I don't actually say it at this line: the night of the performance, I mess up and confuse it with another epithet for the Achaians, κομόωντες, a descriptive participle that means "letting the hair grow out," which Lattimore translates as "flowing-haired." Because I remember that there's an epithet there, and because I remember my motivation in the moment, I flatter, but I forget the shinguards and say, "all you other Achaians with your great hair."

"Great hair" became gender-neutral through my translation, and didn't only apply to those Achaians, but also became interchangeable with the epithet ἠΰκομος, "good-haired." The LSJ clearly genders the epithet, giving the definition: "*lovely-haired*, of goddesses and noble ladies" (Liddell and Scott n.p.). My gender-fluid self wanted to keep it more neutral, and explicitly link back to κομόωντες: I thought, can't everyone in the *Iliad* just have "great hair" like we're in an 1980s teen movie? But more often, I translated ἠΰκομος as "good hair," and, very frequently, with the Beyoncé-inspired "with the good hair." In 2018, I, like so many other people, was still listening obsessively to Beyoncé's brilliant *Lemonade*, where the song "Sorry" features a line about "Becky with the good hair." I loved the line's contempt for a cheater's lover and her conventional beauty standards: "Helen with the good hair" (3.329; 7.355) takes on a different attitude within that pop context. But I also regret the appropriation, as I'd been familiar with "good hair" as a Black American expression at least since Chris Rock's 2009 documentary: as a White person performing to a primarily White audience, I don't think that I had the right to be so flippant with a Black American expression that responds to race-based beauty standards. If I were to perform again, I think I would keep the more neutral "great hair" throughout.

Hephaistos's epithet brought about another issue. The most common epithet that the epic applies to the forge-god is ἀμφιγυήεις, which the LSJ gives as "he that halts in both feet": Cunliffe's Homeric lexicon gives "having a crooked limb on each side." These more literal definitions specifically describing Hephaistos's disability, rather than describing *him*, both fit better with contemporary sensibilities around disability. But the LSJ also gives "the lame one," a now outdated mode of talking about someone with impairments in their legs: Fitzgerald also uses "lame." In his *Iliad*, Lattimore curiously chooses "strong-armed" as a euphemism, erasing the impairment by shifting focus, though he switches to "twice-lamed" in his *Odyssey*. Fagles uses the terrible "crippled." Alexander goes with "crooked-legged." Wilson's *Odyssey* uses "limping." I kept it long and literal, and every time I said Hephaistos, I explained that he had a disability in both legs. I should have really said "impairments in both legs," as the *Iliad* makes the difference between impairment and disability abundantly clear: Hephaistos has purpose-built his own house and workshop with mobility aids, eliminating disability in terms of how he can work at home, despite his physical impairments (18.369–477).

Beyond formulaic epithets, full formulaic phrases show up everywhere in Homeric verse, and again fell victim to my improvisational style. The most common formulaic phrases introduce or conclude direct speech, since direct speech makes up almost 45 percent of the epic. From ὣς ἔφατ' and ὣς εἰπὼν to the longer τὸν δ' ἀπαμειβόμενος προσέφη (107 occurrences), these speech formulae are everywhere. Lattimore actually mixes it up a lot translating these, and perhaps it's no wonder as they occur so frequently. For ὣς εἰπὼν, a participial phrase that literally means "so speaking," Lattimore gives no fewer than eight variations in his *Iliad* translation: "he spoke" (1.446); "so speaking" (2.70; 6.466; 15.352); "speaking so" (4.73); "so he spoke" (4.292; 4.364; 5.460; 5.470; 6.72); "spoke like this" (6.61); "spoke thus" (7.365); "with this speech" (10.131); "he spoke so" (16.751). More, he adds in "so saying" in his *Odyssey* translation. Fagles gets a lot more creative, with a wide range of expressions of speaking that change with the context, from the generic "with those words" (1.446) and "with that" (2.70; 5.460) to the more specific "so he launched" (4.73); "shot back" (4.364); "as Ares whipped" (5.470); "so he ordered" (6.72); "brought his brother round" (6.61)—the list goes on. Alexander sticks to the literal "so speaking" (4.73; 4.292), capturing the present participle; Wilson, again, for the most part, cuts this circumstantial participle altogether, sticking with the main verb of the line. I also cut it several times in my performed translation where the context made it clear that the *speaking* was over. But most of the time, I used the phrase to transition from speaking *as a character* to *speaking as the narrator*. And, from the first week, under the direction of Joseph Shragge, I translated it as "that's what he said." It's both literal and funny, a Michael Scott meme where you least expect it. But then, of course, our serial audience came to expect it, and that formulaic assurance within the performance became funny too.

This tone fits with many of my more casual translation choices for a range of other terms. Compound speaking words often translated as "addressed/spoke forth" (προσηύδα, 6.163; 6.214; προσέειπε, 6.43; προσέφη, 6.108) just became "he was like." When people "insulted" someone else (νεικέω), in my translation, they "started shit" (1.579, 2.221), or they "told them off" (3.38, 3.59), a phrase which I also used for ἐνίπτω (LSJ gives as "reprove, upbraid"; 15.552), and ὀνείδειον φάτο μῦθον (literally "spoke a blaming word," 21.471). Being angry or angered almost always became "pissed" (χολωθείς,1.9), "pissed off" (χολωθείς, 23.88), or, sometimes, even "super pissed off" (χολωσαμένη at 21.479). νήπιος, which Lattimore translates as "fool" when applied to heroes, became "dumbass" (16.46, 16.686); a single, unnamed man, whether in simile or in narration was usually just a "guy"; ἐσθλός ("excellent") became "awesome"; θεράπων ("henchman, attendant, companion-in-arms, squire") became "sidekick." In general, I try to find the most colloquial way to translate as literally as possible.

It's harder when the translation isn't the translation itself, but the cultural connotations that the literal translation expresses and distorts, like with γέρας, "prize." "Prize" sounds so nice—something that you win on a gameshow or take home from a fair. Except that in the *Iliad*, it's most often a woman who has been taken by force after her city has been sacked and all the men in her family killed, and then who has been forced to serve her new master both for sexual satisfaction and for manual labor. So when I first started translating "prize," I said, "I have to make a note here that every time I say prize I'm actually talking about an enslaved woman; this is the shit world that we're in" (1.120). I remind the audience again of this storyworld's literal objectification of women in Book 19, where the narrator lists Agamemnon's material restitution to Achilles:

> Ok, so we've got seven tripods, twelve horses, twenty fiery cauldrons, and you know, you all know of course, in this awful world we're in what comes after tripods, horses, and cauldrons, right? That's right, women. There are seven of them, and they all know how to work with their blameless hands, so that's great, and then there's the eighth, the eighth, who is pretty-cheeked Briseis. (19.243-46)

Lattimore's translation of the same lines sticks to the Greek without comment:

> They brought back seven tripods from the shelter, those Agamemnon / had promised, and twenty shining cauldrons, twelve horses. They brought back / immediately the seven women the work of whose hands was / blameless, and the eighth of them was Briseis of the fair cheeks. (19.243-6)

Comedian Mike Paterson directed my translation of the first half of Book 23, Patroklos's funeral games, and he played with my pushbacks against the

Iliad's in-built misogyny, directing the translation for Achilles's laying out wrestling prizes:

> For first prize, tonight we've got a tripod, now this is the kind of tripod you can put over the fire, and the Achaians value it at twelve oxen; and for the loser, we've got a woman, she knows how to do all kinds of things, and they value her at four oxen (she's no tripod, my friends.). (23.702–5)

> (Lattimore's: There was a great tripod, to set over fire, for the winner. / The Achaians among themselves valued it at the worth of twelve oxen. / But for the beaten man he set in their midst a woman / skilled in much work of her hands, and they rated her at four oxen.)

There's obviously showmanship within this translation, as I went into a *Price Is Right* mode, riffing on our positive cultural connotations of "prize," and the deep irony within that mode that makes it clear how little women's lives are worth in the *Iliad*'s storyworld. As Mike had hoped, the added line got a huge laugh. But again, I wonder about that, and think about popular criticism of *The Handmaid's Tale* in the Whiteness of its feminism. My mostly White-Settler audience laughed because the idea of a woman being just another prize to give away or to win was ridiculous. I'm not sure it would be so funny to other audiences, or in other contexts.

Emily Wilson has done an incredible job in publicly addressing the misogyny of the Homeric world, and of its translators. Performing while translating the *Iliad* adds a new dimension to that, because you have to embody those views. The *Iliad* is still my favorite story, and *telling* it is still better than teaching it or talking about it. But it's a two-edged sword, because for every moment of brutal beauty that thrills to inhabit, there's a deep discomfort in being in that world for too long, in letting that narrator or those characters into my body, in letting them be me, or me be them, in front of others. The language of my *Iliad* reflects that uncomfortable blurring, existing between my vernacular and the Greek. In and out of performing, there are times I feel repulsed at this story and its characters, pissed off at being part of a culture that continues to venerate them, but then, there are times when I just can't help but think how awesome they are, how awesome the whole *Iliad* is. "Rage, goddess, tell me about that destructive rage."

Works Cited

Cunliffe, Richard John. *A Lexicon of the Homeric Dialect: Expanded Edition.* University of Oklahoma Press, 2012.

Homer, *The Iliad*, translated by Richmond Lattimore. University of Chicago Press, 1951.
Homer, *The Iliad*, translated by Robert Fitzgerald. Oxford University Press, 1974.
Homer, *The Iliad*, translated by Caroline Alexander. Harper Collines, 2016.
Homer, *The Odyssey*, translated by Emily Wilson. W. W. Norton & Company, 2017.
Liddell, Henry George and Robert Scott. *A Greek-English Lexicon. Revised and augmented throughout by Sir Henry Stuart Jones with the assistance of Roderick McKenzie*. Clarendon Press, 1940, perseus.tufts.edu.
Romm, James. "Translating the 'Iliad'? Who Isn't." *The Daily Beast,* August 13, 2017. https://www.thedailybeast.com/translating-the-iliad-who-isnt

3

Today in the Temple of Language

Translating Dante[1]

Mary Jo Bang

The book-length poem *Inferno*, the first book in the trilogy *The Divine Comedy*, written between 1308 and 1321 by the Florentine Italian poet Dante Alighieri—who had been exiled from Florence by his political enemies in 1302—begins with a character, also named Dante, finding himself in a dark wood where he suddenly becomes aware that he's lost his way. That book and the next two books, *Purgatorio* and *Paradiso*, track the character as he tries to find his way out of what turns out to be a profound existential crisis. Every subsequent action hinges on that first moment of realization. With my translation of the *Inferno*, I can similarly trace a chain of events back to a particular moment. In June 2006, I picked up a book of poems called *Fig* by the British poet Caroline Bergvall and read a poem titled "Via (48 Dante Variations)." It was a found poem composed entirely of the first three lines of the *Inferno* taken from the forty-seven translations Bergvall had found archived in the British Library in May 2000. Bergvall had arranged the three-line stanzas called tercets alphabetically by the first word of the opening line, with the translator's name and year of publication appended to the end of each selection. Reading the poem, I was fascinated by the fact that while the simple language of the original three lines, which Bergvall gives at the top of the page—"Nel mezzo del cammin di nostra vita / mi ritrovai per una selva oscura / ché la diritta via era smarrita" ("Midway through our life, / I found myself in a dark wood; / the right way was lost")—never changes, no two translations were identical. The poem felt like an object lesson: there

---

[1] This chapter includes portions of "A Note on the Translation," which first appeared in *Inferno*, translated by Mary Jo Bang (Graywolf Press, 2012), and portions of "A Note on the Translation," which first appeared in *Purgatorio*, translated by Mary Jo Bang (Graywolf Press, 2021). Reprinted with the permission of Graywolf Press.

is no single right way to carry what has been said in one language across to another.

Bergvall's poem also reminded me of what I'd learned in a translation workshop I took with William Weaver in 1995 when I was a student in the MFA Creative Writing Program in Poetry at Columbia University. On the first day of class, Weaver brought in copies of the first few pages of three translations of Part I of Miguel de Cervantes's *Don Quixote*, originally published in 1612. They were so different from one another that, at first glance, someone might have thought they were three separate novels. What Weaver wanted to demonstrate for us was how language shifts in register over time, and how, by keeping current with those changes, a translator keeps pulling a text into the ever-evolving present. Reading Bergvall's "Via," I noticed how elevated the language was in all the translations—not only those done many years earlier but even in the more recent ones. *Inferno* was written in the 1300s, but it is also timeless in the way it mimes what it is to be a human being. Dante himself was aware that his poem, which he called *La Commedia* (*The Comedy*)—(the poet Giovanni Boccaccio added *Divina* [Divine] to the title when he gave a series of lectures about the work in 1373)—needed to have warmth if it were to adequately reflect the psychological complexity of human behavior. In Book I of *Il Convivio* (*The Banquet*), written before he began *La Commedia*, Dante explained why the vernacular is more appropriate for poems than the commonly used literary Latin: Latin was so beautiful, virtuous, and noble, its sovereignty would overwhelm the poem and make it feel remote. The vernacular has intimacy, familiarity, and a sense of generosity; it's not reliant on special learning but is simply given to one as a child. Latin is frozen in time and therefore can't change; the Latin of yesterday will be the same Latin of tomorrow; the vernacular is unstable, corruptible, and will change over time. Latin was limited to a small group of readers, the "learned"; the poem needed to be written in a language that could be read by many. Dante's use of the vernacular was so radical that many in other parts of Italy were inspired to learn the Tuscan dialect so they could read his poem.

It seemed to me, reading the Bergvall, that the elevated register of the translations she'd gathered together created the very sense of remoteness that Dante had wished to avoid. Dante's poem in translation sounded the way it might have if it had originally been written in literary Latin. I wondered what might happen if someone were to put those first three lines of the *Inferno* into colloquial spoken English? Would it sound like a cover song, the words of the original unmistakably there, but made unfamiliar by the fact that someone else's voice has its own characteristics? Could it be, like covers sometimes are, a tribute that pays homage to the original, while departing from it? Taking Bergvall's forty-seven variations as examples, I tried putting the three lines into English. Once I gave myself a bit of poetic license, and poetic license seemed essential since what I was translating was a poem, I found there were many different ways to carry the Italian over into English. I paid a great deal of attention to sound. Dante had created an interlocking rhyme scheme especially for the poem, so I wanted to be true to that, but also because sound does a lot of the work in poetry, it contributes to the singularity of the poem and it has tremendous expressive potential. For his *terza rima*, which is nearly impossible to do with elegance in a long poem in rhyme-poor English, I substituted the dominant music of contemporary poetry—assonant echoes, internal rhyme, alliteration. I capitalized the left margin as a gesture toward the English poetic tradition.

After working with the first tercet, I decided to translate the second. For that, I used a 1970 prose translation by Charles S. Singleton that I had on my bookshelf. This was the *Inferno* translation I'd read a decade earlier when a friend and I read *Inferno* together, each of us using a different translation so we could appreciate how two translators approached the challenge of conveying both the meaning and the innovative spirit of the original. Now, leaning heavily on Singleton's translation, tonally elevated and rich with archaicisms, and following the original on the facing page, I translated the second tercet, then a third. It suddenly occurred to me that for the first three lines, I'd had forty-seven models, the variations Bergvall had used to make her poem, and now I had only one. So, I went to the library and selected several translations—ranging in form from those that followed the original *terza rima* rhyme scheme to those that translated the poem into unrhymed prose—and ranging in time from Longfellow's first American translation, published in 1867, to one by Robert and Jean Hollander, published in 2000. Reading all of these, plus their notes, plus Singleton's separate volume of commentary on *Inferno*, I continued translating Canto I, trying to stay scrupulously true to what the poem said, and to what I took to be Dante's intent in writing it, but composing as if I were some hybrid creature, myself plus Dante's text, the two parts behaving as if they had one mind and were living in the present.

After finishing my translation of the first canto, I decided to continue and create an English-language version of the *Inferno* that would adhere to the original but would seem neither remote in time nor elevated in diction. The *Inferno* is a dramatic, harrowing, and often extremely witty demonstration of the timeless pernicious effects of corruption, malice, selfishness, and nefariousness. In that way, the poem remains forever relevant. Dante was a product of his era and his geography: the lens through which he viewed the world was Catholicism. The issues he raises in the *Inferno*, however, are larger than those of a single religious belief system. Dante's poem, a coming-of-age novel of sorts—a lost young man gains emotional knowledge under the influence of a kind but stern tutor—keeps drawing artists to it. I discovered I wasn't alone in my desire to make the poem speak in the language of the present. I found many other revival projects where artists layered a twenty-first-century sensibility over the medieval text, including a 2004 Chronicle Books version of Dante's *Inferno* by Marcus Sanders and artist-illustrator Sandow Birk that sets the poem in contemporary Los Angeles, where abandoned cars and battered signage line the walls of Hell; a 2005 album by the Eternal Kool Project called *The Inferno Rap*, where MicPwr raps Henry Francis Cary's 1805–6 blank verse translation of the *Inferno* over a track composed by Mr. Moe; a 2006 oversized graphic novel, *Jimbo's Inferno* (Fantagraphics), by the punk-pop artist Gary Panter, in which Jimbo—with a crew cut, and wearing only a loincloth—rides a talking suitcase called Valise across a barren landscape to a vertical mall that functions like the *Inferno*. And while I was translating the poem, on February 9, 2009, Dante's Inferno—a video game featuring a hypermuscular action hero named Dante, "a soldier who defies death and fights for love against impossible odds"—was released by Electronic Arts. A Google search at that time for "Dante's Inferno" brought up the game's official website as the first listing; the Wikipedia listing for the *Inferno*, the first book of Dante Alighieri's *The Divine Comedy*, was the second.

I thought one way to make the poem feel relevant would be to allow it to speak with intimacy about the world we live in: the postmodern, internet-ubiquitous present. I wanted the poem to feel familiar and yet not alter Dante's odd fusion of Greek and Roman mythology, Catholicism, and medieval Tuscan politics. The poem rests on those pillars and on their moral lessons. The character Farinata, an arrogant Ghibelline military leader whom we meet in Canto X, needed to remain Farinata, as he had for 700 years: confrontational, unapologetic about the damage he did while he was on earth, self-justifying, reminding Dante that he could have done more harm to the city of Florence but didn't. He's unrepentant and therefore deserving of his end. Virgil, the Roman poet who acts as a guide for Dante in Hell (he will do the same in Purgatory), has to play the role of Reason. God has to look down from Heaven; Satan has to sit at the center of Hell, locked in a block of ice. The characters had to remain as they were in the original but I gave myself permission to toy not only with the sound patterning that makes up the poem's rhetorical surface but with the allusions and similes.

Few of us know what it is to be, or to even see, a peasant and his cart; a simile built on that image risks seeming charmingly antiquated. Even if we work on a farm, we drive a pickup truck or a car to work, or ride a tractor from house to field. The fact is, on the level of language, a peasant is only a refinement of the general category of worker. Similarly, few of us use bows and arrows, so when a boat comes across the pond of Styx "faster than an arrow," the comparison can feel trapped in the distant past. But an Ultimate Aero, one of the fastest production cars in the world, once *the* fastest production car in the world, was an arrow that seemed one with our culture of televised racetracks and glossy magazine ads, one with our personal experience of speed. As I went forward, these were the kind of substitutions I allowed myself—worker for peasant, car for cart, Aero for arrow—ones where the medieval original is embodied in the modern. Of course, these substitutions can seem playful; whenever the classical and the modern meet, there's the potential for a slapstick brand of humor. For that reason, I tried not to draw undue attention to those moments nor to incorporate too many of them into the text. I wanted there to be pleasure in the encounters with the present but wanted that pleasure to be fleeting; the primary role of the substitutions was to demonstrate that Dante's Hell never ages, nor do our basic human failings ever change—they only get enacted against a different background.

In the *Inferno*, Dante paid homage to poets and figures who meant something to him and to his readers; he appropriated stories once told by Virgil, Ovid, and Lucan, and sometimes adapted them to suit his purposes. Another means of bringing the poem into the present would be to include, through allusion, some of the poets and storytellers who have lived and left a mark in the time since Dante wrote his poem. And because the distinction between high culture and popular entertainment has all but ceased to exist, I decided to also include words by poet-songwriters. I would refer to other aspects of contemporary culture as well, just as Dante did. He mentions the annual race at Verona where the winner was awarded a bolt of green cloth; the loser, a rooster that had to be carried around town. He mentions towers, churches, statues, bells, and whistles, both domestic and imported; he includes thinkers such as Euclid, Aristotle, Socrates, and Plato; historical figures like Cleopatra, Caesar, and Hannibal; religious figures and mythic characters. He created a detailed world filled with everyday objects and recognizable people, architecture, and landscapes. I extended that gesture into the present by including references to such figures and objects as klieg lights and cameras, the board game Monopoly, Sigmund Freud, Stephen Colbert, and Eric Cartman from *South Park*.

Walter Benjamin claimed in "The Task of the Translator" that "a translation issues from the original—not so much from its life as from its afterlife . . . a translation, instead of resembling the meaning of the original, must lovingly and in detail incorporate the original's mode of signification, thus making both the original and the translation recognizable as fragments of a greater language" (78). Part of that "greater language" comes from a shared human experience. Over time some elements of human life remain unchanged; other elements get altered. Translation is a method of bringing the past back into the present—across geographies, across different time periods, and across cultural difference—and sharing what is common to all. That act is both homage and theft—the first, a worshipful respect; the second, an oedipal bravado that says everything in the past, no matter who first made it, can be used as scraps, out of which a new suit can be sewn, now with wide lapels, now with narrow. Translation keeps a work of literature alive by simultaneously dismantling and reclaiming it. For the translator, there is an intense—and paradoxical—intellectual pleasure that comes from making a text that has already been made by someone else. It is a strange collaborative camaraderie.

At the end of *Inferno*, Dante emerges from an underground cavern, still shaken by the horrors he witnessed while traveling with Virgil through the nine circles of Hell. Hearing the stories told by those confined there for eternity, he had sometimes found his eyes filling with tears, or, in the case of the two ill-fated lovers, Francesca and Paolo, he was so moved by their story, he fainted. He was chased by demons, had to cross a river of boiling blood on the back of a centaur, was scolded by Virgil for gawking at the petty bickering of a couple of spiteful counterfeiters. Now, having made his way through a dim-lit, winding underground channel, accessed by climbing down the dangling hairy legs of a huge, three-faced Satan frozen in a block of ice called Lake Cocytus, he steps outside. Here is how *Inferno* ends:

Down there, in a remote corner—
The distance of Beelzebub's tomb times two—
Is an area one can't find by sight in that low light

But only by the sound of a stream that,
As it trickles down a slight incline,
Has carved a winding canyon through the rock.

My teacher and I entered that secluded passage
That would lead us back to the lit world.
Not wanting to waste time resting, we climbed—

Him first, then me—until we came to a round opening
Through which I saw some of the beautiful things
That come with Heaven. And we walked out

To once again catch sight of the stars. (330)

Since *The Divine Comedy* is a trilogy, that final scene of the *Inferno* is only the moment when someone hits the pause button; *Purgatorio* is the next chapter in the ongoing story. As I stood with the character named Dante on the hopeful shore of the ocean surrounding Mount Purgatory—and looked up and saw what he saw, the convulsive beauty of the stars in a place where no light pollution washes out the night sky—I wanted to know what happened next. I felt attached to this character in the midst of an existential crisis; I wanted to stay with him to see who and what he would encounter next. I could have simply read an existing translation. But there was still that problem of the elevated register, which is not only a continual distracting reminder of the distance between that long-ago era and today but, more importantly, after having translated the *Inferno*, I could see how the elevation blunts the subtle differences between the voices of the characters, which is a key element of how the poem works. So, in March 2012, before the publication of the *Inferno* translation in August, I began translating *Purgatorio*.

Dante's conception of Purgatory is a seven-terrace mountain, each level devoted to atoning for one of the seven deadly sins; at the top is the Terrestrial Heaven, the ancient, abandoned Eden. As in the *Inferno*, the reader finds, among those on the mountain, enduring examples of the human behaviors that fracture the social fabric into feuding groups, each hell-bent on the destruction of the other, and the myriad types of bad actors who willingly sacrifice everyone—except the yes-men and yes-women who prop them up, and those too are sacrificed if ever a yes isn't forthcoming. Because the characters are meant to represent humanity from the beginning of time until now, Dante draws equally on real people and on invented figures from myth. The drunken, half-man/half-horse centaurs who carry off the bride and bridesmaids at a wedding can serve as an illustration of the dangers of impulsive behavior as easily as an Italian archbishop named Ruggieri degli Ubaldinican can demonstrate human cruelty by locking a former associate in a castle with two of his sons and two grandsons and allowing all of them to starve to death. Dante makes it clear, it's the offense that is the problem, not the perpetrator. Individuals may be punished, yes, but unless society gains insight, spiteful and vicious behavior will simply continue with new players. And so it has. We have only to look at the news.

While medieval Catholicism is both the stage setting for the poems, and source of the character Dante's hope for redemption, for himself and for others, Dante Alighieri, the author, draws on early Christian and non-Christian thinkers to construct his arguments for a better world. He exposes the hypocrisy of the leadership, church and state, demonstrating over and over again the crookedness of the shepherd's rook, the greed, and the meanness of those who wield power. He allows the pagan Roman Poet Virgil to continue to be the voice of Reason until they reach the edge of Lethe, the River of Oblivion, where a woman named Beatrice assumes the role. At the end of the poem, she tells Dante he should have recognized that the features of the Tree of Knowledge, its enormous height, a canopy so wide it overwhelms the trunk, the fact that the branches point up, speak not just to the prohibition to not eat from the tree but to the need for obedience to a moral code that protects society. She instructs Dante to write this poem based on what he's seen and learned.

As in the *Inferno* translation, I tried to bring *Purgatorio* forward into the present by using spoken English and the phonic echoes common to contemporary English poetry. I again extended Dante's cultural reference by including (to name a few) the fable of "The Little Red Hen"; "Goldilocks and the Three Bears"; a photo-op close-up of the MGM logo, Leo the Lion; Tootsie Fruit Chews; and the game of Chutes and Ladders. I again included lines from poems that continue the lineage of Dante and his Roman poets: Shakespeare, Emily Dickinson, Gertrude Stein, Allen Ginsberg, Alice Dunbar-Nelson, and Oscar Wilde, among others. And once again, I incorporated snippets of songs from low-culture poets, the musicians, meant to echo the singers and songs Dante weaves into the poem: Bob Dylan, Cyndi Lauper, Amy Winehouse, John Coltrane, Marvin Gaye, Talking Heads, Richie Havens, and others.

Shared culture creates both a sense of lineage and the illusion of verisimilitude, the way a mirroring store window confirms that the world behind you is today's world. The idea behind including the contemporary allusions is to create a recognizable backdrop against which the reader can appreciate that Dante's remarkable intelligence, considerable humor, vast erudition, and subtly drawn characters are one with our world. A poem is a delicate apparatus—the poet W. H. Auden once called it "a verbal contraption," which is brilliantly apt. How a poem comes to mean can't be totally deconstructed and yet, in spite of that, the translator's task is to find language and pattern it in a way that will echo the effects of the original.

Because my translations are one with this particular historical moment, they are destined to become artifacts of this era. The original poem will continue to exist. There are many other translations that more closely adhere to a literal rendering of the Tuscan dialect in which the poem was written; readers who want something that aspires to the original have many options from which to choose. As John Dryden wrote in his preface to *Fables*—his verse translations of Homer, Ovid, Boccaccio, and Chaucer—I've made my version "for their sakes who understand Sense and Poetry . . . when that Poetry and Sense is put into words which they understand" (Dryden, "Preface" n.p.). My love of Dante's *Commedia* has driven me to unpack the syntax of the ancient original and put it into a spoken form of English that is rich with idiom, and even occasional slang. My hope is that my postmodern, intertextual, slightly slant translations will lure new readers to a poetic text that might seem otherwise archaic and off-putting. And that having read my translation, readers will want to read other translations of the poem. The differences and similarities speak to the way translation works and more generally to how language works.

Works Cited

Bang, Mary Jo. *Inferno*. Graywolf Press, 2012.
Benjamin, Walter. *Walter Benjamin Selected Writings Volume I*; Ed. Marcus Bullock and Michael W. Jennings. Harvard University Press, 1996.
Bergvall, Caroline. "Via (48 Dante Variations)." From Fig. Salt, 2005.
Birk, Sandow and Marcus Sanders. *Dante's Inferno*. Chronicle Books, 2004.
Dryden, John. "Preface." *Fables, Ancient and Modern*. Jacob Tonson, 1700.
Hollander, Robert and Jean Hollander. *Inferno*. Anchor, 2002.
Longfellow, Henry Wadsworth. *Inferno*. Ed. Matthew Pearl. Modern Library, 2003. First published 1867.
Panter, Gary. *Jimbo's Inferno*. Fantagraphics Books, 2006.
Singleton, Charles S. *The Divine Comedy of Dante Alighieri: Translation and Commentary*. 2 vols. Princeton University Press, 1970.

4

True Confessions of a Literary Translator

Arvind Krishna Mehrotra

My earliest memory of translation is when I would translate without reading the original. I would have the original in front of me and I could read the language, but since I read slowly and without understanding all the words, I'd leave it alone and get on with the translation. I was, you could say, translating blind.

I'd been writing since my mid-teens and was eager to write more, no matter how the writing came. When I started doing this thing that I'm talking about, of translating without knowing the original—which was a doha or couplet by Kabir in fifteenth-century Hindi—it in some ways felt similar to what I experienced when I wrote my own poems. There too I tried to see as clearly as I could what was but a floating indistinct shape before me. I could not always tell the two sensations apart, and to help me do so I gave them name tags, calling one Poetry and the other Translation.

The book I was translating from had a bilingual text, so when I read the Kabir doha I was also reading the English version printed below it. But the English was so inflated that it kept drifting away like a gas balloon, much like the Hindi original, though the latter escaped my grasp for different reasons. Kabir's language, as I was to learn, was earthy, whereas the language of the translation seemed not of this earth. Once in a while, in the English, I found something I could hold on to, something recognizable, familiar. I had already discovered Ezra Pound. "Go in fear of abstractions," he'd said. The translation I read consisted of little else. Slowly there emerged through the bilingual fog a few lines of verse, a new poem written 450 years after Kabir's death by a young, inspired, 21-year-old poet who bore my name:

> Be careful of women of gold
> these perfumed mistresses
>
> Never sit by them alone
> even if one is your mother.
> (poem translated in *Delos* #6 136)

Leaving the injunction aside for the moment, I quite liked the urgent pithy quality that one associates with Kabir, whom I'd read in school. He had left a stronger impression on me than the other bhakti poets, which is why I was reading him rather than Mirabai or Surdas.

I have ever since searched for the book in which I first encountered the bilingual text of Kabir. There are in my house in Dehra Dun, gathering dust in a revolving bookrack, a few titles on religion and spirituality published by Bharatiya Vidya Bhavan, Bombay. Bought by my father when I was in my early teens, they seem to have always been around. Their spines are torn, and some of the blue-bordered paper covers are missing, but the signatures and the binding threads are intact. I picked one whose title looked promising: *Ten Saints of India* by T. M. P. Mahadevan. As it turned out, the title was a little misleading; all the saints were from south India. There was no Kabir. I recall searching for the bilingual text earlier too, in an anthology of Indian religious poetry put together by Reverend Ahmad Shah and published by the Baptist Mission Press, Cawnpore, probably in the early 1920s. I cannot locate the book now, but it had many pages of Kabir couplets and songs. However, neither the Hindi nor the English translation seemed to have any resemblance to the poem I'd written.

Once I'd found this new way of writing original poetry, by outsourcing it to Kabir, I wrote several more. If translation is a fight to the death between author and translator, my luck soon ran out. As I translated more poems, Kabir, pushing me aside, took over. He started to speak in his own voice, whereas mine had fallen silent. Here, in these two songs, he is reminding us of the finality that awaits us all, regardless of how it comes or who we are. It's a subject he returned to often:

> you be pauper or prince
> or mendicant-saint,
> once you have come
> you must then end
>
> riding his throne
> one reaches the grave,
> the other is in irons bound
> and limps toward it. (137)

* * *

> The kings shall go, so will their pretty queens,
> courtiers and all proud ones shall go.

> Pundits chanting the *Vedas* shall go,
> and go will those who listen to them.
> Masochist yogis and bright intellectuals shall go,
> go the sun and moon and water and wind.
> Thus says Kabir only those can remain
> whose minds are tied to the rocks. (137)

The contest between Kabir and me, I would still say, had no clear winner. If Kabir, the author, had me, the translator, on the ropes, I was back on my feet quickly. "Masochist yogis" and "bright intellectuals" are phrases that couldn't have been in any original. In boxing terms, one of the phrases might be likened to a jab and the other to a head butt; one is an offense, the other a blatant foul. As a translator, I had in an eight-line poem managed to commit both. Seen in translation terms, this was a point scored.

After I'd done six of these translations, I sent them to a magazine that I'd come to know of on the "little mag" circuit. The magazine, edited by D. S. Carne-Ross and David Wevill and published by the University of Texas at Austin, was *Delos: A Magazine on and of Translation*. The poems were accepted and, in 1971, they appeared in its sixth issue, which also happened to be the last. The US magazines I'd published in till then had names like *The San Francisco Keeper's Voice* and *Salted Feathers*; they were almost always mimeographed and their pages were stapled together, but this one was printed and looked like a book. Along with the issue, *Delos* sent twenty-five offprints and paid seventy-five dollars, my first earnings from writing.

There were, among the six translations, two or three—including "Be Careful of Women of Gold"—that had no resemblance to anything in Kabir that I could find. They were, possibly, fake translations. Little did I know at the time that by passing off my own poems as Kabir's I'd become part of a long tradition whose every poem is written by someone else, or at least none that can be ascribed to Kabir with certainty. Though I had not added the signature phrase, "says Kabir," to some of the poems, I was one of the hundreds of poets who anonymously wrote and still write under his name. The only difference was that I wrote mine in English and the poems were not anonymous.

* * *

Iowa City, Iowa, 1971. I had never been outside India before, but when the Ozark Airlines flight landed in Cedar Rapids, it was like I had come home. Eight dollars per person was all the foreign exchange allowed in those socialist days, and my wife and I still had some saved when we arrived. Someone from the University of Iowa's International Writing Program met us at the airport and drove us to The Mayflower, an apartment building on North Dubuque Street, where we were to live for the next nine months. I had been able to get to Iowa courtesy the Cold War, the Department of State, and Paul Engle, the director of the Program. For the previous two years I'd been badgering him with airmail letters, trying to convince him that he ought to invite me, but he kept saying that I was too young and had not yet published a book, that the Program was for more established writers, all of which was true. Eventually, he relented. The writers who came to the Program were from South and South East Asia, Africa, Eastern Europe, and Latin America, brought to the United States to show them the wonders of the New World. One of the trips we made was to a John Deere factory in Waterloo.

There came to Iowa City one day Robert Bly, and he was reading, among other things, his translations of Kabir. I had all along believed that I would be the first to translate Kabir into the modern idiom but here was this famous American poet who'd beaten me to it. In the same way that I had based mine on someone else's English, Bly, who had no Hindi, based his versions on Tagore's *One Hundred Poems of Kabir* (1915). After the reading, I went up to Bly and, giving him the *Delos* offprint, introduced myself. A few days later Bly's chapbook published by Lillabulero Press arrived in the mail: *Kabir, The Fish in the Sea Is Not Thirsty*. My Kabir project had ended before it had begun.

For decades afterward, my interest in translating Kabir came and went. Other translations appeared, by Charlotte Vaudeville, Linda Hess, and Vinay Dharwadker. I bought whatever Kabir editions were available and read both the text and the commentaries; sometimes, when I liked a poem, I tracked it across editions, which also meant reading different versions. Once in a while I made a translation, half-heartedly. I'd check it anxiously against other translations, whenever others had translated the same poem. I worried about using anachronisms.

In an essay on Eduard Vuillard, Julian Barnes quotes him on the artistic process: "You get there either in a flash or through old age." With my Kabir translations I'd got the register in which to translate him in a flash, but it took me old age to realize this. Forty years after my translations in *Delos* appeared, I published, in 2011, *Songs of Kabir*. To make it easier for bilingual readers to compare original with translation, the Indian edition has the original on the facing page, and both the Indian and US editions give the source of each poem. Here is one of the songs as it appears in *Songs of Kabir*:

> To tonsured monks and dreadlocked Rastas,
> To idol worshippers and idol smashers,
> To fasting Jains and feasting Shaivites,

> To Vedic pundits and Faber poets,
> The weaver Kabir sends one message:
> The noose of death hangs over all.
> Only Rama's name can save you.
> Say it NOW. (Kabir, *Songs of Kabir* 25)

The worry I had about using anachronisms had gone out the window. Fear was replaced with embrace. No poet living in the fifteenth century could have dreamed of dreadlocked Rastas and Faber poets except through the mind of the translator, and therein lies the paradox and mystery of translating poetry: the further you move away from certain originals the closer you get to them, and what appears to be the translator's self-projection is self-effacement. The more you kill the original, that fight to the death, the more it lives.

A. K. Ramanjuan would tell the axe story to illustrate a point about folk tales. A woodcutter was asked how old his axe was. "It belonged to my great-grandfather," he said, "and has been handed down. The axe-head has been changed a few times, the handle has been changed a few times, but it's still the same axe." The story can be adapted to Kabir, to the blues, to anything that is sung or told and is passed from person to person, traveling long distances by word of mouth but seldom in the same form. A Kabir song comes in many versions. Individual singers would change the order and number of lines, and add or drop words at will, as I certainly did, but despite the variations it would, like the woodcutter's axe, remain the same song. Translators are singers too, and sometimes they join in the singing.

* * *

I could read Kabir's Hindi and some of it I could understand. The other language I translated from, Prakrit, though it is written in the same Nagari script, I could not read at all nor understand anything of, unless I had someone to explain it to me. A lot of people have translated in this way, by taking the help of those who are familiar with the original. I sometimes think it may even be better, for a poet, to not know the original except for some scattered words in it. For the rest, she can trust her instinct and feel her way into the lines, just as she would into her own.

The world's literatures make the oddest of pairings. Among the best-known American poems, one that is as iconic as the Coca Cola bottle is William Carlos Williams's "The Red Wheelbarrow":

> so much depends
> upon

a red wheel
barrow

glazed with rain
water

beside the white
chickens. (Williams, *Selected Poems* 30)

A poem that is strikingly similar to Williams's but written 2,000 years before his, which goes like this:

Wings hanging down, necks drawn in,
Sitting on fences as though spitted,
Crows get soaked in the rain. (Mehrotra 45)

Poems like Williams's—clean, minimal, hard enough to drive a nail in and hang your shirt on—have always been around; it's just that they were read differently. Poets notice the same things, and, as these two poems show, the fleeting has a greater chance of being preserved than the momentous. A cyclone that in ancient times flattened a city and killed hundreds leaves no trace in the human record, whereas a spell of rain does.

In Iowa, one of the rooms in the English-Philosophy Building occupied by the International Writing Program was called the book room. It was stacked mainly with only slightly damaged New Directions titles that were donated to the Program. The visiting writers were invited to take whatever they wished from the room and as often as they liked. That's where I found the Carl Rakosi, the Charles Reznikoff, the George Oppen, the Kenneth Rexroth, and of course more Pound and Williams. One of the Williams titles I picked was *Imaginations* (1970), which consisted of five of his early books, including *Spring and All*. Published in 1923, it is a mix of prose and verse. Many of Williams's best-known poems, including "The Red Wheelbarrow," first appeared there. Among the many prose passages that I find I have underlined are the book's opening words, "If anything of moment results—so much the better. And so much the more likely will it be that no one will want to see it." And a little later, "To refine, to clarify, to intensify that eternal moment in which we alone live there is but a single force—the imagination." Referring to Shakespeare, Williams says, "He holds no mirror up to nature but with his imagination rivals nature's composition with his own."

With Williams lines echoing in my head, of both his prose and verse, I translated the crow poem and some 200 others, just enough to make a small book: *The Absent Traveller: Prakrit Love Poetry from the* Gathasaptasati *of Satavahana Hala*.

"The events of amorous life are so trivial," Barthes said in *A Lover's Discourse*, "that they gain access to writing only by an immense effort" (93). The *Gathasaptasati*, or the *Seven Centuries*, is an anthology of 700 verses in the *gatha* form. They are poems "of amorous life," a little like Japanese poetry of the Heian period. In them, no event is too trivial to go unnoticed (a glance, the touch of a hand, a tug at a garment), and the most trivial observation (a woman pointing to a toothmark on a berry) is seen as an event of amorous life. The language of the *gathas*, Prakrit, is, along with Sanskrit, one of the classical languages of India. The anthology was compiled by Hala, a Satavahana king who belonged to a dynasty that ruled over a large part of the Deccan in the early centuries of the Common Era.

Occasionally, we find in the *Gathasaptasati* poems in which something in the natural world is described: it might be a bee sitting on a white jasmine, a sow in a field, a rogue bull, a frog. Since the context is an anthology of love poems, the innocent-looking scene, by intrepid commentators, is transformed into an erotic drawing:

Fore-legs positioned on the bank,
Hinders agitating in the ripples,
A she-frog strokes her own reflection. (Mehrotra 31)

Just as we might say that the Williams poem is about a red wheelbarrow, we might say that this is a poem about a frog sitting by a pond, except that it is not. Gangadhara, who in the sixteenth century wrote a commentary to the *Gathasaptasati*, says of this poem, "The heroine, desirous of 'contrary intercourse', to her lover." What at first appeared to be a description of something observed in nature turns out to be about a sexual position. It is almost as if this were self-evident.

If a frog sitting by a pond, to Gangadhara, suggests "contrary intercourse," what might he make of the crows in the poem quoted earlier?

In his *Autobiography*, Williams says that his goal as a writer was to capture the "immediacy" of experience: "It is an identifiable thing, and its characteristic, its chief character is that it is sure, all of a piece and, as I have said, instant and perfect: it comes, it is there, and it vanishes. But I have seen it, clearly. I have seen it" (289). The crows sitting on a fence, their heavy rain-soaked wings hanging down, can fly away the next minute, just as the chickens can too. But for now, before they vanish, the crows in the Prakrit poem are "an identifiable thing" and "all of a piece" and they are "there" and captured with the same unclouded objectivity that we find in Williams. All this is true, up to a point. Then the differences begin. According to Gangadhara, "By drawing his attention to the rain, the heroine indicates to her lover that their lovemaking need not be rushed through since no one is now likely to disturb them."

Such a reading tempts one to look at "The Red Wheelbarrow" again, this time through Gangadhara's eyes. By drawing his attention to the farmyard scene and the wheelbarrow glazed with rainwater beside the white chickens, what might the heroine, in Williams's poem, be suggesting to her lover? Were we to come across "The Red Wheelbarrow" not, say, in the *Norton Anthology of American Literature*, Vol. 2 but in an anthology of classical Indian verse, we'd read it as a love poem.

* * *

We go through thousands of doors in a lifetime, and the doors keep disappearing behind us, never to return. Then a poet goes through that same door and

> That's no doorstep.
> It's a pillar on its side.
>
> Yes.
> That's what it is. (Kolatkar 45)

Fourteen words to the sixteen in "The Red Wheelbarrow"; two less. The poet is Arun Kolatkar, who knew his Williams as well as he did his *Gathasaptasati*. It was he who in the mid-1980s first told me about the Prakrit poems, reading them out from a Marathi translation and translating into English as he read. The poem that I have quoted, "The Doorstep," is from *Jejuri* (1976), a sequence of poems written after a visit to a temple town near Pune in Maharashtra. The pillar was once part of Jejuri's many temples, but for the pilgrims who come to Jejuri it is another doorstep, till the poet's inspirational eye turns it back into a pillar: "Yes. / That's what it is."

The truth is that ordinary folk live in their fanciful heads whereas it is the poet who sees the world "clearly." Williams's "eternal moment" is a moment of seeing, but refined, clarified, and intensified by what he called "the imagination." Which is why the wheelbarrow is red, the chickens are white, and a pillar is a pillar and not a doorstep.

Literature is not a series of arcs—one arc English, the other Prakrit; one American, the other Indian; one twentieth century, the other second century—but an unbroken circle.

* * *

You could have been traveling west all your life only to realize at journey's end that all the while you've been facing east. It is ironic that I had to learn from Pound and Williams the same lessons that Kabir and the Prakrit poets could have taught me, "direct treatment of the 'thing'" and the music inherent in the spoken voice. Not that it really matters where one learns. The lessons do not change and can be found in many places. Pound himself learned his from the Chinese. "All ages are contemporaneous in the mind," he said.

Translation provides you with a new map of the world of literature. Speaking for myself, living in Allahabad I had stumbled my way to a street in Rutherford, New Jersey, and without leaving it emerged centuries later in the Deccan, not far from Bombay. Every writer carries this map in her head, but even she cannot know all of it for the map, much to Google Earth's consternation is constantly changing.

Works Cited

Barnes, Julian. *Keeping an Eye Open: Essays on Art*. Jonathan Cape, 2015.
Barthes, Roland. *A Lover's Discourse: Fragments*. Trans. Richard Howard, Hill and Wang, 2010.
Kabir. *The Fish in the Sea Is Not Thirsty: Kabir*. Trans. Robert Bly. Lillabulero Press, 1971.
Kabir. *One Hundred Poems of Kabir*. Trans. Rabindranath Tagore. Macmillan & Co., 1915.
Kabir. Poems published in *Delos: A Magazine on and of Translation* #6 (1971), p. 137.
Kabir. *Songs of Kabir*. Trans. Arvind Krishna Mehrotra. New York Review Books, 2011.
Kolatkar, Arun. *Arun Kolatkar: Collected Poems in English*. Ed. Arvind Krishna Mehrotra, Bloodaxe, 2010.
Mahadevan, T.M.P. *Ten Saints of India*. Bharatiya Vidya Bhavan, 1961.
Mehrotra, Arvind Krishna, ed. *The Absent Traveller: Prakrit Love Poetry from the* Gathasaptasati *of Satavahana Hala*. Penguin Classics, 2008.
Williams, William Carlos. *The Autobiography of William Carlos Williams*. New Directions, 1967.
Williams, William Carlos. *Selected Poems*, New Directions, 1968.

What Is a Classic? The Case of Esperanto

Humphrey Tonkin

Before me is a translation of *Coriolanus*, not the best known of Shakespeare's plays, but one of the most interesting and provocative. It is a political play, in which the working classes of ancient Rome confront the patricians, and the patricians try to persuade them to accept the consulship of their military hero Caius Martius, later Caius Martius Coriolanus. The crowd speaks in the accents of early seventeenth-century crowds; the patricians reply in the measured speech that Shakespeare has accustomed us to—measured speech that both reproduces the educated speech of the day and is sufficiently removed from it to convey to the audience a sense of historical distance: this is Shakespeare re-enacting for his audience incidents that occurred a millennium and a half earlier, in another language and another country, but incidents that echo the debates of his own era in which the constitutional role of the commons and the implications of the divine right of kings ran up against one another in a collision that was eventually to lead, thirty years later, to civil war.

The translation, into Esperanto, is not mine, but that of Marjorie Boulton, a British academic, recently deceased, whose luminous poetic talent has enriched the literature of the international language for many years and whose translations from English have unerringly captured the spirit of their originals. At her death, she left unpublished a translation of the Middle English poem *Pearl*, a poem notoriously complex in its prosody, translating one of its 101 stanzas each Sunday for a period of two years as a kind of spiritual exercise. The translation of *Coriolanus* occupied her for almost a decade: she wrote to me about it from time to time, though she never sent me samples of the text. She said that she was inspired to undertake the task in part because of my translations of *Henry V* and *The Winter's Tale*.

The text is written in her careful rounded hand on pages from a notebook. I am looking at the moment at the speech of Menenius in Act 1, Scene 1—the famous story of the belly and the members. Menenius is trying to quieten the hungry crowd with a fable. Fables work well, even if, as in this case, they do not perfectly address the matter at hand: Menenius knows enough about oratory to understand that if one can just hold the attention of the crowd one can both show one's respect for it and quieten it down:

Ĉiuj partoj de la korpo iam
Kontraŭ la ventro ekribelis, tiel
Ĝin akuzante: ke ĝi restas gluta
Meze de l' korpo, pigra, neaktiva,
Ŝranko por la viando, ne portante
Sanan laboron kiel la aliaj,
Dum la ceteraj korpaj instrumentoj
Vidas kaj aŭdas, planas kaj instruas,
Iras kaj sentas, plene kunlaboras
Al apetitoj kaj dezir' komuna
De tuta korpo . . .

The text reads well and closely follows the original. This is clearly a final draft, or close to it. But as I read further, there are more crossings-out, more hesitations. By the time I get to the fourth act, the text is tentative, with gaps and erasures—a first rather than a final draft. In Act 4, Scene 5 the text gives out altogether. *Caetera desunt.* I will have a lot to do to complete the translation and ready it for publication—And one whole act, the fifth, will be entirely mine.

Translating Shakespeare is never easy. Completing someone else's translation is harder still. At the same time it is doubly rewarding. Not only will I, in Keats's words, "once more humbly assay / The bitter-sweet of this Shakespearian fruit," but also I will grow closer to Boulton the poet— her choices, her priorities, her thematic emphases. She will seek to follow Shakespeare, to be sure, but as translator she is also interpreter, finding her way through this most ambiguous of Shakespearean texts. A double pleasure, in short, but also a double challenge.

Shakespeare's primary source for this play was Sir Thomas North's translation of Plutarch. The Roman historian Plutarch (AD 50–130) served as a senior official under the Emperor Trajan and later retired to write his so-called *Parallel Lives*—forty-six biographies of famous Greeks and Romans, most of them arranged in pairs, with one Greek figure matching one Roman figure. They remain eminently readable. In 1579 Sir Thomas North published his translation of Plutarch as *The Lives of the Noble Grecians and Romans*. He used the French translation of Jacques Amyot, a devout churchman whom Montaigne praised for the clarity and purity of his style. So North's version, also widely regarded as a model of Elizabethan prose style, was mediated through the French text. Shakespeare used it for *Julius Caesar* and *Antony and Cleopatra* as well.

In *Coriolanus*, Shakespeare used as much of North as he needed to convey his message and compose a piece for the theater. His Rome is as distant as it needs to be and as much like contemporary London as required. This is late Shakespeare, and so the blank verse is less regular than in his early works, with more run-on lines, contractions, and extra syllables. There is also an abundance of prose, again in a style typical of late Shakespeare, moving freely between prose and the heightened utterances of blank verse as the dramatic moment requires.

And now, Boulton is rendering this in Esperanto, a language that did not exist in Shakespeare's day, indeed has a history of only 130-or-so years, having sprung fully armed (more or less) from the head of its author in 1887.

I am faced with a number of preliminary decisions:

1. To what extent should I attempt to follow the criteria set up by Marjorie Boulton? To do otherwise might require considerable revision of an already established text and would be unlikely to constitute an improvement.
2. What Shakespearean characteristics should I seek to preserve, and what might I pay less attention to? A case in point is the question of stylistic accuracy. My approach to *Henry V* differed from my approach to *The Winter's Tale* in that I intentionally imitated the fluid style of the latter and sought greater regularity in the former—a play written some ten years earlier. How important is it to preserve Shakespeare's late style?
3. Shakespeare was both domesticating Rome—making it England—and also maintaining a certain historical separation. To what extent should I seek to do the same? And, more importantly, what should I aim for in rendering Shakespeare's 400-year-old text in the idiom of contemporary Esperanto? To what extent should I pay attention to earlier widely admired models—Rossetti's *Othello* for example, or Kalocsay's *Lear*, Kellerman's *As You Like It*, Zamenhof's *Hamlet*? Our assumptions about Shakespeare himself and changes in the Esperanto language make the idiom of the 1890s, evident in Zamenhof, or of the 1900s, evident in Kellerman, different from that of the 2020s.

These widely read and admired translations have assumed the status of models of literary translation into Esperanto. The Boulton translation may well do the same. About half of Shakespeare's works have been translated into Esperanto, some of them more than once.[1] Is there a tradition of Shakespeare

---

[1] There are two translations of *Hamlet*, for example: Zamenhof's version, simple but actable, and Newell's version of 1958, which aimed at accuracy and completeness, and, as a result, is more suited to the study than the stage. Zamenhof's version had to wait until 1928 to be presented on the stage, at the World Esperanto Congress in Antwerp in 1928. On Newell and Zamenhof, see Tonkin, "Translation into Esperanto," 181–2. On Shakespeare translations in Esperanto, see Boulton 2019.

in Esperanto to which the translation of *Coriolanus* should conform? Is there a tradition of translating classic works? Indeed, what, in the context of Esperanto, constitutes a classic?

* * *

Can a constructed language, developed for international use, with apparently no past of its own, contain within it the notion of a "classic"? And what might it mean to talk of a "classic" in Esperanto? I am interested both in how classic works from other languages can become assimilated into Esperanto through translation and also in whether it is possible to conceive of a "classic" originally composed in a new language. To answer those two questions we must address two other questions: How did Esperanto come into being? And how did Esperanto, at the time of its founding, relate to the other languages that surrounded it?

On July 26, 1887, a small pamphlet was issued from Chaim Kelter's printing shop at 11 Nowolipe Street in Warsaw, describing a new international language, the work of a certain "Doctor Esperanto." The name was the pseudonym of Dr. L. L. Zamenhof, a somewhat impecunious 28-year-old Jewish ophthalmologist trained in Moscow, Warsaw, and Vienna, whose family had formerly lived a few doors down the street from Kelter's printing works. The author, engaged to marry Klara Silbernik, used part of his new wife's dowry, with the enthusiastic support of her father, Aleksander Sender Silbernik, to finance the Russian-language pamphlet, which, in addition to describing the grammatical rules of the new language and providing a small glossary, contained a pledge to learn the language once a certain number of people did the same. Also included were a few samples of poetry in the new language, a translation of the Lord's Prayer, and examples of commercial correspondence.[2]

The pamphlet attracted the attention of a small but devoted public—enough attention to merit the translation of the pamphlet into a number of additional languages over the next several years. An English-language translation appeared in 1888, the rather unsatisfactory work of a non-native speaker of English. It was replaced by a new translation by the learned and enthusiastic Richard Geoghegan, who had studied philology, classical languages, and Chinese at Oxford, and who became the first "Esperantist" or speaker of Esperanto, in the English-speaking world. At about the same

---

[2] The story has been told many times before. See, for example, Boulton 1960, Korĵenkov 2010, and Schor 2015, in English; Korĵenkov 2009 and 2011, in Esperanto. These are my main sources for Zamenhof's biography.

time, Henry Phillips, Jr., secretary of the American Philosophical Society in Philadelphia, also published an English-language translation with the New York publisher Holt.

Zamenhof's love of language and languages was acquired in part from his father, a teacher of German and for several years Tsarist censor for the Hebrew language. But the immediate stimulus for the new language was, as he was later to explain, Zamenhof's experience as a young boy growing up in the city of Bialystok, in what is now northeastern Poland. The city, a majority of whose population was Jewish, was riven with ethnic rivalries: anti-Semitism was rife, but so was xenophobia in general. Zamenhof attributed much of this unrest to a lack of understanding: Yiddish, Russian, Polish, and a host of other languages were heard on the street, and their speakers kept themselves apart from one another, united only in their mutual hostility.

Zamenhof understood that anti-Semitism ran deeper than some of these other hostilities. As a student in Moscow, Zamenhof was an early enthusiast for Zionism, convening a group of some fifteen Jewish students to discuss the idea.[3] During these years he also compiled a grammar of Yiddish—a language so lacking in status at the time that, while widely spoken, it was regarded not as a full-fledged language but simply as "the jargon" (Zamenhof, *Gramatiko*). The massive outbreak of anti-Semitism in the Russian Empire following the assassination of Tsar Alexander II on March 1, 1881, caused Zamenhof to return home and continue his studies in Warsaw. At one stage he had dreamed of writing poetry in Russian—and his work on Yiddish included exploration of the poetic qualities of that language as well.

It was a time of upheaval both positive and negative. If the Russian pogroms represented a visceral fear of change and the rise of an exclusionary nationalism, these same years saw fundamental changes in communications of all kinds. Zamenhof traveled to study at the Imperial Moscow University in 1879 by train, when the Warsaw–Moscow line had been open for only eight years. Technology was changing the world at a rapid pace, bringing people together as never before—both in person by railroads and steamships and virtually through the telegraph. Education systems, though expanding, could not keep up; knowledge of foreign languages remained low. Such massive upheavals were a major reason for Zamenhof's interest in creating an international language.

Following the publication of what came to be known as the *Unua Libro*, the First Book, of 1887, a second publication, the *Dua Libro*, was published in

---

[3] Korĵenkov *Homarano* 46, quoting from Zamenhof's 1907 interview with the *Jewish Chronicle* (Zamenhof "Esperanto and Jewish Ideals"). On Zamenhof's ideas on religion and language, see Kiselman, "La evoluo de la pensado de Zamenhof."

January 1888, this time not in Russian but in the new language. Zamenhof's following grew slowly but surely. He himself was preoccupied at the same time with establishing his career, though he carried on a voluminous correspondence with his followers, who soon numbered several hundred in the Russian Empire and, increasingly, beyond (Warsaw was on the western edge of the Pale of Settlement, in which Jews were permitted permanent residence, and relatively close to the border with Prussia). Soon the language of Doctor Esperanto became, in common parlance, the language of Esperanto and, before long, simply the Esperanto language.

Attracting several hundred users of the language was itself a remarkable feat. People have been inventing languages almost from the beginning of time—and also collectively creating transactional languages for the purpose of trade, like Swahili, Hausa, Malay, and the so-called Lingua Franca used in the Middle Ages by sailors in the Mediterranean basin. The Abbess Hildegard von Bingen invented something she called the *lingua ignota*, a form of simplified Latin, in the twelfth century, but its influence, if any, was unrecorded. Many of the scientific thinkers of the seventeenth century were interested in the development of linguistic systems that might serve as mirrors of thought and logic. Francis Bacon took an interest in such so-called philosophical languages, as did René Descartes, Isaac Newton, and Gottfried Wilhelm Leibniz, who imagined a linguistic system that might parallel mathematical logic. John Wilkins, the first secretary of the Royal Society, actually produced such a project in his *Essay Towards a Real Character and a Philosophical Language* (1668). He was preceded by the *Logopandecteision* of 1653, the work of the enigmatic Sir Thomas Urquhart (who, it was alleged, died in a fit of laughter on hearing of the restoration of Charles II).

Such universal linguistic systems, imagined by philosophers steeped also in the classical tradition, were intended not for general use but as *a priori* grammatical and lexical representations of universal order. They were very different from the a posteriori projects for international languages created in increasing numbers in the nineteenth and twentieth centuries in response in part to changes in patterns of communication, in part to the expansion of the study of philology. These projects, based on existing languages, were intended, with varying degrees of ingenuity and earnestness, to overcome differences of language in a world increasingly interconnected but linguistically divided. As international and regional commerce increased and an enfranchised and educated middle class with a curiosity about the world grew larger, differences of language became more and more problematic.

* * *

Three major languages competed for attention: French, German, and English.[4] Nineteenth-century French thinkers, members of a nation whose language more closely resembled classical Latin than did German or English, stressed an intellectual continuity from the Roman Republic, by way of the Franks, to Enlightenment thinking, and beyond to French republicanism. As we have noted, the Latin language and its legacy were seen as direct influences on the writers and philosophers of late-sixteenth- and seventeenth-century France—Montaigne, Corneille, Racine, Descartes—and on Diderot and Voltaire and the other major Enlightenment figures of the eighteenth century. Latin during the Revolution was regarded as "an instrument for inculcating a love of republican virtue" (Prendergast 89), and regard for Latin authors continued to shape French intellectuals into the nineteenth century, established as a fundamental element in the system of public education that emerged from the Revolution.

This theory of an unbroken line from the Romans to contemporary thought underlay the method of Charles Augustin Sainte-Beuve, perhaps the most influential of the mid-century French critics. His essays "Qu'est-ce qu'un classique?" and "De la tradition en littérature" (1858) saw tradition as "a controlling element in literature" and literature as an ever-evolving continuum (Prendergast 14; Mack 10–11). A classic was a model, a work of enduring value that at the same time invited imitation yet controlled the flow of literary output and informed later sensibilities. Of course, the tradition also had its less salubrious aspects: as Prendergast points out, "the evocation of Latinity was one way of conferring the aura of the past on the dubious legitimacy of imperial modernity" (Prendergast 89). Above all, the French language was seen as a language of clarity of thought, whose antecedents stretched back to the thinkers and doers of ancient Rome. Of the major languages of Europe, French was the one that carried the highest prestige—and it also dominated in international affairs: it was the virtually unchallenged language of diplomacy and international negotiation, until the settlement of the Great War in 1919 led to parity with English and the founding of the bilingual League of Nations. Promotion of French overseas had a long history: the exclusive use of French was the norm in schools in the French colonies, the language was widely taught in European schools, and French often served as a lingua franca in gatherings of scholars. The Alliance Française was founded in 1883 to further the use of French.

---

[4] On this "war of languages," see, for example, Harper.

German emerged as a major European language long before the establishment of a united Germany.[5] In some respects it saw itself as an international language from the beginning. Goethe dreamed of an emerging *Weltliteratur*, a kind of international exchange—an intellectual and aesthetic economy in which publishing crossed national boundaries, translation brought about a cross-fertilization of ideas, and a common core of great works might be established. Indeed he went further, embracing intellectual exchange in all fields: "It is to be hoped that people will soon be convinced that there is no such thing as patriotic art or patriotic science. Both belong, like all good things, to the whole world, and can be fostered only by untrammelled intercourse among all contemporaries, continually bearing in mind what we have inherited from the past" (qtd. in Strich 35).

In this intellectual exchange there would be a special role for the German language:

> I am convinced a universal world literature is in the process of being constituted, in which an honorable role is reserved for us Germans. All nations are paying attention to us; they praise and criticize, accept and reject, imitate and distort, understand or misunderstand us and open or close their hearts to our concerns. We must accept this with equanimity because it is of great value to us. (Goethe 225)

Goethe was hardly alone in such views of the German language. German-speaking universities established themselves as centers of learning under the leadership of such figures as Wilhelm Von Humboldt early in the nineteenth century. Their combination of research and teaching, in which the former drove the latter, established them, and the German language, as powerhouses of science and medicine—but also of classical studies and philology. German philologists seized on the work of Sir William Jones, who, recognizing similarities among Sanskrit, Persian, and the languages of Europe, posited the existence of an Indo-European "family" of languages, and thereby expanded the legacy of Greece and Rome to embrace the ancient civilizations of the Middle East. German archaeologists and philologists sought connections and continuities between these civilizations and the Germanic tribes at the fringes of the Roman Empire, culminating in the emergence of the German language and its codification in the fifteenth and sixteenth centuries. Such thinking, and such reordering of history, led not so much to a rejection of the Roman legacy as to an elevation of its antecedents in Greece, particularly

---

[5] On the status of German in the world, see Ammon. On the tension between German as an international language and as an expression of German nationalism, see Damrosch.

in the thinking of German and British writers, Matthew Arnold prominent among them.⁶

Above all, the discovery of Indo-European led to a reordering, a reinvention, of the history of language and languages, on to which were grafted the prejudices, aspirations, and preconceived notions of those engaged in the reinvention. The broadening of the intellectual and linguistic legacy led also to the serious study of German antecedents and the gradual emergence of the idea of the *Volk*, the assumption that language was the expression of the particularity of a given people. In his *Fourth Discourse to the German Nation* (1808) the philosopher Johann Gottlieb Fichte argued for the construction of a German nation based on the "living" organism of German as compared to the "dead" language of French. Thus the idea of linguistic internationalism emerged in parallel with the idea of linguistic nationalism, leading Michel Bréal, almost a century later, in his essay "Le langage et les nationalités" (1891) to denounce the idea of "a particular trademark imposed by nature on different ethnic groups" and John Stuart Mill to describe such ideas as "a poison released into the atmosphere" (Prendergast 98). In his work for the East India Company, Mill espoused the importance of learning other languages not for their inherent linguistic qualities but as a way of coming to understand the peoples who spoke them. Such attitudes were opposed by Thomas Babington, Lord Macaulay, whose famous Minute on Education led to the passing of the English Education Act of 1835 whereby funds were withdrawn from multilingual education in India and reinvested in English-only schooling.⁷

As for English, its quest for world dominance was driven above all by the expansion of industry and the establishment of a network of supply chains that linked the colonies with the mother country.⁸ At the same time, British scholarship, led initially by the Scottish universities and, later in the nineteenth century, by Oxford and Cambridge and the newly established University of London, gained increasing influence on the continent of Europe and in the colonies. In the United States, stimulated by the Morrill Act of 1862 that established the first of the land grant universities, and by private research universities that followed the German model, often with funding from private philanthropy, scholarship expanded rapidly. While a knowledge of German remained an important advantage in science and medicine, and a knowledge of French was essential to the study of the humanities, English increased its influence in every sphere, aided also by the growing respect paid

---

⁶ See his *On Translating Homer* 1867 and Chapter 4 of *Culture and Anarchy* (1869).
⁷ On language and empire, see Phillipson.
⁸ On English as a global language, see Crystal.

to its leading literary figures, particularly Shakespeare, who in Germanized form was virtually adopted as an honorary German—as he was also embraced as a Russian by the Russians.

The search for a solution to the linguistic deadlock was driven, then, by two contradictory impulses. The first impulse was essentially imperial: the consolidation of empire manifested in the emergence of a united Germany, the expansion of French overseas territories, and what James Belich (2009) has called the "settler revolution"—the British planting of English-speaking settlers all across the world from the sixteenth century on, but particularly in the wake of the Industrial Revolution of the eighteenth and nineteenth centuries, and the consequent development of strong self-governing—and English-speaking—countries: Canada, Australia, and New Zealand. Nor can we forget the United States, colonized initially in the seventeenth century and independent, but Anglophone, as of 1776.

The second impulse was, broadly speaking, internationalist. Peyser quotes the American social reformer Raymond Bridgman (1905): "Joint action by the nations of the world would not be possible unless there were an identity in the world corresponding to the identity of any one people but greater. . . . National self-consciousness has been attained but world self-consciousness has not. Will it ever be attained?" (109). The second half of the nineteenth century saw the emergence of international institutions and multinational governance: in an attempt to expand and rationalize a number of bilateral agreements reached in the previous fifteen years and intended to set standards for the newly discovered telegraphy, the International Telegraph Union came into being in 1865. The Universal Postal Union followed in 1874. The International Red Cross was established in its original form in 1863–4; the first Geneva Convention dates from 1864.

While multilateralism does not in itself represent the emergence of a "world self-consciousness," indeed may be seen simply as an attempt by the great powers to establish some rules within which, or through which, to compete (a case in point is the emergence of World's Fairs, beginning with the Great Exhibition at the Crystal Palace in 1851,[9] which both promoted global trade and stoked global rivalry), there were certainly plenty of idealists with aspirations for world unity. A thin line separated the imperial civilizing impulse evident particularly in British thinking at the time from the meliorism espoused by contemporary social reformers.

* * *

[9] For example, New York 1853, Munich 1854, Paris 1855, Philadelphia 1876, St. Louis 1884, Chicago 1893. See Geppert.

It perhaps comes as no surprise that this period was also a period of language invention—indeed not singly but in battalions. Stojan's bibliography of 1929 lists hundreds of projects, and Dulichenko provides information on almost 1,000 (see also Blanke, *Internationale Plansprachen*, and *International Planned Languages*). Most were the work of language enthusiasts or professors of linguistics whose command of system exceeded their interest in expansion, or whose conviction of their own rightness rendered them unable to consider the possibility of improvement by others. While they espoused to varying degrees the need for international cooperation, they tended to focus on the linguistic qualities of their projects rather than their communicative goals. Such products of the study had, in the majority of cases, no adepts at all, beyond their creators. Others displayed linguistic incompetence of an order that exceeded even the enthusiasm of their creators. Only a few—notably Volapük (1881)—gained much traction. Volapük, the creation of the German cleric Johann Martin Schleyer, enjoyed a few years of popularity, but ran up against two obstacles: its inherent difficulty (it was, following the German model, highly inflected, and hence had an unnecessarily high threshold to be crossed by the learner before it became useful[10]), and the proprietary attitude of its inventor, who insisted on maintaining control of its development. While it was still expanding when Esperanto came along, internal stresses were already evident, and Schleyer's resistance to change only led to greater agitation by its speakers, leading to new experiments and fragmenting priorities among the enthusiastic apostates who pursued them. Ultimately, the language collapsed under its own weight.

Most of these linguistic inventions were based on major European languages—particularly German, French (and its Latin heritage), and the Slavic languages.

Creating a new language is a complex task, not least because of an inherent resistance to the idea of artificially creating something that should, by rights, grow, as Keats would say of poetry, as naturally as leaves to a tree. We do not like to think that language is made by humans, shaped by human design, constantly changing to fit human needs. All languages have a past, and while we use language to shape things never before seen or imagined (as Sir Philip Sidney reminds us of the practice of poets, in his *Apology for Poetry*), we do so by recourse to words and figures of speech long established: while language may look to the future, it is always retrospective, because based on its own history. Languages, as Samuel Johnson observed, are the pedigrees of nations.

---

[10] By contrast, Zamenhof's grammar was simple, English being his model (Korjenkov 59).

This realization was perhaps Zamenhof's greatest and most important discovery: to create a language of the future, one must create a history as well. But history is itself a language: we define who we are in the present by defining (in the present) who we were in the past. As students of nationalism and community, such as Anderson and Hobsbawm, have clearly established, we *invent* the past. It was Zamenhof's particular contribution to so-called interlinguistics (the study of constructed languages and their feasibility) to recognize that languages are continua and that learning a new language means entering a space informed by history: even a constructed language must construct a history. One way in which it does so, of course, is through the translation of classic works from other languages. Indeed, that is one of the lessons of the effort of Francophone scholars to create continuity between Latin culture and their own: they were reordering and reprioritizing the past.

A second awareness relates to the aesthetics of language. While plenty of language projects produce texts that look utterly unlike languages we know or have known, Zamenhof took pains to make his language look and behave like other languages. Of course, once one becomes fully familiar with any language, and lives, as it were, within it rather than outside it, its oddities cease to be odd, and its uniquenesses become opportunities rather than stumbling blocks. However, the higher the threshold of unfamiliarity, the greater the sense of commitment needed to overcome it. Zamenhof wanted his language to be easy to explore and rewarding to use. Thus, in his First Book, while he goes to great lengths to explain the simple and regular grammar of Esperanto in terms familiar to his reader, he directs very little of the reader's attention to the lexis and semantics of the language (Zamenhof, *Originala verkaro*). He provides a brief dictionary, to be sure, but in essence he carries over into the language the common semantics of European languages, essentially leaving it up to the community of speakers to tighten and expand the dictionary definitions and to assign definitions to their derivatives. In so doing, he embraces this common semantic history: his words are not new, but variants of past meaning, of the common stock of European languages. In short, he *invents* a linguistic past and lays bare a network of paths to connect his new language to its antecedents. He also writes poetry in the language and translates poems from other languages into Esperanto: Esperanto is not a barren system, he insists, but potentially can develop its own aesthetic.[11]

---

[11] Particularly remarkable is the *Proverbaro Esperanta* (1910), a collection of proverbs in Esperanto, drawn primarily from Russian, Polish, French, and German, and based on work by Zamenhof's father, Markus. They constitute a kind of instant folklore for the new language.

A third and crucial awareness relates to community. A disciple of Ferdinand de Saussure *avant la lettre*, Zamenhof understood that languages are constructed not so much by individuals as by collectives. A language spoken by a single individual is not a language at all: a language spoken by a group belongs not to any individual in that group but to the group as a whole, and its use is a form of performance. No sooner was Esperanto launched than Zamenhof encouraged others to refine and expand it. Antoni Grabowski, believed on somewhat imprecise authority to be the first person with whom Zamenhof conducted a conversation in the new language, published *La Neĝa Blovado*, his translation of a Pushkin short story, as early as 1888, one year after *La Unua Libro*. He followed it with a translation of Goethe's one-act play *Die Geschwister* the following year. And in 1889 the first periodical in Esperanto, *La Esperantisto*, began to appear in Nuremberg, fostering the spirit of community that Zamenhof encouraged and publishing news of the Esperanto movement, linguistic advice, and literary translations. While Zamenhof provided a basic vocabulary in the First Book, and followed it up with a more extensive Russian and Esperanto dictionary, he left the expansion of the vocabulary in the hands of the community of Esperantists—and encouraged them to contact one another by issuing an *Adresaro*, a collection of postal addresses of the first thousand-or-so enthusiasts, most of them in the Russian Empire.

Zamenhof, almost unique among such linguistic experimenters, came to his project not as a professional linguist but as a lover of languages for what they were capable of, both technically and, above all, in human terms. His early writings attest to his broad humanistic ideals, born (as we can now observe) of his own early experiences as a Jew in the rampantly anti-Semitic environment of the Russian Empire: Zamenhof had fled Moscow only to live through the Warsaw pogrom of December 1881—and to observe growing anti-Semitism in Vienna in 1886 as Jews of Eastern Europe fled westwards to escape persecution. He was later to write:[12]

> Se mi ne estus hebreo el la ghetto, la ideo pri la unuigo de la homaro aŭ tute ne venus al mi en la kapon, aŭ ĝi neniam tenus min tiel obstine en la daŭro de mia tuta vivo. La malfeliĉon de la homara disiĝo neniu povas senti tiel forte, kiel hebreo el la ghetto.

> If I were not a Jew from the ghetto, the idea of the unity of humankind would never have come into my head, or never held my attention so

---

[12] Korĵenkov *Homarano* (2009), 8, quoting Zamenhof's letter to Alfred Michaux, February 21, 1905. See also Zamenhof, "Esperanto and Jewish Ideals."

firmly throughout my life. No one experiences the sadness of human separation as strongly as a Jew from the ghetto.

and again

> mia hebreeco estis la ĉefa kaŭzo, kial mi de la plej frua infaneco fordonis min tutan al unu ĉefa ideo kaj revo—al la revo pri la unuiĝo de la homaro. Tiu ĉi ideo estas la esenco kaj celo de mia tuta vivo, la afero Esperanta estas nur parto de tiu ĉi ideo—pri la tuta cetera parto mi ne ĉesas pensi kaj revi.
>
> My Jewishness was the main reason why, from my earliest childhood, I totally dedicated myself to one idea and dream—the dream of the unity of humankind. This idea is the essence and goal of my entire life; the matter of Esperanto is only part of it: I never stop thinking and dreaming of the entire rest of that idea.

These impulses led Zamenhof to abandon the Zionism of his student days (rooted in the belief that escape from one nationalism might lead to the establishment of another) for a new internationalism that neither abandoned the idea of patriotism (love of the place in which one is born) nor embraced the idea of national superiority.[13] While many of his followers did little more than tolerate his spiritual journey toward what he called "homaranismo"[14]—a version of that "world self-consciousness" that Bridgman was describing at about the same time, this belief in the unity of humankind was a driving force in his thinking, including also an awareness of the inherent goodness and unity of all religious faith if its commonalities rather than its differences could be laid bare.

⁂

He began with the language. As its basis Zamenhof chose French over German, or, more precisely, the familiar Latin heritage of the modern European languages over a reworking of the modern languages themselves. It was, after all, Latin that had sustained the intellectual commerce of Europe until printing and the reproduction of localized texts drove it from a position of dominance. It was prestigious, and it was widely accepted as a foundation

---

[13] Zamenhof's most extensive discussion of patriotism and nationalism can be found in his speech at the London Guildhall, August 21, 1907. See Zamenhof *Originala verkaro* 381–3.
[14] See Kiselman.

of scholarship. No other language contained so much of the history of European languages—not only of Romance languages but, in a measure, of Germanic and Slavic languages as well. And, above all, it served as a departure point for most European linguistic investigation, for the entire discipline of comparative philology, and for that field of study that became known in the nineteenth century as classical studies. Latin was also a relatively flexible language, with an affixing system easily regularized and adapted to fit a new language, allowing for creative word-building and a consequent reduction in the size of the basic vocabulary.

Zamenhof was insistent on the importance of literature, both original and translated, to his project.[15] Literature stretches and tests a language, forcing it into expressions of experience hitherto unknown in that language, deepening its semantic base, and building a prosodic and conventional foundation. Not only did Zamenhof himself write a number of poems mostly related to the growth of the Esperanto movement, but he also embarked on a translation regimen of great ambition. A few literary translations appeared in the pages of the periodical *La Esperantisto* and elsewhere, their authors seeking to show that translation was possible, to share their own literatures with others, and to improve their command of the language. Translation was an important part of Esperanto from the beginning.

Some seven years after the publication of the language, Zamenhof announced a particularly ambitious undertaking: the launch of the *Biblioteko de la lingvo internacia Esperanto*, containing representative works drawn from the literatures of the world.[16] In effect, it was an attempt to construct for Esperanto at least a sample of that *Weltliteratur* of which Goethe had dreamed. Later, the French publisher Hachette contracted with Zamenhof to publish his translations. From the beginning these translations were seen not only as classics of world literature rendered in Esperanto but also as classics of Esperanto style. Zamenhof did not shrink from offering guidance on the use of Esperanto: that was the intention behind his *Lingvaj Respondoj*, responses to inquiries from individual Esperantists published in various Esperanto periodicals and collected in book form in 1910. But his translations were his principal models.

Zamenhof's first major literary undertaking was a translation of *Hamlet*—singled out, no doubt, not only because of the challenge it presented but also because, of all works that formed part of the common canon of European literature, the story of Hamlet and his single-minded search for truth perhaps

---

[15] On the history of Esperanto literature, see Minnaja and Silfer; Sutton.
[16] Between 1894 and 1898 some thirty-four works were published, not all of them literary, by a range of authors and translators, including Zamenhof.

best expressed the spirit of the times. It has been said that behind every European revolution there lies a performance of *Hamlet*. It was the best-known work of the best-known classic of European literature. To translate *Hamlet* was to conquer Everest.[17]

Given the roots of the language in French and Latin, we might have expected Zamenhof to start there. But his purpose was, as much as anything, to establish Esperanto's *bona fides* not just in French but in English and German as well. If these three were in competition for dominance, all three should receive recognition in the language designed to take their place as the international language. In the event, Zamenhof likely based his translation of *Hamlet* on the German translation by August Wilhelm Schlegel, perhaps with some reference to the original (he had studied English but did not know it as well as French or German).[18] The result was, and is, generally regarded as a triumph—an eminently playable and relatively faithful text that at the same time expands the range and expressibility of the new language.

The text of Zamenhof's translation of *Hamlet* is not as dense as the original: not only is Esperanto more polysyllabic than English, but also many of the flexibilities that have been added to Esperanto over the years, allowing for greater precision and expressiveness, were not yet present in Zamenhof's usage, so concision won out over completeness. One of his particular gifts to the language was the creation of a relatively flexible structure that allowed, within certain limits, for linguistic change and allowed for the introduction of new lexical roots: most of Esperanto's lexis was created not by Zamenhof but by his successors, products of a linguistic marketplace in which terms compete with one another until one form wins out, while the language grows increasingly adaptive and flexible over time.

Zamenhof went on to pay homage to Goethe and Schiller in translations of *Iphigenie auf Tauris* and *Die Räuber*. He also translated the widely popular fables of Hans Andersen, and the novel *Marta* by his Polish contemporary Eliza Orzeszkowa (one of the first, by the way, to condemn the Warsaw pogrom of 1881). Finally, he set about translating the entire Old Testament, published in parts over a number of years and eventually gathered by the British and Foreign Bible Society into a complete Bible with a New Testament rendered by a team of translators. His particular interest in drama sprang perhaps from an awareness that the language was first and foremost a written

---

[17] On Shakespeare in Eastern Europe, see Stříbrný.
[18] On Zamenhof's choice of a German translation, see D. B. Gregor's introduction in Zamenhof, *Hamleto* iii–vii. For additional references on the role of the work in the development of Esperanto, see my afterword: Zamenhof, *Hamleto* 207–23.

language, and that the written language should, as far as possible, offer models for speech.

Translation and the importance of translation have remained hallmarks of Esperanto ever since. Zamenhof's contemporary Kazimierz Bein not only translated Boleslaw Prus's historical novel *Faraon* but also launched the first work in what was to become a kind of tradition in the Esperanto movement: an anthology of Polish literature translated into Esperanto—a tradition that still continues. Literally dozens of such translated anthologies have appeared over the years: the *Encyclopedia of Esperanto* of 1933 lists Catalan, Bulgarian, Belgian, Estonian, and Hungarian anthologies; since then, among the national literatures covered have been Hungarian, English, Scottish, Australian, Japanese, Chinese, Lithuanian, Macedonian, Italian, and numerous others. Translations of key works of national literatures have also been produced. One of the earliest was Kofman's partial translation of the *Iliad* (1895–97), soon followed in 1906 by Vallienne's complete *Aeneid*. The East-West Series of literary translations, launched by the Universal Esperanto Association in 1961 with a translation of Rabindranath Tagore, consists of fifty-seven exemplary book-length translations from all parts of the world.

While original literature in Esperanto is more abundant than translated literature, the early translations helped shape literary style, literary conventions, and prosody. The development of original literature was highly dependent on these translated models—and even today the relationship between translation and original writing remains close and reciprocally beneficial. Many of the finest Esperanto poets, among them William Auld, Marjorie Boulton, Baldur Ragnarsson, and Kálmán Kalocsay, have also been prolific translators—for, as Auld rightly remarks, they, unlike most translators, are translating out of their own languages when they translate into Esperanto.

Less successful have been attempts to translate out of Esperanto and into other languages. The concision of Esperanto poetry, assisted by a highly flexible system of roots and grammatical endings, is hard to render in other languages. Indeed, those who write in Esperanto often say they have been drawn to it by these unique characteristics. So we look in vain for classics of Esperanto in other languages—though several writers (István Nemere, Trevor Steele, Anna Löwenstein, among others) write in both Esperanto and their native languages.

The root *klasik-* first appears in Esperanto in 1889, two years after its founding. Today it covers both the Graeco-Roman tradition and the idea of "a model of style universally valued." And, if Zamenhof originally chose French and Latin as the basis of his language, today Esperanto has become fully internationalized in the sense that it has speakers of all linguistic backgrounds. So broad a diversity of speakers might seem a challenge for the translator. What, after all, do these individuals have in common? And, given that Esperanto aspires to universality, how can any kind of common cultural understanding (and hence common cultural reference points) be established? A constant debate in Esperanto circles concerns the extent to which Esperanto can be said to possess a common culture. With over a century of convergent communication behind it, and a history to match—and with an affirmative desire to understand and be understood—the language and the movement accompanying it have created a certain core of common cultural values in which, among other things, there is a constant fruitful interaction between original and translated works and a reservoir of common experiences. In a sense, as I have suggested elsewhere (Tonkin, *Translation into Esperanto*), this is a *translated* culture, in which everyone is in some sense a translator, mediating between his or her native idiom and the practice of international community. As such, it presents unique challenges and unique rewards to the translator, not least in recognizing the importance of linguistic diversity to a sense of belonging in a particular location and culture at a particular time, and of linguistic unity in an overarching worldwide community of shared interpreted experience.

* * *

I am looking at a blank page. Beside me is the speech of Aufidius that ends Act 5 Scene 6 and thus the tragedy of Coriolanus. We are at the end, and it is a bleak ending—Aufidius, Fortinbras-like, clearing the stage and at the same time lamenting the death of the soldier Coriolanus whom he has defeated not on the field of battle but through the agency of a pair of nameless conspirators hired for the purpose, who cut him down in cold blood in Aufidius' presence. Such are the wages of pride.

By now, I can hear the voice of Marjorie Boulton guiding my choice of words, helping me reorder the verse to have it sound and signify right in a new language. But the spare words of Aufidius at the end of the play cause me to hesitate, not least because I am wondering what is going through Aufidius's mind, how invested he is in his words, and how much he cares that Coriolanus should be memorialized at all. Fortinbras, I think, cares. But I don't know about Aufidius.

> My rage is gone
> And I am struck with sorrow. Take him up.
> Help three o'th' chiefest soldiers; I'll be one.
> Beat thou the drum that it speak mournfully.

Trail your steel pikes. Though in this city he
Hath widowed and unchilded many a one,
Which to this hour bewail the injury,
Yet he shall have a noble memory.
Assist.

The first line and a half are all monosyllables, but for the word "sorrow." Given its use of grammatical endings, all adjectives in Esperanto are at least disyllables, as are all nouns except for the occasional nominative elision. I can find a way of reducing the beginning of the first line from three feet to two feet, giving me three feet for the second half: "Kolero mia ĉesis" (accent in Esperanto is always on the second-to-last syllable). What is meant by "chiefest soldiers"? Outstanding soldiers? Soldiers of highest rank? I settle for "ĉefsoldatoj," chief soldiers. And "I'll be one"? "Mi estos unu" sounds wrong. "Tri ĉefsoldatoj helpu, kaj mi kvaros," I'll be the fourth. Normally one would say "Mi estos unu el ili" or "Mi estos la kvara," but the compression works well.

There's an appropriateness, following this scene of violence, in personifying the drum, which "speaks mournfully" as if in reluctant response to a battery of punches ("Beat thou . . ."). But how to convey that in Esperanto? And "mournfully"—more than sadly (triste): surely mourning a death (funebre): "Tamburon batu ĝis funebra krio" or is a cry too incoherent, or insufficiently verbal? "Tamburon batu ĝis funebra ĉanto"? Still we are missing the sense of movement in the verb "speak." There's an adjective "morna"—used particularly in poetry to convey extreme sadness: "Tamburon batu ĝis ĝi morne ĉantas." The line moves more smoothly. And perhaps the imperative form at the end: "ĉantu." No: not chanting but sighing: "ĝis ĝi morne ĝemu."

To trail a pike is to reverse it, point toward the ground. The conflict is over, the mourning begins. We could argue about the meaning of the word "pike" and whether "halebardo" or "pikstango" or "lanco" best conveys the meaning—but we are overwhelmed with monosyllables again. The steeliness must go: splendidly cold though it is, there is no room: "Renversu lancojn." "Unchilded" is an unusual locution, used only here in all of Shakespeare's plays, but readily rendered in Esperanto "seninfanigis"—made (-ig) childless (sen-infana, without children). But this is five syllables. There is room if we reverse the order to maintain the rhythm: "Renversu lancojn. Kvankam li ĉi-urbe / Seninfanigis kaj vidvigis multajn / Kiuj pri l'ofendo ploras ĝis ĉi-horo / Tamen li restu nobla en memoro." Do the final lines rhyme (injury / memory)? Is the slant rhyme intentional? I decide that it is—and I let the extra syllables in the next-to-last line stand: this is late Shakespeare, and the slight irregularity fits the mood.

And so I reconstruct this final speech:

> Kolero mia ĉesis
> Kaj frapis min aflikto. Levu lin.
> Tri ĉefsoldatoj helpu, kaj mi kvaros.
> Tamburon batu ĝis ĝi morne ĝemu.
> Renversu lancojn. Kvankam li ĉi-urbe
> Seninfanigis kaj vidvigis multajn,
> Kiuj pri l'ofendo ploras ĝis ĉi-horo,
> Tamen li restu nobla en memoro.
> Asistu.

I put away the paper. I will look at it again tomorrow. Do the lines move smoothly? Are they comprehensible to a non-English speaker, to a non-European, yet evocative enough to rise above the mundane? Do they, in short, convey to us the sense of a classic—removed in time, but present; exemplary, yet vital?

Works Cited

Ammon, Ulrich. *The Position of the German Language in the World*. Trans. David Charlston, Routledge, 2019.
Belich, James. *Replenishing the Earth: The Settler Revolution and the Rise of the Anglo-World, 1783–1939*. Oxford UP, 2009.
Blanke, Detlev. *International Planned Languages: Essays on Interlinguistics and Esperantology*. Ed. Sabine Fiedler and Humphrey Tonkin. Mondial, 2018.
Blanke, Detlev. *Internationale Plansprachen. Eine Einführung*. Akademie-Verlag, 1985.
Bridgeman, Raymond L. *World Organization*. Ginn, 1905.
Boulton, Marjorie. "La evoluado de Esperanto observita tra tradukoj de Ŝekspiraj dramoj." In *Centjara Esperanto*. Ed. Geraldo Mattos. Fonto, 1987, pp. 39–62.
Boulton, Marjorie, trans. *Perlo*. Mondial, 2019.
Boulton, Marjorie. *Zamenhof, Creator of Esperanto*. Routledge & Kegan Paul, 1960.
Crystal, David. *English as a Global Language*. Cambridge UP, 1997.
Damrosch, David. *Comparing the Literatures: Literary Studies in a Global Age*. Princeton UP, 2020.
Duličenko, Aleksandr. *Mezhdunarodnye vspomogatel'nye jazyki*. Valgus, 1990.
Eliot, T.S. *Selected Prose*. Ed. Frank Kermode, Harcourt Brace Jovanovich, 1975.

Geppert, Alexander C.T. *Fleeting Cities. Imperial Expositions in Fin-de-Siècle Europe*. Palgrave Macmillan, 2010.
Goethe, Johann Wolfgang von. *Essays on Art and Literature*. Ed. John Gearey, Ellen von Nardroff and Ernest H. von Nardroff. *Goethe's Collected Works*, Vol. 3. Suhrkamp, 1986.
Harper, T.N.. "Empire, Diaspora, and the Languages of Globalism 1850–1914." In *Globalization in World History*. Ed. A. G. Hopkins. W. W. Norton, 2002, pp. 141–66.
Kellerman, Ivy. *Kiel plaĉas al vi de William Shakespeare*. Sesa Internacia Kongreso de Esperanto, 1910.
Kermode, Frank. *The Classic*. Faber & Faber, 1975.
Kiselman, Christer. "La evoluo de la pensado de Zamenhof pri religioj kaj la rolo de lingvoj." *Religiaj kaj filozofiaj ideoj de Zamenhof: Kultura kaj socia fono. Aktoj de la 32-a Esperantologia Konferenco, Bjalistoko, 2009*. Ed. Christer Kiselman. Rotterdam: Universala Esperanto-Asocio, 2009, pp. 39–61, www.cb.uu.se/~kiselman/bjalistokoueak.pdf.
Korĵenkov, Aleksander. *Homarano: La vivo, verkoj kaj ideoj de d-ro L. L. Zamenhof*. Sezonoj / Litova Esperanto-Asocio, 2009.
Korĵenkov, Aleksander. *Homarano: La vivo, verkoj kaj ideoj de d-ro L. L. Zamenhof*. 2nd ed. Sezonoj / Litova Esperanto-Asocio, 2011.
Korĵenkov, Aleksander. *Zamenhof: The Life, Works and Ideas of the Author of Esperanto*. Trans. Ian Richmond. Mondial, 2010.
Mack, Peter. *Reading Old Books: Writing with Traditions*. Princeton UP, 2019.
Minnaja, Carlo and Giorgio Silfer. *Historio de la esperanta literaturo*. Literatura Foiro, 2015.
Peyser, Thomas. *Utopia and Cosmopolis: Globalization in the Era of American Literary Realism*. Duke UP, 1998.
Phillipson, Robert. *Linguistic Imperialism*. Oxford UP, 1992.
Prendergast, Christopher. *The Classic: Sainte-Beuve and the Nineteenth-Century Culture Wars*. Cambridge UP, 2008.
Rossetti, Reto, trans. *La tragedio de Otelo*, by William Shakespeare. Stafeto, 1960.
Schor, Esther. *Bridge of Words: Esperanto and the Dream of a Universal Language*. Metropolitan Books/Henry Holt, 2015.
Sidney, Sir Philip. *An Apology for Poetry*. Ed. Geoffrey Shepherd. Nelson, 1965.
Stojan, Petr E. *Bibliografio de internacia lingvo*. Universala Esperanto-Asocio, 1929. [Rpt., with a bibliographical supplement by Reinhard Haupenthal, Olms, 1973].
Stříbrný, Zdeněk. *Shakespeare in Eastern Europe*. Oxford UP, 2000.
Strich, Fritz. *Goethe and World Literature*. Trans. C. A. M. Sym, Routledge, 1949.
Sutton, Geoffrey. *Concise Encyclopedia of the Original Literature of Esperanto*. Mondial, 2008.
Tonkin, Humphrey. "Hamleto en Esperanto." *Multilinguismo e Società*, vol. 1, 2008, pp. 45–55.

Tonkin, Humphrey, trans. introduction and notes. *La vivo de Henriko Kvina*, by William Shakespeare. Universala Esperanto-Asocio, 2003.

Tonkin, Humphrey, trans. introduction and notes. *La Vintra Fabelo*, by William Shakespeare. Universala Esperanto-Asocio, 2006.

Tonkin, Humphrey. "Translation into Esperanto." In *The Translator as Mediator of Cultures*, eds. Tonkin and Frank, 2010, pp. 169–90.

Tonkin, Humphrey and Maria Esposito Frank, ed. *The Translator as Mediator of Cultures*. Benjamins, 2010.

Zamenhof, Ludoviko Lazaro "Esperanto and Jewish Ideals: Interview for the Jewish Chronicle with Dr. Zamenhof." *Jewish Chronicle*, September 6, 1907, pp. 16–18.

Zamenhof, Ludoviko Lazaro. *Gramatiko de la jida lingvo*. Monda Asembleo Socia, 2019.

Zamenhof, Ludoviko Lazaro, trans. *Hamleto* de William Shakespeare. 9th ed. Universala Esperanto-Asocio, 2006.

Zamenhof, Ludoviko Lazaro. *Originala verkaro*. Ed. Johann Dietterle. Ferdinand Hirt, 1929.

6

The Russian Canon in Retranslation

Marian Schwartz

Russian literature, perhaps more than any other, is known and sustained in English by its classics. For more than a hundred years, American and British readers alike have eagerly read Dostoevsky, Tolstoy, Pushkin, and Chekhov—authors who spanned less than a century of Russian literature. This steady and concerted interest has sustained a deep tradition of retranslation into English. New translations of the most famous Russian canonical works appear with remarkable frequency, sometimes in flash floods: witness the four new translations of Leo Tolstoy's *Anna Karenina* that have come out in the twenty-first century.

Why do we persist in retranslating the prerevolutionary Russian and Soviet canon when there is strong reason to believe that good and in some cases excellent translations already exist of them all?

Russian classics get retranslated for largely the same reasons all classics get retranslated, reasons that generally boil down to a translator's conviction that she can do a better job and/or a publisher's belief that there is an untapped market for a new translation. Translators and publishers feel a strong attachment to a given work and want to put their hand to it, regardless of existing translations. But the classics of Russian literature are something of a special case due to their unusual dominance in the world's engagement with Russian literature.

It is worth taking a step back to consider how these mostly nineteenth-century writers—Fyodor Dostoevsky, Leo Tolstoy, and Anton Chekhov, but also Ivan Turgenev, Ivan Goncharov, Mikhail Lermontov, and, of course, Alexander Pushkin[1]—in particular became household names and perennial favorites. For this we can look primarily to one person: Constance Garnett, whose translations of Dostoevsky, Tolstoy, and Chekhov (two of whom were her contemporaries) and indeed her entire body of work of more than seventy volumes (including translations of Turgenev, Goncharov, Ostrovsky, and

---

[1] Glaringly absent are women prose writers of the period, who only recently have started to gain visibility in English, for example, Pavlova, *A Double Life*.

Herzen as well) constituted early on a friendly portal into Russian literature that has been accessed by a vast number of people ever since. Her work ignited an Anglophone love affair with Russian literature. Even today, her translations serve well for the most part, especially in their revised editions. Over time, though, the precise but unobtrusive language she used to such great advantage has become dated and is often cited by translators as justification for producing new translations of the novels for which she is best known.

Garnett's translations were many readers' introduction to what would become the foundation of the Russian canon, but she also can be viewed as standing at the head of the century and more of retranslations that followed. Garnett's 1914 translation of Fyodor Dostoevsky's *Crime and Punishment* (1866) was preceded by Frederick Whishaw's in 1885—and followed by eleven more. Her 1904 translation of Leo Tolstoy's *War and Peace* (1869) was the fourth into English, to be followed by seven more. Her translation of Ivan Turgenev's *Fathers and Children* (1862) was published in 1895, following a first translation by Eugene Schuyler and preceding a full fourteen more!

This is not to argue that Garnett was always retranslating, especially with writers more contemporary to her. For example, she appears to have been the first to translate, in 1916, one of Anton Chekhov's best-known stories, "The Lady with a Dog" (1899), written during Garnett's active career as a translator, and there must have been many similar instances.

Garnett may have been there at the beginning, but the flow of retranslated Russian classics has continued unabated into the twenty-first century. I myself have retranslated three prerevolutionary and two Soviet-era Russian classics, all of them since the turn of this century—only one of them also a part of Garnett's bibliography.[2]

Of my five retranslations, only one—*Anna Karenina*—was at my initiative and arose out of a very personal aesthetic response to Tolstoy's bold and innovative writing in that novel.[3] The other four came at the invitation of publishers who felt there was a market for a new translation, but in each case I felt my new translation could address particularly stylistic deficiencies in previous translations.[4]

My first retranslation was Mikhail Lermontov's *A Hero of Our Time*. The dominant translation of this book, by Vladimir Nabokov, "in collaboration

---

[2] Lermontov, *A Hero of Our Time*; Olesha, *Envy*; Bulgakov, *White Guard*; Goncharov, *Oblomov*; and Tolstoy, *Anna Karenina*.
[3] For a full discussion of my approach to *Anna Karenina*, see my "Translator's Note," in Tolstoy, *Anna Karenina* xxii–xxv.
[4] In *Oblomov*, *White Guard*, and *Anna Karenina*, I had the opportunity to discuss my approach and decisions in a substantial Translator's Note, to which I refer the reader interested in further detail.

with" his son Dmitri, bears Nabokov's imposing stamp: he refused to translate Lermontov's verse as verse and peppered his endnotes with highhanded criticism of Lermontov's skill as a writer. Most egregious of all was Nabokov's decision to commandeer to his own endnotes a brilliant footnote of Lermontov's that is in fact an integral part of the text.

My decision to translate this elegant short novel came easily—and yet. And yet. The Nabokov translation will always be the most popular and sell the best because it is Nabokov. One could hardly expect otherwise.

Undoubtedly my least favorite retranslation project was a staple of Russian literature syllabi, Yuri Olesha's *Envy* (1927)—least favorite because the more I read the book, the deeper my experience of it as a devastating harbinger of the great Soviet atrocity just getting under way. This slapstick-rich social satire unnerves with its sparkling prose, comical ditties, spot-on characterizations, and venomous undercurrents. To my mind, none of the previous translations captured the sparkle and pace I aspired to provide.

The opening sentence brilliantly demonstrates Olesha's light touch throughout the novella. Not only is it markedly concise, but it scans— eight syllables, every other one stressed, setting a jaunty tone for the entire novella.[5] Previous translations doggedly mirrored the sentence's original word order, which led to a string of clumsy prepositional phrases and got bogged down by the notion of a WC. My solution has the lilt of the Russian original: "Mornings he sings on the toilet." Similarly, in previous translations the comical ditties were anything but comical.

White Guard was known in English by the wonderful read that is Michael Glenny's translation, which, for all its merits, is a pale shadow of the glorious original, ignoring the obvious fact of Bulgakov's ornamental prose and skipping entire difficult experimental passages. Glenny's end result reads fluently but is a serious misrepresentation of the original text.

There is an argument to be made for a work's first translation's need to ease the reader into a work that is not only foreign but also possibly demanding from the standpoint of style or ideas. If Glenny's translation was, as I believe, the first English translation of this novel, then he certainly did just that, leaving it to subsequent translators to illuminate the layers and nuances of what is in fact a much more complicated—and intriguing—work.

This phenomenon—of retranslations adding more information to the reader's understanding of a text—is universally true of retranslations. Just as no two readers will perceive a text identically, neither will any two translators

---

[5] Он поет по утрам в туалете: on po-YOT po u-TRAM v twa-LYET-ye. Word for word: "He sings in the mornings in the WC."

(being the closest of readers). Each retranslation reflects the translator's reading as well as writing skills and tastes.

Style being as much a component of content as narrative and characterization, a retranslation can not only fill in gaps left by a previous translation but also sharpen the reader's focus by introducing new precision to the book's language. My translation of *Oblomov* is a case in point.

In writing this translation, my primary objective was to right the wrong that the Western eye has done the title character, whom the Western reader often dismisses as a slacker, a man too lazy to get off the couch and save himself from being taken advantage of, from losing the love of his life, from falling in social status. Previous translations have presented Oblomov as someone so two-dimensional as to be ridiculous, contemptible even. It can be nigh impossible for the Anglophone reader to appreciate Oblomov's strong positive qualities or indeed to understand why he is so beloved by the book's other characters. My translation was written with the intent of demonstrating the profound, tragic character of Oblomov and his life, so rich in detail, the embodiment of subtle social commentary.

It would take a new translation to add the missing third dimension and place Oblomov in the same positive light in which Russians view him. A new translation would have to bring out his gentle humor, especially as brought out in the dialog and his interpersonal relationships. It would have to clarify an obsession of his with which the twenty-first-century reader can easily identify: food. Oblomov's menus mirror his personal fortunes, so my translation for the first time maintains that intricacy, contrasting the French cuisine of his prosperity to the traditional Russian dishes of his impoverishment, even adding to the apparatus a Gastronomic Glossary (written in collaboration with Russian historian and gastronomic authority Darra Goldstein). This kind of detail helps bring this iconic protagonist of Russian literature to life for non-Russians.

The book's original publisher, Seven Stories Press, is to be commended for including considerable useful apparatus in the edition. In addition to the Gastronomic Glossary and my Translator's Note, the distinguished contemporary writer Mikhail Shishkin was induced to write an Afterword that explicates the Russian understanding of the book. Shishkin's opening statement places Oblomov in his historical and political context:

> Oblomov is one of the great Russian thrillers.
> We have direct evidence of a crime. Someone has been accused. Is he guilty? Innocent? Each generation of readers has a different answer to this question.
> The crime is Russian life—which is to say, no life at all. The title of Alexander Herzen's famous mid-nineteenth-century novel, *Who Is To*

> *Blame?* has been the most burning of Russian questions for nearly two centuries. Who is to blame for Russia's notorious roads? For its graft and embezzlement? For its idiot officials? Who is to blame for its pervasive slave mentality, no matter what the regime or economic structure? Who is to blame for its bloody history and for the way human dignity is trampled at every step?
> We have people galore to accuse—and just as many accusers.
> One of the most famous defendants to be put on trial for this is Ilya Ilich Oblomov, caught by Goncharov's pen *in flagrante delicto*—on his sofa. (Shiskin 545)

One of the joys of translating contemporary fiction is the opportunity one sometimes has to interact with the author. One of the joys of retranslating classic fiction is the opportunity to interact not only with scholars but also with translators past and present. Translating *Anna Karenina* brought me in contact with both scholars and translators, past and present, over the course of more than ten years that elapsed between my initial drafts and eventual publication.

In the late 1990s, I reread *Anna Karenina*, which I had not reread for decades; I was bowled over by Tolstoy's stylistic innovations and felt compelled to try to convey these innovations in English. In addition, at the time of my initial proposal, there had not been a new translation of the novel in forty years, and most Slavists were recommending even earlier translations, very often Garnett's.

From my point of view, a scholarly edition was unnecessary; there was an abundance of commentary already available. What no one had done yet was to convey Tolstoy's (to me) strikingly modern and muscular style. What had until then been viewed as carelessness or mistakes on Tolstoy's part struck me as intentional and in fact the whole point of Tolstoy's approach.

So I turned to Tolstoy's correspondence from the period leading up to his writing of the novel and found not only confirmation for my hunch but also insight into Tolstoy's motivation for writing his new novel as unconventionally as he did.

Anna Karenina, which came after another masterpiece, *War and Peace*, is Tolstoy's last major work before he underwent a major spiritual conversion. That Tolstoy was getting restless was made clear in his correspondence at the time[6] and would become very plain in the new novel. Essentially, he felt that he could not continue to write conventionally beautiful Russian. Tolstoy's

---

[6] On March 22, 1872, Tolstoy wrote to his editor, N.N. Strakhov, asserting that the Russian writer was "unfree" and called literary Russian "repulsive." Tolstoy made it clear that he abhorred affectation on moral as well as aesthetic grounds and sought to express what was true, rejecting literary conventions and embracing what was "specific, clear, beautiful, and temperate"—language he associated positively with the peasant and negatively with "society." Tolstoy's language became an instrument of his worldview.

biographer, A. N. Wilson, also asserts that Tolstoy was looking for "a new source of vigour in language," the only possibility for writing in Russian being to "discover a plain, unvarnished style" (255)—not the language of peasants, but a language comprehensible to peasants.[7]

The key point here is that Tolstoy wrote *Anna Karenina* as he did, without conceding to literary conventions, with a full intention born of moral as well as aesthetic considerations. Not only did he find conventional literary language affected, but, as I came to understand, he believed it stood in the way of the moral arguments he needed to make.

Tolstoy, at the height of his powers, did something very (if not completely) different from what he or anyone else had done before (as I describe at length in my Translator's Note), and did so with the utmost purpose. Herein lies the guiding premise of my translation—the assumption that anything unconventional was intentional and not the result of error or carelessness—a premise wholly unlike that of all the many translations that came before or after mine.

Previous translations persisted in "fixing" Tolstoy, to the point of obscuring specific ideas and observations conveyed by Tolstoy through style rather than direct explanation.

If interaction with scholars has been a general positive in my career, in this translation of *Anna Karenina* I found a literary soulmate in Gary Saul Morson of Northwestern, a preeminent scholar of Russian nineteenth-century literature and of Tolstoy in particular. After Yale University Press accepted this project, Morson took on the serious task of combing through the translation and providing both additional notes and an unusual and compelling introduction. He and I spent the fall of 2013 in an intense discussion of virtually every word of the novel. The experience was absolutely thrilling.

One passage gave rise to extensive discussion, specifically because it posed a difficulty that previous translators had failed to address in such a way as to make Tolstoy's point clear.

At the beginning of the novel, Stiva is upset because his wife Dolly has discovered his affair, and Matvei, his valet, tries to reassure him, but reassure him in such a way as to be sure to draw attention to himself. Tolstoy underscores Matvei's perpetual attempts to stand out as clever by noting the poses he strikes: "Matvei put his hands in his jacket pockets, drew one foot to the side, and regarded his master silently and good-naturedly, barely smiling," and later in the passage, "putting his hands in his pockets and cocking his

---

[7] Wilson claims that Tolstoy even entertained the notion of writing in some other language altogether.

head to one side"—anything but your typical valet's posture. Indeed Stiva is aware of this quality: "Stepan Arkadyevich [Stiva] realized that Matvei was trying to be funny and attract attention" (Tolstoy, *Anna Karenina*, trans. by Schwartz 6).

Matvei reassures Stiva about the disaster with Dolly by saying, *Obrazuetsia*. As Tolstoy tells us later in the novel, the word was invented by another servant in the household, in imitation of the fancy words she'd heard spoken all around her all her life. Matvei, appreciating its cleverness, has appropriated it for his own ends—and catches Stiva's attention with it, just as he had hoped.

Today, *obrazuetsia*—a verb from the root "form" or "shape"—is a perfectly normal expression meaning that all will be well, but as is obvious in the novel and confirmed by the most authoritative dictionary of the period, it was not a common expression when Tolstoy used it. At the time, the word had only the concrete sense of something physically being shaped or formed, not, as it has come to mean, that things will turn out all right.

The word sticks in the back of Stiva's mind, where he keeps delighting in it and trying to figure out how he can introduce it into his own conversation, as a demonstration of his own wit. He returns to it several times as he mulls over some way to use it to his advantage in conversation. Stiva has no trouble understanding the word's meaning, so the translation has to be equally understandable. But it also has to be slightly pretentious and striking.

Had Morson—who has taught the novel annually for decades—not pointed out the subtlety of this passage, I might have overlooked it as all my predecessors had. Once I understood the terrific wit on display, though, there was no hiding it under a bushel. The solution I chose—*shapify*—was in fact Morson's suggestion, but though he deserves all the credit, it's a solution I wholeheartedly embrace precisely because, though not a real word, it is readily understood and "fancy."

Reviewers have not always warmed to this approach precisely because the word is invented and fancy. They prefer translations along the line of "things will work out"[8]—although that phrase is not even remotely clever, or new, or potentially useful to Stiva's line of repartee. This neutral choice actually

---

[8] A few examples: "shape up" (Tolstoy, *Anna Karenina*, translated by Pevear and Volokhonsky 5); "sort itself out" (Tolstoy, *Anna Karenina*, translated by Zinovieff and Hughes 7); "shape themselves" (Tolstoy, *Anna Karenina*, translated by Louise and Aylmer Maude 4); "come right" (Tolstoy, *Anna Karenina*, translated by Magarshack 21); "shape up" (Tolstoy, *Anna Karenina*, translated by Bartlett 7).

muddles the picture and makes Matvei's action and Stiva's reaction simply confusing.

This is far from the only instance in *Anna Karenina* when Tolstoy makes a point by showing rather than telling, by introducing something arrestingly odd without explicitly describing it as such. "Shapify" is not the only possible solution to this translation, but it is the only one devised so far that even begins to address Tolstoy's point.

Retranslation is a matter not merely of fixing the mistakes of earlier translations but of uncovering previously overlooked treasures, then. Presumably, a work that has entered the canon offers multiple facets for the translator to highlight. At its best, a retranslation tells readers more about the work than they already knew from previous translations and brings new luster to an important work of literature. Given the outsize presence of retranslation in Russian literature, one can only hope the tradition will be preserved as twentieth-century authors enter the canon and the public domain.

Works Cited

Bulgakov, Mikhail. *White Guard.* Translator Marian Schwartz. Yale UP, 2008.
Dostoevsky, Fyodor. *Crime and Punishment.* Trans. Frederick Whishaw. 1885.
Dostoevsky, Fyodor. *Crime and Punishment.* Trans. Constance Garnett. Heinemann, 1914.
Goncharov, Ivan. *Oblomov.* Trans. Marian Schwartz. Seven Stories Press, 2008; Yale UP, 2010.
Lermontov, Mikhail. *A Hero of Our Time.* Trans. Marian Schwartz. Modern Library, 2004.
Olesha, Yuri. *Envy.* Trans. Marian Schwartz. New York Review of Books, 2004.
Pavlova, Karolina. *A Double Life.* Trans. Barbara Heldt. Columbia UP/Russian Library, 2019.
Schwartz, Marian. "Translator's Note." *Oblomov*, by Ivan Goncharov. Yale UP, 2008, pp. vii–xii.
Schwartz, Marian. "Translator's Note." *Anna Karenina*, by Leo Tolstoy. Yale UP, 2014, pp. xxii–xxv.
Schwartz, Marian. "Translator's Note." *White Guard*, by Mikhail Bulgakov. Yale UP, 2008.
Shishkin, Mikhail. "Afterword." *Oblomov*, by Ivan Goncharov. Trans. Marian Schwartz. Yale UP, 2008.
Tolstoy, Leo. *Anna Karenina.* Trans. David Magarshack. Signet Classic, 1961.
Tolstoy, Leo. *Anna Karenina.* Trans. Louise and Aylmer Maude. W.W. Norton, 1970.
Tolstoy, Leo. *Anna Karenina.* Trans. Rosamund Bartlett. Oxford UP, 2014.

Tolstoy, Leo. *Anna Karenina*. Trans. Marian Schwartz. Yale UP, 2014.
Tolstoy, Leo. *Anna Karenina*. Trans. Richard Pevear and Larisa Volokhonsky. Viking, 2000.
Tolstoy, Leo. *Anna Karenina*. Trans. Kyril Zinovieff and Jenny Hughes. One World Classics, 2008.
Tolstoy, Leo. *War and Peace*. Trans. Constance Garnett. Heinemann, 1904.
Turgenev, Ivan. *Fathers and Children*. Trans. Constance Garnett. Heinemann, 1895.
Turgenev, Ivan. *Fathers and Sons*. Trans. Eugene Schuyler. Ward, Lock & Co., 1867.
Wilson, A.N. *Tolstoy*. Norton, 2001.

7

Translating Yiddish Classics

Redefining Tradition in Modern Yiddish Literature through the Prism of Kadya Molodowsky

Chantal Ringuet

> One language has never been enough for the Jewish people.
>
> —Shmuel Niger

Yiddish, a Germanic language with a dynamic though dramatic history as the language of Ashkenazi Jewry, has known an exceptional development from the period of the Haskalah or the Jewish Enlightenment at the end of the eighteenth century until the Second World War. The language of a people without a land, Eastern European Jews living in the Pale of Settlement under the rule of the tsar, Yiddish has been associated to strong political, ideological, and cultural movements promoting liberal and democratic ideas. Yiddish has also been a vehicle for a diversity of literary genres and styles pervaded by modernism and the avant-garde. However, with the destruction of the Yiddishland during the Holocaust, its number of speakers declined dramatically in the following decades. No longer linked to a vibrant and dynamic cultural life, Yiddish thus evoked "the old smoke-ochre of the morning" (Ozick) coming out of the chimneys of Auschwitz and other concentration camps where millions of Jews perished under the Nazi occupation while "the world remained silent" (*Un di velt hot geshvigen*, 1956), as Elie Wiesel originally phrased it.[1]

---

[1] Elie Wiesel's indispensable account of Holocaust literature is also known in English under the title *Night* (1960). After its original publication in Yiddish, the book was rewritten in French and published in a shorter version by Les Éditions de Minuit in 1956 under the title *La nuit*. The French edition was then translated into English by Stella Rodway and published under the title *Night* by Hill & Wang in 1960. Right from the start, the title *La nuit/Night* reveals a standardization of the discourse which was central in the "remaking" process by which the text was made available for Western readers. On this topic, see Roskies and Seidman.

In the postwar years, Yiddish, it seemed, was destined for an irreversible decline. Native speakers of the *mame-loshn*—an expression used to describe the Yiddish language *and* culture—were now older generations of Jews, often survivors of Nazi camps who first became refugees and then immigrants, individuals who felt tragically ambivalent toward the destiny of their uprooted and "murdered" language.² Therefore, it has been qualified as a "death-defying language" (Lerman). In this context, the act of translating Yiddish literature can be defined, to a certain extent, as a task sullied by a burden, the collective trauma of the Holocaust and the hollow presence of the Yiddishland, a postwar neologism used to describe an engulfed world. While new generations of Yiddish scholars and translators have made tremendous efforts to keep the language alive in the last decade and tend to demonstrate that they have overcome this trauma, often in new territories unmarked by the presence of the Second World War, like the United States, one fact remains: it is no longer possible to live or to be in contact with society more broadly defined in Yiddish.

This chapter seeks to present a brief discussion of the major issues pertaining to the translation of Yiddish literary "classics" today. First, it sheds light on the relationship between a European language forged by exile and migration, spreading over a wide diaspora—a context involving the presence of many linguistic variations and dialects—and the notion of "classic" in literature. Second, while analyzing the paradoxical dimensions of a "Yiddish classic," I intend to reclaim this foundational concept for women writers in an international frame, as illustrated by the work of Kadya Molodowsky (1894–1975). How can a young literature evolve in a context of constant instability, a situation that characterizes the diaspora frame of reference, while still producing works of its own? How can these works be qualified as "classics," a concept which usually refers to pre-eminently European or national literatures instead of transnational or international ones? While approaching these interrogations, this chapter addresses a broader and much discussed question: How does non-dominant and minor literatures make their way into translations in dominant and major languages?³

---

² Cynthia Ozick described Yiddish as "a murdered language" during the Second World War. See Cynthia Ozick, "Envy; Or, Yiddish in America." See also Rachel Ertel, "Introduction," *Royaumes juifs. Les trésors de la littérature*, X.
³ It should be noted that translation is considered here both as an inherent component of Jewish culture and as a cultural process.

Contextualization

To broach some of the crucial issues involved in translating a "classic" of Yiddish literature in other languages, it is essential to map out the language's position within the Indo-European languages and in the Western world. Born in the Rhine Valley, approximately in the year 1000, Yiddish is one of the youngest European languages; furthermore, it is a Jewish language (such as Hebrew and Ladino) requiring the use of the Hebrew alphabet. Throughout its modern history, which spreads from the 1780s to 1939, it has been the vernacular language of Ashkenazi Jews living in the diaspora. Like many other "minor" languages, Yiddish has been depreciated, if not ostracized, by speakers from other communities in Central and Eastern Europe. Over many centuries, it was qualified as a "corrupt form of German," as a "bad German written in a Jewish idiom" or simply as a *zhargon*. In other words, it was perceived as the language of "Unbildung," the non-educated masses. For many Jews assimilated to European cultures, Yiddish was the language which they did not want to be associated with, to the point that it aroused fear. As Franz Kafka wrote in 1912, "But dread of Yiddish, dread mingled with a certain fundamental distaste, is, after all, understandable, if one has the good will to understand it" (Kafka, "An Introductory Talk on the Yiddish Language" 263).

On the European continent, Yiddish literature did not get the support of official cultural institutions and elites,[4] a situation that increased its fragility. Since its grammar and spelling were standardized as late as in the 1930s by linguist and founder of YIVO Max Weinreich, this context of instability highly contributed to widen the gap between this vernacular language and the "learned" ones. By contrast, it is interesting to note that French, the most widely used language of Europe from the Middle Ages to the eighteenth century, had its own academy since 1634–5.

For these reasons, as a "literary" language, Yiddish has emerged quite recently in history. The apparition of modern Yiddish literature is generally dated to the publication of Mendele Moykher Sforim (born Sholem Yankev Abramovitsch)'s *Dos kleyne mentshele* ("The Little Person") in 1864, which depicts the world of the *shtetl*, the small Jewish town in Eastern Europe, versus that of the city, and often illustrates the sociological and ideological tensions between Jews living under Russian rule in the Pale of Settlement. Its literary production embraces multiple styles, from modernism and symbolism to

---

[4] The long-term conflict between Hebraists and Yiddishists, which has led to the 1908 Conference in Czernowitz, illustrates this situation among Jewish "enlightened" intellectuals.

the avant-garde, as well as a diversity of influences. As neither classicism nor romanticism pervades Yiddish belles-lettres, this expression has long been considered by many as a contradiction in terms or as an example of "miscommunication."

Yiddish and the Classics of European Literature

While discussing the translation of Yiddish classics in other languages, it is important to recall that many classics of European literature have long been translated into Yiddish. At the end of the nineteenth century, Jewish readers had access to classics of Western literature through literary translation. From Shakespeare to Molière and Romain Rolland, European classics were available to readers who were native speakers of the *mame-loshn*. This situation mirrors the high-level of literacy and plurilingualism that characterizes Yiddish culture, as well as the open-mindedness of the readers themselves who were constantly welcoming modernity in its various forms of literary and artistic expression in order to absorb them on their own. However, as Alyssa Quint has noted, Yiddish translators were then more interested in "distilling an entertaining Yiddish-language version of a play with which to pack Yiddish theater" (Quint) than in parsing the beauty of its literary qualities. Thus, the common expression used about Shakespeare's dramas in Yiddish as being "ibergezetst un farbesert" ("translated and improved") did not refer to their literary qualities—since the texts were usually downgraded to a lower level— but to its power of entertainment.

Classics in Yiddish literature began in the 1860s with Mendele Mokher Sforim and in the 1880s with Sholem Aleichem. What characterized the production of these authors is the influence of Russian fiction and the way they present a mix of realism, humor, and social commentary. Later, I. L. Peretz brought modernism to Yiddish literature. During this period, the birth of the Yiddish press in Russia contributed greatly to the dissemination of this literature all over the world. In parallel, starting in the 1880s, several waves of Jewish immigration to North America brought Yiddish speakers to the United States (New York), among whom were numerous poets. Then, with the Russian Revolution of 1905, other migration waves brought Jewish newcomers in Canada (Montreal, Toronto, Winnipeg). In these cities, the Yiddish press continued to bloom through publications such as *Di Forvets* (NY) and *Der Keneder Adler* (Montreal), quickly leading to the emergence of Yiddish literature in North America. Among the renown figures were poets like Mani Leib and Jacob Glatshteyn, who belonged respectively to the groups *Di Yunge* (The Young Ones) and *Di Inzikhistn* (The Introspectivists),

Celia Dropkin, Anna Margolin, Malka Heifetz Tussman, and, of course, Kadya Molodowsky. Later contributions were made by novelists I. J. Singer and his brother I. B. Singer, who received the Nobel Prize in Literature in 1978. The same phenomenon took place in Montreal with poet J.-I. Segal and Ida Maze and later with Rokhl Korn and Chava Rosenfarb, and in Tel Aviv after the Second World War with Avrom Sutzkever.

For a long time, the "classics" of Yiddish literature were exclusively books written by men. From Sholem Aleichem, I. L. Peretz, Mendele Moikher Sforim, the founding fathers of Yiddish literature in Europe, to Avrom Sutzkever and Isaac Bashevis Singer, one of the major writers of this literature in the twentieth century, the "canon" was indisputably masculine. Therefore, historians and critics (all men themselves) were paradoxically reproducing toward women the situation that had long been prevalent for Yiddish in the diaspora: marginalization and exclusion. While Yiddish, the language of the *heym*, was deeply associated to the familiar and the feminine, the most illustrious representatives of its literature were all men, so much so that women, even if they approached a vast range of topics—from major events of Jewish history to the challenges of daily life—went largely unrecognized. While Judaism is based on a long tradition of patriarchy, and the exclusion of women from the "canon" is prevalent in many literatures of the Western world, it seems strange retrospectively to encounter such a situation, all the more so as questions of genre and gender pervade Yiddish literature.

Another difference considering the "classics" of Yiddish in its recent history relate to literary genres and the phenomenon of migration. While the European "classic" writers were practicing more established genres such as novel and prose, North American writers were often more accomplished in poetry than in prose, Mani Leib and Jacob-Isaac Segal being noteworthy examples. Yiddish women writers, who emerged mostly in the 1930s in Europe and America, have usually favored poetry instead of prose. European-born Kadya Molodowsky and Rokhl Korn, as well as American born writers Celia Dropkin and Anna Margolin, all wrote poetry that was very modern and innovative, challenged the norms of their time, and played major roles in founding a modern Yiddish literary tradition.

Crossing Frontiers between Memory and History

Right from the start, it is essential to stress that translating Yiddish is a delicate task, emotionally loaded because of the dramatic events of modern history, a situation not usually found in other European languages. This act of translation raises an issue of historical consciousness and it involves the crossing of multiple frontiers. First, a frontier between generations: since the majority of Yiddish translators are descendants of native speakers who have inherited the language as young adults, translating Yiddish reinvigorates a link with older generations. In other words, it is a form of meshing (or "remaillage"), a revival of a language that is no longer spoken in everyday life and of a world that has ceased to exist. It is a reality that American intellectual Marianne Hirsch attempted to come to terms with in her concept of "postmemory," which describes "the relationship that the 'generation after' bears to the personal, collective, and cultural trauma of those who came before—to experiences they 'remember' only by means of the stories, images, and behaviors among which they grew up" (5). Second, a frontier between cultures: for a few Yiddish translators who don't have the language in their cultural or family background, the act of translation is loaded with a deep cultural signification. While contributing to the preservation and transmission of memory, it builds a dialog between cultures that had been historically divided by religion and language and inaccessible to each other (Ringuet; Simon). Such an approach denotes the profound meaning of the expression "affiliative familial postmemory" (Hirsch, *Generation* 22). Third, a frontier between "learned languages" and "popular languages." On account of its diverse linguistic components, Yiddish, as a "language of fusion," lends itself to a certain flexibility. In terms of translation, this implies a variety of possibilities and nuances that can be explored easily in a recent language that doesn't belong to a well-established European tradition. American English, today the language of most of the descendants of Yiddish speakers, provides another example of such recently appeared idioms, as shown in the various texts included in the anthology *How Yiddish Changed America and How America Changed Yiddish* (Stavans and Lambert). However, it remains complex to render the inflections and colors of Yiddish as well as its "roughness" into a high European language infused with classicism such as French. Therefore, the act of translating Yiddish into standardized French involves crossing a frontier between "learned languages" and so-called "popular languages."[5] Thus, it is easy to imagine that in such a case, a certain "fear" of standardization can inhabit scholars and readers of Yiddish literature.

Issues and Challenges

Since Yiddish is a flexible language that comprises a variety of dialectal forms, translating it raises specific issues pertaining to the famous "loss" inherent

---

[5] On this subject, see Gepner 43–7.

in the very act of translation. According to professor and translator Anita Norich, "Yiddish readers fear that what is lost is not only culturally specific nuances, the *tam* (taste, flavor) of the original, but the history and culture of a people" (Norich, *Writing in Tongues* 9). Yet the *tam* doesn't reside only in the vocabulary but in a certain number of connotations and in the organization of the language. In his canonical book *The Meaning of Yiddish*, Benjamin Harshav explains this situation in the following terms:

> The vocabulary of Yiddish is rather poor in comparison with English or Russian, but each word has an aura of connotations derived from its multidirectional and codified relations not just within a semantic paradigm, as in other languages, but to parallel words in other source languages, to an active stock of proverbs and idioms, and to a typical situational cluster. (Harshav 39)

While the limited vocabulary of the language generates a higher dependence of words on their multilingual context of emergence, their emotive and semantic directions are not deprived of irony. Thus, translations of Yiddish literary works should be as multilingual as the originals; in other words, they should be achieved without "uprooting" the language from its linguistic, geographical, and cultural anchorages.

In consequence, Yiddish should not be standardized to the point of erasing the many references to religion and ethnicity that are often a component of the text (Rosenwald). These references, which are not rare in secular Yiddish, include a set of terms for naming persons and things specifically connected with religion. These are, on the one hand, "the names for the constituent parts and rituals of the sabbath and the holidays, for this life and the life to come, for such religious functionaries as rabiners and *rebeim* and *rabonim* and *tsaddikim*" (Rosenwald). On the other hand, these references include a set of interjections toward one's own attitude toward situations that have been mentioned or are about to be described. James Matisoff, in his book *Blessings, Curses, Hopes and Fears*, calls these "psycho-ostensive expressions" in the book's subtitle. Such expressions are used in order to recognize, summon, or avert God or evil in relations with others. The most popular of these is probably *keyneynhore* or "no evil eye," which is used "in mentioning any gratifying achievement," as Uriel Weinreich points out in his Yiddish-English dictionary (Weinreich, *Yiddish-English Dictionary*).

The typical "lost in translation" problem takes on additional levels of signification here. The act of translating Yiddish literature, classic texts or not, thus obeys many requirements, and its paradigms varies according to the constraints and the context in which translations are being made, as Rosenwald explains:

> Translators of Yiddish writers should retain both these aspects of their characters' Jewish competence. This is not an easy task, because doing so can make the translated texts more resistant and unfamiliar to the un-comprehending Jewish or Gentile reader. But to do otherwise uproots and flattens the characters. (Rosenwald)

A Feminist View on the "Classics"

Since the last decades of the twentieth century, one of the major issues pertaining to the translation of Yiddish women writers consists in developing a feminist approach. As in many other Western literary traditions, women were marginalized of the mainstream currents of Yiddish literature on the pretext that women writers were addressing mostly domestic topics instead of "important" subjects related to society and politics, history and culture, as well as to tradition. As we can judge by looking at the anthologies of Yiddish literature published up to the 1980s and 1990s, which focused mostly on male writers, this prejudice has lasted for a long time. Although Ezra Korman in his essay "Yiddishe dikhterins" (Yiddish poetesses) (1928) provides the first framework to examine the history of Yiddish women poets, it took many decades to establish a tradition of Yiddish women writers, as Kathryn Hellerstein mentions in her book *A Question of Tradition*. However, this was truly a misconception of Yiddish women writers' achievements, since many of them expressed either in prose or poetry a strong voice perceived as "masculine" while approaching topics not related to domesticity. This was particularly the case of Kadya Molodowsky, Rokhl Korn, Celia Dropkin, Anna Margolin, and Chava Rosenfarb, among others, whose writings are today considered "classics" of modern Yiddish literature. Therefore, to rehabilitate their voices through literary translation has become an urgent task. As Madeleine Cohen notes, "The long-lasting consequences of excluding women from the literary canon can be measured in part through the availability of their work in translation" (Cohen n.p.), which were rare until very recently compared to their male counterparts.

Kathryn Hellerstein, an American scholar who started translating Yiddish women writers in 1985 and contributed to introduce Molodowsky's works to the American readership, recalls her own journey in the following terms:

I realized that women poets in Yiddish had been sparsely represented, received with prejudice, and only partially heard and understood by their contemporaries and mine. It seems necessary, even urgent, to bring to light—that is to read, write about and translate—as much Yiddish poetry by as many women as possible, in order to see what was there and to define and examine the traditions of writing in which women were engaged. (Hellerstein, "Translating as a Feminist" 193)

Yet, while one of the main difficulties that a translator of Yiddish literature encounters is rendering the specific Jewish elements of the language into languages such as French or English; Yiddish poetry sometimes leads the translator back to the cultural roots of the text. This might involve the religious traditions against which the poems are opposing a dissident voice. For this reason, as Hellerstein states, "The translator needs to learn the traditions in order to understand the significance of the secularization of Yiddish culture in the twentieth century and therefore to be able to translate poetry" (Hellerstein, "Yiddish Poetry," 76). In this perspective, the poem "Froyen-lider," part of a poetry book entitled *Kheshvandike nekht* (Vilnius 1927), remains an excellent example of "classic" text, since it deals with the tension between tradition and modernity, a situation exemplified by the narrator's resistance to specific practices deriving from Jewish law and embodied by the use of Hebrew words and expressions serving as metaphors.

"Froyen-lider" ("Women-Poems")

An excellent example of a Yiddish text which delves into different traditions and expresses the tension between tradition and modernity is Molodowsky's poem "Froyen-lider" or "Women-Poems," a poetic suite of eight poems in which a young woman finds herself torn apart between tradition and modernity and describes her nightly visions. While illustrating the "disruptive power of a series of Hebraic words," this poem confronts the translator with two different levels of language and reference: the first associated with traditional narratives in which the narrator finds herself limited as a woman who can't express her own subjectivity freely; the second with modernism and self-expression, which is clearly her own path. These two registers remain distinct and are illustrated by use of many Hebrew words and expressions in the Yiddish text. While it is not unusual to find Hebrew expressions in a Yiddish text, Molodowsky integrates them as if those were signs drawing the attention on themselves, thus participating in building a narrative in which "language itself becomes a metaphor" (Hellerstein, "Hebraisms as Metaphor" 144).

"Froyen-lider I" is divided into two parts. The first part of the poem depicts a woman's vision at night, and the second recounts the dreamer's refusal to accept its meaning. Her female ancestors come to her and exhort her to keep her virtue. One of these women is an *agune*, a word signifying a woman abandoned by her husband or whose husband disappeared without granting her a divorce. She finds herself in the desperate situation of being unable to remarry and forced to stay husbandless. In the end, the poem remains unresolved and, on the existential level, illustrates the paradox and harrowing situation in which the woman finds herself. How can we translate such a term? Since there is no readily available translation of this word, which relates to Jewish law, and since it has no equivalent in neither English nor French, the best solution seems to be keeping these Hebrew words and expressions in the English or French translation, and providing a glossary explaining their meaning to a broad readership. Moreover, keeping the original names and expressions in Hebrew (and sometimes in Yiddish) has the advantage of putting the reader in contact with words loaded with a deep emotional and historical depth. In other words, they resonate beyond "untranslatability."

This poem depicts a young woman torn between tradition and modernity at a historical turning point of Yiddish literature, the interwar period representing both the emergence of women's voices and the end of the golden age of Yiddish literature (which ended abruptly with the Second World War and the destruction of Yiddish culture and European Jewry). Its title, "Women-Poems," depicts the very essence of Yiddish women writers, poetry being an essential, organic component of their lives, while Jewish law and traditions were restrictive toward the expression of a literary or artistic self among women. It draws our attention on the crucial question of genre and gender, a distinction that was not yet operative and that pervades Yiddish literature. In short, "Froyen-lider" is a groundbreaking piece that invites us to redefine the parameters of the "classics" in Yiddish literature, a word that often refers to a work of literary fiction and that, by extension, tended to exclude Yiddish women writers.

Yet, some women writers have written novels that have been rediscovered in literary translation. This is the case of Molodowsky's novel, *A Jewish Refugee in New York: Rivke Zilberg's Journal*, recently translated by Anita Norich, which represents, according to Norich "a turning point for 'assumptions about genre and gender in Yiddish literature'" (qtd. in Cohen) (Norich) or Blume Lempel's *Oedipus in Brooklyn and Other Stories* (2017), translated by Ellen Cassedy and Yermiyahu Ahron Taub. Also worth mentioning are *Confessions of a Yiddish Writer and Other Essays* (2019) by Chava Rosenfarb, translated by Goldie Morgentaler, and Miriam Karpilove's novel *Diary of a Lonely Girl, or The Battle against Free Love* translated by Jessica Kirzane. These books are new accounts following the publication of anthologies such as *Found Treasures: Stories by Yiddish Women Writers* (1994) edited by Frieda Johles Forman, Ethel Raicus, and Sarah Silberstein Swartz; *The Exile Book of Yiddish Women Writers* (2013) edited by Frieda Johles Forman; and *Women Writers of Yiddish Literature* (2015) edited by Rosemary Horowitz.

In conclusion, translating the classics of Yiddish literature raises specific issues pertaining to the status of Yiddish as a language of the diaspora: that is, as a language without national and geographical frontiers, which has spread over the five continents and therefore embodies all the characteristics of a major world literature. Its longtime status as "wandering language" reflects its contact with many cultures and languages, which must be considered in order to grasp its influence in literary works. This act of translation also requires a deep knowledge of the religious vocabulary often found in the language, despite its very secular nature. The same can be said about Jewish humor, which is both colorful and unique, often described as "untranslatable" because of its specific expressions and of the use of diminutives and of words and expressions borrowed from different languages. Moreover, "classics" of Yiddish literature must include women writers, whose voices have long been marginalized and put aside to the point of falling into oblivion by lack of translations available. It is now the task of the translator to contribute to shed light on women's voices, notably those who now deserve to be qualified as classics of modern Yiddish literature.

If Yiddish literature reached its golden age between the Jewish Enlightenment at the end of the eighteenth century and the Second World War, we could question the relevance of translating texts in the 2020s. Why translate today the works of a literature that some won't hesitate to call outdated? To this question, we will answer by another one: Could we imagine not having access to Dostoyevsky's or Marina Tsvetaeva's works on the pretext that there are no translations available? This points to another aspect of the act of literary translation, especially when it comes to revealing and rediscovering a world literary heritage that, like the language itself, might still fall into oblivion. And to fight against its disappearance. As both a European literature and a world literature, Yiddish is unique among diaspora literatures. Thus, the translator's task consists in passing its scintillation or, as I. L. Singer would have written, its "inner illumination," along to readers.

Works Cited

Cohen, Madeleine. "The Feminine Ending. On Women's Writing in Yiddish, Now Available in English." *Los Angeles Review of Books*, April 10, 2020, larev iewofbooks.org/article/the-feminine-ending-on-womens-writing-in-yiddish-now-available-in-english/.

Ertel, Rachel. *Royaumes juifs*. 1 et 2., Éditions Robert Laffont, coll. « Bouquins », 2008/2009.

Forman, Frieda Johles, ed. *The Exile Book for Yiddish Women Writers: An Anthology of Stories That Looks to the Past So We Might See the Future*. Exile Editions, 2013.

Forman, Frieda Johles, Ethel Raicus, and Sarah Silberstein Swartz, eds. *Found Treasures: Stories by Yiddish Women Writers*. Second Story Press, 1994.

Gepner, Corinna. "De la trahison à la métamorphose." *TransLittérature*, Special issue, *Traduire le yiddish*, vol. 42, no. 1, 2012, pp. 37–56.

Harshav, Benjamin. *The Meaning of Yiddish*. University of California Press, 1990.

Hellerstein, Kathryn. "Finding Her Yiddish Voice: Kadya Molodowsky in America." *Revue d'études anglophones*, Summer 2002, pp. 48–68.

Hellerstein, Kathryn. "Hebraisms as Metaphor in Kadya Molodowsky's Froyen-Lider I." *The Uses of Adversity: Failure and Accommodation in Reader Response*, Ed. Ellen Spolsky. Bucknell University Press, 1990, pp.143–52.

Hellerstein, Kathryn. *A Question of Tradition. Women Poets in Yiddish (1586–1978)*. Stanford University Press, 2014.

Hellerstein, Kathryn. "Translating as a Feminist. Reconceiving Anna Margolin." *Prooftexts*, vol. 20, no. 1–2, Winter–Spring 2000, pp. 191–208.

Hellerstein, Kathryn. "'A Word for My Blood': A Reading of Kadya Molodowsky's 'Froyen-Lider.'" *AJS Review*, vol. 13, no. 1–2, Spring–Autumn, 1988, pp. 47–79.

Hellerstein, Kathryn. "On Yiddish Poetry and Translation of Yiddish Poetry." *I Radical Poetics and Secular Jewish Culture*, Ed. Stephen Paul Miller and Dan Morris. University of Alabama Press, 2009, pp. 70–78.

Hirsch, Marianne. "The Generation of Postmemory." *Poetics Today*, vol. 29, no. 1, 2008, 103–28.

Hirsch, Marianne. *The Generation of Postmemory*. Writing and Visual Culture after the Holocaust, Columbia UP, 2012.

Horowitz, Rosemary, ed. *Women Writers of Yiddish Literature*. McFarland and Cie, 2015.

Howe, Irving and Eliezer Greenberg, eds. *A Treasury of Yiddish Stories*. Viking, 1954.

Kafka, Franz. "Rede über die Jiddische Sprache." *Prague*, February 18, 1912, *Hochzeits-Vorbereitungen auf dem Lande und andere Prosa aus dem Nachlass, Gesammelte Werke*. Herausgegeben von Max Brod. Taschenbuchausgabe in acht Bänden, Fischer Taschenbuch Verlag, 1983.

Karpilove, Miriam. *Diary of a Lonely Girl, or The Battle against Free Love*. Trans. Jessica Kirzane. Syracuse UP, 2020.

Korman, Ezra. *Yiddishe dikhterins. Antologye*. L.M. Shtayn, 1928.

Lempel, Blume. *Oedipus in Brooklyn and Other Stories*. Trans. Ellen Cassedy and Yermiyahu Ahron Taub. Mandel Vilar Press, 2016.

Lerman, Anthony. "Yiddish is No Joke." *The Guardian*, March 5, 2010, www
.theguardian.com/commentisfree/belief/2010/mar/05/yiddish-jewish-culture
-zionism.
Matisoff, James. *Blessings, Curses, Hopes and Fears: Psycho-Ostensive Expressions
in Yiddish*. Stanford UP, 2000 [1979].
Molodowsky, Kadya. "Froyen-lider, I-VIII." Kheshvandike *nekht*, Vilnius, 1927,
pp. 1–19.
Molodowsky, Kadya. *A Jewish Refugee in New York: Rivke Zilberg's Journal*.
Trans. Anita Norich. Indiana UP, 2019.
Norich, Anita. "Kadya Molodowsky. A Woman Novelist Rediscovered." *Pakn
treger*, vol. 76, winter 2017, www.yiddishbookcenter.org/language-literature
-culture/pakn-treger/kadya-molodovsky-woman-novelist-rediscovered.
Norich, Anita. *Writing in Tongues. Translating Yiddish in the Twentieth Century*.
U of Washington P, 2013.
Quint, Alyssa. "Translated and Improved." *The Edward Blank YIVO Vilna Online
Collections*, April 5, 2017, vilnacollections.yivo.org/Translated-Theater.
Ozick, Cynthia. "Envy; Or, Yiddish in America." *Commentary*, November 1969,
pp. 33–52.
Ozick, Cynthia. "Washington Square." *A Cynthia Ozick Reader*, Ed. Elaine M.
Kauvar. Indiana UP, 1996, pp. 279–84.
Ringuet, Chantal. "Les aventures d'une traductrice dans le Yiddishland à l'ère
postvernaculaire." *Convergences francophones*, vol. 2, no. 1, 2015, pp. 72–90.
Rosenfarb, Chava. *Confessions of a Yiddish Writer and Other Essays*. Trans.
Goldie Morgentaler. McGill/Queen's University Press, 2019.
Rosenwald, Larry. "Four Thesis on Translating Yiddish Literature in the 21st
Century." *Pakn Treger*, vol. 18, Summer 2002, www.yiddishbookcenter.org
/language-literature-culture/pakn-treger/four-theses-translating-yiddish
-literature-21st-century.
Roskies, David G. *Again the Apocalypse: Responses to Catastrophe in Modern
Jewish Culture*. Harvard UP, 1999.
Seidman, Naomi. "Elie Wiesel and the Scandal of Jewish Rage." *Jewish Social
Studies*, vol. 3, no. 1, 1996, pp. 1–19.
Sforim, Mendele Moykher. "Dos kleyne mentshele." *Kol Mevaser*, vol. 2, no.
45 through vol. 3, no. 6, November 12 [24] 1864–February 4 [16] 1865.
Stavans, Ilan and Joshua Lambert, eds. *How Yiddish Changed America and How
America Changed Yiddish*. Restless Books, 2020.
Weinreich, Uriel. *Yiddish-English Dictionary*. Schocken, 1977.
Wiesel, Elie. *La nuit*. Les Éditions de Minuit, 1958.
Wiesel, Elie. *Night*. Trans. Stella Rodway. Hill & Wang, 1960.
Wiesel, Elie.*Un di velt hot geshvigen*. Central Union of Polish Jews in Argentina,
1956.

8

Víctor Català's *A Film (3,000 meters)*
Translating a Catalan Classic

Peter Bush

The year 2023 will see the publication of my translation of Honoré de Balzac's *The Lily in the Valley* by the New York Review of Books. Balzac is an author firmly established in the Western literary canon: he is unquestionably a writer of French classics. Reviewers and readers will have some inkling of what lies in store and where it comes from, even if they may actually be surprised by what they find. In 2022, Open Letter published my translation of Víctor Català's novel, *A Film (3,000 meters)*. Català's novel *Solitude*, translated by David Rosenthal, came out in 1992 (Readers International) and *Silent Souls and other stories*, translated by Kathleen McNerney (MLA) in 2018. So Català (1869–1966) now exists in English and the slow struggle for readers and recognition begun in 1992 goes on, without the existing cultural capital a new Balzac translation enjoys.

In any case, translated Catalan classics must compete, as all translations must, with the existing might of English-language classics that dominate reading programs in schools and literary studies in universities in the English-speaking world. Nor should we forget that the fact that Català wrote in Catalan brings a host of other historical hurdles. Francisco Franco's dictatorship did its best to ban the language from public spaces, though a trickle of literary work by Catalan writers was published by small presses like Biblioteca Selecta. Franco didn't die until 1975, though Francoist attitudes toward the Catalan language didn't die with him, and are still an influential presence, complimented by the cultural centralism of all Spanish political parties; Catalan language and literature has a minimal presence in Spanish universities and schools.

One aftermath of the civil war in the literary sphere meant both that the readership for Catalan literature was restricted and undermined: three generations had no access to general literacy in the mother tongue that they spoke at home. Another was that the civil war created enduring political divisions and enmities that led to a severely fractured cultural life both in Catalonia and the rest of Spain: writers would be published or not, read or not, favorably reviewed or not, beyond the inevitable Francoist censorship, within non-Francoist literary communities. This had some impact on Víctor Català who welcomed Franco's victory, though she was a champion of the Catalan language and critical values that had nothing in common with the dictatorship's ultra-catholic nationalistic version of fascism. Seen as bourgeois and well-to-do by anarchists, like Josep Pla, she faced and escaped death-threats during the war. That there are now finally translations into English speaks to a *domestic* revaluation of her work and also a greater sense of cultural and political self-confidence in Catalonia. Undoubtedly, the highly controversial invitation to Catalonia to be guest country at the Frankfurt Book Fair in 2007 multiplied the number of Catalan books translated into other languages. It was also helped by a strategic change in the policy of the Institut Ramon Llull, the Catalan cultural funding and promotion body, to prioritize the translation of prose work by modern authors, and with foreign publishers and translators, to begin to give visibility internationally to a range of Catalan fiction.

Born into a middle-class, land-owning family from the small Costa Brava fishing port of L'Escala, Català was accustomed to living in a small community where everybody knew everybody and their histories, where constant contact existed across social classes, political positions could range from anarchist and republican on the left to Carlist on the right, and where there was always trade with the rest of Europe, and movement out along the coast to France: outlooks weren't simply provincial and inward-looking. She wasn't a member of the Catalan elite and wasn't a writer who was nurtured as part of the Barcelonan literary establishment.

She embraced literary modernism and was opposed to *noucentisme* that was championed by Eugeni d'Ors and others from 1906. The statelessness and oppression of the Catalan language predated the civil war by hundreds of years, and it was only in the nineteenth century with the *Renaixença* movement that literary Catalan was revived and developed in ways that encompassed romantic, realist, and modernist approaches. *Noucentisme* was a reaction against that openness and tended to be backward-looking and favored a style of language that looked to the Middle Ages, subjects that were elitist and historical, with conservative moral perspectives. It was a proponent of a normalized, "pure" language that didn't reflect the realities of Catalan in the street, the inevitable contact with Spanish, and the varieties existing across class-divides and Catalan-speaking areas. The *noucentistes* frowned on literature that dared to reflect any of those nuances, and thus encouraged a static, censorial attitude to literary writing in Catalan.

Víctor Català didn't go to university. Her republican federalist family in L'Escala regularly received daily newspapers, literary and other magazines, and the latest published books from a bookseller in Figueres. They encouraged her to be an autodidact. Among her papers is a note under the heading "I must study and do," detailing "Spanish classical theatre, History of Art, French, Spanish and Italian grammar, geography, physics, arithmetic and logic," and "read Hegel, Schopenhauer, Voltaire, Leopardi" (Muñoz i Pairet, 16). She later had a flat in Barcelona and lived there for some time, and was friends with writers like Narcís Oller, the realist novelist, and spells out her strongly independent anti-*noucentiste* literary views in correspondence with him and other leading writers like poet Joan Maragall. From the start she had to confront other prejudices: the machismo and clericalism rife in Catalan society. In 1898, at the age of twenty-two, she anonymously submitted a poetic monologue, *La Infanticida*, to a literary competition in Olot. The work won a prize but the story of a mother killing her baby shocked the Catholics of Olot, and they were even appalled when the author was revealed to be a woman, Caterina Albert. As a result of the furor she decided to adopt the literary pseudonym of Víctor Català that she would use throughout her life, though it was soon to become public knowledge that the name belonged to a woman, Caterina Albert. When interviewed by the poet Tomàs Garcés in 1926, she commented:

> Apparently there were convoluted discussions about who the author was. Seemingly it was a daring monologue. I'd not realized that. When they found out the author was a woman, the outcry was even greater. They didn't think it was right for me to tell the story of an infanticide. Yet can the work of an artist be curbed? I don't think an artist should be curbed by moral norms. I think it is fundamental to defend the independence of art. Thanks to this independence I have been able to be faithful to my calling, that everyone would have liked to restrict. The only norm I recognize is good taste, what is immoral is only what is useless. Thus, it is only poorly conceived work that is immoral. (Casacuberta 21)

Víctor Català published several collections of short stories and the novel *Solitude* in the first seven years of the new century that rapidly established her as rising literary star in Catalonia and in Spain, as they were quickly translated into Spanish. The subjects were set in rural contexts and that enabled critics, readers, and publishers to pigeon-hole her as a writer of rural dramas, though her style and treatment of themes weren't narrowly rural, but used the rural to focus on issues of oppression, emotion, and relationships in a way that transcended immediate physical contexts and challenged conventional literary and moral stances. Then ten years passed without any new publications, and nobody was expecting *A Film (3,000 meters)*, that began to be published in the new literary magazine *Catalana* in 1918 with the final part coming out in June 1921. In her prologue, Català is at pains to point to the light-hearted nature of her new novel that is inspired by the cinema: "For both our sakes, let this long, inconsequential sequence of scenes without excess dressing or substance prevail a while and relax your brain" (p. 15).[1] The novel is set on the Costa Brava and Girona but mainly in Barcelona. The protagonist Ramon Nonat Ventura, also known as El Senyoret (The Little Gent), rises from hapless orphan in a Catholic orphanage in Girona to criminal gang leader in Barcelona in a plot inspired by picaresque and noir literary narratives, nineteenth-century serial fiction and penny dreadfuls as well as the new movies that were becoming so popular in Catalonia. Critical reaction was almost uniformly negative, and there was horror at the very idea of a female, rural novelist from L'Escala daring to venture into such male territory as urban low-life and the *noucentistes* loathed any genre aspiring to reach "the masses."[2] It is largely true to say that the novel was well and truly buried until Maria Bohigas at Club Editor embarked on a program to reclaim Víctor Català as a leading Catalan writer of the twentieth century by re-publishing *Un film (3000 metres)* in 2015 and three volumes of her short stories (*Tots els contes*, 2018–19). On a visit for publishers to Barcelona organized by the Institut Ramon Llull, Chad Post and Kaija Straumanis of Open Letter at the University of Rochester heard writer Jordi Nopca enthused about the novel and decided it was for their list and commissioned me to translate it.

I spent months on the translation during which I also read some of the recent scholarship inspired by Català's writing, and her stories. It's gone through eight drafts and my editors' edit. As you'd expect, the whole process of re-reading and re-writing has led me to make hundreds of thousands choices, interpretations, and revisions. There have been moments when I have thought it is impossible to translate the book. I've despaired. It's not an uncommon feeling for literary translators facing a demanding classic and, exacerbated by the desire to get it "right" as much as I can, particularly as the novel has never been translated into English before, and it's taken a hundred

---

[1] All page references are to the translation published in May, 2022.
[2] Good, Writing Methods: Models of Literary Creation: Models of Literary Creation and Reception in the work of Caterina Albert i Paradís/Víctor Català. This thesis is an excellent introduction to Víctor Català's work, as are the earlier two works by Catalan scholars. It is available on the web and, as such, an invaluable aid to English readers of Català who want to know more.

years to get to this point. I'd like to explore some of the ideas about the novel that the translation process has generated.

The six parts of the novel follow the life of the male protagonist, Ramon Nonat Ventura, from birth to death but each part has a specific focus that takes the reader into a different historical or social milieu with a wide range of characters offering a critical reflection on their relationships from the perspective of gender or class: a central story that frames a series of stories, a kaleidoscopic effect within a Thousand and One Nights narrative: fictional tropes of orphans, spinsters, maids seduced by masters, crooks, go-getting provincials in the metropolis combined with realist depictions of factory workers, haberdashers, street-porters, and corrupt politicians and Belle Époque high society. The reader is grabbed both by the desire to know what Nonat's next steps will be and by the mini-dramas his career will abandon or galvanize. Víctor Català proclaims in her prologue: "the lethal leaps made beyond the realms of verisimilitude, the many twists and turns, tell you it's neither an exquisite nor a fully fashioned fantasy, and you're freed up, for a while, from the torture of straining your eyes in attempt to catch all the threads" (p. 13), knowing full well that her readers will in fact become obsessed with tracing all the threads and trying to tie them up. The irony of her mock modesty becomes obvious to the reader from the opening pages. I will detail a few key aspects in the interplay between the theme of the bastard's meteoric rise and the counterpoint of myriad mini social dramas, between literary tropes, historical context, class, and gender.

After ten years without a new book from Víctor Català her readers will have been reassured when starting the first episode in the new serial novel. A retired fisherman Jepet and his wife Maria la Gallinaire the Chicken Woman live in a small fishing village on the Costa Brava. Maria is the dominant partner, "wears the trousers," and made money selling chickens and other goods, while Jepet was away on long fishing voyages, as she couldn't stand the boredom of a purely domestic role. The only thing she is missing is a child (she's sure Jepet is to blame) and laments not holding onto that orphan she looked after for a time. As the gale blows, that boy now returns as a smart young man wanting to find out who his parents were.

Stories are swapped and we learn that Maria took him to be baptized before leaving him in the orphanage as Ramon Nonat Ventura. This name is hugely symbolic and the reference will have immediately been recognized by Catalan readers in 1918. Sant Ramon Nonat was a Catalan saint born between 1200 and 1204, in the village of Portell in the region of Urgell. There are differing stories about him, Catholic and non-Catholic. He was born via a caesarian section, possibly carried out by the count who fathered him, and his mother, the daughter of a local farmer, died as a result. He was thus called

"Nonat," or "not born." His father saw to his bastard son's education and he eventually worked for the Mercedarian Order in Barcelona helping to free Christian prisoners being held in Moorish prisons in Arab parts of Spain and North Africa. He was himself captured and his jailors made holes in his lips by using red-hot skewers and padlocked his mouth because he was always pontificating. He was eventually made a saint in 1657, and became the patron saint of orphans, midwives, victims of gossip, and of silence. There are Nonnatus Houses in the United Kingdom and United States that are orphanages and refuges for unmarried, pregnant mothers and one features prominently in the popular BBC TV soap, *Call the Midwife*, now in its ninth series. Ironically, the adolescent is rescued from the Girona orphanage by a locksmith who trains him as an apprentice, and later he is reduced to silence in court and prison by a bullet that shatters his mouth.

It is in Girona that the author and her fiction first enter into a new, surprising territory: the world of the industrial working class. On the one hand, religious myth in a name and, on the other hand, a gesture to immediate historical reality. That world gains further prominence when Nonat moves to Barcelona, a center of working-class struggle. Víctor Català was beginning to write her novel when the international impact of the Russian Revolution strongly reverberated in the city where direct-action and syndicalist anarchism had had a strong presence from the late nineteenth century and spear-headed an insurrection in Barcelona in 1917.[3] Peroi who finds Nonat a factory job in Barcelona reads radical newspapers and is influenced by anarchist trades-unionism and tells his friend that "the era of the working-man is the epoch of equality" (p. 97). The ruthless Nonat had already abandoned and broken the heart of the locksmith in Girona who had rescued him from the orphanage and doted on him as the son he had never had. He now rapidly rises in the Barcelona factory to a position of manager usurping the role of Rovira, who had helped establish him, leading to the latter's sacking, madness, and suicide. In all of this, Nonat shows himself to be a skilled worker, staying on after hours at the factory and developing projects of his own to earn money, and a man of ideas as he thinks up schemes to bring work to the factory through a network of rag-and-bone men combing the city for scrap metal and cheap antiques he then helps renovate and satellite workshops beyond the factory. He assumes the general role of manager of

---

[3] Victor Serge, *Birth of Power*. Serge was in Barcelona in 1917 and participated in the anarchist uprising. His novel, based on that experience and in Petrograd, was published in French in 1931 as *Naissance de notre force*. His descriptions of what happened and the reactions of the Catalan bourgeoisie give a good idea of the historical situation informing Víctor Català's experience and novel.

these projects but at the same time uses the entry they give him to enter new households to steal. In his thoughts he employs the vocabulary of anarchism as he toils to bring about his own "emancipation," which can only be fully achieved by realizing the radical, anarchist slogan "No more masters!" However, his way forward is not to fight for a classless society, but to become himself a master, and so he buys a small factory which he rapidly turns into the base for his criminal activity as he develops a gang that terrorizes the city now employing all the metal-beating and organizing skills he learned in his war against the upper classes. This revenge against his putative aristocratic forebears and by extension, his war against Barcelona's high society, reaches a climax when he sets in motion a series of jewel and antique heists from wealthy acquaintances of an old Madrid roué he is convinced is his father. After that familiar opening sequence with Maria and Jepet Víctor Català's picaresque noir subject-matter was thus set to shock and discomfort readers and critics: she relishes describing the male proletarian ambience of small factories and capturing the fraught atmosphere, carnival of disguises, and class tensions on the city's streets, in its households, Liceu opera house, and theaters. Nonat's consciousness embraces class hatred but he is no anarchist: he desperately longs to be aristocratic—witness his dandy appearance, visits to the opera, and love of horse-riding—and the violence of his simmering frustration is stoked by his knowledge that it is an impossible dream.

I will detail just one of the many stories that stem from Nonat's criminal strategies that offers, as they all do, ambiguous riffs on the vagaries of birth inheritance, social rebellion, and gender, and in this case, a parody of a typical *roman feuilleton* situation. Well into Part Four of the novel the narrative suddenly and without explanation switches to the era of the French Revolution and a smugglers inn near the French frontier. In the middle of the night the innkeeper hears a rap on the kitchen window and when he goes outside, he finds a man who has been stabbed. Once the man is dragged inside, a baby is found in the folds of his greatcoat, and the dying man has just enough life left to tell his audience of miscreants that the baby is the only survivor of an aristocratic family of five who were all beheaded, and that his name is Laurent Philippe de Grisau. The innkeeper takes in but doesn't adopt the child who will marry his daughter and inherit the tavern. In Part Five we are fast-forwarded to modern times and introduced to Senyor Grisau, the French aristocratic orphan's grandson. Grisau is a silversmith and a lecher. His "fondness for a bit of skirt" leads him to steal from the jewelers where a successful career seemed guaranteed. However, he is detected and blacklisted in the guild and ends up begging on church steps where he catches the eye of Senyora Pepa, one of the myriad many female characters caught in Nonat's nets, whose biography offers another facet in the novel's kaleidoscopic representation of Barcelona society. Senyora Pepa had been the housemistress and mistress of a priest at the Santa Maria del Mar church who had racked up a considerable fortune in money and property; Senyora Pepa signed many of the related documents and was the single beneficiary of the priest's will. Like many of the women in the novel Senyora Pepa doesn't like to be idle and further invests her inheritance; she also wants her success to be her last laugh at the expense of those who decried her as the kept woman of a corrupt priest. She sets up Senyor Grisau with a small jewelry shop in the district of Gràcia and a young man, Bielet, with a shoe-shine salon. Both will become key elements in Nonat's mafiosi empire, whereas Senyora Pepa is murdered when the dandy and his main henchmen burgle her house.

However, I want to focus on the scenes where Grisau's grooming of a young seamstress leads to him being hounded out of his shop by local women. The aristocratic orphan's grandson falls foul of female "street" justice.

Decades before Mercè Rodoreda's *In Diamond Square* or Rosa Maria Arquimbau's *Forty Lost Years*[4] Víctor Català is drawn to a district of the city famed for its political radicalism and artisan workshops as well as its textile merchants. The initial tone is one of light-hearted irony as she delineates the family of a salt-cod seller:

> Senyora Quimeta, the salted cod seller, was a widow with six daughters and a son. All set to be a salted cod seller the son helped his mother with all shop tasks. Her daughters came in every kind and for every taste. The eldest was married to a civil guard; the second was courting a lad from a grocery-store the third had taken to the church and spent her days daydreaming and pondering whether she would be more amenable to God if she became a Sister caring for the poor, or a nun in an enclosed order. The fourth was studying to be a piano teacher; she wore her hair gathered with a big bow and spent the whole day practicing scales and other exercises that hugely endeared her to the ears of neighbors. The fifth was a manic housekeeper, and, finally, the youngest... "What shall we do with the young'un?" Senyora Quimet had wondered, the moment that little clod of earth popped out. (p. 238)

And this continues as her sixth daughter begins to work as an apprentice for a dress-maker whose workshop is round the corner from her salted cod shop. The seamstresses stroll by Senyor Grisau's jewelry and mock the sixty-year-old and his lecherous glances at them. Her daughter, they nickname "Nadala"

---

[4] *In Diamond Square*, Virago, 2013 and my translation of Arquimbau's novel (Fum d'Estampa,2021).

("Daffodil"), with Rosa, her friend and fellow apprentice—both, in turn nicknamed "Bouquet"—go to tease "the dirty old man" every afternoon, put their faces close to his window, stick their tongues out, licking and steaming up the pane before he chases them off. When Rosa's family moves to a different part of the city, Nadala's relationship with the yellow-coated jeweler evolves: she eyes his bracelets and necklaces affectionately, and he invites her in, promises to make her a pretty medallion, touches her hair, takes her on his lap, so that when the seamstresses next walk by and mock him:

> "Girls, take a look at that little egg yolk!" shouted one seamstress.
> "Looks like a plastic canary!" said another.
> "And what a schnozzle! Like a chunk of spicy sausage!" added a third.
> "Not one I'd like a bite of!" quipped another.
> The whole posse burst into laughter. (p. 274)

But not Nadala who bursts into tears. Her mother can't understand why she is so late home and never wants her supper, and after weeks of accepting her daughter's lies about the over-time she's doing, a neighbor finally tells her to be wary of Senyor Grisau's interest in her daughter. She goes to have a look and finds her daughter on the lecher's knee. Mother and sisters kick up a fuss, neighbors join in, and Grisau is attacked with iron bars, weights from scales and "Frenchy's grandson" abandons his shop and a drawer full of money. This story develops over two parts of the novel and is intercut in cinematic style with episodes in which Nonat begins to take stolen goods to Grisau to sell on, and on a stormy night he meets Senyora Pepa when he takes shelter in her shoe-shine business. When the gang is finally broken up, Grisau escapes relatively lightly and returns to begging. Català bids an ironical farewell to the blue-blooded, picturesque beggar:

> scrambled like an egg yolk, Senyor Grisau, in the entrance to Santa Maria, holds out a greasy cloth cap to passersby on a gnarled hand dotted with spikey hairs. As he is a *decorative* pauper, an ancien régime painter occasionally uses him as a model. (p. 432)

Later, there is another grooming episode when the younger, rebellious daughter of a woman who runs an ironing shop is courted by a commercial rep in textiles who regularly calls on a tailor in the same street. She eventually runs away with him when he has to travel and, after a riotous, debauched tour of Spain and Europe, she ends up back in Barcelona, pregnant and abandoned, soon to become the first woman in the city's premier criminal gang though on her way to a tragic, bloody end. The literary figures of seamstresses and working-class women actively using rich men to further their opportunities in life—as opposed to being groomed—become central in the pre- and post-civil war fictions of Rosa Maria Arquimbau.[5] The dressmaking industry brought the female skilled workers into direct contact with economic disparities as they made the clothes for wealthy women, and seamstresses played a leading role in the struggle for women's right to vote and the election of the Second Republic.

Víctor Català infuses the rapid succession of interconnected scenarios and characters, as in an action-packed movie or serial fiction with dialogues with a broad range of literary devices and linguistic pointers. The most obvious is her use of Spanish for the speech of most of judges and other members of the establishment and the Catalan flecked with Spanish employed by working-class characters. Nonat himself resolutely prefers to use Catalan and feels at a disadvantage with upper-class Spaniards he meets, because he can't engage perfectly in Spanish, and that detracts from the otherwise sophisticated façade he maintains as a proper gentleman; a similar sentiment makes him terminate his activities in foreign parts that, as far as he is concerned, includes the Spanish-speaking area of the Peninsula. At the same time, there is extensive use of inner monologues in the novel, as, for example, when Nonat walks the streets of Girona and dwells on the symbolic charge of the architecture or the historic feel to his bedroom in the tavern. Or when he is returning from Lleida by train in a compartment shared with a magistrate who recognizes him from Girona and a murder scene there and ends up being the judge in his final trial. The thief doesn't recognize the magistrate immediately and sinks into an observation of the man and his suitcase that becomes increasingly abstract, if not Cubist:

> That traveler seemed to look at him not only with his eyes, but with his every feature, his shirt collar, his hat, his whole person; you might have said all of him was a gaze, a kind of emanation that was pinning him down. So much so that, for a second, the bastard had the absurd sensation that the suitcase was staring at him too. That inanimate object, curled up like a tame pet at its master's side, appeared to enjoy a mysterious life of its own, bound to the latter by a magnetic current that transmitted the commands from a superior will, forcing it to support him, to stare at their traveling companion too, with an entirely conscious insistence. (p. 368)

[5] Comanegra has recently re-published short stories and novels by Rosa Maria Arquimbau with introductions and a biographical, historical volume by critic Julià Guillamon *Cor lleuger i altres narracions de l'era del flirt*, 2016 (stories from 1930 and 1933); *Quaranta anys perduts*, 2016 (first published in 1971), *L'enigma Arquimbau*, with *Història d'una noia i vint braçalets*, 2015.

Such passages reflect the reactions of Nonat, and Víctor Català teases the reader by developing the noir thread of the investigating magistrate who fancies himself as an amateur sleuth, hinting ambiguously at a connection between this magistrate from Girona and the magistrate father of Nonat's biological father who sacked her as a maid, or does the color of his eyes suggest he might even be his father? She tantalizes the reader trying to tie up threads.

In the concluding passages an abstract pictorial triangle frames the thoughts of the consul's wife—the sacked maid—as she reviews her turbulent life before the final debacle:

> Now and then the maid's monotonous singing drowned out the clink of crockery; the clatter of the billiard balls slowed, as if they were exhausted, the leaf fluttering at the top of the branch finally stilled, as if it were asleep. Inside that imaginary triangle, the consul's wife's memory, the only wakeful item in that drowsy siesta, kept unreeling visions by the hour, and the weight of the past, always uneasy within her body oppressed by so much fat when disturbed by new impressions, rose hazily, cloud after cloud, misting a comatose present now half-lit by so many painful filters. (Part 6, p. 40)

Any sentimental gloss on her search for lost time is cut dead by "so much fat." The consul's wife, surrounded by luxury in her mansion, longs for her first lover and her first child. She muses that her lover was killed in the war in Cuba, unaware that she will soon be reunited with her long-lost son in a fratricidal climax that will drive her to lunacy and Nonat to prison and death.

The translation of *A Film (3,000 meters)* makes available in English for the first time what is an entertaining, experimental novel by Víctor Català, the leading Catalan woman writer of the first half of the last century, and a very different kind of "classic" to her short stories and other novel, *Solitude*. It joins the growing body of Catalan modern classics available in English that will help readers and critics appreciate the distinct contribution that Catalan writers have made and are making to the canon of modern fiction. These are literary discoveries and pleasure much deferred by civil war and dictatorship even in Catalan. Translators, publishers, and scholars of Catalan literature can only hope that the volume of work being translated will establish once for all internationally that Catalan writers like Víctor Català, Josep Pla, and Mercè Rodoreda belong to the same culture and deserve to be recognized alongside Salvador Dalí, Joan Miró, and Antoni Gaudí.

Works Cited

Arquimbau, Rosa Maria. *Història d'una noia i vint braçalets* and *Cor lleuger i altres narracions de l'era del flirt*. By Julià Guillamon. Comanegra, 2016.
Arquimbau, Rosa Maria, with introductions and a biographical, historical volume by critic Julià Guillamon, *L'enigma Arquimbau*, with, 2015.
Arquimbau, Rosa Maria. *Forty Lost Years*. Trans. Peter Bush. Fum d'Estampa, 2021.
Arquimbau, Rosa Maria. *Història d'una noia i vint braçalets*. Ed. Julià Guillamon. Comanegra, 2015.
Arquimbau, Rosa Maria. *Quaranta anys perduts*. Ed. Julià Guillamon. Comanegra, 2016.
Balzac, Honoré de. *The Lily in the Valley*. Trans. Peter Bush. New York Review of Books, 2023.
Call the Midwife, created by Heidi Thomas. Neal Street Productions, 2021–.
Casacuberta, Margarida. *Víctor Català, l'escriptora enmascarada*. L'Avenç, 2019, p. 21.
Català, Víctor. *A Film (3,000 meters)*. Trans. Peter Bush. Open Letter, 2022.
Català, Víctor (Caterina Albert). *Silent Souls and Other Stories*. Trans. Kathleen McNerney. MLA Texts and Translations, 2018.
Català, Víctor. *Solitude*. Trans. David Rosenthal. Readers International, 1992.
Català, Víctor. *Tots els contes*. Club Editor, 2018–19.
Català, Víctor. *Un film (3000 metres)*. Club Editor, 2015.
Good, Kate. "Writing Methods: Models of Literary Creation: Models of Literary Creation and Reception in the work of Caterina Albert i Paradís/Víctor Català." Ph.D. thesis. University of North Carolina, 2018.
Muñoz i Pairet, Irene. *Caterina Albert-Víctor Català (1869–1966)*. Edicions Vitel·la, Bellcaire d'Empordà, 2016.
Rodoreda, Mercè. In *Diamond Square*. Trans. Peter Bush. Virago, 2013.
Serge, Victor. *Birth of Power*. Trans. Richard Greeman. Spectre, 2015.
Serge, Victor. *Naissance de notre force*. CLIMATS, 2004.

9

Translation as Storytelling

Susan Bernofsky

Translation is a form of storytelling, a way to give an account of something you've read in another language. Translating, you put into words—your own words—what you found in a foreign work, doing all the voices as if sitting with listeners around a campfire. Even though almost all translations are by definition based on texts written by someone else, the translator's own subject position unavoidably enters into the translated text, adding an implicit second layer of narration. This complex structural relationship involving original, translator, and translation is most readily visible in the case of retranslations, especially of classic works that already exist in several different translations in a given language.

I've been thinking a lot about the stories I tell when I translate because I'm in the early stages of a massive new retranslation project: Thomas Mann's monumental novel *The Magic Mountain* (*Der Zauberberg*), first published in 1924. There are two earlier published translations of this novel, each admirable in its own way. The first, published by Helen Lowe-Porter in 1927, was done in consultation with Mann and helped secure his international reputation. (It more recently served as an inspiration for Kate Briggs's *This Little Art*.) And in 1995, John E. Woods published a much-lauded retranslation that was celebrated above all for capturing Mann's irony and humor. So given that the novel doesn't "need" a new translation—as it might have if it had been poorly translated in the past—when I was invited to prepare a new translation of the book for Norton, the first thing I asked myself was whether I had stories to tell about this book that I felt needed telling. This train of thought derived directly from previous retranslations I'd done of classic works: Hermann Hesse's *Siddhartha* and Franz Kafka's *The Metamorphosis*. In each case, I discovered a story I wanted to tell about the work that I felt would shed new light even after their earlier English translations.

In the case of Hesse's *Siddhartha*—a quest narrative in which a young man spends years searching for the right sort of life—my story had to do with the relationship between the state of grace the protagonist seeks and the lyricism of the prose describing his search. Regardless of how one assesses

Hesse's profundity as a novelist, he was a highly gifted prose stylist whose German sentences are almost aggressively melodic: heavy on the assonance, occasionally even cloying in their lushness. In *Siddhartha*, his Orientalist fantasy of South Asia, I felt Hesse was using a sense of harmonic balance in his sentences as a correlative to his novel's vision of the world. It's important to remember that this novel was written in the immediate aftermath of what at the time was still being called the Great War. The unprecedented violence of this war fought with twentieth-century technology—including chemical weapons as well as tanks and bombers—killed millions of combatants and left many survivors either physically maimed and/or psychologically scarred. The word "shellshocked" was coined in 1915 to describe the condition of those who had been through that experience.

Hesse began *Siddhartha* in 1919 and finished it in 1922. So at a moment when all of Europe was still reeling from the war—and from the influenza pandemic that followed immediately after—Hesse presented a radical alternative to grievous injury and death, giving his young protagonist all the time in the world to search for his true calling. And the prose that accompanies this project—melodically flowing sentences held together by assonance—represents Hesse's vision of a state of nirvana, a universe in balance. Everything is about harmonious balance and dignified pacing.

I kept this understanding of Hesse's book in mind as I worked sentence by sentence on my translation, cultivating as much lyricism as I could. Here, for example, is the book's final sentence, in which Siddhartha's friend Govinda realizes that Siddhartha has achieved enlightenment and gazes on him in wonder:

> Tief verneigte er sich, bis zur Erde, vor dem regungslos Sitzenden, dessen Lächeln ihn an alles erinnerte, was er in seinem Leben jemals geliebt hatte, was jemals in seinem Leben ihm wert und heilig gewesen war.

> Deeply he bowed, bowed to the very earth, before the one sitting there motionless, whose smile reminded him of everything that he had ever loved in all his life, everything that had ever, in all his life, been dear to him and holy. (Hesse, *Siddhartha*, translation 126; original 472)

The first line of my translation is augmented with additional words because I wanted to slow down the pacing of the phrase in which Govinda bows. The English phrase was in danger of having too few syllables, making the action and its narration feel too hasty. To help create the sense of gravitas the moment requires, I doubled the one-syllable verb "bowed," even though the three-syllable word it translates ("verneigte") appears only once in German. I also added an emphatic "very" to the phrase "to the earth"—mostly for rhythm but also to remove the ambiguity from the preposition "to": Govinda bows so low that his forehead touches the ground, but he is bowing to Siddhartha, not to the earth. The "very" interrupts the possible misreading of the phrase.

The repetition of "bowed" also helps to make up for a chiastic structure I elided later in the sentence ("in seinem Leben jemals [. . .] jemals in seinem Leben"). I chose not to reproduce it exactly because of the oddness (corniness?) of writing "in his life ever" in English, so instead the words "ever in all his life" appear in two slightly different configurations. My sentence has two sets of repeated elements where Hesse's only had one—I'm emphasizing what I want to show the reader about his prose. These repetitions rhetorically represent the sense of balance I've been discussing.

My last tweak to the sentence was in the syntax of the final phrase, which I rearranged because I didn't think the last words of this book should be "to him," even though the final words in German are the equivalent of "had been." In German, in which so many sentences end on conjugated auxiliary verbs—whose low information content makes them functionally invisible—the last words that stand out emphatically are "wert und heilig," and that's where I wanted to end my translation, too, on the resonant word "holy."

In Kafka's *Metamorphosis*, I had a very different sort of story to tell. My reading is based on my conviction that Gregor Samsa is a hysterical drama queen, that the story is a comedy—if admittedly a very, very dark one—and that the joke is always on him. Kafka's humor here is deadpan and invariably situational, rooted in the disconnect between Gregor's frantic attempts to do the right thing and his grotesque physical state. As the very model of a company man, he is so horrified at the prospect that he might be late for work that he disregards the far more serious problem that his body has been monstrously transformed; this characterization spoofs the very notion of dutifulness. His humiliation is funnier yet (and also sadder) because we can see that in some spiritual sense he has brought this curse down upon himself through his fanatical obedience, which is extreme to the point of absurdity. The funniest part of the story, in my opinion, is when Gregor's father pulls out a safe full of family documents to review their finances after Gregor's transformation, discovering that the family had plenty of money all along. This comes after Gregor's explanation that he had no choice but to work like a dog to repay his parents' crippling debts. Turns out they didn't have any. Once more, the joke's on him. This is a melodramatic sort of humor, so I worked to make the melodrama as clear and obvious as I could everywhere in the translation.

Often that meant finding deadpan humor in the use of overly formal language and precise enunciation (playing off the contrast with Gregor's new body), as when his sister has finally found food disgusting enough to be to monstrous Gregor's liking: "'Might I be less fastidious than before?' he thought, already sucking greedily at the [moldy] cheese" (Kafka 58). Here the humor comes from the contrast between "might" and "fastidious" (elevated discourse) and "sucking greedily" (low).

One instance of drama-queen melodrama arises from Gregor's fear that his firm's general manager—who has come to his home to see why he's late for work—will make a negative report about him to his boss: "Gregor realized he could not possibly allow the general manager to depart in his present frame of mind if his own position at the firm was not to be put in the gravest jeopardy" (Kafka 46). The inflated language of "gravest jeopardy" brings out the melodramatic edge I'm looking for.

At one point in the story I used the same doubling-the-verb technique as in *Siddhartha* to slow down action that was happening too quickly because the English words in question have fewer syllables than their German counterparts. Gregor has emerged from his room, hoping to coax the general manager into staying to hear him out, but his father chases him back inside. Gregor had gotten through the narrow doorway (one of the double door's wings is still bolted closed) by slipping through sideways, and when he now tries to retreat through this opening on all sixes (and at his full lateral width), he gets stuck and has to be pushed. Violently, his father provides this assistance.

The phrase describing this action in German is, "da gab ihm der Vater von hinten einen jetzt wahrhaftig erlösenden starken Stoß." The word "Stoß"— meaning "push," "shove," or "thrust," with sexual connotations—is preceded here by three modifying words (an adverb and two adjectives: wahrhaftig, erlösenden, starken) that add up to nine syllables, creating a bit of suspense in the sentence. I was able to get up to eight syllables with "genuinely liberating," but decided to translate the verb twice to heighten the drama and make sure the sexual overtones were clear without fully dominating the passage. In my translation the father "administered a powerful shove from behind, a genuinely liberating thrust," to free his monstrous offspring from the doorway (Kafka 51).

So these are two examples of how an interpretation of a work can become a storyline that plays out in many small translation decisions on the sentence level. To be clear, I don't advocate adding syllables in every single sentence one translates from German to English, even though the English translations inevitably come out shorter in terms of syllable count; I do so only where it seems important to preserve what I understand as the rhetorical strategy at key points in the text.

* * *

Now to *The Magic Mountain*, a truly monolithic work of German literature. It's going to take me a while to finish deciding exactly what sort of story I want to tell in my translation, and my story may change in the course of working on these thousand pages. One of the ideas I do already have about it is that the book is one huge, inflated fairy tale, as suggested by a remark in the prologue: "Besides, it's not out of the question that this story of ours, in its innermost nature, will bear some resemblance to a fairy tale" (Mann 10). There are a number of points even early in the book where my translation choices reflect this reading.

One of the first problems in *The Magic Mountain* I puzzled over is the translation of the simple little word "einfach" (literally: "simple") that appears both in the first line of the prologue and the first line of Chapter One. In both cases, it's used as part of the unit "ein einfacher junger Mensch" (literally: a simple young person/man) (Mann 9, 11). And in my first draft I wrote "simple young person," and then started trying to find a better word to replace that "simple" with, since after all, surely the protagonist of Thomas Mann's great novel isn't a simpleton. I ticked through a number of possible synonyms: "regular," "ordinary," and so on—my partner even suggested the twenty-first-century equivalent "basic"—before settling on "unremarkable," an appealing word that fits well with the arched-eyebrow, we're-both-in-on-the-joke-here ironic tone Mann is cultivating.

But then I started thinking about it more. In what sense is young Hans Castorp unremarkable? He's not an average sort of person; the first thing we learn about him is that he's rich, or at least wealth-adjacent: he's carrying a traveling bag fashioned of pricey and exotic crocodile skin that, as we're immediately informed, was given to him by a consul with a fancy-sounding name who is both his uncle and foster father. Clearly his family story is anything but simple. Of course, the word might well be meant ironically. Does Mann really expect us to be reading in high-gear irony mode already by the second word of Chapter One? Maybe. But I started to hunt around in period dictionaries to learn how the words "einfach" and "simple" were used early in the twentieth century, and lo: both words were often understood (according to dictionary definitions) to mean "guileless" or "artless," that is, a person "senza alcun sospetto" (like Dante's famously unsuspecting Paolo and Francesca who fell in love over a book). And this makes sense. Isn't *The Magic Mountain* the story of an unsuspecting young person who boarded a train to pay "a three-week visit" and then got lots more than he bargained for? I really do think this is the story Mann is telling. So keeping in mind the bit in the prologue where the narrator coyly points out that there's something of the fairy tale in the book he's presenting, what if the translation of "einfach" really is literally "simple"? Don't many fairy tales start out with a "simple young person" setting out on a journey? And if the secondary meaning "not so clever" creeps in as well, maybe that's not inappropriate, given the narrator's general tone of mildly amused detachment.

Continuing to ponder, I recalled Emily Wilson's brilliant analysis of the opening of Homer's *Odyssey* that prompted her to describe Odysseus as "a complicated man": she notes the etymological derivation of this English word from the Latin "plicare" (to fold). Odysseus is both many-layered (like a cloth folded over on itself) and one who has journeyed hither and yon (many turnings in his past). He is "with pleats," the *com* and *pli* of "complicated" (Wilson). And it turns out that the *ple* of "simple" comes from "plicare" as well (*sim* signifies "self-same," i.e., "one"). The simple is that which has only a single turning or fold. Technically, one might object, the simple ought to be "without folds," just as complicated is with them (com = con = with), or, to use a different sort of example, shouldn't that excellent product we refer to as "two-ply toilet paper" actually be called "one-ply"? Well, at a certain point, the word designating a fold came to mean a layer as well, making "simple" the clear opposite of "complicated." Which also makes it a not-bad metaphorical equivalent for the German "einfach," which literally means "one compartment." I'm still at the beginning of my *Magic Mountain* explorations, but for now I'm going to call the fellow "a simple young man."

When working on a new translation of a previously translated work, I make a point of not spending too much time looking at the earlier translations, out of fear that this might interfere with my getting a grasp on my own vision of the book. Thinking about "einfach"/"simple," however, prompted me to consult the two previous translations. The Helen Lowe-Porter translation uses "simple-minded" in the preface and "unassuming" in Chapter One. To me, that looks like a copy-editing casualty rather than a conscious decision on her part; translators weren't always able to control the final edit of their translations as is commonplace now. John Woods uses the word "ordinary" in both passages, in keeping with his foregrounding of the book's ironic tone.

As I work on my translation, I keep finding more passages that confirm the importance of the notion of the fairy tale in Mann's novel. For example, the house in which Hans Castorp spends most of his early childhood is described as "in einer trüben Wetterfarbe gestrichen" (literally: painted a somber weather-color). In an early draft of my translation, I wrote "painted a glaucous hue," since the weather in Hamburg as Mann describes it is often gloomy and gray. But then I started thinking harder about that word "Wetterfarbe"—a strange word, certainly. I couldn't find it in a single German-language dictionary, even the nineteenth-century ones. Eventually I did find it though: in an anonymous nineteenth-century German translation of Charles Perrault's fairy tale "Peau d'Âne" (Donkey

Skin) (Anon., *Echte und wahrhafte Feen-Mahrchen* 104). This is the story the Brothers Grimm famously reworked under the title "Allerleirauh" (All Kinds of Fur), but the word doesn't appear in their adaptation of the story ("All Fur (Allerleirauh)" 216–20). In the Perrault tale, a girl threatened with incest (her father wants to marry her) tries to save herself by inventing trials for him, and the first of these is the challenge to bring her a dress "the color of the weather" ("une robe de la couleur du temps")—later revealed to be of a sky-blue hue (Perrault 221). I'm guessing that Mann read this story in German as a child (or had it read to him) and that this intriguing fairy-tale color stuck with him. (That the French word "temps" signifies "time" as well as "weather" lends another hidden irony to this story, in which time is also an important theme.) So the house in my translation is currently described as "somberly painted the color of the weather."

Another story I want to tell about Mann's novel has to do with tourism. We are frequently reminded that the book's protagonist comes from Hamburg in the German north and experiences the novel's Swiss setting as exotic. He waxes rhapsodic at his first glimpse of the Alps, and finds it delightfully quaint that a server in Davos is referred to not as a "Kellnerin" ("waitress") but a "Saaltocher" (literally "hall daughter," a common word for "waitress" in Switzerland in those days). Given that I've spent a lot of time in and thinking about Switzerland in connection with my decades-long work on Robert Walser, I feel a particular affection for the novel's setting and want to make a point of describing this landscape touristically, as Hans Castorp and Mann—both hailing from the Baltic coast—would have experienced it at the time. For one thing, I'll probably be calling most things in this multilingual setting—remember that Switzerland has four official languages—by their German-language names (e.g., Graubünden rather than Grisons). One of the reference works I'm consulting is a turn-of-the-twentieth-century Baedecker.

I'm also looking to shape my translation in terms of a really precise accounting of the book's cultural artifacts. Ironically this is easier for me than for either of the book's previous translators because of the internet and twenty-first-century library access. Helen Lowe-Porter translated the book soon after it appeared and had access to Mann himself, but I can't imagine he was interested in explaining every detail of every reference to her; and John Woods was translating seventy years later but before the internet had become the powerful reference library it is today. *The Magic Mountain* is exceptionally full of things that need looking up, and I've been doing a lot of that—both online and in period reference works on paper.

For example, Hans Castorp's cousin—the tuberculosis patient he's come to Davos to visit—tells him about a fellow patient who speaks in an endless series of malapropisms. One particularly awkward linguistic mistake she makes, "Steriletto" (Mann, 29), involves something called a "Sterilett," which she confuses with the word "Stilett" ("stiletto"). At the time of Mann's writing, "stiletto" still meant only "thin dagger"—it was not yet connected to footwear—and would have seemed a fairly exotic word to a German speaker from a sheltered background like the person being mocked here. Unfortunately the word she confuses with it is one improper for use in polite company: a "Sterilett" (coming from the French "stérilet") is a precursor of the IUD, the same device the early-twentieth-century feminist Margaret Sanger promoted in her 1921 pamphlet, "The Use of the Pessary" (Sanger 754–7). In translating this passage, I considered defaulting to the same period malapropism ("steriletto") as Lowe-Porter, but ideally this moment in the translation would be more legible to twenty-first-century readers as what it is: a truly cringeworthy gaffe. Woods translates the word as "stirletto," capturing the mispronunciation but not its unseemliness. For now, I've been playing around with variants on "switchblade" (having been unable to find a satisfactory one based on "stiletto"); switchblades were first offered for sale around the time the book is set, and some of them were marketed to women. The best knife-themed malapropism I've found so far is "snatchblade," which I think shows the cruelty of the men's Schadenfreude-driven humor at the expense of this unworldly woman—an important element for establishing the atmosphere of Mann's book.

This, then, is an initial account of how I am approaching this Swiss fairy tale made in Germany. My ideas about the book may change and develop as I work; the point of this snapshot of my work-in-progress is to offer an example of how such a project can be approached. Thinking in terms of the stories we intend to tell about a work is a good way to focus our labors. It also helps ensure we call things by the names it's most appropriate in the space of our translations for them to have.

Works Cited

[anon]. *Echte und wahrhafte Feen-Mährchen*, 2nd ed., vol. 1. Franz Heinrich Köhler, 1839, pp. 100–16.
Grimm, Jacob, et al. "All Fur (Allerleirauh)." *The Original Folk and Fairy Tales of the Brothers Grimm : The Complete First Edition*. Princeton UP, 2015, pp. 216–20, search-ebscohost-com.ezproxy.cul.columbia.edu/login.aspx?direct=true&db=e025xna&AN=795265&site=ehost-live&scope=site.
Hesse, Hermann. *Siddhartha. In Sämtliche Werke*, 2nd ed., vol. 3. Ed. Volker Michaels. Suhrkamp, 2003.
Hesse, Hermann. *Siddhartha*. Trans. Susan Bernofsky. Modern Library, 2006.

Kafka, Franz. *The Metamorphosis*. Trans. Susan Bernofsky. W.W. Norton, 2014.

Mann, Thomas. "Der Zauberberg." *Große kommentierte Frankfurter Ausgabe*, vol. 5.1. Ed. Michael Neumann. S. Fischer, 2002.

Perrault, Charles. "Peau d'Âne." *Contes*. Ed. Marc Soriano. Flammarion, 1989, pp. 217–32.

Sanger, Margaret. "The Use of The Pessary." (lecture). November 11, 1921. Typescript, Margaret Sanger Papers, Sophia Smith Collection, Smith College, Margaret Sanger Microfilm, Smith College Collections S67, pp. 754-7.

Wilson, Emily. "The Odyssey: A Reading and Discussion." (lecture), Bread Loaf Translators' Conference, Middlebury, Vermont, June 2, 2018.

10

In Terror and Pandemic
Translating García Lorca's *Poet in New York*

Mark Statman

At the time of this writing, the world has been half a year into the coronavirus pandemic, a global disaster unlike anything I've ever seen in my lifetime and unlike anything seen by anyone I know. Even my mother, a Great Depression baby, a child of the Second World War, who remembers all kinds of epidemics and disasters, can't make any comparisons.

With tens of thousands already dead, with rising millions infected, and with news of more death and infection arriving every day, it's hard for me not to find resonant, eerie echoes of Federico García Lorca's *Poet in New York* (Grove 2008), which I translated with Pablo Medina. The coronavirus is certainly different than the root causes of the horror Lorca first saw when he arrived in New York in June 1929, almost five months before the Depression. Not knowing exactly what to expect, Lorca was stunned by the city's sheer size, by the degrading effects of capitalism on the people who lived there, by the hypocrisy, the racism, by religion without God. In New York, Lorca was exposed to a city that had been infected by greed and superficiality, an unnatural city whose grandeur, whose wealth and sophistication, masked the city's greatness. His own engagement with *duende* in New York, that great wounding force that leads to creation, led him to understand New York, to be able to write his New York. And it allowed him to leave, a greater poet, a more complete self.

And there is a way in which that struggle, that need to look deeply, fearlessly, creatively, is the struggle to which the pandemic has brought us. Because what the virus has done in the present day has been to fundamentally change not only a city but all cities, not only a country but all countries. It was this kind of experience, of deep and lasting and unwelcome change, and how individuals, society, and societies respond to that change, which initially led Pablo and myself to this most beautiful and disturbing text of modern literature.

* * *

> I defend myself with this look
> that pours from the waves where dawn dares not go.
> I, armless poet, lost
> in the vomiting crowd.
>> ("Landscape of the Vomiting Crowd [Twilight at Coney Island]," *Poet in New York* 51)

When Pablo and I began our translation of *Poet in New York*, it was not because we had some idea of publishing it. It was because we discovered, after the attacks of September 11, 2001, in particular on the World Trade Center and New York City, that both of us had each turned to *Poet in New York* to make sense of what had happened. We each had lived for most of our lives in the city and, as poets, it was in poetry we thought we might find some answers. As we wrote in our introduction:

> Seeking solace we read the literature of New York: the poetry of Whitman, the chronicles of José Martí, Hart Crane's "The Bridge," E.B. White's extraordinary essay "Here is New York" the myriad novels and plays the city has inspired, and we dove into Ginsberg, Corso, Koch, O'Hara—in short, into the body of work that informs and defines the spiritual fabric of our city. Then we came to García Lorca's Poet in New York and saw reflected in this book the range of emotions we ourselves felt and images strangely reminiscent of the ones we witnessed of September 11 and its aftermath.
>
> One afternoon, a couple of years later, we realized a new translation of Poet in New York was needed that showed the city, not just as it was then but as it became after September 11, riven by tragedy, burdened by rage, humbled by grief. Who would be better suited to the task than two New York poets, neither of whom was a professional translator or scholar but who were for decades (still are) devoted readers of Lorca? (xvi)

Our goal was not necessarily to translate a "classic" and to render it a classic once again—we hardly even talked about the fact of its literary significance. Rather it was to take a text that had illuminated our current lives and to translate it in that context, one of a city that had been somehow beaten down but would recover and thrive. New York is a city symbolic for its cultural and historic significance, as well as its capitalistic and consumerist ones, so much so that terrorists thought the city and the World Trade Center, in particular, deserving of destruction. Could we, as Lorca did in Spanish, represent the city, in all its glory and despair, and make a *Poet in New York* in English, as beautiful and fierce as his?

* * *

Poet in New York has a distinct plot and reflects very much on Lorca's own life. The poet of the book may or may not be Federico García Lorca, and the story of the book may not be Lorca's as well. What does happen for Lorca is that he arrives in New York in late June of 1929, shortly before the Great Depression. Having just turned thirty-one years and already known as a poet and playwright in Spain, he was, in theory, going to study English uptown at Columbia University. He knew he would be leaving New York in March 1930 to give a series of readings and lectures in Havana. The structure of the book reflects this: the book opens with "Poems of Solitude at Columbia University," then the poet travels through the city, from Harlem to downtown Manhattan and Brooklyn. The poet will then leave the city and visit upstate New York and Vermont. He will then return to the city, and ready himself to leave for Cuba.

This sets up the physical geography of the book. But the aesthetic, emotional, and spiritual plot is much more complicated. When Lorca arrives at Columbia, he is overwhelmed by the city, by the sheer size of it, by the way architecturally the sky, so much a part of his life in Spain, has turned from friend to assassin. Everything he sees is unfamiliar. Disturbing. Here is the whole of the first poem in *Poet in New York*. It sets the stage (the dramatist in Lorca was forever setting the stage) for what's to come:

Back from a Walk

Murdered by the sky.
Among the firms that move toward the snake
and the forms searching for a crystal
I will let my hair grow.

With the limbless tree that cannot sing
and the boy with the white egg face.

With the broken-headed animals
and the ragged water of dry feet.

With all that is tired, deaf-mute
and a butterfly drowned in an inkwell.

Stumbling onto my face, different every day.
Murdered by the sky.

("Back from a Walk," *Poet in New York* 5)

The walk, near Columbia University, on Broadway, Riverside Drive, has shown the poet nothing he knows. This world has trees with no limbs, animals broken, a mysterious, blank child. The poet is tired and deaf, and he can't speak. The butterfly is not flying but has drowned in the inkwell, the inkwell from which a poem might be written. Even the poet is unrecognizable to himself, his face different every day.

The poet goes to Harlem. There he sees things he suspects those who are not citizens of Harlem can't see. He identifies with the oppressed because he sees what is hidden and the silencing cruelty of racism. He names the oppression and challenges it.

Oh Harlem! Harlem!
There is no anguish compared to your oppressed reds,
to your blood shaken inside the dark eclipse,
to your garnet violence, deaf and mute in the shadows,
to your great prisoner king in his janitor's uniform.

("The King of Harlem," *Poet in New York* 27)

But the poet imagines a time in which these oppressed will rise up. Not just the citizens of Harlem, but all those who he sees as victims of the injustice of the world economic order at which New York is the very center. And that the natural world will reclaim what has been lost by the world of what Lorca elsewhere calls one of machines. With great clarity, he names the enemy.

In time the cobra will hiss in the final floors,
the nettles shake the patios and porches,
the Market become a pyramid of moss,
the reeds follow the rifles,
and soon, very soon.
Oh, Wall Street.

("Dance of Death," *Poet in New York* 29)

Lorca dates this poem December 1929. It is just a few months after the stock market had crashed. Lorca claims to have seen stockbrokers jumping out of buildings in despair, an awful image similar to those of the 9/11 victims who jumped from the towers to escape the flames, the collapse. Pablo and I lived in this New York. For months after, the smell of the dead was in the air, coming from the buildings which continued to burn.

As with the city Lorca saw, our city had been altered, the people as well. Walking the streets it seemed as if, despite the helicopters that routinely flew over the city, the city was filled with a kind of silence. A silence of grief. We were learning of the dead, of our friends, of the family and friends of friends. We wondered why this had happened. An attack on the capitol of capital?

> You'll have to travel into the eyes of idiots,
> open fields where the tamed cobras of barbed wire hiss,
> landscape full of graves that yields the riches apples,
> so that behind the magnifying glass
> comes the blinding light that rich men fear,
> the smell of a single body with the double slope of iris and rat.
> They burn, these people who can piss around a moan
> or on windows where we understand the never-repeated waves.
> ("Landscape of the Urinating Crowd [Nocturne of Battery Place]," *Poet in New York* 53)

In a certain way, Lorca's initial response to New York shows us someone whose only response can be to show, imagine, and name. The "armless poet" is one who experiences it all but is unable to do more than that. Lorca can describe what he sees, he can name the grief:

> Everyone understands the grief that comes with death
> but true grief is not present in the spirit.
> it isn't in the air or in our lives
> or in these terraces full of smoke.
> True grief that keeps things awake
> is a small infinite burn
> in the innocent eyes of other systems.
> ("Blind Panorama of New York," *Poet in New York* 67)

That burn, small and infinite, is the powerful wound that will need healing. To heal, the poet has to leave New York City. His goes north, first to upstate New York, then to Vermont. But the effect for which the poet hoped, through exposure to the natural world, doesn't yield the recovery the poet expected. There are many layers of *Poet in New York*. They are religious, political, and sexual, and they are fundamental to Lorca's own developing identity. Lorca's biographers have noted Lorca's time in New York as significant because of how more politically outspoken he became after his time in the city, as well as how he increasingly became public about his homosexuality. In upstate New York, the small *p* poet of the book becomes the larger *P* Poet. He becomes one not only who describes, imagines, and questions but who has answers.

He becomes a Poet who echoes Whitman, of whom he writes about in the section, "Two Odes." He becomes willing to take on the mantle not simply as chronicler of but as voice for. He is a Poet for those who can't speak for themselves.

In the section just before the climactic "Two Odes," "Return to the City," the Poet begins with this great denunciation:

> I denounce all of the people
> who ignore the other half,
> the unredeemable half,
> who raise their mountains of cement
> over the still-beating hearts
> of small forsaken animals
> and where we are headed
> in the final feast of jackhammers.
> I spit on your faces.
> The other half listens to me,
> devouring, urinating, flying in its innocence,
> like the boys in the doorways
> who place fragile sticks
> into holes where the antennae
> of insects rust.
> This isn't hell, it's the street.
> This isn't death, it's the fruit store.
> There is a world of broken rivers
> and infinite distances
> in the cat's leg crushed by a car,
> and I hear the worm's song
> in the heart of many girls.
> Rust, ferment, shaken earth.
> Earth yourself swimming
> through the numbers in the offices.
> What can I do, bring order to the landscape?
> Bring order to the many loves
> who will, in time, turn to photographs
> and then pieces of wood and mouthfuls of blood?
> No, no. I denounce.
> I denounce the conspiracy
> of those deserted offices
> swept clean of agony
> that erase the designs of the forest,

and I offer myself to be eaten by the crushed cows
when the screams fill the valley
where the Hudson gets drunk on oil.
("New York: Office and Denunciation," *Poet in New York* 125-7)

A denunciation and then comes the willingness to sacrifice himself, to offer himself. In poems that follow, "Jewish Cemetery," "Small Infinite Poem," and "Crucifixion," the Poet draws a deep connection between the sacrifice of Christ and what the role of the Poet is going to be. And the next section, of the great odes, we see how in "Cry toward Rome (From the Tower of the Chrysler Building)," the Poet becomes willing to take on the Catholic Church itself, certainly heresy for the religious Lorca if he is wrong. It isn't hard here to see a parallel between the Chrysler Building, then the tallest building in the world, and the World Trade Center. Again, the Poet speaks for the silenced and the oppressed and, even more, he calls them to speak and act as well:

Meanwhile, meanwhile, meanwhile,
the blacks who empty the spittoons,
the boys who tremble before the pale terror of managers
the women drowned in mineral oils,
the masses of hammer, violin or cloud,
must cry although their brains are smashed against the wall,
must cry before the domes,
must cry maddened by fire,
must cry maddened by snow,
must cry with their head full of excrement,
must cry with all the nights broken together,
must cry in a voice so broken
the cities will tremble like girls
and break the prisons of oil and music,
because we want our daily bread,
alder flowers and perennial threshed tenderness,
because we want the Earth's will be done
to give its fruits to all.
"Cry toward Rome (From the Tower of the Chrysler Building)," *Poet in New York* (145-7)

In this poem, read in the context of the attacks of 9/11, and in light of the coronavirus, as well as the "Ode to Walt Whitman" that follows, in which Lorca raises his voice in defense and praise for that most singular of American voices, it is impossible to ignore the majesty of the Poet's cry. Like the prophets of the Old Testament, the Poet reminds us that, in adversity, whatever it might be that can cause us to fall cannot and will not prevent us from rising. The economic and political worlds may fail us, may fall, but we of this earth do not have to fail and fall with them. There is more greatness in life than money or fame or land or power: there is the daily bread, the tenderness, the fruits for all.

When the poet of *Poet in New York* leaves New York, like Federico García Lorca, he leaves quietly, with a sense of greater self and at peace. Lorca had written that he could have called the book New York in a Poet. And what he takes from that, what he is able to hold of New York, sustains him greatly as a writer. After *Poet in New York*, he will go on to write his greatest plays (*Blood Wedding*, *Yerma*, and *The House of Bernarda Alba*), as well as the moving *Lament for Ignacio Sánchez Mejías*, *Diwan of the Tamarit*, and the *Sonnets of Dark Love*. Yet, to my mind, nothing he ever wrote has seemed so beyond time and place.

* * *

Our pandemic times—I would love to be able to write "moment," but the experts out there are warning that there will only be more of the same happening with the degradation of this earth household—will be made bearable, survivable, and will certainly be illuminated by the poetry of the present. That poetry will speak directly to what we are living through and how we will live in the future. The poetry of the past, what we name our classics, will do so as well, not only because of the ways in which the poetry still speaks for its times but for the ways in which it has lasted over time, for all time. Our classics, and *Poet in New York* is clearly one of them, endure because they represent the best part of what we hope of our civilization endures.

I close with the last paragraph of our introduction to *Poet in New York*. Change the attacks for the pandemic, change 9/11 to the present, and change New York for the world.

> To read *Poet in New York* in the version we offer here is to read not prophecy but chronicle, not the future but the present. We have lost the New York City of September 10, 2001. What we gained is a New York in some ways wiser, sadder, and perhaps better able to deal with triumph and tragedy. We cannot quantify grief nor can we quantify hope. They are not found in mourning prayers or in hate, not in the call to arms or in prejudice, not in money or fast cars or the most glittering jewels for the tallest buildings or in the smartest books. These are ancient lessons

Lorca learned well in New York, and we, lulled into complacency by our collective wealth, forgot and relearned in a nightmare of fire and ash. To read this book now is to see Lorca's eyes—eyes of a child—staring from the anonymous grave into which he was thrown after his murder and to hear the black sounds of *duende* carried by the Spanish breeze above our buildings and streets got a place where true grief and hope, twin sisters, reside. (xxiii).

—April 2020, Oaxaca de Juárez and San Pedro Ixtlahuaca, Oaxaca, México

Work Cited

Lorca, Federico García. *Poet in New York*. Trans. Pablo Medina and Mark Statman. Grove Press, 2008.

11

Stopping at the Surface

Translating Clarice Lispector's *The Besieged City* and *A Breath of Life*

Johnny Lorenz

I just pass my hands over the surface of things.

—Andy Warhol (Goldsmith 88)

My partner, who holds an MFA in drawing, once brought an apple to her class of high school students and placed it on her desk. She asked the students to draw the apple. After they had completed their work, she turned their attention to a curious fact: the students had drawn apples, yes, but no one had drawn the apple in front of them. They drew what they believed an apple "should" look like. Not the bruised, imperfect fruit—the thing sitting on her desk; that very real apple had been ignored. If I may put it this way, the students drew the apple that had already been imagined for them. It seems to contradict common sense, but seeing what is in front of us can be exceedingly difficult. It demands an unusual attentiveness.

It is precisely this problem of seeing that interests our protagonist, Lucrécia, in *The Besieged City* (1948), by the great Brazilian novelist Clarice Lispector: "The difficult thing is that appearance was reality. Her difficulty in seeing was as if she were painting" (*The Besieged City* 99). Lispector encourages us, in so much of her work, to think not only about what we see, but *how* we see. The title of *The Besieged City* might suggest advancing military columns and the din of weaponry. It's not, dear reader, *that* sort of book. The siege of the book's title is entirely conceptual, while the city, it would seem, is really "there"—but then again, with Lispector, what's really "there" is precisely the question. Lispector's novels are characterized by profound ambiguity and an astonishing exploration of the most vexing ontological and epistemological questions; for the translator, there is hardly any opportunity to fall back on plot, or to describe, in plain terms, physical action represented on the page. The action on the page is the action of the mind. Translating the work of Clarice Lispector has meant, for me, living in her luminous rooms of abstraction, a condition both inspiring and, at times, incredibly exhausting. In Lispector's novels, vision is not passive or immediate; seeing becomes a kind of imaginative, even spiritual, work. Would Lispector's devotees accept my work of translation, or would I be guilty of undermining these sacred texts?

Throughout *The Besieged City*, Lucrécia engages in an unrelenting experiment with vision:

> It was a new way of seeing; limpid, indubitable. Lucrécia Neves peered at an orange on the plate. Farther on the bin for bottles, the wooden crate, the decaying ledger, a dirty rag and the orange once again. The gaze was not descriptive, what was descriptive were the positions of the things (98).

In this "new way" of seeing, Lucrécia is attempting to see without describing, without imposing meaning; it's an (almost?) impossible wish, a radical openness to the world. Here is another example from the book, when Lucrécia, referred to as a "creature," is at her sink, washing dishes, gazing at the surfaces around her:

> Nothing was happening though: a creature was facing whatever it was seeing, taken by the quality of what it was seeing, with its eyes obfuscated by its own calm way of looking; the light in the kitchen was her way of seeing—things at two o'clock seem to be made, even in their depths, of the way their surfaces are seen. (*The Beseiged City* 95)

Lucrécia tries, constantly, to re-orient vision. She even attempts to obliterate her own subjectivity in order to become another object in the room: "behold, behold, all of her, terribly physical, one of the objects" (75). This desire to see herself as an object does not mean to "objectify" herself in that familiar sense of degrading herself before the patriarchal order. She imagines, rather, being neither a woman nor a man, but something outside those categories. In a way, vision brings us closer to the objects around us (I see the apple on the desk), while simultaneously creating distances (the apple is "over there"). Vision establishes where one is (in a classroom, for example), but to see is to be simultaneously *a part of* the room and *apart from* the room. Here and not here. This frustrating paradox informs much of Lispector's work.

At the time of the book's publication, critics didn't know what to make of *The Besieged City*; they struggled for a way to even talk about it. One bewildered reviewer, cited by Benjamin Moser, described the novel as hopelessly hermetic: "May someone find the key" (Moser ix). Another critic, Temístocles Linhares, complained that the book offered "no apparent meaning," only "a certain morbid taste for a phrase for the phrase's sake" (Linhares 208). Lispector, years later, in an open letter, would deny this accusation of linguistic self-indulgence: "I still think of my words as being naked" ("Delayed Letter" 209).The book's experiments with vision demand a new syntax; the question the text poses for its protagonist, Lucrécia, is a question the author seems to be asking herself: "So what would she say if she could go, from seeing objects, to saying them" (*The Besieged City* 68). Like Emily Dickinson before her, Lispector awakens us to the reflexive patterns of syntax by constantly disrupting them. Her writing never allows us to read with anything less than full attention.

I'm tempted to say that Lispector's work is impossible to "skim," but this is where our metaphors get us into trouble—for to "skim" is a metaphor of water, a metaphor that serves as an implicit criticism of those lazy minds that remain on the surface of things. Lispector, however, is obsessed with surfaces. In some sense, she asks us not to penetrate the surface but (a more subtle challenge) to *arrive at* the surface. Our lexicon of metaphors assumes we must begin at the surface and then, like muscular swimmers, dive deep into the waters of complexity—but the surface, actually, can be a very difficult place at which to stay. Swimming across the surface of the water, or merely staying afloat during the tempest—this requires tremendous effort.

Can Lucrécia (or anyone, really) look at some *thing* without either falling short of it—or going beyond it?: "Her fear was that of surpassing whatever she was seeing" (*The Besieged City* 100). Lucrécia must constantly re-learn this way of seeing, recommit herself to it, but success is fleeting: "She could still see, and was seeing. She'd fallen however from the surface of things to the inside" (130). Lucrécia may lack "the futilities of the imagination" (94) but in spite of this, or perhaps because of it, she, more than anyone else in the city of São Geraldo, sees what is "there," if only briefly. At one point, Lucrécia begins contorting her body, imitating the pose of an ancient Greek statue, trying to destroy the distance between herself and the world, to become a thing, a thing with eyes of stone: "When she was ready she'd look like an object, an object of São Geraldo" (30). She stares at a framed photograph of herself; her face, transformed into pure object, gazes back at her: "the picture was the unreachable surface" (148). Again and again, what seems unreachable in Lispector's work is not the buried treasure of meaning but rather the surface itself. That unreachability is precisely what the translator must come to terms with when trying to grasp Lispector's language. What is required, as Nietzsche declared in *The Gay Science*, is to be superficial, but "superficial" as a powerful attentiveness to surfaces:

Oh, those Greeks! They knew how to live. What is required for that is to stop courageously at the surface, the fold, the skin, to adore appearance, to believe in forms, tones, words, in the whole Olympus of appearance. Those Greeks were superficial—*out of profundity*. (Nietzche 38)[1]

Lucrécia attempts to see what is there, without too quickly dismissing it by conceptualizing it, by understanding it: "The hard thing is that appearance was reality" (*The Besieged City* 68). Why does it take courage or audacity to stop at the surface? It's as though we've turned every image into a symbol—at the expense of the image itself. In my "Introduction to Poetry Writing" class, for instance, students' poems are full of flowers—flowers as symbols, symbols intensely felt, and yet, one suspects, most of these enthusiastic poets have not taken the time to look at flowers or study their quiet habits. The surface is not cliché; what is cliché is the easy metaphor of roses. What is cliché is the deep feeling.

Stopping at the surface—there is a lesson here for the translator, the translator who might be thinking: *What the novelist really meant to say was* . . . . Lispector's syntax can be so strange, so odd in its movement, that the translator is tempted to beautify, or (if you permit me to indulge in metaphor myself) to airbrush the jagged edges. But what if Lispector's language is itself a jagged edge? The translator would be undermining Lispector's project by committing to lovely prose or the elegant turn of phrase, hallmarks of "good writing." The translator—if overly concerned with the judgment of the Anglophone reader, if too anxious that the weird syntax will be read as a flaw in the translation—might be tempted to "smooth" the surface, when, of course, it is precisely this surface Lispector wants us to see. We are not speaking here of a commitment to surface as a commitment to shallowness; these are precisely the pre-packaged metaphors that get us into trouble. In Lispector's *The Passion According to G.H.*, a novel I didn't translate (it was superbly translated by Idra Novey), our narrator is surprised by a cockroach; her challenge to herself is to see the cockroach before her: "I had never actually seen a cockroach" (*The Passion According to G.H.* 48). How is this possible, we might ask, for someone living in the tropics? Lispector's text wants us to look at the roach—but it also wants us to look at the process of looking. In a sense, we are back in that drawing class, trying to see the apple. We have merely switched categories; what we call "beautiful" gives way here to the "ugly." If, like the narrator of *The Passion*, we already know, or claim to

---

[1] I thank Benjamin Moser, the Clarice Lispector Series editor for New Directions, not only, of course, for his assistance in translating Lispector's work but also for sharing with me this passage from *The Gay Science*.

know, long before the cockroach crawls into the room, what a cockroach is, what it represents, if we already know that the appropriate behavior involves fleeing the roach or smashing it—how do we ever see the *thing* itself? With the roach, as with so much else, we see what we are conditioned to see. Vision becomes a form of blindness.

Of course, for the reader and for the translator, the degree of engagement with a text can be so intense, so heightened, that to stay "on the surface" of language might not strike us as a viable (or even desirable) option. Oh, how these metaphors get us into trouble! Any metaphor for language, no matter how compelling, seems doomed to fail. I'm trying to articulate here the importance of the "surface"—and, in a sense, to consider the question of "style," to which we can barely refer without condescension. Too often our metaphors do our thinking for us: in a literary context, we want what's "beneath the surface"; we want to get to the "bottom" of things; we don't want to seem "superficial"; we privilege "deep" thoughts. Lispector's work reminds us that the surface is not easy, and that we cannot ever separate style from content. Lispector reminds us that the surface of the water is water.

Let us consider now another book by Lispector, *A Breath of Life* (1978), her posthumous novel, a book I've also translated for New Directions. Its narrator, in the very first chapter, makes the following assertion: "I want every sentence of this book to be a climax" (6). Whether we are contemplating a narrative or sexual climax, we are faced here with a rather daunting test of endurance. A sexual climax that involves no foreplay, and, by the same token, no release, no post-coital resolution—such a climax, enduring and insistent, becomes a kind of torment; it's not sustainable. One would need to disengage, to separate. In the context of the literary experience, one would need to put the book down. Not long ago, I was invited by The New School in New York City to give a lecture on *A Breath of Life*. The students in attendance had been assigned the novel ahead of time. On the day of the event, the professor who'd invited me to speak informed me of something that caught me off guard: a student in the class had provided a doctor's note explaining that *A Breath of Life* was just too upsetting, and, consequently, the student would not be attending my lecture. Now, please keep in mind that *A Breath of Life* is not the sort of book we might associate with "trigger warnings"; it does not depict, for example, graphic violence or sexual abuse. The trauma of the book, if I might put it this way, is the trauma of *being*. This psychological violence is built into the syntax of Lispector's language. The way her language moves can be, it would seem, powerfully unsettling.

A Breath of Life begins as "the cry of a bird of prey" (3), an urge to break free of one's own linguistic system; the book begins with a return to the body, to the cry that predates syntax.² The book concludes (if it "concludes" at all) with an ellipsis, a not-saying on the final page, something deferred, an inability to find resolution or accept death, a death that would be marked by the grammatical period. It's worth noting that Lispector was working on this book while she herself was dying of ovarian cancer. *A Breath of Life* returns us to the violence of our own existence, that fundamental rupture, the oppressive fact that we did not decide to *be*, and rather than bring us into a sense of belonging through the imaginative powers of language, Lispector rips at the reassuring comforts of narrative.

What sort of comforts does narrative provide? Let's consider the courtship novel—the emphasis on heteronormative, erotic love, the happy resolution provided by marriage, and the glorious spectacle of a wedding day. Lispector's *The Besieged City* seems to operate, on the one hand, like a courtship novel: Lucrécia is a young, single woman living with her mother, and she considers several suitors until, eventually, she lands the richest of the bunch. Romantic courtship, however, is hardly the focus of the book's attention; in fact, the grand spectacle of a wedding never actually occurs. When Lucrécia finally marries, the marriage is a purely bureaucratic affair, occurring in the novel's shortest chapter, in which the groom doesn't even make an appearance; instead, he's represented by his attorney. It's as though Lispector had written a courtship novel that has no patience for courtship novels. The text is more interested in those moments when, as mentioned earlier, "nothing was happening" (95) (for instance, the scene in which Lucrécia is washing dishes), moments of tedium and yet, somehow, moments of ecstasy.

Allow me to focus here on a small example of the "nothing" that is happening in *The Besieged City*, as it would also allow me to discuss how, as a translator, I approach the nitty-gritty of translating Lispector's unique syntax:

> tudo o que ela via era *alguma coisa*. Nela e num cavalo a impressão era a expressão. (*A cidade sitiada* 22)

---

[2] Hélène Cixous famously argued in her essay "The Laugh of the Medusa" that a woman's writing must return to her body and that, in the sound of a woman's laughter, in the sound of the orgasmic cry of pleasure, there is something subversive to the patriarchal order. An admirer of Lispector, Cixous published a book-length study of Lispector's work, *Reading with Clarice Lispector*. Elaine Scarry's *The Body in Pain* also explores the relationship between language and the body, arguing that, as a response to pain, the body's cry is an utterance that signals the destruction of language.

everything that she was seeing was *some thing*. In her and in a horse the impression was the expression. (*The Besieged City* 15)[3]

Another translator might have rendered the first sentence thus: "everything she saw was *something*." My own translation is, admittedly, less elegant. To borrow my students' preferred criticism of a piece of writing: my translation here doesn't "flow." But if language can be like water, let's remember that water doesn't merely flow—it slams, floods, freezes, trickles, pushes, explodes. The imperfect indicative of "to see" in the phrase "ela via" is going to sound awkward in English if we opt for the past continuous verb tense: "she was seeing." In English, we like the act of seeing to be instantaneous: "she saw." However, I needed the sense of duration, and exertion, implicit in "was seeing." Perhaps it's my fault—or is it the fault of the English language?— that the line is clumsy in translation. Additionally, English speakers tend to refer to "something" (a compound word) rather than "some thing." It's not the dazzling metaphor that keeps the translator up at night; it's a seemingly insignificant something, or *some thing*. Lispector's obsession with "things"— with the "thingness" of a thing—justifies the subtle separation, the slightest pause, between "some" and "thing." Speaking through the character of Angela in *A Breath of Life*, Lispector refers to her own obsession with the "thing," that which exists outside the self, what can never truly be known, what is real but not human: "The object—the thing—always fascinated me and in a certain sense destroyed me" (*Breath of Life* 101).

What of the next sentence?: "In her and in a horse the impression was the expression." The strangeness of Lispector's diction is never gratuitous; it is strange by necessity. Here, I ask that we not blame the translator—or the English language—for the weirdness. The sentence imagines a kind of seeing not informed by language; it imagines an unmediated transformation from (passive) impression to (active) expression, undermining the distinction between these two kinds of engagement with the world. This difficult concept, this seemingly impossible simultaneity, is perhaps not even the strangest aspect of the sentence: to my mind, at least, the strangest aspect is simply beginning a sentence with the phrase, "In her and in a horse"— that almost nonchalant leveling of the human and the equine. This sentence is quintessentially "Clarice"! (I should mention that Brazilians tend to refer to her by her first name, not as "Lispector.") Now, I am sure some critics

---

[3] Marília Librandi's *Writing by Ear: Clarice Lispector and the Aural Novel* concludes with a fascinating discussion of *The Besieged City*; Librandi argues that Lucrécia's project is to imitate a horse's way of seeing and, by doing so, "overcome the gap between language and perception" (165).

would think of the previous sentence, in the original Portuguese or in my translation, as a sentence badly written; I can imagine a composition professor striking it with an unforgiving pen. As we know, critics at the time of its publication thought of *The Besieged City* as hopelessly flawed by its idiosyncratic phrasing. Is the aforementioned passage an example of "bad writing"? It's a question that Lispector herself invites us to ask, as we shall see.

First, let us return, briefly, to *The Passion According to G.H.*, in which we are asked to look at the ugly cockroach, and to keep looking at it, arriving at the point where the roach becomes strangely beautiful, where it becomes a "bride in black jewels" (*The Passion According to G.H.* 67), and then, in an attempt to reorganize vision itself, the book takes us to the point where even that trick—turning the tables on beauty—is no longer sufficient, no longer sustainable: "farewell beauty of the world. Beauty that now is remote to me and that I no longer want" (80).[4] We arrive here at the point where beauty is no longer a goal at all; it is a limitation. In the very first chapter of *A Breath of Life*, the text greets the reader with this astonishing assertion: "I am making a really bad book on purpose in order to drive off the profane who want to 'like'" (12). The translator of Clarice Lispector must be willing to accept "bad" writing and follow it to that point on the horizon where the concept becomes fundamentally unstable. *A Breath of Life* is essentially doing to *itself* what *The Passion* did to that cockroach: the book presents itself as something outside the interpretive categories that would frame it. If the text purports to be a "really bad book," it goes on to assert that the writing is, ultimately, "neither 'bad' nor 'good'" (12). Once again, Lispector's tactic (or that of her narrator) is to confuse a binary opposition deliberately, undermining and destabilizing it, in order to dispense with it altogether. It's the book's assault, however, on "liking" and, by extension, "not liking," that I find most disruptive. Liking would seem to be a necessary crutch. Without liking, how do we even begin to speak of creative work? Lispector troubles common sense. As we've grown accustomed to consuming art as opportunities for publicly "liking," we limit the aesthetic experience. As we've learned to enthusiastically deploy the thumbs-up icons and the quantifiable, imaginary stars made available to us, it becomes increasingly difficult to respond to art outside of "liking," to be radically open to art and allow ourselves to be opened by it. It becomes increasingly difficult to see what is there.

---

[4] Adorno discusses the concept of "the ugly" in his *Aesthetic Theory*. In an article entitled "Aesthetic Violence: The Concept of the Ugly in Adorno's 'Aesthetic Theory,'" Peter Uwe Hohendahl offers this helpful and relevant synopsis of Adorno's approach to the ugly: "The subversive force of the advanced work of art violates conventional aesthetic norms by foregrounding the ugly and rejects the false reconciliation of the beautiful" (186).

Works Cited

Cixous, Hélène. "The Laugh of the Medusa." Trans. Keith Cohen and Paula Cohen. *Signs*, vol. 1, no. 4, Summer 1976, pp. 875–93.

Goldsmith, Kenneth. *I'll Be Your Mirror: The Selected Andy Warhol Interviews.* Carroll and Graf Publishers, 2004.

Hohendahl, Peter. "Aesthetic Violence: The Concept of the Ugly in Adorno's 'Aesthetic Theory.'" *Cultural Critique*, vol. 60, Spring 2005, pp. 170–96.

Librandi, Marília. *Writing by Ear: Clarice Lispector and the Aural Novel.* University of Toronto Press, 2018.

Linhares, Temístocles. "The Spell of the Phrase." Appendix to *The Besieged City*.

Lispector, Clarice. *The Besieged City*. Trans. Johnny Lorenz. New Directions, 2019.

Lispector, Clarice. *A Breath of Life*. Trans. Johnny Lorenz. New Directions, 2012.

Lispector, Clarice. *The Passion According to G.H.* Trans. Idra Novey. New Directions, 2012.

Moser, Benjamin. "Obyezloshadenie." Introduction to *The Besieged City*.

Nietzsche, Friedrich. *The Gay Science*. Trans. Walter Kaufmann. Vintage, 1974.

Scarry, Elaine. *The Body in Pain: The Making and Unmaking of the World*. Oxford University Press, 1987.

12

Tanizaki's *The Key* in Translation

Will You Still Need Me, Will You Still Read Me, When I'm (Over) Sixty-Four?

Anna Zielinska-Elliott

In 1956, Japanese novelist Jun'ichirō Tanizaki published his controversial novel *The Key* (*Kagi*). Its explicitly erotic scenes and themes of "perversion" and marital infidelity created considerable scandal in Japan, reaching all the way to the chambers of the Japanese parliament, where Tanizaki was lambasted by lawmakers for promoting immorality among youth. The book's instant notoriety, along with its unusual narrative structure and psychological drama, not to mention the fame of its author, has guaranteed its place as a modern classic of Japanese literature.

A little more than sixty-four years after its publication, *Kagi* remains one of Tanizaki's most widely read works. It has been translated into over twenty languages, in some cases more than once; but not, as it happens, into Polish. Thus, when I undertook the first Polish-language translation of *Kagi* in 2019, I felt no small burden of responsibility. Tanizaki is well known in Poland: a number of his works appeared in translation in the early 1970s, earning him recognition among connoisseurs of world literature. I could expect, then, that readers would have high expectations, and that some might have read the book in other languages and would want to compare. I knew also that some aspects of the book would present translation challenges, including stylistic questions that would require me to decide whether to make characters speak in a Polish that was closer to the language of the 1950s. As I began to work on the translation, I became curious about the circumstances of the book's creation and subsequent translations, looking for clues that would help me in my own endeavor.

This chapter touches on some of the issues I encountered in the process of translation. I begin with a short overview of Tanizaki's place in the twentieth-century canon, offering then a brief account of *Kagi*'s publication and translation history, focusing on the English translation, and following with examples of the difficulties the book has presented to the translator over the decades, including to the present author.

Opening the Door to Controversy: Tanizaki Produces *The Key*

One of the greatest Japanese writers of the twentieth century, Jun'ichirō Tanizaki (1886–1965) is counted together with Yasunari Kawabata (1899–1972) and Yukio Mishima (1925–70) as one of the "Big Three" writers during the first "Golden Age" of translated Japanese literature in the United States, introduced to foreign audiences in the 1950s and 1960s (Fowler 3). Thanks mainly to Knopf's sustained publishing and marketing efforts, contemporary Japanese fiction was brought to readers at that time in translations done by academics at leading American universities. It was in those early years that Tanizaki's works were first translated into English, starting with *Some Prefer Nettles* (1929) in 1955, followed by *The Makioka Sisters* (1948) in 1957, both the work of Edward Seidensticker. In the early 1960s, three more books appeared, all translated by Howard Hibbett: *The Key* (1956) in 1961, *Seven Japanese Tales* (published in Japan between 1910 and 1959) in 1963, and *Diary of a Mad Old Man* (1962) in 1965.

Before discussing translations of *The Key*, it is worth saying a little about the book itself and its reputation in Japan.

The novel consists entirely of alternating diary entries written by a husband and wife, constituting a record of their sexual relations over a period of several months. The diaries are supposedly written in secret, but it gradually becomes clear that both husband and wife read each other's notes and use them as a way to communicate and manipulate each other, often engaging in deception. Tanizaki started writing *The Key* in the late summer or fall of 1955 and intended to publish it in installments in *Chūō Kōron*, an influential monthly magazine. The first installment appeared in the January 1956 issue. In February and again in March, the magazine published notices from the editor apologizing for the interruption of the book's serialization; in the April issue came another apology, this time from Tanizaki himself, who blamed the delay on his health and on preexisting obligations (*Chūō Kōron* 71.4: 215). Finally, a second installment appeared in May, and publication continued without a break until December. The May installment—which in fact hit the newsstands in April—included explicit sexual scenes, causing an uproar in Japanese cultural and political circles.

The trigger might have been a special report published in the April 29 issue of *Shūkan Asahi*, titled "Between Obscenity and Literature: The Case of *The Key* by Jun'ichirō Tanizaki." In part as a result of media interest, *The Key* drew the attention of lawmakers and was the subject of discussion during debate about a proposed Prostitution Prevention Law, which took place in the Judicial Affairs Committee of the National Diet on May 10–12, 1956. The debate turned the issue from a social and artistic one to a political one. The parliamentarian who introduced the topic claimed that the promotion of morality was necessary to prevent prostitution and, giving the example of *The Key*, asked: "To what lengths will it spur on youth, who are already burning with passion and brimming with the spirit of adolescence?" Perhaps because the story was richly illustrated, it was also compared to *shunga*, erotic woodblock prints. It was further suggested that Tanizaki should be called to the Diet to explain himself (Diet Records: May 10, 1956/044–8).

This was not the first time Tanizaki had run into trouble with the authorities. In the 1910s, some of his works had been censored, and in the 1930s he removed from his modern-language translation of the eleventh-century novel *The Tale of Genji* parts "unsuitable for direct transplantation into the current times," anticipating the objections of the authorities (Ito, 186). Later, in 1943, military authorities stopped the publication of *The Makioka Sisters* (*Sasameyuki*), claiming it was unsuitable for wartime consumption, mainly because it made virtually no reference to the war (Ito 190).[1]

It would appear that reports on this parliamentary debate had a material effect on Tanizaki's artistic choices for *The Key*. A few years after the affair, the extent of the author's unwillingness to testify before the Judicial Affairs Committee became clear. In a live radio conversation between Tanizaki, *Chūō Kōron* editor Hōji Shimanaka, and critic Shinpei Ikejima that aired on NHK on September 27, 1960, Tanizaki admitted to having rewritten the rest of the book:

Oh, that? Yeah, well, I changed my plan a bit in the middle of it. It didn't work out the way I had meant it. As Mr. Shimanaka knows, up to the second or third installment.... After that it was a bit different, different than the original plan. It became a problem in the Diet, and I would rather have died than be dragged into a place like that ... (*laughter*). Anyway, I thought I might just stop publishing it and asked Mr. Shimanaka's advice. But he said he wanted me to continue no matter what... (*laughter*). (NHK 113–14)

---

[1] In 1920, Tanizaki even wrote a story titled *Censor* (*Ken'etsukan*), a comic dialogue between an author and a censor.

The prospect of having to defend his book and prove it was a work of literature to a group of conservative parliamentarians must have been unimaginable to Tanizaki, by then the grand old man of Japanese letters. Perhaps understandably, he preferred to change his concept for the novel instead of putting himself through potential public humiliation.

Translations of *The Key*

As mentioned earlier, *The Key* has been translated from Japanese into over twenty different languages by now. The earliest translation seems to have been into Korean in 1960.[2] Several more translations into that language followed in later years. The first, and so far sole, English translation appeared in 1961. Other early language translations included Finnish (from English), also in 1961; Swedish, Danish, and Dutch in 1962 (all from English), and Italian and French in 1963 (both from Japanese).

The English translation was initiated not by Hibbett but by Harold Strauss, then editor-in-chief at Knopf. Having been stationed in Japan at the end of the Second World War, Strauss conceived a lifelong interest in modern Japanese literature and is widely recognized as having played a key role in fostering the tastes of American readers in the postwar years. As Donald Keene noted in his obituary of Strauss, "It was he, more than any other person in publishing, who made it possible for modern Japanese literature to take its place among the literatures of the world" (Flint). A year after *Kagi* appeared in Japanese, Strauss wrote to Hibbett, asking whether it was worth translating. Hibbett replied:

> It is written in a swift, lucid style and needs to be read in one or two sittings in order to appreciate its complexities and its strengths. Of course it is not Tanizaki's masterpiece, but neither is it the elderly fling at sensationalism that many Japanese critics have alleged. . . . I do like the novel and would certainly recommend it for translation.[3]

Strauss thanked Hibbett for his letter, noting, "It is too early to decide as yet, but I rather think we shall publish *Kagi* one day."[4] That "one day" came

---

[2] *Yŏlsoe*, trans. by Yi Wŏnsu and published by Chŏngunsa. I am grateful to Yun Soon Yang for this information.
[3] Hibbett to Strauss, November 30, 1957. I am grateful do David Hibbett for permission to quote from his father's letters.
[4] Strauss to Hibbett, December 4, 1957.

sixteen months later, in April 1959, when Strauss asked Hibbett to translate the book, asking him not to "worry about censorship" and to translate "as forthrightly as possible."[5] Hibbett agreed conditionally to undertake the translation in a letter of May 4, saying that he wanted to try translating one of the "embarrassing" passages first. He stressed that he did not mean erotic scenes, but others, such as when the wife talks to Kimura, her lover-to-be, about her "virtue" having been preserved. Hibbett wrote, "These, I think, read well enough in Japanese, but may seem a bit ludicrous in English." He also expressed doubts about some passages being lengthy and too repetitious. But he concluded his letter on a positive note: "I am actually much enticed by the thought of translating *Kagi*—not least if it will épater le bourgeois in Boston."[6]

In his response, Strauss gave Hibbett the freedom to make whatever adjustments he considered necessary in the name of readability:

> While we believe that if a book is worth translating, it should be translated as it was written, nevertheless certain minor adjustments are desirable and acceptable. What we are after is the faithfulness of total effect. When you say that certain passages "read well enough in Japanese," I think you ought to try to achieve the same total effect in English.[7]

About a year later, in June 1960, Hibbett reported that he had mailed the translation to Strauss by special delivery the night before. He continued: "I hope you like it. I'm glad to have had the chance to do it for you—I greatly enjoyed it. . . . I made no 'expurgations,' nor do I think any are needed. But you and your staff will be a better judge of that."[8] The manuscript then went into production, and printing was finished by the middle of December of that year.

Hibbett's translation was well received. In his review, Edwin McLellan wrote that Hibbett "has somehow managed to retain not only the starkness of the original but the cruelty and the intelligence. His translation is a work of remarkable skill and taste" (211). Donald Keene commented in the *New York Times* that Hibbett "beautifully captures the interplay of the male-female diaries" ("Recorded Passion" 291). In a talk given many years later, Hibbett spoke about his experience translating *The Key*, pointing out that, despite the scandalous nature of the book, he did not introduce any changes. He added:

---

[5] Strauss to Hibbett, April 29, 1959.
[6] Hibbett to Strauss, May 4, 1959.
[7] Strauss to Hibbett, May 8, 1959.
[8] Hibbett to Strauss, June 7, 1960.

"The lawyers did go through it and, as I recall, the only thing they wished to remove, which was alright with me, was a single drop of saliva that occurred at one point in the text" (Richie 40). I reviewed the Japanese original, but couldn't find the drop of saliva supposedly missing from Hibbett's English translation. I did, however, find some other passages and phrases missing, to which I will return later.

Unlocking *The Key*

What, then, are the challenges that *Kagi* presents to the translator? In my opinion, there are two different kinds of difficulties. The first has to do with the look of the original text; the second has more to do with the content itself.

The fundamental structure of the book—diary entries of a husband and wife—was explained earlier. Tanizaki's original text made the difference between "his" and "her" entries typographically immediately apparent by employing different syllabaries to accompany the Chinese characters: *katakana* for the husband and *hiragana* for the wife. The result is that the entries (which generally follow in alternating order) are presented on the page in a visually distinctive fashion. Thus, the first sentence of the husband's diary looks like this:

一月一日。………僕ハ今年カラ、今日マデ日記ニ記スコトヲ躊躇シテイタヨウナ事柄ヲモ敢エテ書キ留メル ̄ニシタ。(8)

[New Year's Day. This year I intend to begin writing freely about a topic which, in the past, I have hesitated to even mention here (3)].

The same sentence written in the system used by the wife would look like this:

一月一日。………僕は今年から、今日まで日記に記すことを躊躇していたような事柄をも敢えて書き留めることにした。

As can be seen, the husband's writing in *katakana* is more angular, while the wife's *hiragana* script is rounder. Both phonetic systems of writing are equally old, and both ultimately derive from Chinese characters. Traditionally, they were used for different purposes and bear a gendered character: *hiragana* was historically more used by women, while *katakana* was perceived as more masculine, and in fact was still quite commonly used by men in the early twentieth century. (It remains in wide use to write words of foreign origin.)

In working on the English translation, Hibbett decided not to differentiate the two diaries visually by using different fonts. When asked about this problem later, he replied, "I really didn't think it would be efficient to put one of them in italic, but I wondered whether [instead] I might be able to convey a sort of feminine style" (Richie 40). Many other language versions (such as Italian, Spanish, Catalan, and Turkish) followed the English example and used just one font. One wonders, though, why Hibbett felt that using a different font for the two diaries would not be "efficient," as this very approach has been used unproblematically in some European languages, in Russian, and in the Chinese translation published in Taiwan.

The translations of *Kagi* into French and German (of which there are two each, all translated from Japanese) offer a window onto how these choices seem to have changed over time. The French versions, one from 1963 (titled *La confession impudique*, by Gaston Renondeau) and the other from 1998 (*La clef*, by Anne Bayard-Sakai), were both published by Gallimard. The German translations, both titled *Der Schlüssel*, came out in 1971 (by Sachiko Yatsushiro and Gerhard Knauss, published by Rowohlt) and 2017 (by Katja Cassing and Jürgen Stalph, published by Cass). While, like Hibbett's, the first translations in both languages did not graphically differentiate the two diaries, the second versions both did, using different fonts. In the second French translation, the husband's diary was printed in italics, which, according to the translator, Bayard-Sakai, "made the reading much easier for the reader."[9] In the new German version, the husband's diary is printed in small caps. It is also worth noting that the translators in that case divided the labor, with Katja Cassing translating the wife's entries and Jürgen Stalph translating the husband's entries—a brilliant way to effectively differentiate the two styles.[10]

Another striking feature of the original Japanese text that the translator must grapple with are the frequently-appearing rows of nine dots (which can be seen after the first four characters—the date—in the sentence quoted earlier). Identical series of dots can be found in more than 250 other places in the text. What role do they play? As Japanese friends confirm, in an average diary, a date will often be followed by some brief remark on the weather. However, there are none of these remarks in the book, leading one to wonder if the dots are there to indicate that such mundane observations have been removed. The suggestion that sections of the diaries have been deleted is encouraged by the wife's reference, near the end of the book, to having written

---

[9] Private e-mail communication with A. Bayard-Sakai, February 23, 2020.
[10] Private e-mail communication with J. Stalph, February 19, 2020.

in her diary every day for four months starting on January 1. Yet by late April, instead of getting 120 entries, the reader has seen only a little over 30—some merely one line in length, with dots at the beginning and end of many of them. These would seem to be places where text has been removed, leaving only the passages directly or indirectly related to the sexual relationship between the husband and wife.

But if these nine-dot ellipses do indeed indicate cuts, the question necessarily arises, who removed the missing passages?

One obvious explanation is that the missing passages were removed by the author, to make the reader think that Tanizaki somehow came across real diaries and edited them for the reader. Another possibility, suggested by Anne Bayard-Sakai (who rejected Tanizaki as the potential editor), is that the cuts were done by the wife, who, in her final summary after the husband's death, compares the two diaries, and decides what to leave and what to cut. That would also explain why the husband's and wife's entries alternate (Bayard-Sakai 97–8).

Although these long ellipses (assuming that is what they are) are perhaps visually distracting, they are undoubtedly of some real significance in the telling of the story. For this reason, it is a little surprising that many translations choose to ignore them altogether or only include some of them. For instance, the dots are not present in the English, Spanish, Catalan, or Turkish translations. Most—not all—of them remained in the new German translation (except for the ones following dates in the beginning of entries). They have been kept in the new French version, in the Italian, Taiwanese, Chinese, and Russian versions.

The second aspect of the book that might potentially present difficulties for the translator is its erotic content. The novel does not include any profanities or words for genitalia, but given its explicit focus on the nature of mature sexuality, one could be forgiven for asking whether translators—perhaps, like Tanizaki, anxious about the censor—made any cautionary cuts or changes to the bedroom scenes. Indeed, it seems that such emendations were made in at least some cases, where certain passages were changed or removed. To explore this question, let us look at the husband's entry of January 29. Having gotten his wife drunk and given her sleeping pills, the husband at last has the chance he has long sought to see his wife naked with the light on. Bringing a fluorescent lamp into the room, he takes advantage of this opportunity to carefully examine her body:

JPN: 僕ハ彼女ヲ俯向キニサセ、臀ノ孔マデ覗イテ見タガ、臀肉ガ左右ニ盛リ上ッテイル中間ノ凹ミノトコロノ白サトイッタラナカッタ。(27)

ENG: I turned her face down, and even peered into the hollow where the white flesh of her buttocks swelled up on either side. (29–30)
FR (1963): Je la retournai sur le ventre, je l'examinai jusque dans son derrière. Partout sa peau était d'une blancheur inimaginable. (32)
FR (1998): J'allais jusqu'à la mettre sur le ventre pour examiner le trou de son postérieur, mais même le creux dans la raie de fesses était d'une blancheur inouïe. (36)
GER (1971): Ich drehte sie um und untersuchte ihren Rücken und die unberührten Flächen zwischen ihren Beinen. Auf den sanften Rundungen ihrer Hüfte fand ich das Fleisch so weiss und rein, wie ich es noch nie gesehen hatte. (22)
GER (2017): ICH DREHTE SIE AUF DEN BAUCH, ABER SELBST ZWISCHEN IHREN POBACKEN UND UM DEN ANUS HERUM WAR NICHTS DERGLEICHEN ZU ENTDECKEN. (38)
SP (2002): Le di la vuelta, colocándola boca abajo, e incluso contemplé la cavidad entre las blancas redondeces de sus nalgas. (23)

The early French and German translators, like Hibbett, chose euphemisms rather than state explicitly, as the Japanese text does, that the husband inspects his wife's anus. Perhaps it was not considered erotic enough for the rest of the scene? Or perhaps "anus" was the "drop of saliva" to which the Knopf lawyers objected? Interestingly, the 2002 Spanish translation also follows the more demure early translations.[11]

In my own translation, I have decided to keep all the dots, on the grounds that they are crucial to understanding the basic premise of the book. I also translated the bedroom scenes without removing anything: sixty-four years later, I couldn't imagine the Polish publisher being concerned about the book's indecency. In terms of language, I chose to use a neutral late twentieth-century Polish, although I did include a few slightly old-fashioned expressions that might remind the reader of the way grandma and grandpa used to speak.

Conclusion

Translating a book notorious for its descriptions of late-middle-aged sexual fantasies requires maintaining a "clinical" distance that allows the work to

---

[11] For reasons of space, I am unable to include other, similar examples where the English translation omits something and the Spanish follows suit, as with the phrase *kahanshin* ("lower half of the body"), missing both from English and Spanish in pp. 27 (JPN), 29 (ENG), and 23 (SP), while it is kept in both French and German versions.

be seen as more of a psychological novel than as pornography; and in this regard, I would argue that the technical challenges are in some ways more daunting than the linguistic challenges. As I have tried to show, typography plays a key role (pun intended) in upholding the conceit of the novel as something that is not the product of the author's imagination, but is instead his discovery—a case of psychological obsession embodied in twin diaries that he is merely bringing to light and sharing with an interested public. By means of different typefaces and implied evidence of supposed editorial choice, Tanizaki deliberately puts some distance between himself and the text, murmuring fascinatedly alongside the reader, "How interesting! How bizarre!" as if he had nothing to do with creating the story in the first place.

Recognizing the tortured process whereby the book came into being, the translator of *The Key* also has more than the usual obligation to pay attention to the historical circumstances surrounding the production of the text, as these appear to have shaped in fundamental ways both the story's plot and language. Lest we fall into the assumption that Tanizaki was somehow lacking in resolve, or that he was dealing with a quaintly conservative legislature that was behind the times, we should recall that *Lady Chatterley's Lover* was only published in an unexpurgated version in the United Kingdom in 1960 (and controversially at that), four years *after The Key* appeared in print in Japan; and that the very next year, Grove Press was sued in the United States for its publication of the full version of Henry Miller's *Tropic of Cancer*—this, of course, being the same year that Hibbett's translation of Tanizaki's novel came out. In some ways, the biggest challenge for the twenty-first-century translator of this classic is to try to recreate the author's sense of daring, of taboo-breaking, and brave venturing into forbidden territory while maintaining the same cool, distanced language of the original.

Works Cited

Bayard-Sakai, Anne. "Tanizaki Jun'ichirō ron: 'Kagi' no futōmeisei to jojutsu sōchi." *Kokubungaku kaishaku to kyōzai no kenkyū*, vol. 43, no. 6, 1998, pp. 92–98.

"Between Obscenity and Literature: The Case of *The Key* by Jun'ichirō Tanizaki." *Shūkan Asahi*, Special Issue, April 29, 1956.

Flint, Peter. "Harold Strauss, Editor, Dead: Brought in Japanese Literature." *New York Times*, November 30, 1975.

Fowler, Edward. "Rendering Words, Traversing Cultures: On the Art and Politics of Translating Modern Japanese Fiction." *Journal of Japanese Studies*, vol. 18, no. 1, 1992, pp. 1–44.

Ito, Ken. *Visions of Desire: Tanizaki's Fictional Worlds*. Stanford UP, 1991.
Keene, Donald. "Recorded Passion." *New York Times*, February 19, 1961.
McLellan, Edwin. "The Key." *Monumenta Nipponica*, vol. 16, no. 1–2, 1960, pp. 11–20.
Richie, Donald, ed. *Words, Ideas and Ambiguities: Four Perspectives on Translating*. Imprint Publications, 2000.
National Diet Records. Record of May 10, 1956, debate. kokkai.ndl.go.jp/#/detail?minId=102405206X03219560510&spkNum=0&current=1.
NHK. "Tanizaki Jun'ichirō hen." *NHK hen bundan yomoyama banashi*. Vol. II. Tokyo: Seiabō, 1961, pp. 104–26.
Tanizaki, Jun'ichiro. *Diary of a Mad Old Man*. Trans. Edward Seidensticker. Knopf, 1965.
Tanizaki, Jun'ichiro. *Kagi. Futen rōjin nikki*. Shinchōsha, 1968. Originally published 1956 *Chūo koron*, January–December, 1956.
Tanizaki, Jun'ichiro. *The Key*. Trans. Howard Hibbett. Tuttle, 1971. Originally published Knopf, 1960.
Tanizaki, Jun'ichiro. *La clef*. Trans. Anne Bayard-Sakai. Gallimard, 1998.
Tanizaki, Jun'ichiro. *La confession impudique*. Trans. Gaston Renondeau. Gallimard, 1963.
Tanizaki, Jun'ichiro. *La llave*. Trans. Keiko Takahashi and Jordi Fibla. Siruela, 2014. Originally published El Aleph, 2002.
Tanizaki, Jun'ichiro. *The Makioka Sisters*. Trans. Edward Seidensticker. Knopf 1957.
Tanizaki, Jun'ichiro. *Der Schlüssel*. Trans. Sachiko Yatsushiro and Gerhard Knauss. Rowohlt, 1971.
Tanizaki, Jun'ichiro. *Der Schlüssel*. Trans. Katja Cassing and Jürgen Stalph. Cass, 2017.
Tanizaki, Jun'ichiro. *Seven Japanese Tales*. Trans. Edward Seidensticker. Knopf, 1963.
Tanizaki, Jun'ichiro. *Some Prefer Nettles*. Trans. Edward Seidensticker. Knopf, 1955.
Tanizaki, Jun'ichiro. *Yŏlsoe*. Translated by Yi Wŏnsu. Chŏngunsa, 1960.

13

An Essay on Nichita Stănescu

The Classic and the Personal in Translation

Sean Cotter

What is a classic? To paraphrase Roland Barthes's definition of literature, "La littérature, c'est ce qui s'enseigne, un point c'est tout"—the classic is what is translated, that's all (qtd. in Appiah 340). What we call "classical" literature, from Ancient Greek and Latin, is something the vast number of people read in translation. Translation distinguishes "classic" from "canonical." While it is easy to name canonical texts of American literature, we do not refer to "classics of American literature" nearly as often as we do "classics of world literature"—those canonical books we read in translation.[1] This fact of circulation dovetails with the metaphorical translation that also seems important to our use of "classic": re-reading a work in a new context. The text functions like a classic when readers return to the book in different periods of their lives, or after "tectonic shifts," in David Damrosch's term: "Works that attain a lasting status as classics of world literature are ones that can weather a variety of tectonic shifts in the literary landscapes" (187). Translated texts are retranslated when recontextualized. The first shift of context happens in the translation from one language to the next; the second when a reader returns to the work later in life. The text that weathers its literal and the metaphorical translations is the classic.

Yet in asserting this definition, I am haunted by Barthes's idea that "literature is what is taught," not what is made. If "literature" requires ancillary labor from educators, if a text becomes literature only through the

---

[1] Roughly half as often, according to the Google Ngram viewer. https://books.google.com/ngrams/graph?content=classics+of+American+literature%2C+classics+of+world+literature&year_start=1800&year_end=2019&corpus=26&smoothing=3&direct_url=t1%3B%2Cclassics%20of%20American%20literature%3B%2Cc0%3B.t1%3B%2Cclassics%20of%20world%20literature%3B%2Cc0#t1%3B%2Cclassics%20of%20American%20literature%3B%2Cc0%3B.t1%3B%2Cclassics%20of%20world%20literature%3B%2Cc0.

collaboration of various parties, then we must consider how much effort (and from how many translators) is needed to create the classic. It takes not a village but a planet to make a classic. This definition creates a certain anxiety for me as a translator from Romanian, one of a small group laboring to recreate Romanian works in English. Is it possible for a work written in a language with few speakers to become a classic? Each language may elect its canon, but this is a local question, and the local is not the international circulation of "the classic." Continuing the passage I quoted, Damrosch, with an almost athletic indifference to effort, defines the classic on the basis of not only its circulation in translation but also its retranslations:

> Works that attain a lasting status as classics of world literature are ones that can weather a variety of tectonic shifts in the literary landscapes. As they do so, their translations change along with their interpretations.... New translations of Dante appear almost annually; Seamus Heaney's *Beowulf* and Robert Fagles's *Iliad* are released on tape in readings by Hollywood actors. (187)

Damrosch's prioritizing of the persistence through change is a useful definition of "the classic," but the mountains of cultural capital that underwrite Derek Jacobi and Maria Tucci's recordings of Fagles's translation, it pains me to admit, seem out of reach for writers from Romanian, a language of roughly 30 million speakers in the world. While even Heaney has dabbled in Romanian (via Ioana Russell-Gebbett's unpublished translations), retranslations of Romanian texts hardly appear annually. Does this mean a Romanian work cannot become a classic?

One response might point to the thousands of works, in large and small literatures, that never garner the attention and labor to become classics. On this macro-scale, Romanian literature is only a subsection of all the under-read artistic writing in the world. Yet this position amounts to a shrug. What if, more productively, we examined the classic function of certain texts on a micro-scale, on the scale not of a planet or village but of a single person. Texts may perform the work of weathering translation, of lasting through tectonic shifts, whether or not they are read, re-read, and recorded by Hollywood actors. The numbers of these works are, of course, many times greater than the numbers of world literature classics. Changing the scale of our analysis will uncover a slew of translated texts that are important, for strong or weak reasons, to individual people. A thorough investigation of the classic function requires we make space for the personal classic.

This shift in scale invites a shift in method. Rather than arguing objectively and persuasively for the macro-value of a Romanian text,

I intend to argue subjectively and suggestively, using autobiography and literary history-cum-anthropology, to show how a small, four-line poem has stretched through different periods of my life like a long, taut guitar string. I can sense the poem has performed the classic function for me, because in whatever period of my life, when I accidently brush against this string, it reverberates in all the periods at once. My opposition here, between the macro-canonical and the micro-personal, might recall the arguments for autobiography from the 1980s and 1990s, which leveraged accounts of personal experience against English department preferences for *Beowulf* and the *Iliad*. Yet these arguments often aimed to challenge the imaginary apolitical scholar of literature, the individual reader abstracted from the social, and to reveal the interpellation of the individual within unjust structures of power. Those individual reader positions, male and white, were revealed to be easily explicable effects of the same power structures that supported the literary canon. My aim is not to subvert canonical works but to work at the conjuncture of social structures, because translation happens at this intersection. These conjunctures create a more complicated site for the formation of the individual. In fact, my point is that the confluence of conflicting ideologies makes the personal a site of associative thinking and affective attachment, where competing systems, like tectonic plates, slide past each other in productive ways.

Nichita Stănescu's "Poem," first published in 1960, has persisted through discontinuous contexts in my life, weathering a series of tectonic shifts in my personal landscape. Before I chart the two decades between 1994, when I first encountered the poem, and 2012, when I read my translation one night in New York, I want to examine the diminutive text, whose size itself seems to argue against its status as a classic of world literature. The poem has only four lines, no rhyme, and if we believe the ellipses, no ending:

Poem

Spune-mi, dacă te-aş prinde-ntr-o zi
şi ţi-aş săruta talpa piciorului,
nu-i aşa că ai şchiopăta puţin, după aceea,
de teamă să nu-mi striveşti sărutul? . . .
(Stănescu, *Opera poetică* 124)

I no longer have the version I read in 1994, or the trot I would have had to make for myself, muddling word by word through one of the first two Romanian literary texts I ever read. This is the version I published in 2012.

A Poem

Tell me, if I ever caught you
and kissed the arch of your foot,
wouldn't you limp a little after that
for fear of crushing my kiss? . . .

(Stănescu, *Wheel* 31)

This poem imagines a love encounter, a pursuit and its consequences. It playfully flips the speaker over, who imagines he catches the Daphnean addressee and then dives to a position as far beneath her as possible. The lines flip as well: line one suggests the aggression of a long-standing pursuit, only to switch to submission in line two; only to return, in the implication of a wound in line three, to a form of aggression; only to switch again in the last line to submission, in the vulnerability of an easily crushable kiss. The last line of the Romanian is more tentative, more vulnerable than this English version: five words hesitatingly approach the verb "strivești," as though afraid to admit the ease (indicated by the alliteration with "sărutul") with which "you crush the kiss." The ellipses suggest this pattern of switching places might never end. The speaker and the addressee might become coupled in the endless oscillation of their roles. We can hear their constant alternation as a vibration. Seen from the perspective of eternity, the amorous pair creates a hum.

This image of eternity, the notion that one small moment of contact might resonate through a lifetime, is an apt image of the classic, or at least, of the personal version of the classic I want to claim exists. The other important aspect of this poem is also small: it is all a hypothetical, starting with "if." This small poem suggests, promises, tantalizes with the idea of the eternal, yet even these four lines do not have the temerity to be certain of this outcome. This poem is no *Iliad*. As Sappho, via Anne Carson, writes, "Some men say an army of ships is the most beautiful thing / on the black earth. But I say it is / what you love" (27). Stănescu's love poem is not an epic but a classic on the scale of the personal. My goal is explicitly not to convince the world that Stănescu is a neglected classic and that Jacobi and Tucci should rush to the nearest sound booth to record him. My goal, rather, is to convince the world that personal experiences of small literatures' small poems should be valued the way we value classics.

* * *

When the Peace Corps brought me to Romania in 1994, I didn't know who Stănescu was, and I had only a dim idea where Romania was. I was staying with a host-family, studying Romanian twenty hours a week as part of the Peace

Corps training, and romanticizing my experience in notebooks of poems. The family I stayed with was involved in transportation: the father drove a truck, the son a taxi, and the mother used to operate a tram. The father was gregarious and funny, about as tall as me and much larger, with energetic white hair, and a puffy, handsome face. His frequent laughter exposed the yellow-fringed triangular gap that years of pulling smoke into his mouth had worn between two of his upper teeth. For convenience, he would wedge his cigarette in the gap, so he could talk and laugh without it falling. I liked him, and he took his role as host to heart. He would take me fishing, or sit with me at the window, pointing out things in the street and telling me their Romanian names.

Our relationship underwent a dramatic change one Sunday at mid-day dinner. Their granddaughter, all of four years of age and forty tons of cute, had learned a poem by heart. She stood and adopted a rhetorical posture: feet at ninety degrees to each other, hands clasped horizontally across her chest. She then declaimed, with terrifying intensity, a series of rhyming lines. I did not understand what she said—I learned later the lines were from the nineteenth-century poet Mihai Eminescu—but I was impressed by the fact that a poem had been given its moment during the family meal. This was my first encounter with the high status of poetry in Romania.

My second came immediately afterwards. Enthused by the granddaughter's performance, I stated to the family that I wrote poetry. My host-father became suddenly serious. "Prove it," he said, and the mother, son, and granddaughter looked at me, all equally stony. I went to my room and brought the father some pieces of paper. He looked at the English lines, turned his head from the table with an air of resignation, and let the pages fall from his hands. I could tell this was for him significant and unexpected news. My host-mother changed the topic, and since it was already late, the dinner soon ended. For the remaining two months, the father treated me differently: delicately, protectively, reverently. He shoo-ed people out of the room if I was writing. He literally tip-toed past my door, leaning back as he placed the balls of his feet down one by one. He told visitors that he was hosting an American poet, and when I left, the family threw a party for me and all the other Peace Corps trainees.

He was one of many such encounters: the people in a train compartment who gave up their seats to a poet who entered, offering him food and booze; the taxi driver who offered me a free trip to the airport, as long as we talked about poetry the entire ride. In time, I learned the clichés: "A Romanian is born a poet" and "For every two Romanians, there are three poets." I learned that in 1989, when someone was needed to announce on television that Ceaușescu's rule and his life were over, a group of soldiers drove a tank through Bucharest, looking for a poet.

I owe my first encounter with Stănescu to this same veneration of poetry. The Romanian language teachers working for Peace Corps dedicated a day to two poems, "Și dacă..." ("And If...") by Eminescu and "Poem" by Stănescu. This choice ran counter to the exceptionally practical, explicitly American methods of our language training. A typical lesson would cover the vocabulary for market shopping, which we practiced by going to the market outside our training site. In fact, the language training had another goal, in addition to teaching us the language: it would teach us to teach. The language training we received was meant to model the up-to-date English-language teaching we would perform, as volunteers in our jobs in Romanian schools, and the methods we would teach to our colleagues in those schools. We were taught that "communicative" methods had superseded the outmoded "grammar/ translation" method, which would use literary texts when teaching a foreign language—a still common method in Romanian classrooms. Thus, this day of poetry challenged American Peace Corps pedagogy and job training. These poems that we could understand only with the help of trots, and that we translated in a group phrase by phrase as though we were studying Latin, were a Romanian contribution in both content and method. This challenge demonstrates the strength of Romanian poetry ideology, as it existed at that time.

The choice of these two poets is significant: Eminescu is (still) Romania's "national poet" and Stănescu a "genius" whose public persona, during the Ceaușescu period, was modeled on the first. Thus, what these teachers asserted against an American training program was in part a Romanian national symbol. The possibility of this symbol is the result of almost two centuries of language ideology that I can only sketch out here: Romantic assertions of identity that ultimately stem from Johann Herder's belief in a necessary connection between the place and the language that there develops. Romanian language ideology follows other nineteenth-century national movements of Central and Eastern Europe, which advocate for what Benedict Anderson terms the "vernacularization" of the languages of power, making the struggle for local control of state functions synonymous with the advocacy of local languages. "These languages became surrogate national homes and the seedbeds for future national states," writes Zygmunt Bauman. "Nowhere else in modern times has there developed such a deep belief in the well-nigh magical power of the word and of cultural symbols in general; nowhere else have such far-reaching hopes and formidable fears surrounded their use" (Bauman 78–9). Eminescu himself read extensively in German Romanticism, especially Friedrich Schiller, whose slogan, "Bildung ist Freiheit," gave culture in general and poetry in particular a role in freedom from imperial influence. If the people are housed within their language, then the poet elevates that language, authorizing the nation as he authors his poetry. The "myth of Eminescu," as Lucian Boia has called it, develops at the end of his life and the end of the nineteenth century, transforming him into "the extreme representative of Romanianness" (43). The epitome of his connection to the Romanian land is a linden tree in the city of Iași. According to the myth, Eminescu picked this tree out from the many growing in the park, and he wrote many of his poems here, sometimes in the company of his beloved Veronica Micle. Even today, the tree is still the center of this major city park, rooted to the earth, supported by steel rods and straps, beside a bronze bust of the poet.

While the political structures changed over the twentieth century, the nationalist structures become only more important. As Katherine Verdery has argued, Ceaușescu self-consciously employed the symbols of the Romanian nation to bolster his regime, even at the price of undercutting the ideals of communism his regime ostensibly pursued (Verdery 138–9). Thus we find Eminescu continuously foregrounded as the national poet, for example the introduction in a landmark 1974 anthology of Romanian verse:

> Up to and including today, the greatest poet of our people, who expressed its essence philosophically and formed its language with the highest music and meanings. The broad awareness of his belonging to a superior matrix of existence and creativity, the Romanian one, gave the poet wings. (Dumnitrescu Bușulenga 126)

Yet the Ceaușescu regime always insisted on corollary validation through its ability to generate its own national symbols. To this end, in the 1960s it licensed a new generation of poets, whom the regime insisted on marshaling within national poet roles. They entered literary careers, therefore, within the parameters and vocabularies of a state-controlled publishing system. These young poets proved adept at balancing the state's conflicting desires for aesthetic validation and ideological support. It was a conflicted system, in which each party attempted to profit from the other's participation.

Nichita Stănescu dominated this literary and cultural context, from his debut in 1959 until his death in 1983. When I claimed earlier that Stănescu's public persona was modeled on Eminescu, I am not referring to his writing style or content but to his function. Stănescu was marketed to Romanian readers as their contemporary national poet. Early in his career, he was willing to write poems around vocabulary controlled by the state, such as "luminous" and "peace," and like Marin Sorescu, Ana Blandiana, and others of this group, his style was unadorned and direct, an aesthetic novelty that inspired other writers and appeared unaesthetic, practical, and positive to the state editors. As a result of his skilled poetry diplomacy, Stănescu won many prizes, entered school textbooks, traveled abroad, and appeared on state television. The poet Nichita Danilov recalls the extreme height of Stănescu's reputation as evidenced in the register of a typical poetry reading introduction: "Remember, my friends. Take a good look at this man. He is a genius. Rejoice that you were able to meet him! That you lived at the same time as he did!" (qtd. in Cotter 307). Stănescu's reputation benefited from the state, and the state bolstered the reputation of poetry, drawing on old ideas, to maintain the presence of the Romanian nation.

Eminescu was Stănescu's companion during this journey. Stănescu was said to have memorized many of Eminescu's poems, even, on a trip to Belgrade, to have repeated one poem ("A Dacian's Prayer") from memory, over and over, for ten hours. Even though he was known to spend time with many different women, the state media portrayed his relationship with Dora Tăriță as an example of Romantic devotion, an equivalent to Eminescu's relationship with Micle. Stănescu publishes articles on Eminescu, including one, "Eminescu the Great," in which Stănescu reflects on the linden tree growing in front of the magazine office where he works. The smell, he states, overwhelms him, and "suddenly, I understand Eminescu's epithet for the linden: *the holy linden*. All at once, I perceive the depth of Eminescu's perception of the linden. Yes, the holy linden, the holy linden, the poetic linden—ineluctable, disturbing" (Stănescu, *Cartea* 76). If the linden travels from Iași to visit Stănescu's office in Bucharest, his poems take the reverse course. During a late television interview, the reporter informs Stănescu that a kindergarten teacher in a village near Iași was so moved by Stănescu's poem, "The Land," that she set it to music. The national overtones of the poem's title are amplified by recognizable tropes: the proletarian composer, the erotic appeal of the actor, and the recording's organic, rooted setting. As a performance begins, the reporter states that the site he chose for the performance is the home of "the poetic thrill for all the people of the Romanian land." We cut to an actor, Valeria Seciu, singing the poem with her acoustic guitar, beneath the holy linden.

"Poets as national symbols" goes a long way toward explaining how Eminescu and Stănescu end up in a 1994 Romanian language classroom: the teachers were presenting those poems they had been taught to think of as the best, most representative Romanian poetry. These poets' value withstands the American pedagogical program. At the same time, it is inevitable that this idea leaves much outside of this portrait of the teachers, especially as the explanation implies a passivity that the teachers did not demonstrate. The bare fact that they had agreed to work for a US government agency, in the heady period just after Ceaușescu's execution, when most Americans were considered spies, shows the teachers' adventurousness. The fact that a few years later, this same group of teachers went on strike to demand compensation proportionate with their level of experience, also demonstrates their initiative. (They were all fired.) I do not know these teachers well enough to understand the ways their lives intersected with the Romantic ideology of national poetry.

But even if I did, there remains a theoretical objection that gets at the heart of the question, "What is a classic?" The form of the national poet might explain canonicity, but to think of it as a classic requires translation. The work needs to weather a shift, to move out of precisely this national context that seems so convincing. Contextual analysis has trouble with translation, the practice that changes a work's linguistic and cultural context in the most complete way imaginable. My point is not only the trite but true observation that one context does not explain another, that the state support of Stănescu does not explain his adoption by translators who did not participate in that history of Romania. The problem lies in the translators themselves. Their position within the overlap of contexts makes them less available to contextual explanations, no matter how convincing and powerful these contexts' ideologies may seem. As I have tried to demonstrate so far, the story of a classic in translation is the story of heterogeneous, conflicting situations.

My own participation in the Peace Corps, for example, was not driven by a version of nationalism, a desire to come to the aid, metaphorically, of Eminescu's linden tree, in some national-spiritual communion with "the people of the Romanian land," nor was it driven by the goals Peace Corps identified for itself, which were also explicitly national. In this organization's self-definition, the actual aid provided is only one of its hallowed "three goals," while the other two are cultural:

> To help the people of interested countries in meeting their need for trained men and women.
> To help promote a better understanding of Americans on the part of the peoples served.
> To help promote a better understanding of other peoples on the part of Americans. (Peace Corps)

This third goal received an overwhelming emphasis during the three months I spent in training, and it was a constant refrain of the subsequent two years I spent in Romania as an English teacher. (I know as well that my subsequent work as a translator since that time has been counted toward measures of "third-goal" success in Peace Corps reports.) Yet as a volunteer, I did not want to make the United States better known abroad—I would confess rather than profess my country of origin. The same reluctance to participate in the national extended to "promoting better understanding" of other peoples on the part of the United States.

My motivations were different, as far as anyone can account for their own motivations, and twofold, both of which were surprisingly difficult to explain to the Romanians I lived with. First was the value of service I had learned growing up in the Episcopal Church, through group activities such as Habitat for Humanity work-trips, and the similar emphasis I encountered attending Loyola University, New Orleans. I joined Peace Corps in part from the idealistic notion that I would use my time (free from family or job) to help people. When I explained this idea to my host-family, they nodded and called it "munca patriotică." At first I thought that I could accept "patriotic work" as a translation of what I did, because I was working for a government agency, after all. I later learned that this term in fact referred to the compulsory, unpaid labor Ceaușescu had required of Romanians, service in the fields during a harvest, for example. My host-mother would use the same term to ask for her daughter-in-law's help folding laundry. The idea of working for two years for free, in order to satisfy a norm for altruism, was foreign to them.

My second motivation was a desire to travel, to live abroad for an extended time, as I had done my junior year of college. This desire was also difficult for my host-family to digest, but the problem was not a holdover from communist-era passport control. What I was doing looked a little like tourism, but I was staying too long. It most resembled traveling abroad for work, which many Romanians my age pursued, but as my host-family brother repeatedly explained, "Everyone here wants to get out of Romania. Why do the Americans want to get in? We are a poor country. If you're not going to make money where you go, why not stay home, with your friends, your family? Why come here?" Talking with him became more and more frustrating by the day, as he kept bringing up the same questions. I imagine he thought he was demonstrating sincere interest in my answer, a curiosity that went beyond politeness (and coupled with his own desire to emigrate to the United States). For me, I felt so hounded that one afternoon, in a fit of pique, I agreed to tell him the real reason I had come. He sat stock still, listening without talking, for what seemed like the first time. I told him that I had been involved in an accident, and a man had died. It wasn't my fault, but still it was better if I was out of the country for a while. Either because he had received a satisfying explanation, or because he now believed he was living with a murderer, he never brought up the question again.

My motivations were different than my teachers' and unintelligible to my host-family, and there I was in a Romanian language class, there I was reading

Eminescu and Stănescu. Here it begins, in this conflicted space of shifting tectonic plates. The small poem takes on the effect of a classic over the ensuing decades, for me, on the scale of an individual life. From that moment in the classroom, the poem lazes in my heart and accumulates a heap of emotional resonances. The first time I remember understanding a joke in *Academia Cațavencu*, the Romanian satirical newspaper, it was parodying Stănescu's "Poem." I remember flirting in a Romanian disco, with a woman who seemed impressed I could recite the poem from memory. When I returned to the United States and began graduate school in translation, I turned to Stănescu, only to find a famous visitor to the translation workshop, at the other end of the seminar table, flirting with me. When I began to teach translation, Romanian texts such as this one were pedagogically useful because they created a level field—the great majority of my students do not know the language. I created a translation exercise around the poem's four lines, so that students could practice translating the shifting tone (is the first word, "speak" or "say" or "what if"?). I taught this class many times, until the course was removed from the catalog, and I estimate that by 2011 over 450 students had translated "Poem," making it what has to be the most translated work of Romanian literature in history.

In 2011, Jill Schoolman, editor of Archipelago Books, had dinner with a Romanian ex-patriot doctor, writer, and translator who bent her ear about his favorite Romanian poet. Jill and I met at a conference, and she proposed I translate a selection of Stănescu's poems, which ended up numbering about 200, one of which was "Poem." Of all the texts in *Wheel with a Single Spoke*, I felt most overwhelmed by these four lines, one of the shortest in the collection. In fact, I have never had, and cannot imagine having a translation experience similar to this attempt to translate this poem that had been my companion for many years. When I tried out an English phrase to match the Romanian, I felt as though I plucked a guitar string, but a string where one end was tied to the bridge in the present, and the other end was not tied to a tuning peg but to a far-off Romanian classroom, one that leaned and rolled toward me and away, slackening and increasing the tension, resounding in vibrations only I could hear, because only I had lived through them.

The first word, "Spune," recalled our Romanian language lessons on vocabulary for shopping, because Bucharest market vendors and shop clerks alike address clients with the "polite" form of the same imperative, "spuneți." My Peace Corps cohort, used to American capitalism's "may I help you," thought it was delightfully rude to be addressed with, "Say it." We liked it so much we named our newsletter, "Spuneți." There's an aggressive solicitation in the first word that a "literal" translation, "say," would not create. I hesitated over the first word of "Poem" the longest: speak? hey? My choice of "tell me" seemed to me as much imperative as reflexive, a ringing bell that tells for the speaker. The link to neophyte Americans' encounters with post-Communist market merchants is so attenuated in the published version as to be inaudible. For me alone, our bemusement resonates in a welcome way with Stănescu's self-ironizing tone.

The effect of the 450 students who translated the text is easier to notice: they taught me to hear a particular lightness. They worked from a trot I prepared, and we discussed the text in class, working through each line to the tricky dative of possession in the last ("you to me crush the kiss" meaning "you crush my kiss"). They revised their translations in groups, comparing their solutions to those of their classmates. The readings and solutions they produced, even in their lack of knowledge of Romanian, were so convincing that they made me believe in the "translator's clairvoyance" Wai-Lim Yip diagnoses in Ezra Pound. Several students, over the years, offered the insight that Stănescu's title, "Poem," seemed off-hand, as though there were nothing to say about the text aside from naming its genre, in the broadest possible way. Yet in English, "Poem" sounded lapidary; it seemed to promise not nothing but everything, a summation of the genre. To avoid this tone, all that was needed was the indefinition of an indefinite article: "A Poem." Translation choices are often as small as this, as a single letter. That "a" stands in my translation as an acknowledgment of my students' work.

Yet Stănescu's poem didn't fully become a personal classic until a moment in New York, in 2012. Jill Schoolman and Corina Suteu, the erstwhile, stellar director of the Romanian Cultural Institute, arranged a launch for *Wheel with a Single Spoke* at Poets House, in lower Manhattan, hosted by Stephen Motika. Earlier that day, I had lunched with a friend and his girlfriend; I knew him from graduate school, and he shared a name with the poet I would read that evening. My friend's life had changed since he finished his doctorate: he had left the academy and parted with his wife, and now worked in sickness and in health as a lawyer. While he was in the bathroom, his girlfriend asked me probing questions about his capacity to love. Feeling nostalgic and disoriented, I wandered afterwards through this city I did not know, where each turn in Central Park reminded me of a Woody Allen movie, or *Home Alone II*. After a quick dinner, I met Jill, Corina, and a Romanian actor at the venue, a glass-wrapped building overlooking the Hudson.

The evening was scheduled to include a presentation about Stănescu, my reading from the translation, and the originals read by a Romanian actor—not Derek Jacobi but an ex-pat drama student. I had sent a list of poems I intended to read, but the actor, I learned, only received them shortly before the evening of the launch and had not rehearsed all of them. In particular, he had not prepared "Poem." I winced. I asked him politely if he could add those four lines to the list. He winced. But his generosity won out, and he began to read the poem over and over, out loud, first with the page and then by memory, repeating the poem more than a hundred times. I thought of my students translating the poem over and over, and of Stănescu reciting Eminescu from memory, over and over. With everything arranged and the evening descending outside, the actor's low voice droned around me as I gazed over the people slowly arriving in the hall. My eyes rose to look through the large window that gave onto the river and the lights of traffic on the opposite bank. When I focused again on the interior of the hall, I saw, in the last row of chairs, a Romanian friend whom I first met in 1994, the language tutor Peace Corps had hired for me after training. I went to greet her, not completely sure she was really present, as though I were reaching for a ghost. She had immigrated to the United States some ten years before, was now a citizen and teaching English as a second language in Brooklyn. She sat in that seat all during the reading, including the moment when the actor read "Poem" and I read "A Poem," and I felt that all of us were the hum of a string that stretched out far behind us, and ahead of us, until it faded from view.

Given the changes involved in even an ordinary life such as mine, I prefer this version of the micro-classic to the macro-classic. This version is a complicated and conflicted alternative to the canonical. While the points of resonance I feel may be idiosyncratic, I value them more for their aleatory progression. I value them for the translations they produce. "Poem" is different than "A Poem." The first is a very well-known poem in Romania, but not here. I know the relationship of the first and the second in a way I can only describe as personal—a classic only I know. This difference in translation is one of many such shifts I've tried to describe, and changes that continue to accrue: I've stopped teaching the translation class, Peace Corps is no longer in Romania, my host-father and host-mother have died, their daughter-in-law was committed to a mental hospital, I've lost touch with the son, and the earlier passage, about Eminescu's linden, is the first of Stănescu's writing I have translated in nearly a decade. Yet this personal classic persists, even as I take up, in a digressive manner, Nichita's poem as its definition. If this collection calls us to define the classic, I answer: a hum.

Works Cited

Anderson, Benedict. *Imagined Communities*. Rev. ed. Verso, 2016.
Appiah, Anthony Kwame. "Thick Translation." *The Translation Studies Reader*, Ed. Lawrence Venuti. 3rd ed. Routledge, 2012.

Bauman, Zygmunt. "Intellectuals in East-Central Europe: Continuity and Change." *In Search of Central Europe*, Ed. George Schöpflin and Nancy Wood. Barnes and Noble Books, 1989, pp. 70–90.
Boia, Lucian. *Mihai Eminescu, romanul absolut: Facerea și desfacerea unui mit*. Humanitas, 2015.
Cotter, Sean. "Translator's Afterward." In Stănescu, *Wheel*.
Damrosch, David. *What Is World Literature?* Princeton UP, 2003.
Dumnitrescu Bușulenga, Zoe, ed. *Antologia poeziei românești*. Editura Didactică și Pedagogică, 1974.
Peace Corps. "Changing Lives The World Over." www.peacecorps.gov/about.
Sappho. *If Not, Winter: Fragments of Sappho*. Trans. Anne Carson. Vintage, 2003.
Stănescu, Nichita. *Cartea de recitire*. Cartea Românească, 1972.
Stănescu, Nichita. *Opera poetică*. Humanitas, 1999.
Stănescu, Nichita. *Wheel with a Single Spoke*. Trans. Sean Cotter. Archipelago Books, 2012.
Verdery, Katherine. *National Ideology under Socialism*. U of California P, 1992.
Yip, Wai-Lim. *Ezra Pound's Cathay*. Princeton UP, 1969.

14

From Arabic to English, What Is a Classic?

Michelle Hartman

"It's the political rather than the personal that's most engaging for the foreign reader, since there are some truths only a storyteller can tell," reads the *New York Times*'s review of a novel I recently translated from Arabic to English, *The 99th Floor*, by Jana Elhassan. But contrary to this reviewer's confident assertion, I in fact chose to translate this novel precisely because of its in-depth exploration of "the personal." An intimate portrait of how traumatized people can (and cannot) love after living through some of the world's cruelest violence, it was the exploration of the psyche of the novel's characters that drew me in. Indeed, much to the contrary of what the reviewer states, the exploration of what is overtly "political" in the *99th Floor* is not important in and of itself but only insofar as it engages the personal. But then again, the personal is political—as the feminist slogan we have heard repeated since the 1960s goes.

Can we separate the personal and political? And even if we could, why would this "foreign reader" prefer the political to the personal? I dwell on the *New York Times* reviewer's declaration and its underlying assumptions because I find it indicative of the wide gulf separating an understanding of Arabic literature on its own terms, in its own contexts, and the reception of Arabic literature when it travels to English-language audiences. It also raises a question I will not spend time here on here: Who, exactly, is this "foreign reader" so interested in the political but not the personal? This crude division between the "personal" and "political"—neatly separated in Arab contexts for this purported "foreign reader"—has the effect of depersonalizing, decontextualizing, and even dehumanizing Arab people: quite the opposite of what we usually understand the role of literature in translation to be.

It is within this fraught context that the translation of the classics of Arabic literature happens. The importance of what this literary tradition is, and what is important, interesting, or engaging about it in English translation, clearly is easily lost in translation. This makes it all the more crucial to think about how we define what a classic of Arabic literature in English is in the first place.

Thus, I framed this chapter as a question: What is a classic? In what follows, I explore some of the dynamics of how Arabic works are considered classics in English translation. I also examine the role translation plays in making works into classics (or not!) in the twenty-first-century context that is so impacted by the globalization of literature, literary markets, and capital flows. Following this, I look in detail at the role gender, genre, and region all have in the making of what a classic is, from Arabic to English.

Arabic Literature and the *Arabian Nights*

As my comment about Jana Elhassan's novel indicates, I am a translator of Arabic fiction into English, specialized in women's writing, particularly from Lebanon, Syria, and Palestine. In English-speaking circles what I do is often received as unusual, overly specialized, and even rarefied. Years ago, when asked what she did, my colleague Bouthaina Shaaban was continually met with the question "Arab women writers, are there any?" She wrote about this in an article of the same name in 1993 (Shaaban). While I have not been asked this so bluntly, the general lack of knowledge in the English-speaking world about the active and diverse Arabic literary scene is still striking. This is as true of my university colleagues who work in other areas of literary studies as it is the educated general public. Suffice it to say that only last year, in response to me introducing myself and what I did to a colleague, a literature professor in another department of my university replied, "So you translate Arabian literature then?"

Mistaking Arabian for Arabic is not just a slip of the tongue. It indicates something about the conflation of a rich and long literary tradition produced in a language—Arabic—and the single text that is understood to be the classic work of this tradition—the *Arabian Nights* (*Alf layla wa layla*, also known as the *1001 Nights*). An entire tradition collapsed in one work might indicate this work's status of a classic, I believe. If there is one single work translated from Arabic into English and well known in a wide range of English-language contexts, it is this one.

To anyone knowledgeable about Arabic literary traditions, this points up the dissonant fact that the *1001 Nights* is simply not considered "a classic" in Arabic. It is not that these stories are not well known or well loved, but rather that they are not considered great, or even good, Arabic literature, regionally, nationally, or in pan-Arab contexts. A literary work with a fascinating translation history not only in English but also in French, the *Arabian Nights* took on a considerably different life in European contexts than it ever did or has in the Arab world. This meant the work rose to a status in those languages it still does not have in Arabic. In Arab contexts, these are tales a grandparent might tell before bed—relegated to the role of cultural artifact, but not Literature with capital L.

The contrast between charming folk tales and a great literary classic recalls the *New York Times* reviewer's interest in politics over the personal in that both show a profound difference in what is considered important. Many people have written about this disconnect in relation to the *1001 Nights*; there are a quite a few studies detailing the translation history of this work from Arabic into English. Several factors converge to produce this work as a classic, not the least of which is the appetite for exotic stories of the East, replete with the Orientalism and attendant racism that Edward Said named in his work of the same name in 1978.

A convergence of factors therefore shapes the answer to the question that I am asking in this chapter: What is a classic from Arabic to English? The first is an understanding of what is literary in Arabic and in English. There is a basic lack of education in the English-speaking world about what makes Arabic literature literary—partly because English and Arabic works define the literary differently. Another factor is a general lack of attention to the poetics and aesthetics of Arabic literary works in favor of other concerns, particularly politics, cultural difference and understanding, or exotic explorations. The long history of Orientalism and racism toward Arabs overcodes English-language responses to literary works in English translation.

The *1001 Nights* is an obvious example of these processes at work. Like classics written in other languages, there are multiple translations of this work into English. And all of these are very different. Comparing them can help to make clear some of the dynamics in the process of translating this work "as a classic." But other examples of Arabic literature—even those considered classics in Arabic—have received nowhere near the same amount of attention. Indeed, there is very little Arabic literature in translation at all. Moreover, many works considered undisputed "classics" in Arabic literature have never been translated, or published, in English and there are very few retranslations or multiple translations of texts—ancient or modern.

Making Classics: From the *Nights* to Naguib Mahfouz

At the same time, translation into English is very important to the Arabic-language literary scene today. The global dynamics of capitalism and globalization, together with English-language hegemony and US imperialism, allow translation to play an increasingly important role in actually making works into "classics." Arab writers accrue social and literary capital—if relatively little monetary compensation—through the translation of their work into English. Arabic literary works gain credibility through their translation into English, as well as by winning the newly proliferating prizes, some of which explicitly promote translation like the so-called Arab Booker Prize (or more formally, the International Prize for Arab Fiction [IPAF]). All this gives disproportionate power to English-language translators, critics, and even professors of literature to state and determine what is and what should deserve to be considered a "classic."

I can supplement this with another concrete example from my experience. A few years ago, I edited a book, *Teaching Modern Arabic Literature in Translation*, which was published by the Modern Language Association in 2018. This was an exciting project to be involved in. It was only the second volume dealing with Arabic literature ever published by this prestigious association, which dominates the study and teaching of literature in the United States. The volume preceding this one was dedicated to teaching the works of Naguib Mahfouz, published in 2012, which many felt was itself overdue coming twenty-four years after his Nobel Prize. To date, of course, Mahfouz is still the only Arabic-language author to have won the award. From the time he won the Nobel, Mahfouz has been the go-to representative modern Arab author, leading to the canonization of his works in the West. Probing more deeply, others have suggested his gentle challenges to patriarchy while ultimately upholding it, his fetishization of a bourgeois image of Egypt's past and his "Western friendly" attitudes that uphold a certain status quo also contributed to his lionization in translation and subsequent fame.

My proposed volume on teaching modern Arabic literature in translation covered a range of more and less known works—I chose pieces that engage a wide and diverse, but also representative, range of Arabic literature, including prose and poetry, works by men and women, more and less canonical. But it must have been Mahfouz's fame that led the editorial board of the MLA to insist that I could not publish the volume without at least one chapter dedicated to Naguib Mahfouz. Whatever the reasons, a group of US-based literary scholars decided that Mahfouz's works were such important "classics" that no volume on modern Arabic literature could be published without him.

I challenged the recommendation of the board and won my appeal. This process caused me to reflect on my time as a university student of Arabic literature in the wake of this prize in the 1990s. We were reminded regularly by our professors of Arabic literature that Mahfouz was not the stylist of the under-translated Edward al-Kharrat, or as popular as the better-known Ihsan Abdel Quddous—a glaring example of a widely known and respected author whose works have not yet been translated at all in 2020. And just to put this into a broader perspective given the range and breadth of Arabic literature—all three of these are Egyptian male authors, the dominant gender writing in the most prominent location in the Arab world. One thing our teachers missed out, as I will suggest later, is the works of Latifa al-Zayyat, for example, which could be considered just as much "classics" as that of these men. Her impact on generations of writers, both male and female, who came after her is massive. While her output may not be as prolific, it is certainly as profound. Furthermore, why is it so rare to consider works from Arab locations outside Egypt as classics? In what follows I discuss what makes a classic by examining three things: Arab women's writing, regions of the Arab world, and genre—and thinking about classics of poetry and prose.

Arab Feminist Classics: Are There Any?

While it may be widely recognized today that there is a great deal of Arab women's writing, defining these works as Arabic "classics" presents a greater problem. As mentioned, Latifa al-Zayyat's works might be understood as classics of Arabic fiction; *The Open Door* (*Al Bab al maftuh*, 1960) certainly is a feminist classic. A sweeping tale of a woman's personal and political coming-of-age story against the backdrop of Egypt's anti-colonial struggles in the 1940s and 1950s, it bears all the hallmarks of a work that will stand the test of time. Translated into English by well-respected translator Marilyn Booth and published by the American University in Cairo Press in 2012, it was reissued and made more widely available in paperback by their Hoopoe imprint in 2017.

Even as I propose this novel as an Arab feminist classic, I am once again aware of the translational dynamics between Arabic and English that make other works much better known and visible than al-Zayyat's. Even with this paperback version available, it has only been in print for three years and her two other shorter works—*The Owner of the House* (*Sahib al-bayt*, 1994) and *The Search* (Awraq Shakhsiyyah: *Hamlat taftish*, 1992)—are both out of print in North America. Contrast this with the more prolific Nawal El Saadawi based in North America before her passing, who is much more likely to be recognized and recognizable in the English language. The author of numerous memoirs, semi-autobiographical novels, and other fictional works, Saadawi made a name for herself in and through translation. In addressing her exposure and fame in English, an even more vehement case against Saadawi has been made by Arab critics than the one against Mahfouz. While some of this is overlaid with overt and implicit sexism, several critiques do hold—her work does dovetail with stereotypes and assumptions about "oppressed" Arab women, even if some of this is produced in the translation process. It is then all the more interesting to note that the themes and issues that have brought Saadawi attention in translation contrast with those most prominent in the work of al-Zayyat. The women depicted in her work are more easily pigeonholed into the three classic categories Arab women occupy in translation according to critic and poet Mohja Kahf: victim, escapee, and pawn.

As a translator of women's fiction, I am struck by not only how little work by Arab women is translated but also how remarkably powerful the hold of these limiting categories is in English-language environments. So many works that one might think of as Arab feminist classics are still not translated. The novel I was somewhat obsessed with in graduate school, Layla Balabakki's "I Am Alive!" (*Ana Ahya!*, 1958) thought to be one of the first fully formed women's novels in Arabic, is still not translated into English. It is often mentioned in the same breath as Colette Khuri's "Days with Him" (*Ayyam ma'hu*, 1961), which has not yet appeared in English either. The year 2020—in which I am writing this chapter—saw the first translation into English of a work certainly considered to be a feminist classic, Palestinian Sahar Khalifeh's *Passage to the Plaza* (*Bab al-Saha*, 1990). These classics are not the only works by women to be overlooked in English, I will return to another example in the section on poetry later.

Can the (So-called) Peripheries Produce Classics?

All the authors I have mentioned thus far hail from what one might call the "center" of the Arab world, rather than the "peripheries," if these are indeed the right terms to use. Poets and novelists who would be easily recognized as authors of modern classics might include Naguib Mahfouz, Ihsan Abdel Quddous, or Edward al-Kharrat; women writers like Nawal El Saadawi, Latifa al-Zayyat, Layla Baalbaki, Colette Khuri, and Sahar Khalifeh; poets such as Mahmoud Darwish and Nizar Qabbani, who I will discuss later; even the newer author Jana Elhassan whom I translated—all of these writers hail from Egypt, Syria, Lebanon, or Palestine. The importance of region may be largely overlooked in English translations where the Arab world tends to be conflated as one homogeneous, faraway place, flattening its contours and distinctions. Deeming works from these locations as able to produce classics, with few exceptions, is even more notable as translation becomes more important and shapes the local consumption of Arabic literature.

An author who can help us to think through some of these processes is Sudanese Tayeb Salih. His *Season of Migration to the North* (*Mawsim al-hijra ila al-shamal*, 1966) has circulated in English very successfully, as a postcolonial novel. A favorite of literature classes focusing on works from non-Western locations, it is read as Arab and African in turn, and can be seen in this way as a "postcolonial literary classic." While Saleh certainly is respected and has a following in Arab literary circles, perhaps even enough to make his work a classic, I would classify him as the exception that proves the rule of center—periphery dynamics.

Another case that will be interesting to follow, in the coming years, is the 2019 Booker International prize-winning novelist Jokha al-Harthi. Her *Celestial Bodies* (*Sayyidat al-qamar*, 2010) surprised the Arabic literary world by bringing home this important international prize. An Omani author whom many Arab readers and even critics were unfamiliar with, al-Harthi tells a multigenerational tale of three women's lives, impacted by histories of slavery, in the rapidly modernizing Omani society of the twentieth century. Will *Celestial Bodies* become known as a classic because it won such a large prize, following the example of Mahfouz? Can his happen even though her author is Omani and a woman? Or will she remain somewhat peripheral to the Arabic literary scene as predetermined by the geographical marginalization of her region?

Genre

While gender and region both have a strong pull over how literary works are read and understood as important, genre determines what is and is not a classic in Arabic in even more striking terms. It is not an exaggeration to say that in relation to the Arabic literary tradition overall, poetry is by far the more important genre and the one deemed to have produced most—of not all—Arabic classics.

But up to this point I have hardly mentioned poetry! Like so many Arabic-English translators working today, I am rather biased toward novels. This is partly because poetry is beyond the scope of my translational expertise. Moreover, I focus here mainly on the modern, partly because there are few if any novels produced in Arabic before the twentieth century. The question of period is important here—in this chapter I have only talked about "modern classics," it would take another person with different expertise to write about "classical classics." But it is so crucial here to mention period in relation to genre, because the vast majority of literary work in Arabic considered "classic" by Arabs is poetry.

Likely none of the classic Arabic-language poets are household names in English-speaking environments, whereas Imru al-Qays, Abu Nuwas, al-Mutanabbi, or even al-Khansa' are names that trip off the tongues of most Arabs even if they are not particularly interested in literature. There are many modern poets who are well regarded across the Arabic world—like Mahmoud Darwish and Nizar Qabbani to name only two—as well as others with more local or regional fame. But it is important that in English even the collections of the most famous modern poets like Darwish and Qabbani would likely not be understood as "classics," except in specific contexts or for particular reasons.

We like novels better in English, in general. The genre of the novel is familiar, recognizable, and more respected in English than in Arabic. Because the content of a novel is often easier to understand and digest than a poem, or collection of poetry; novels tend to travel in translation better. Even without the specific challenges that Arabic poetry poses to the English translator, poetry is more about language, style, and form, rather than "content" or a story.

But in Arabic, what is understood as classic in any real sense is always poetry. The dearth of poetry in translation in English then is even more striking in trying to think about what is a classic. There are many academic studies of classical Arabic poetry that have translations in them. There are some attempts to capture poetic beauty of the pre-Islamic *Mu'allaqat*, as in the case of Michael Sells's *Desert Tracings* (1989), but by and large there is very little available.

If this is the case of the classical classics, then what of the modern classics? When I started teaching Arabic literature in English in 1999, I could not assign the works of Mahmoud Darwish—there was no collection of his poetry in print in North America at the time. This has since been corrected, but few other Arabic poets have appeared in English translation. No example here is better to bring together how classics do and do not become known in translation than Nazik al-Mala'ika. An Iraqi woman poet, al-Mala'ika is widely viewed as the founder of the free verse movement in modern Arabic poetry. Her work is as important to the development of modern poetry in Arabic as that of any other poet. Then why is it that the very first collection of her poetry is only published in 2021, under the title, *Revolt against the Sun* (*Thawra 'ala al-shams*)?

What Is a Classic?

This chapter has perhaps asked as many questions as it has answered. And my working through some of the ways in which Arabic literary works are and are not considered classics is highly selective. While the specific examples given here can be critiqued, debated, and replaced, the broad stroke of what I am presenting in relation to the translation of modern Arabic literary classics into English is less controversial. The state of Arabic-English translation and the ways in which it forms and shapes the production of works as classics overcode everything I am writing about here. I may not have answered what a classic is from Arabic to English, but hope to have provided some ways to think about this question and the process of translation itself.

Works Cited

Baalabakki, Layla. *Ana Ahya!* Dar al-Adab, 1958.
al-Harthi, Jokha. *Celestial Bodies*. Trans. Marylin Booth. Sandstone P, 2018.
al-Harthi, Jokha. *Sayyidat al-qamar*. Dar al-Adab, 2010.
Khuri, Colette. *Ayyam ma'hu*. Dar al-Anwar, 1958.
al-Mala'ika, Nazik. *Revolt Against the Sun: Selected Poetry of Nazik al-Mala'ika.* Saqi Books, 2021.
Salih, Tayeb. *Season of Migration to the North*. Heinemann, 1970.
Sells, Michael. *Desert Tracings: Six Classic Arabian Odes by 'Alqama, Shanfara, Labid,'Antara, al-A 'sha, and Dhu al-Rumma*. Wesleyan UP, 1989.
Shaaban, Bouthaina. "Arab Women Writers: Are There Any?" *Washington Report on Middle East Affairs*, February 1993, pp. 36–7.
al-Zayyat, Latifa. *Al-Bab al-maftuh*. Al-Ha'iah al-masriyyah al-'amah lil-kitab, 1960.
al-Zayyat, Latifa. *Awraq Shakhsiyyah: Hamlat taftish*. Al-Ha'iah al-masriyyah al-'amah lil-kitab, 1992.
al-Zayyat, Latifa. *The Open Door: A Novel*. Oxford UP, 2004.
al-Zayyat, Latifa. *The Owner of the House*. Quartet, 1997.
al-Zayyat, Latifa. *Sahib al-bayt*. Dar Hilal, 1994.
al-Zayyat, Latifa. *The Search: Personal Papers*. Quartet, 1996.

15

Translating a Classic into the Future

Tómas Jónsson—Bestseller

Lytton Smith

A 36-inch wooden statue on a mantelpiece, a neatly bearded gentleman holding a book in one hand and a fine sword in the other hand. Don Quixote, the eponymous protagonist of Miguel de Cervantes's novel—that first European novel, the original. This statue was a remnant of a time my father had lived before I was born, and it sat on the mantelpieces and sideboards of the houses we called home in Spain, in England, and in Germany. This statue seemed, sometimes, to be my whole childhood. The games of balloon soccer were never allowed to knock it over; it repelled horseplay. There, always, in the foreground or the background, the statue was the story of reading, of imagining, of not being able to unimagine.

The statue was Don Quixote but, I would learn, Sancho Panza, a peasant laborer, was missing. My parents had been able to afford one statue of a set of two for sale in a high-end department store; they brought home the Don. Cervantes, whom the late Harold Bloom called "the central western author" (alongside Shakespeare), cannot have imagined this mantelpiece statue, the boy looking up at it, noting its absent companion, can he? I was too young to understand the complex figurations that took place as I regarded a wooden statue that literalized a character from a novel I'd yet to read, a novel in which "the spiritual atmosphere of a Spain already in steep decline can be felt throughout" (Bloom, again), "thanks to the heightened quality of her diction"—her being the translator, Edith Grossman (Bloom, "The Knight in the Mirror" n.p.).

* * *

In "Mess with a Classic," a series of 2019 *Paris Review* columns, the writer Elisa Gabbert "revisits canonical works of literature and addresses the anxiety of confronting the art of the past" (Gabbert, "Proust and the Joy of Suffering," n.p.). Gabbert writes that "my husband and I and two friends decided to start a 'Stupid Classics Book Club,'" comprising "all the corny stuff from the canon that we really should have read in school but never did" (Gabbert, "The Stupid Classics Book Club" n.p.). Gabbert clarifies "stupid" not as a synonym for idiotic but for "rehashed into cliché over time by multiple film adaptations and Simpsons episodes" (Gabbert, "The Stupid Classics Book Club"). The "stupid classic" reveals the way culture treats classics rather than passing judgment on books like *The Strange Case of Dr. Jekyll and Mr. Hyde*, *Frankenstein*, and *The Bell Jar*.

When we read a classic, even or especially a "stupid classic," we often encounter the distortions and diffractions arising from versions of the story we think we know, versions we've heard from friends, teachers, television shows, memes, and so on. Classics, endlessly parodied, adapted, versioned, and pastiched, end up a part of us even if we've never cracked the spines of their books. Reading *The Strange Case of Dr. Jekyll and Mr. Hyde*, Gabbert at first finds it "pretty much aligned with the version I'd absorbed through cultural references and cartoons." However, the familiarity of Stevenson's story breaks at the last chapter, the moment the "classic" deviates from the popular version of the classic: "I had no inkling of this part of the story, which now seems to me infinitely richer and more complex than I'd imagined" (Gabbert, "The Stupid Classics Book Club"). Gabbert discovers that a classic is hidden from us by our preconceptions of it. We believe we know a story because we've heard so much about a classic book—but it's precisely because we've heard so much about a book that we don't know its story. In a sense, a classic book seems to exist entirely in the past; it has no future for us, for it seems there's no need to read it.

For a translator, this presents a particular problem quite unlike, say, a *Simpsons* riff on *The Shining*. A translator is almost by definition working with material that's not familiar to their imagined readers. While re-translations pose an exception, with any translator of *Don Quixote* having to contend with the versions a reader knows or thinks they know, translators often bring into the reader's language a work that is by and large new to it: lexically, culturally, and geographically. The book may be a classic in the language the translator is working from and may aspire to obtain classic status within the target language's cultures, but at the moment of translating it, the translator complicates its status in both cultures, destabilizing any secure sense of what a classic is.

Take the case of Guðbergur Bergsson's *Tómas Jónsson Metsölubók*, first published in Iceland in 1966 and which I translated for Open Letter forty years later, its first Anglophone publication, in 2017. The book's very title, *Tómas Jónsson—Bestseller*, invokes and plays with ideas of popularity and personality, suggesting a work haunted by ideas of reception. Is the book in the reader's hands a bestseller? Is Tómas Jónsson himself a bestseller? If—and it is *if*—the book is an Icelandic bestseller, is it an Anglophone one? At the time of writing, the book's lone, 1-star Amazon.com review, courtesy of Mrs. J. Cooke of the United Kingdom, responds "Awful. I don't think I got beyond the first couple of chapters. Just weird and twisted—might be to someone else's taste[.]"

That review and the questions of taste it raises are eerily in line with the book's own, diffident relationship to notions of what a classic is or should be—and whether the term is even wanted in the novel's world. *Bestseller*, weighing in at over 400 genre-confounding pages with little coherence in narrative perspective or plot causality, published in three Icelandic editions, each revising the previous, resists many readers. Like *Finnegan's Wake* or *Infinite Jest*, *Bestseller* is a book that people might be more likely to own than have finished, falling neatly into Gabbert's "should have read" category. Ostensibly telling the story of a solitary, memory-challenged, disgruntled, retired bank clerk who is guilty of reprehensible actions yet capable of profound meditation, the novel is marked by elusive discursion and self-correction more than by plot. As the critic Birna Bjarnadóttir explains, the novel

> stirs up long-standing notions about certain classical literary values [...] and undermines the kind of rhetoric that has been thought to secure cultural values in Iceland. (*Recesses of the Mind* 195)

Part of the challenge *Bestseller* lays down for the reader (and the translator) is its relentlessly ironic and disruptive quality. At one point, the novel's narrator, ostensibly but not self-evidently the Tómas Jónsson of the book's title, reflects on the relationship between life and writing, reaching two conclusions. First, he appears to reject fictive invention in favor of factual writing: "nothing should be left but writing biographies," he decides, because "fictions are useless to every *living* human" (*Tómas Jónsson—Bestseller* 98):

> Should a writer, however, construct some narrative that does not exist in reality but rather takes reality's place, i.e. the only true *fiction*, fantasy and imagination, then no one can understand it but the writer himself. (*Tómas Jónsson—Bestseller* 97–8)

The potential of fiction, Tómas contends, is also its impossibility: the more a writer succeeds in imagination, the further they get from a reader. Tómas's understanding of imaginative writing as leaving the reader behind prefigures our relationship with classic books: their reputations, seeming to precede them, replace their being read—or, if read, being read with fresh eyes.

Tómas's second conclusion directly addresses this notion of the classic:

> I never felt the day had properly reached evening unless I had read a few pages, sometimes starting in the earliest morning. Here I refer of course to reading good books, classic works, edifying subjects, preferably scientific literature written for the masses; or, something that allows the reader access to the dream world that is the future. (*Tómas Jónsson—Bestseller* 98)

"Góðra bóka, sígildra verka, uppbyggilegra viðfangsefna" (*Tómas Jónsson Metsölubók* 122)—good books, classic works, and edifying subjects—are Tómas's staples. *Sígildur* is one of two words chiefly used for "classic" in Icelandic, the other being the German-derived *klassiker*. *Sígildur* connotes a thing of lasting value; *gildur*, from which it is formed, has the sense of valid, prominent, valent, as well as thick or fat.[1] Even as Tómas repeats the cliché that a classic is something popular, "for the masses," he also imagines it is biographical and scientific, conveying a knowledge that is new for the reader. It's precisely this potential for a book that underpins the meaning of *sígildur*: it derives power from its prominence, from being "something that allows the reader access to the dream world that is the future."

Given Tómas's rejection of "fantasy or imagination," what might he mean by this dream world? What he sees in it, I'd argue, is a glimpse of futurity, of something yet to come. The classic *sígildur*, with the prefix *sí-* connoting something "always, continually," operates less as a work that has stood the test of time—rooted in mythologic status, set on a pedestal—than as one that conjures a world to come, the dream world, *draumaheima*.

Tómas does not, then, observe a binary between fiction and nonfiction, imagination and scientific accuracy. He instead conceives of reading and writing as essentially prefigurative acts. The novel's opening chapter is titled "Ævisaga," biography, the word Tómas also uses in his theory of what should be written. Three words into the book's fifth sentence, however, its incipient narrative breaks:

> I am descended from the bravest, bluest-eyed Vikings. I am related to courtly poets and victorious kings. I am an Icelander. My name is Tómas Jónsson. I am old
>
> no, no (*Tómas Jónsson—Bestseller* 3)

---

[1] "Sígildur" in Hólmarsson, Sanders, and Tucker.

Tómas is quite literally, on a syntactical level, breaking with the past, rejecting a sense of illustrious lineage. Instead, Bergsson's novel offers a series of seventeen "composition books," as if not actually meant for publication. Discussing *Bestseller* subsequently, Bergsson would encase it in a set of nesting dolls of authorship: "*Tómas Jónsson Bestseller* is not composed by Tómas Jónsson, a bank employee, but its material is separate from him, comes from notebooks. The work was written by two men [Hermann and Svanur] who had rented from him in the basement apartment; they loosely arrange the material" ("Formáli" ["Foreword"], *Tómas Jónsson Metsölubók* 10).

Bestseller is a kind of escapist autofiction in which Tómas tries to write himself out of his own decay, despondency, and imminent death. What is at stake isn't immortality but a kind of melding of the biological with the biographical. Throughout his composition books, Tómas repeatedly obsesses with a book being written about him, or writing a book about himself, mapping his own body onto the act of writing: "Ég er að skrifa af mér vörtur, kynfæri og útlimi og tunguna líka til þess að ég ljúgi ekki í skáldverkinu Tómas Jónsson metsölubók" (*Tómas Jónsson Metsölubók* 389) ("I am writing about my warts, genitals and limbs and tongue also so that I do not lie in the novel, Tómas Jónsson, Bestseller" (*Tómas Jónsson—Bestseller* 346). His attempts to be as physical as his book, or for his book to be as physical as him, lead to its existence, enacting a metafictional and self-fulfilling prophecy: Tómas writes his own *draumaheima* only to find himself living in that future through the "loosely arranged" work produced by his tenants, Hermann and Svanur, who turn his notebooks into a book that both is and is not a biography and anatomy of Tómas in all his effluvia.

At the time of publication, *Bestseller* was described by critics in seismic terms, with Sigfús Daðason suggesting that it had "broken new reality into Icelandic literature."[2] The theme of a creation that breaks was taken up by several other early reviews, including Ólafur Jónsson, who wrote of how the book will be "with the passing of time considered groundbreaking in literature: the first truly contemporary Icelandic novel."[3] Jónsson's formulation here is telling: at the moment of its publication the "bestseller" classic can only anticipate being a classic, not claim that status. The classic is paradoxically defined, at least by Daðason and Jónsson, in terms of how

---

[2] "Guðbergur Bergsson hefur í ritum sínum brotið nýjum veruleika braut inn í íslenzkar bókmenntir." Quoted in Thorsson, Guðmundur Andri, "Regnbogar næturinnar" ("Night Rainbows") in *Tómas Jónsson Metsölubók* (2012), 464.
[3] "Þegar frá líður talin tímamótaverk í bókmenntunum: fyrsta virkilega nútímasagan á íslenzku."

alien it at first is—and, as Gabbert's experience reminds us, the classic often becomes strange, a new kind of species, when we do actually read it.

The act of translating a book is a particular, intense instance of the classic's unanticipated futurity, its status as yet-to-come. The leading scholar of modernism and of Icelandic literature, Ástráður Eysteinsson, has noted that the 1970s, just after *Bestseller* was published, saw a wave of translations into Icelandic, including in 1978 Bergsson's own translation of Gabriel García Márquez's *One Hundred Years of Solitude* (1967). This led to associations between Márquez's magical realism and Bergsson's own aesthetics; Eysteinsson himself writes of Bergsson as "diverting the Icelandic novel of contemporary life," a spatial metaphor that suggests a shift in the landscape, perhaps even in the country, of Icelandic literature (Eysteinsson, "Icelandic Prose Literature" 439). Eysteinsson reinforces that topographic metaphor as he describes the book as managing

> to leave the landscape of the Icelandic novel much altered. This revolution blew up the existing epic horizon of the novel, opened its form and structure, leaving no laws of tradition unquestioned. ("Icelandic Prose Literature" 423)

While Bergsson himself, reflecting on the book between its second and third editions, in 1992, recognized the alteration in physical space associated with it—the physical translation it represented—his own take at first seems rather less global and comparative. He grumbles, via the passive voice, "it was claimed that I had created in my works a village similar to Márquez's Macondo, only my village was Grindavík," a traditional Icelandic fishing town (Bjarnadóttir, "Recesses of the Mind" 62). For all that *Bestseller*'s readers and critics have frequently seen it as neorealist and revolutionary, Bergsson seems here to return it to something homespun, supremely realist, rather than aligning it with the metafictional possibilities of García Márquez and Cervantes, whom Bergsson also went on to translate.

Yet, as with Tómas's theory of art, something more complex is at stake here in Bergsson's aesthetics, with fascinating repercussions for our understanding of the translated classic. Bergsson follows up his rejection of Macondo in favor of Grindavík not with a rejection of magical realism but with a resituating of it:

> I think Icelandic readers did not have to go to South America to find a model or a similar technique in novel writing. This is also one of the many characteristics of the Sagas of the Icelanders [. . .] The method is Icelandic [. . .] to unite events, places, and times in the web of fate. (Bjarnadóttir, *Recesses of the Mind* 62)

Bergsson's point, I think, is not that *Tómas Jónsson—Bestseller* offers something fundamentally new in Icelandic literature, but something old—classical, we might say—yet forgotten and so new in spite of being old. Bergsson reclaims and rejuvenates Icelandic sagas and familiar motifs from Icelandic culture that have become hackneyed as much from a lack of clear-eyed engagement on the part of readers as from over-use by writers. We might think, here, of Gabbert's moment of recognition of what's surprising in *Dr. Jekyll and Mr. Hyde*: the classic text retains its potential to surprise precisely because we don't expect its innovations, thinking it exists in our past, not in our future. Could it be that what defines the classic is its potential to call into being some kind of *draumaheima*?

Translation becomes a part of the would-be classic's would-be future because it necessarily involves an encounter with the possibilities and potential of a book rather than with its meme-version. This dynamic encounter stems in part from the meanings proliferated between and across the languages a translator works in. For instance, "Tómas's Seventh Composition Book" begins with the Icelandic sentence "Ég, Tómas Jónsson, hertygja mig gegn lausung" (*Tómas Jónsson Metsölubók* 166): I, Tómas Jónsson, armor myself against . . . what? One option, "laxity," invokes the laxative, appropriate for a book whose narrator is happy to recount how "I energetically farted," a book which repeatedly discusses bodily emissions. Another, "permissiveness," spoke more to the narrator's sexual peccadilloes, his perversions and licentiousness. "Falseness," a third meaning of *lausung*, fits with the book's concern with the fictive and with the reliability of truth. The published translation reads, "I, Tómas Jónsson, armor myself against laxness" (*Tómas Jónsson—Bestseller* 140). "Laxness" offers a word with meaning both for Anglophone and Icelandic readers. In English, laxness, though partially obsolete (the Oxford English Dictionary's last quoted usages are, fittingly, from the late 1960s), is clear in meaning: Tómas is steeling himself to avoid unruly behavior. That reading is in keeping with the book's uneasy fascination with the sensory aspects of domestic space: at one point, Tómas listens in excruciating details to his lodgers having sex and joins in from the other side of the wall, imagining the wife's sweat stain against the wall. Tómas, enigma that he is, both gives in to secretions and seeks to "armor" against them, to keep prim and proper: "I have striven to create an ordered, organized home," he continues (*Tómas Jónsson—Bestseller* 140).

In an Icelandic context, "laxness" will also resonate as the last name of Halldór Laxness, the only Icelandic Nobel prizewinner in Literature. (Icelanders like to point out that, per capita, they've won more literature Nobel Prizes than any other country bar St. Lucia: 290 to St. Lucia's 533, with Sweden a distant third at 81 prizes per capita.)[4] Laxness's presence in translation isn't

---

[4] Source: https://stats.areppim.com/stats/stats_nobelxlitxcapita.htm.

a fortunate coincidence. In the previous chapter, a petit bourgeois group the book calls "The Board," who plot the future of the Icelandic nation and its culture over lunches in a Reykjavík canteen, have been discussing literature, with two of the men at the table "weigh[ing] in with moist sentences from a newly published Laxness novel" (*Tómas Jónsson—Bestseller* 120). The Board's discussion of politics, economics, and gender is impossible without their wrestling with Laxness's Nobel status, even to the extent that certain views about his work get the two men branded "stealth commies" (*Tómas Jónsson—Bestseller* 121). Literature, in this vision, is sociopolitical, the "class" in the classic. While *lausung* isn't a Laxness reference, and while there's not a pun on "lax" behavior and Laxness in Icelandic, the association of literature with bodily emissions and the challenges of avoiding being lax is something that troubles Tómas repeatedly. In one of the book's more fabulous passages, he describes inventing a device to seal around his nostrils during a shower and prevent water getting in them; his identity as a writer is never far from being bound up with all manner of bodily seepages. If translating *lausung* as laxness reveals this, it only does so in the unstable space between existing in Icelandic and in English.

Put another way: for *Metsólubók* to become *Bestseller*, whether or not it becomes a bestseller, and regardless of whether it was *Metsólubók* in 1960s Iceland, it also has to remain *Metsólubók*. If "laxness" belongs to "my" translation, it also belongs to Guðberger's novel, in various versions across its three editions, and to Tómas's composition books. In translating between languages and contexts, never settling only into one of them, "laxness" exists as a demonstration of what translating is: the threshold where we are neither in one language nor another, flickering between cultures that are themselves already altered from being national by global sites of cultural production. Grindavík is not Macondo, Bergsson insists, but in a strange quirk of futurity it was Macondo before Macondo was part of Bergsson's aesthetics, his Grindavík. That is, Bergsson can only recognize Iceland as being magically realist on its own terms before he ever read and translated Márquez because he went on to read Márquez; Grindavík, in being not Macondo, is a translation of Macondo, forever in a relationship with it, but never identical to it.

Iceland itself, whose tourist offices often style it in oxymoronic terms, "land of fire and ice," is a particularly fertile context for thinking about translating in such restless terms, a way of existing in more than one state or identity at once. Settled by exilic Norwegians at the expense of its few hermitic Celts; beholden variously to Norway and Denmark as sovereign powers and to Stockholm, Paris, and Rome as religious and cultural centers; shaped by its own seafaring threshold-crossing; geologically being slowly pulled apart by the tug of the so-called American and European tectonic plates: Iceland, only partly covered by ice, unlike Greenland, remains *sui generis*.

Tómas Jónsson—Bestseller, person and book, are indeed restless, never quite resolving into settled identity; one might read this novel as a series of energetic pulses more than as an Aristotelian achievement of beginning, middle, and end. At times, Tómas carries the flag for Icelandic nationalism, in ways that reject any diversity or heterogeneity; at others, he is a Puckish chameleon, ever reinventing himself in dialog with a world beyond Icelandic shores ("where Laxness is in order of world-famous writers" (*Tómas Jónsson— Bestseller* 323). In some senses, his awareness of European literary centers and influences anticipates his being translated into English. And yet his very laxness suggests he also remains fundamentally Icelandic, almost disinterested in what's beyond Iceland's shores other than oceans. Nevertheless, this is a book which ends with a ship out on those Icelandic oceans, an ending that recalls nothing more than *Moby-Dick*. Neither Bergsson nor Tómas wants to give up on Iceland or see it compared unfavorably to the world beyond it, and yet they also need that world beyond it in order to define Iceland's own *dramaheima*.

The lesson *Tómas Jónsson—Bestseller* teaches us about what a classic is, then, is less about whether a translation can be a classic than what we've misunderstood about classics. In 1966, as Bergsson published *Bestseller*, translating *One Hundred Years of Solitude* lies in his future, as does a translation of Don Quixote from 1981 to 1984, retranslated twenty-some years later, in 2002. Any translation of *Don Quixote* wrestles with the fact that it is *a* translation, not *the* translation of that "first" modern novel, first translated in 1612, just seven years after its Spanish publication. Tómas enacts an analogous process by constantly redefining and recasting himself and, in so doing, Icelandic literature and culture. Tómas's elusiveness as a character is an antidote to a fetishizing of the "original," a disruption of even the softer source versus target language, which still presupposes a unidirectional teleology for translation.

By contrast, the model Tómas offers for translation is one that reminds us of the historical and geographical crossings translating keeps making, as well as linguistic ones. Translating is what's yet to come, even after the book's been translated, just as *Tómas Jónsson's* future relies not on its being written in its seventeen composition books but in its fictional characters arranging them into a novel (or a biography, or a biology) that its factual author, Bergsson, publishes.

For the classic to have a future in translation, it must also await the reader who will be its translator. This Tómas imagines too: "Buy the bestseller by Tómas Jónsson, a book about a jerk that is being translated into seven foreign languages" (*Tómas Jónsson—Bestseller* 237). I was born the year Bergsson first translated *Don Quixote* into Icelandic, and Don Quixote was for much of my life my own "stupid classic": my father's favorite book, one he'd read in both Spanish and English (but not in Icelandic), its plots and language everywhere around me. I knew what it was to be quixotic or to tilt at windmills well before I was out of elementary school. I grew up thinking of *Don Quixote* as classic and, as in the past, kept alive by its adaptations and versions, the Broadway musicals and by a carved wooden statue of the Don himself, some three feet tall, on the mantelpieces of our childhood homes. *Don Quixote* both never needed to be read, being ever present in our home, and always lays in my future the missing puzzle piece to the story of my father's past.

My father never succeeded in tracking down the missing statue of Sancho Panza. Perhaps that's fitting given that *Don Quixote* is, among other things, the ur-text for failed or misprisioned quests. Bergsson, retranslating *Don Quixote*, enacts that process over twenty years, and embodies the sense that there is always a future where there is a classic: not a future for a classic as much as a future through or because of a classic.

In Icelandic, the word for world, *heimur*, shares something of the word for home, *heimili*, and the adverb *heima*, at home—although the correspondence might well strike a translator's eyes more than an Icelander's ears. A *draumaheima* is a dream world, but for the translator it might also be a dream one is at home in. Translating is an attempt to bridge home and world. At the end of *Bestseller*, three figures end up adrift on a lifeboat "on a sea of fog and darkness." None of them is Tómas, quite, but they are still "three drunk and doubting Tómases" (*Tómas Jónsson—Bestseller* 411). They contemplate sinking; they contemplate being rescued. They are on the threshold of the future, as Iceland was in the 1960s. Like a classic—like *Moby-Dick*, perhaps, like a wooden statue inspired by a classic novel—this ending is familiar. And yet its future is not. And yet it must be, if its story is to be (future perfect progressive tense) a classic.

Works Cited

Bergson, Guðberger, trans. *Don Kíkoti*. By Miguel de Cervantes. Ab, 1983; JPV, 2005.

Bergson, Guðberger, trans. *Hundrað ára einsemd*. By Gabriel Garcia Marquez. Mal og Menning, 1967.

Bergson, Guðberger. *Tómas Jónsson—Bestseller*. Trans. Lytton Smith. Open Letter, 2017.

Bergsson, Guðberger. *Tómas Jónsson Metsölubók*. Forlagið, 2012 [1966, 1987].

Bjarnadóttir, Birna *Recesses of the Mind: Aesthetics in the Work of Guðberger Bergsson*. McGill University Press, 2012.
Bloom, Harold. "The Knight in the Mirror." *The Guardian*, December 13, 2003, www.theguardian.com/books/2003/dec/13/classics.miguelcervantes.
Eysteinsson, Ástráður. "Icelandic Prose Literature, 1940–80." *A History of Icelandic Literature*, Ed. Daisy Neijmann [General editor: Sven H. Rossel. Histories of Scandinavian Literature. 5.] University of Nebraska Press in cooperation with The American-Scandinavian Foundation, 2006.
Gabbert, Elisa. "Proust and the Art of Suffering." *The Paris Review*, May 28, 2019, www.theparisreview.org/blog/columns/mess-with-a-classic/.
Gabbert, Elisa. "The Stupid Classics Book Club." *The Paris Review*, April 23, 2019, www.theparisreview.org/blog/2019/04/23/the-stupid-classics-book-club/.
Hólmarsson, Sverrir, Christopher Sanders, and John Tucker. *Íslensk-ensk orðabók / Concise Icelandic-English Dictionary*. Iðunn, 1989, adigicoll.library.wisc.edu/IcelOnline/Search.TEId.html.
Thorsson, Guðmundur Andri. "Regnbogar næturinnar" ("Night Rainbows") in *Tómas Jónsson Metsölubók*, 2012.

16

Love, Anger, Madness Making a Classic
Amplifying Marie Vieux-Chauvet's Haitian Trilogy

Carolyn Shread

What does it take to make a classic? Haitian author Marie Vieux-Chauvet offers a case study in what it is to garner global recognition in spite of violent forces of suppression. Putting aside a larger question about whether we in fact want to retain the category of "classics" at all, for the moment let us begin from the premise that if at least the canon of classics is to be an inclusive one, rather than a mirroring of privilege, we do well to consider authors like Chauvet. The history of her arrival among world classics emphasizes the main point of this chapter, namely that a classic is not born but made. Acknowledging the fabrication of classics dismantles essentialist claims to literary excellence that can mask little more than a reiteration of the interests of an elite who have laid claim both to these texts and their interpretation. The modes and conditions of the fabrication of a classic are various, the stakeholders multiple, and the paths leading to consecration, including the significant investments and returns of translations, differentiated. Although I am the translator of an unpublished manuscript of Chauvet's short novel *Les Rapaces* (1986),[1] my role here is to amplify Chauvet's voice and claim her space by telling the story of her trilogy, *Amour, Colère et Folie*, published in 1968 by the prestigious French press Gallimard, yet only appearing in the English translation of Rose-Myriam Réjouis and Val Vinokur as *Love, Anger, Madness* some four decades later. The reasons for this long delay illuminate our understanding of the making of classics and the ways in which unique voices are heard against hegemonic pressures that stifle them.

---

[1] I am not alone in having an unpublished Chauvet translation. The difficulty of securing rights has produced a history still to be written of her translations that never went to press, although Thomas C. Spear offers a good start to that translation history in "Marie Chauvet: The Fortress Still Stands."

Along with their titles, most classics are signaled by an instantly recognizable name. Yet identifying *Love, Anger, Madness* must begin with the caveat that even the author's name suffers obfuscation. Marie Chauvet, as she is still most commonly referred to in Haiti, published an early work under the pseudonym Colibri (French for hummingbird), before appearing as Marie Chauvet for the trilogy published with Gallimard and other prior publications in Haiti, then as Marie Vieux for her final work, *Les Rapaces*, written in exile in New York and published posthumously. More recently, with the republication of her works both in Haiti and abroad, she appears alternately as Marie Vieux-Chauvet (hyphenated) or Marie Vieux Chauvet. Such instability is partially a consequence of writing in an era in which, while men retain their names for a lifetime, women's last names are frequently altered according to marital status.[2] What man has ever signed a work with the type of pronouncement included on the back cover of the 1986 publication of *Les Rapaces*?

> Marie Chauvet signs her last novel: MARIE VIEUX [...]
>
> The public is hereby informed that all works by **Marie Chauvet** republished hereafter will bear the writer's maiden name: **MARIE VIEUX**.[3]

This performative conferral of the author's name was not of the author's doing; rather, it was her children, the heirs to the rights to her work, who implemented the name change following the fallout over the original publication of the trilogy, including the author's divorce from Pierre Chauvet. The family's impact on the making of this classic is considerable, complex, and no doubt still misunderstood.

Uncertainty continues to mark the author's work, as shown when scholars invariably slip from Marie Vieux-Chauvet to Marie Chauvet when discussing her, if not on the page, at least in unguarded moments of conversation when her work is claimed most intimately. While this slippage is indicative of the ways she has been appropriated by an inner circle who refer to her with a mixture of respect and familiarity, it is also a reminder of the halting,

---

[2] Another reason for this, according to Spear, is that "the hyphenated last name Vieux-Chauvet was invented to serve as a compromise among Chauvet's three children," and he adds, "It is not the least unfortunate twist the family has left on their mother's publishing legacy" see Spear, "Marie Chauvet: The Fortress Still Stands" 23.

[3] "Marie Chauvet signe son dernier roman: MARIE VIEUX [...] Le public est ici informé que toute œuvre de **Marie Chauvet** qui sera rééditée portera désormais le nom de jeune fille de l'écrivain: **MARIE VIEUX**" (my translation), back cover of *Les Rapaces* (Henri Deschamps, 1986).

confused way in which her voice has come to be heard on the world stage. Indeed, the way this author is cited is, in itself, often reflective of the way the speaker is positioned, either within the specialized group of Chauvet scholars and Haitian readers—those who claimed her as a classic from the start— or those beginning to discover her in world literatures via translations.[4] The making of a classic is an uneven process, both temporally and spatially discontinuous. Even so, to trouble the nomenclature system in this way is an indication of the upheaval this particular classic brings to established literary systems and to our understanding of just what a classic is.

These opening comments on Chauvet's signature emphasize that while among an educated Haitian readership, concentrated primarily among the North American diaspora, her triptych, with its searing critique of the Duvalier dictatorship, has long been celebrated as a cult classic, mainstream circulation has only recently gained momentum. How do we explain this discrepancy and lag? The conceit of a hidden classic is not uncommon and, indeed, this status often serves to heighten the reputation of a text. Certainly, this is the frame within which Chauvet is often referenced by critics, starting with those who read her in Haiti. When Haitian author Dany Laferrière describes his first encounter with the novel, he finds it "in the old wardrobe, carefully hidden under the clean sheets" (Laferrière 494; "dans la vieille armoire, bien caché sous les draps propres"; my translation). His account of a sequestered treasure is repeated in countless variations among his compatriots who often evoke their initial, compelling, clandestine encounter with the book when it appeared during the dictatorship, only to be immediately pulled from distribution, and in the years afterwards when it remained impossible to find, save in two bookstores, one in New York, one in Port-au-Prince, where it was sold under the counter. Subsequently, the publication of the translation of Chauvet's work into English coincided with a general discourse claiming her as that paradoxical entity: the unrecognized classic. Several reviews of the translation of the three novellas highlight this aspect of the work,

> Withdrawn just after it was published in France in 1968 following a government warning that it would endanger the author's family, Marie Vieux-Chauvet's Haitian trilogy, "Love, Anger, Madness" has been an underground classic ever since. ("Meanness of the Heart" 66)

---

[4] I myself have alternated between several of these appellations in the course of my publications and public presentations; in the present context, I revert to the shorter Chauvet.

The time has come, thanks to the first English translation of this hidden classic by Rose-Myriam Réjouis and Val Vinokur, professors at New York's New School. (Marxsen 6)

For the last thirty years of the twentieth century, Marie Vieux-Chauvet's *Amour, Colère et Folie* was legendary for being lost. (Smart Bell 30)

While these three reviewers present the author to an international audience as a hidden gem, in her preface to the English translation Edwidge Danticat, celebrated Haitian-American author and de facto Haitian cultural ambassador in the American diaspora, does not hesitate to name this work "the cornerstone of Haitian literature" (Danticat vii). For Haitians, at home and abroad, her status is uncontested. To cite another definitive statement, Laferrière, now elected as simultaneously the first Haitian and first Quebecois member of the *Académie française*, affixed the following seal of approval to the work in his Afterword to the republished French edition: "Yes, Marie Chauvet did write *the* novel of the dark years of the Haitian dictatorship" (Laferrière 493; "Marie Chauvet a bien écrit le grand roman des années noires de la dictature haitienne" my translation). It is worth noting, again, the familiarity with which Laferrière names her— Chauvet, *tout court*. This lauding by an *immortel* (as members of the *Académie française* are known) shifts the implied location of the pronouncement to the institutional site in Paris and hence to a wider sphere of recognition.

In the present collection of essays, in which the classics in translation span the entire world of languages and cultures, it would be remiss not to explain the context of Chauvet's writing, namely Haiti of the 1950s and 1960s. Chauvet's formative experiences took place under the national wound of an American Occupation that lasted fifteen years (1915–34). Later she witnessed the horror and violent oppression of "Papa Doc" François Duvalier who came to power in 1957. Upon his death in 1971, this ruthless dictator transferred his hold over the country to his nineteen-year-old son Jean-Claude Duvalier, "Baby Doc," thereby imposing a thirty-year stranglehold that ended only in 1986. Chauvet's work emerges as a direct response to these sociopolitical realities, although it is not reducible to them.

Significantly for the translational history of this text, the consecutive dictatorships were responsible for the waves of immigrants in exile, first in the 1960s and 1970s from a privileged upper stratum of society that was viciously attacked by Duvalier's private army of *tonton macoutes*, and then in the 1980s by less fortunate migrants, fleeing economic oppression and continued state violence. These two waves formed the considerable Haitian diaspora that concentrated in large North American cities such as Montreal, New York, and Miami, but that extended as far around the world as Congo. Chauvet's primary readership is constituted as much by this extensive network across the diaspora as from Haiti itself.

In *What Is a Classic? Postcolonial Rewriting and Invention of the Canon* (2013), Ankhi Mukherjee posits that "the classic is primarily a singular act of literature, while the canon [. . .] is 'an aristocracy of texts'" (31). Even as we acknowledge that Chauvet has long been excluded from the canon club as a result of systematic discrimination against writers of color and women, we can also ask what it is that makes *Love, Anger, Madness* a classic. In what does her singularity inhere? For if a classic is to be made—if stakeholders are to hold it up and declare "This is a classic"—there must be grounds on which to lay their claim.

In a short, incisive commentary, Stéphane Martelly proposes that it is precisely a contest of singularity that plays out in Chauvet's work in as much as the project of a dictatorship itself is to impose a singular meaning. Martelly reminds us of how the functioning of signs intersects with the arbitrary affixing of meaning by a system in which the power of life and death lies with "the only great hermeneut, the dictator himself" (Martelly 144; "le seul grand herméneute est bien le dictateur"; my translation). Such is the definition of totalitarianism, whose reality is too easily forgotten, Martelly argues. Chauvet's first achievement is thus to "trouble the fate of a word saturated [. . .] to upset the imprisoning of meaning, interrupt the zombifying voice of the father-dictator by offering a variation" (145; "interrompre le destin d'une parole saturée [. . .] troubler l'emprise du sens, interrompre la voix zombificatrice du père-dictateur et introduire une variation"; my translation). Obviously, Chauvet is far from the only author to have challenged tyrannical power with the pen, but this is the framework in which her trilogy must be read. And the stakes are considerable, for as Martelly says: "it's inevitably in the pages of a great book that an attempt to master and control meaning fails *absolutely*" (149; "c'est immanquablement dans les pages d'un grand livre qu'échoue *absolument* une recherche de sens maitrisé et contenu"; my translation). Chauvet's classic thus stands first and foremost as a claim to the right of each individual to a singular voice.

In an interview that dates back to 1992, Yanick Lahens, a Haitian author who became the first Francophone Worlds chair at the Collège de France in 2019, explained how Marie Chauvet's writing innovates formally through interior monologue, abandoning a traditional collective "we" to become "one of the first novelists to write in the first person in Haitian literature" (Taleb-Khyar and Lahens 442). Lahens describes the revolutionary uniqueness of that "I":

Why is it that a Third World writer cannot, before saying "I am black or I am a Marxist," say simply "I am" [. . .] Chauvet understood this, and she traced a new path with *Amour, Colère et Folie* [. . .] Never has a French writer needed to begin with "I am French, I am white." (442–3)

Lahens has remained one of Chauvet's closest readers and critics, with a keen eye for what it is in the work itself that distinguishes it. In another interview, she puts her finger on why the I written by Chauvet is so compelling:

> Our identity has always been defined and lived through an Other, one exterior to ourselves, hostile yet fascinating, since alienation shall always come with the quest for a "pure" identity [. . .] we must now recognize that otherness lives within ourselves. (Zimra 80)

Indeed, Chauvet's innovative portrayal of a female self is groundbreaking in the way that it reworks a heritage rooted in slavery—including the proud revolutionary tradition of the first Black republic declaring its independence from the French colonial empire in 1804—in order to explore the complexities of the inner self. In this process, Chauvet evokes female protagonists, such as Claire Clamont in *Love,* who, as Lahens clearly states, "dares name her own desires" (85). Against the backdrop of a small town terrorized by a violent thug now empowered as Commandant, Calédu, Chauvet takes readers behind the blinds and into the bedroom where the spinster Claire indulges lonely erotic fantasies about her brother-in-law. Claire is not offered as the object of the reader's prurient curiosity; rather, as critic Betty Wilson puts it, Chauvet

> empowers her transgressive protagonist and makes her a figure to be reckoned with: not only does she control the narrative (her voice/ her point of view is the only one we hear), but she also controls and manipulates the other members of her household. (412)

Through her diary writing, Claire's powerful voice and raw lucidity produce her own self-definition. While generating her own reflection, she also unmasks, with unwavering and brutal honesty, the terrorized lives of those around her. Fearlessly, she draws up the pitiful picture of a people crushed variously, in every social rank, by the violently oppressive circumstances of a nation under siege. Forsaking all allegiances, her intimate understanding of the mechanisms of such social distortions and cruelties spares no one and, because Haiti has no exclusive claim to such operations, lays bare a universally recognizable human fallibility in the face of such challenges. This ability to speak beyond circumstance, even as it is captured in all its specificity, is one of the hallmarks that makes a classic.

There is still considerable work to do to rise to the challenge Chauvet's work presents its readers, whatever their situation in the world, for as Lahens puts it, "This trilogy still asks questions that we have not yet answered" (Lahens 133; "Cette trilogie n'a pas fini de nous poser des questions auxquelles nous n'avons pas encore répondu"; my translation). The searing revelations of *Love, Anger, Madness* lay bare our failures to interrupt the destructive functioning of power. Yet the claustrophobia that is one of the recurrent themes of Chauvet's writing—be it Claire in *Love* in her bedroom, the family imprisoned by the "men in black" in their house in *Anger*, or the sequestered poets in *Madness*—all point to the human imperative to break down the walls that divide and rule us. Chauvet knows that the misuse of power in all its manifestations is intolerable; her readers each bring their own experiences of rejecting abusive force, along with their unresolved political, social, or individual dilemmas.

Thanks to scholars working in the archives, notably Régine Isabelle Joseph, we now have some insight into Chauvet's unflinching intent to portray moral depravity: "If I sought to cry out truth obliquely, my hope was to awaken the consciences of my fellow citizens by making them touch their very cowardice and lustful desires" (Chauvet qtd. in Glover, "Marie Chauvet" 27; "Si j'ai pris des biais pour crier la vérité, au moins avais-je l'espoir de réveiller la conscience de mes compatriotes en leur faisant toucher du doigt leur lâcheté et leur concupiscence"; my translation).[5] The intense psychological acuity of her text derives from this overarching ideal. Even as Chauvet exposes violence, her rigorous ethics also involve the revelation of uncomfortable complicities with violence; this painful reckoning is all the more revolutionary in that she dared speak about how it intersects with women's sexuality.

True to most classics, Chauvet's abilities to speak truth to power exceed those of most of her critics. If she named the taboo, by exposing, for instance in *Anger*, the torture and rape repeatedly suffered by Rose Normil, another female protagonist, more often than not, her critics do not have the same nerve. As Régine Jean-Charles points out in "They Never Call It Rape: Critical Reception and Representation of Sexual Violence in Marie Vieux-Chauvet's *Amour, Colère et Folie*": "much has been written about Vieux-Chauvet's daring use of sexuality or her creation of a violent universe, but there has been very little exploration of the portrayal of sexual violence" (7). Jean-Charles is quite right to emphasize what makes Chauvet's work so important as a cultural project to alter discourses about sexual violence and how critics have failed to rise to her challenge.

---

[5] Letter from Marie Chauvet from January 16, 1968.

This reticent prudery, not to say complicity with patriarchy, continues in the reception of her translations, as seen in the euphemistic erasure of rape in a review that appeared in *The Economist* in 2009: "The middle-class family in 'Anger' is torn apart when the 20-year-old heroine, Rose, is forced to sleep with a soldier to stop the regime from seizing their land" ("Meanness" 66). Just who forces Rose into this position? The responsibility for her prostitution lies within the family, ready to sacrifice her to save their land. A sacrifice whose discomfort arises from Rose's own assumption of her role and an uncertainty among critics of how to interpret her experience. Call it what it is: rather than "sleeping with" a soldier, a man brutally rapes Rose. Not just once. This torture, often implicitly characterized as a religious martyrdom, is a repeated nightmare. This isn't just, as *The Economist*'s review title suggests, "meanness of the heart"—though there is also plenty of that—this is in the category of a crime against humanity. We are referring to a regime that systematically maintains control over a population by subjugating women through rape. Chauvet's achievement is to bring the case forward by revealing all the structural, societal, familial, and individual complicity that circulates sexual violence and imposes it upon a particular demographic far before most of her readers or critics were willing to do so.

A frank acknowledgment of Chauvet's status as a classic has been a long time coming. In the 1970s Pradel Pompilus and Raphaël Berrou, authors of what for many years was viewed in the Haitian education system as the authoritative three-volume guide to the national literature, devoted a mere six lines to Chauvet, whom they deemed a minor writer.[6] Still today Chauvet's fictional intervention into the dictatorship elicits a wary response, as Kaiama L. Glover explains in "'Black' Radicalism in Haiti and the Disorderly Feminine: The Case of Marie Vieux-Chauvet" when she notes that Chauvet is missing from contemporary analyses such as Matthew Smith's *Red and Black in Haiti* (2009). Glover argues that the regular inclusion of the "pantheon of engaged writers" (*Daughter of Haiti* 154) such as Jacques Roumain, Jacques Stéphen Alexis, and René Depestre follows a logic that defines them as "committed" due to their "political activity" ("'Black' Radicalism in Haiti" 9). Glover's intersectional analysis of the way politics and gender compound exclusion helps explain both how Chauvet herself has been marginalized and how this same process is dramatized in her texts: "Chauvet presents an isolated woman character whose political ambivalence implicitly critiques the coercive communities that seek to determine her existence" ("Daughter of Haiti" 155). On the grounds that Chauvet's protagonists present an activism

---

[6] *Histoire de la littérature haïtienne illustrée par les textes.* See vol. 3, 584.

defined by the constraints of gender and that the author is treated in a similar manner by some critics, Glover challenges the tradition of Black radicalism to rethink certain premises:

> while Chauvet's women may not be "black" or "radical" in any "traditional" way, might not their—and her—resistance to explicit political identification illuminate the limitations of radicalism within the historically gendered space of political engagement. ("'Black' Radicalism in Haiti" 21)

In short, Glover argues, Chauvet pays not just for exposing the Haitian elite as much as she does Duvalier but also for her political non-alignment, again the singularity with which she speaks.

Having discussed some of the contents of Chauvet's trilogy that place it firmly among the literary classics, I shall now address the linguistic factors to which her translations respond. Not only is the linguistic situation of Haiti particular, it also suffers from widespread misperceptions. Let's start with the fact that while Haiti is often referred to as a Francophone country, in part due to its tremendous literary heritage of writing in French, this descriptor elides a linguistic reality, namely that everyone in Haiti speaks Creole, while only some 15 percent of the population also knows French. The implications of the ways in which this linguistic landscape has evolved with French spoken and written by an educated, largely urban elite while Creole remains the traditional oral language of the nation, are considerable. As one critical sociolinguist put it succinctly, these "language policies keep the working masses in their place just as effectively as a gun" (Jacobson 14). Language is power in a very tangible way in this context.

What does the linguistic landscape of Haiti mean for this author? First and foremost, let it be understood that as a bourgeois author in mid-twentieth-century Haiti, Chauvet's literary language, the language of her written texts, was naturally French, due to her education and cultural background. Chauvet would have been hard pressed to write in Creole, even had she wanted to. The first-ever book published in Haitian Creole, Frankétienne's *Dézafi*, was published only in 1975. Haitian Creole orthography had not yet been standardized; indeed, Creole did not become the second official language of the country until 1987, some fifteen years after Chauvet's death. The author dramatizes the linguistic dilemma of her country in the third book of her trilogy, *Madness*, in which four poets hide out from the dictatorship, lost to the insane lucidity of their situation. One of them recounts his language background, which presents a linguistic schism familiar to so many Haitian authors.

My black mother, who didn't know how to read and who sold trinkets at the market, slaved away to make a scholar of her son. I left Creole and voodoo [sic]⁷ behind by going to school, and she, who was never able to say a French word to me, would beam when she heard me recite lessons she did not understand. (Vieux-Chauvet, *Love, Anger, Madness* 291)

La négresse, ma mère, qui ne savait pas lire et qui était vendeuse de pacotilles au marché, a trimé dur pour faire de son fils un savant. Je suis sorti du créole, sorti du vodou en m'instruisant, et elle qui n'a jamais pu m'adresser la parole en français souriait fièrement en m'entendant répéter des leçons qu'elle ne comprenait pas. (Vieux-Chauvet, *Amour, Colère et Folie* 301)

This is a recurrent story in Chauvet's work: in *Les Rapaces* the poet Michel tells the same tale. While at that time French was the only language of education, as well as the key to social mobility, the relationship between an abandoned maternal tongue and the prestige language haunts those whose childhood appropriation or mastery of French secures their unquestionable claim to it. A little later in *Madness*, the poet laments that he is "hog-tied to the tempting rhymes of a loaned-out language, tossed between Creole and French like those rowboats over there on the sea" (Vieux-Chauvet, *Love, Anger, Madness* 291; "amarrée corps à corps aux rimes tentantes d'une langue d'emprunt, ballottée entre le créole et le français comme ces barques là-bas, sur la mer" 304). Chauvet's keen critique spares nothing, and certainly not the tortured linguistic heritage that is hers. Nonetheless, while Creole culture and expressions are present on occasion in Chauvet's own writing, the overwhelming impression of her trilogy is that of classical French.⁸ For this reason, her work is ready to travel widely across the Francophone world precisely because it conforms to the predominant standards and thus enjoys the cultural capital of the dominant form of French.

When it comes to the translation of Chauvet's work, the language panorama becomes even more complex. Focusing on the translation from French into English, we could start by asking, who does this translation

---

⁷ Although *Love, Anger, Madness* was published in 2009, it is regrettable that "vaudou" is translated as "voodoo" throughout. In 2011, following the petitioning of scholars and practitioners, the Library of Congress changed its subject heading in the catalog to "Vodou," which is now the accepted spelling. For a discussion of this translational question, see Meï and Dize.

⁸ In my translation of *Les Rapaces*, however, I did introduce Creole into the text along with English as a means of connecting with a diasporic American readership that may not know French but that does use Creole within the community. See Shread, "La Traduction métramorphique."

make the work accessible to? Usually a translation serves to amplify a text beyond its original linguistic and cultural sphere. However, in this instance, a translation actually becomes necessary in order even to reach a first audience of Haitian origin among an Anglophone diaspora that has been detached from its French heritage. This classic must exist in English in order to respond to linguistic dislocations that reflect a long history of colonization and exile. This is how translations map the scars of a history of empire, oppressive dictatorship, and failed state, reflecting what Mukherjee aptly describes as "the unique time, irregular geography, and the collective life of literature" (13). In an interview published on the blog *H-Net Haiti in Translation*, one of the most well-known translators of Haitian literature into English, Carrol F. Coates, explained the motives of those interested in acquiring his translations:

> I anticipated that a significant number of my potential readers might be younger Haitians not schooled in French. The validity of these expectations was at least moderately shown when I was invited to present the translation at the Embassy of Haiti in Washington D.C., in March 2000. A number of Haitian parents asked me to autograph a copy for their children so they could read an important writer from their own culture. (Meï n.p.)

Another translator of Haitian literature, Kaiama L. Glover, reiterates the point that translation is a necessary step for the reception of classics such as *Love, Anger, Madness* given the linguistic discontinuities existing within a diasporic audience:

> Bringing this novel to English-speaking audiences has particular resonance for me, a Caribbean literature scholar teaching in a New York City institution. New York is one of the primary sites of the Haitian diaspora and, as such, many of my students are first-generation Haitian Americans who read and write in English—not French. And so I've been a firsthand witness to the broader phenomenon whereby a transnational population is cut off from certain aspects of its cultural heritage. (Depestre 256)

Translation is thus critical to the survival of this author's work as a direct result of its dislocated home audience. It is important to bear in mind that the English of North America is not the only English; indeed critics such as Marie-José Nzengou-Tayo have called attention to the fact that translations must be heard across the Caribbean in the idioms of a regional readership. There is an Anglophone Haitian diaspora in places such as Jamaica or the

Bahamas, as well as Hispanophone diasporas, notably in the Dominican Republic. Translations thus provide multiple vectors for the amplification of Chauvet's voice beyond its initial context. Jacques Derrida famously argued that any text depends for its survival on a translation, as demonstrated by these diasporic demands. But while Derrida's point is well taken, let us not forget that a translation also depends on the survival of the original text. It is to this aspect—the text to be translated—that I now turn.

The title of this chapter insists that a classic is made, that it can't simply be, precisely because the story of Chauvet's trilogy emphasizes the precarity of her work—a precarity that begins with the material artifact of the manuscript. The survival of the text precedes its long and complicated publishing history that includes a stubborn resistance to granting rights for either republications or translations. For a classic to be translated, it must be available. However, before it even arrives at its translations, the story of *Amour, Colère et Folie* illustrates the perilous ground on which translations depend. Chauvet narrates this same anxiety both within the trilogy, among the tormented poets of *Madness*, and in her last novel, *Les Rapaces*, in which Michel's manuscript is entrusted to Anne, and, following her murder, is taken into safekeeping by her father who is first transformed by reading it and then vows to publish it. The material transferal of the text recounted here is not so far removed from the transmission of Chauvet's own book.

"Despite it all the manuscripts did survive" (Joseph, Introduction n.p.; "Les manuscrits ont quand même survécu"; my translation). Such is Régine Isabelle Joseph's conclusion in her Introduction to a letter Marie Chauvet sent to editor Gaston Gallimard. Joseph's archival research draws attention to the anxiety surrounding a manuscript in a pre-digital era before reproduction became a millisecond matter of cut and paste (Joseph, "Letters of Marie Chauvet and Simone de Beauvoir").[9] When Chauvet sent her book to Paris in search of a publisher, she sent her sole manuscript,[10] and she did so at a time of intense vulnerability, as her comment even about this letter shows: "I will entrust this letter to a friend to send from New York. Since the mail is

---

[9] Joseph cites her source as the *Fonds Simone de Beauvoir,* BNF NAF 28051. Simone de Beauvoir, "Lettres reçues de lecteurs" 25.
[10] Interestingly, in interview, the Haitian author Frankétienne offers a genealogy I have not heard elsewhere: "elle avait envoyé des copies à plusieurs maisons d'édition. Je crois qu'elle avait envoyé des copies à Grasset, au Seuil et à Gallimard. Grasset avait déjà accepté de publier le livre. Mais elle a fait le choix de Gallimard qui était une plus grande maison d'édition," "she had sent copies to several publishing houses. I believe that she had sent copies to Grasset, Seuil and Gallimard. Grasset had already accepted the book for publication. But she chose Gallimard, which was a larger publishing house" (my translation). If such is the case, it invites further research into the Grasset and Seuil archives in order to tell the full story of the making of *Love, Anger, Madness*. See Frankétienne 85.

searched, it would be dangerous to post it to you from here" (Chauvet qtd. in Joseph, "Marie Chauvet" n.p.; "Je vais confier cette lettre à une amie qui part de New York. La correspondance étant fouillée, il serait dangereux de vous l'expédier d'ici par poste"; my translation). Likewise, had her classic been intercepted, or simply lost, we might never have known it.

Chauvet dispatched her precious manuscript to Simone de Beauvoir, not directly, but via Gallimard publishers. The following extract from a letter Chauvet wrote to her intermediary illustrates the fragility of the book at this critical juncture:

New York, May 2, 1967

Dear Madam,

I received your April 29th note, and I thank you. I admit I was slightly disconcerted by your silence because I was at least expecting a delivery confirmation.

The manuscripts were expedited c/o Gallimard 3 weeks ago by air and by certified mail. They should already be in your possession.

I did not and still do not know your address, since you have not given it to me. Counseled by some French friends, I thought I did well by going through Gallimard.

I am counting on another word from you to reassure me, since these are my only copies.

I will return to my country around May 15th. If ever you do write, avoid, I beckon you, all commentary about politics. [In Haiti] letters are searched.
    (Joseph, "Letters of Marie Chauvet and Simone de Beauvoir" 33)

Fortunately, Chauvet's work was protected and her voice amplified through a system of solidarity Joseph aptly describes as global feminism at work. Through close textual analysis of the epistolary exchange, Joseph presents Chauvet's canny cultivation of a "transnational literary *compagnonage,*" (26), or mentoring relationship, with de Beauvoir. Raising her voice outside the stifling context in which she found herself, she appealed to de Beauvoir by sending her the manuscript via Gallimard and asking for intercession on her behalf. In the process, she developed "a sincere friendship that was, nevertheless, carefully and strategically cultivated" (37). Joseph proposes an insightful reading of the rhetorical strategies Chauvet deployed in her letters:

a lesson in the art of solicitation, a lesson that shows how a Haitian writer—writing in French, but from across the Atlantic—asserts her agency in a presumably peripheral space via an epistolary form located outside the publishing institutions of Paris and other circulating centers of cultural production. (31)

This is indeed a classic that was made against the odds and despite forces of opposition among stakeholders, starting with the regime, then the author's family, along with institutional sexism and racism at a global level. Joseph's unearthing of the correspondence reveals the way in which de Beauvoir was far more than a mere transmitter of Chauvet's manuscript; instead, Chauvet engaged her as an interlocutor who successfully ensured that the Parisian press would give her work its due regard.

There is still extensive research and ordering to be done in the archives following Joseph's initiation of this line of exploration. One question that does not seem to have been raised and whose answer is relevant to the history of this classic is: Why did Gallimard want to publish this book? What was their investment and interest? Aside from the seal of approval from one of the most famous French intellectuals of the time, how did the editors envisage positioning this book for their market in France and beyond? We can surmise, given that the date of publication coincides with the revolutionary moment of May 1968 in France, and indeed around the world, that the French editors read Chauvet as a timely voice not just in Haiti but, and no doubt more importantly for them, in France itself. We know that foreign literature in translation often serves to introduce uncomfortable innovations with the protection of an alibi that it comes from elsewhere and thus relates ambiguously to the target audience. In this instance, even before the translations, were the taboos about women's sexuality that Chauvet broke viewed as answering a need in France via the cover of Haiti, which acts as an alternative French space? In light of recent movements to recalibrate the relationship between literature from France and from the French-speaking world, there is certainly work to be done on how this classic is situated within the French pantheon. Yet, this line of enquiry has been neglected due to the fact that the book was immediately withdrawn from circulation upon publication, not just in Haiti, but also in France. As Glover comments:

> Gallimard's publication of her trilogy would have all but guaranteed her an immediate international celebrity and definitely inserted her into both Haitian and extrainsular literary canons. Would have. As it happens, though, Chauvet's success was thwarted by Haiti's political reality of the late 1960s. (Glover qtd. in Jean-Charles 61–2)

The effect of erasure at the moment of publication continues to the present day. One of Joseph's important observations is the imbalance of the current situation in which de Beauvoir's work "is actively maintained in Paris by a leading institution of knowledge production and preservation" while there remains a notable "absence of a similarly robust and accessible Chauvet archive" (Joseph, "Letters of Marie Chauvet and Simone de Beauvoir" 29). Moreover, Joseph points out the incongruous fact that Chauvet's letters to de Beauvoir are categorized in the last of three divisions among the "Letters received" archive: "Letters received from intellectuals," "Letters received from writers become correspondents," and "Letters received from readers" (29). This clear miscategorization gives us pause to think about Chauvet's continued suppression and the efforts still needed for her work to be recognized appropriately. In the future, Chauvet's own papers owned by the family will no doubt help fill in the story of the making of this work.

Before continuing with the publishing history of *Amour, Colère et Folie* and its translations, I would like to acknowledge Régine Michelle Jean-Charles's article "Naming, Claiming, and Framing Marie Chauvet" as another significant contribution to the effort to clear the way to Chauvet's classic. Jean-Charles argues that discourses surrounding the trilogy and especially its fabled publication are a serious distraction from the work itself. She targets "the effects that the cult of drama can have on Chauvet criticism" (59). This drama—which I am about to recount—produces a mythification that overshadows the classic itself. Jean-Charles's perceptive critique determined my own presentation of Chauvet's masterpiece in the present context, prompting me to start with what formal and narrative elements in this text offer grounds for calling it a classic before explaining its publishing story. However, since my argument is that a classic is made, it does require a telling of its fabrication. In doing so, I draw extensively on *En Amour avec Marie*, a collection of twenty-eight homages to Chauvet by authors who knew her and by scholars.[11] While this book offers valuable firsthand testimonies and astute critical analyses, it is also exemplary of the mythification of Chauvet. Moreover, Jean-Charles rightly raises an eyebrow to comment: "One wonders if a critical volume on Jacques Roumain or Jacques Stéphen Alexis would use 'being in love' with the author as an organizing principle" (55). Redirecting our critical attention away from an excessive fascination with circulating rumors ensures that the person of the author and the history of her text do not determine the literary response the work receives. For if a

---

[11] Emmelie Prophète, ed., *En Amour avec Marie*, 2016.

classic is anything, it is writing that endures on merits celebrated by multiple stakeholders.

To turn now to the story of the making of *Love, Anger, Madness*, we must start with a long period of silence. Spear recounts that "the only article published in Haiti about Chauvet in the entire decade of the 1970s appears to be that of Ginette Plummer Adamson" (Spear 15). In 1983 Laferrière characterized an initial "lukewarm" reception of the trilogy in Haiti: "the right repressed her, the center ignored her, and the left sniffed at her" (Laferrière qtd. in Jean-Charles 62; "Ainsi la droite la refoulée, le centre l'ignoré et la gauche reniflée"; my translation). Evidently, the work disturbed readers on all sides—not just the dictator. The hushed response has many causes, but, according to the architect of the digital archive *île en île*,[12] Thomas Spear, who has been involved with those advocating for the book since the mid-1980s, there is one overriding factor in its restricted circulation: "More than politics or sexism, the primary silencing of Chauvet's works has been editorial" (Spear 23). Spear places the responsibility for the delayed reception of this classic squarely with the family as heirs to the rights, without which the book was stopped in its tracks. Wading into the murky debate about who exactly was responsible for removing the book from circulation no sooner was it off the press, he is adamant that "it was not the Duvalier régime that censored the trilogy or suppressed its publication: the pressure to stop distribution of the text came from the author's family" (9). At the time of the dictatorship, such hesitation is understandable: several members of Chauvet's family had already been killed and the family feared further reprisals (12–14)[13] Once the dictatorship was over, however, from 1986, such obstinacy is more difficult to fathom.

This case demonstrates that the survival of a translation does, in fact, depend on the existence of a text to translate, and then on the manner in which the rights to that text are managed. As Spear explains, "the author's heirs had purchased the rights, keeping Gallimard and anyone else from republishing the work" (15). The consequence of this obstruction was an effective quashing of the trilogy since it ensured that "no one could republish, sell or translate for decades" (14). Without rights, there is no making of a classic, since it can't make its way to readers.

I recall I first heard about the trilogy in the early 1990s from a French professor at the University of Massachusetts Boston. Living in Paris at the time, I scoured the bookstores, but to no avail. On my return to the United

---

[12] See ile-en-ile.org/.
[13] Spear reports that Didier and Paul Vieux were killed in 1963. Her sister's son Raymond and cousin Michael Corvington were also killed in 1968.

States, I triumphantly found a copy of *Les Rapaces* on the twelfth floor of the W.E.B. Du Bois Library at UMass Amherst, but inevitably the copy of *Amour, Colère et Folie* was missing—they all are. After all, the frequency with which a book is stolen is also indicative of a certain status. Readers have often had to wait a very long time to access this book. Here I add another tale to the long myth surrounding Chauvet's work; the mystification that Jean-Charles diagnosed is as real as it is compelling. Such is the life of literary classics.

In 2016 an article by Thomas Spear helped set the record straight for the making of this classic by offering a fairly comprehensive catalog of failed republication and translation efforts. Spear describes the frustration of a first translator of the trilogy, Lizabeth Paravisini-Gebert, in the mid-1980s when it became apparent that Gallimard did not, in fact, have the rights to the text. Various publishing houses, including the University of Virginia Press imprint CARAF Books, sought to bring a translation to light in the 1990s. Spear laments that a golden opportunity to publish "a critical edition of *Love, Anger, Madness* with the 'Archives' series published by ALLCA in Madrid" (17) was also lost. Translation initiatives were coupled with the ongoing inaccessibility of the original French, even when, at the turn of the century, a collaboration between editor Rodney Saint-Éloi of Mémoire d'encrier and Pierre Astier's Le Serpent à Plumes seemingly had secured a contract with Chauvet's family to publish the author's entire corpus. Eventually, it was another peculiar twist in the tale that provoked the breakthrough: in September 2003 an unauthorized edition of the trilogy was put out by the "Albanian publishers Voix de Femmes" (9). This action, celebrated by those keen to get their hands on the infamously elusive text, precipitated the end of the family's unwillingness to relinquish the rights.

In 2005, almost forty years after the original publication emerged, before being immediately removed from the market, *Amour, Colère et Folie* was finally republished by another Parisian-based publisher, Emina Soleil. It was accompanied by a preface entitled "In the Name of Truth and History."[14] Signed by three members of the Chauvet's family, the one-page note seeks to set the record straight and calm the scandal, although as Jean-Charles ponders, we might ask whether we should accept "the author's offspring as authoritative figures on her biography and legacy" (Jean-Charles 67). An air of dissatisfaction continued to surround this publication in that the production value was not necessarily equivalent to the caliber of the work. While Spear acknowledged in 2016 that the trilogy "remains in print in hardcover,

---

[14] Preface "Pour la vérité, pour l'histoire" (my translation) written by her two daughters and son, Marilyse Charlier, Régine Charlier, and Pierre Chauvet, in the French republication of *Amour, Colère et Folie* 5.

paperback, and eBook formats" and that this is "a status unmatched by most of her works in French" (20), he nonetheless expressed some bitterness in regard to:

> the extent to which Chauvet's family resorted to cheap and poorly edited editions when publishing anything at all in French, rather than accept concrete offers from prestigious publishers with serious editorial and distribution policies. (21)

Spear's expression of frustration and long disappointment is shared by others, including Anaïse Chavenet, head of the book distributors Communication Plus in Port-au-Prince, whose interview in *Le Nouvelliste*, the Haitian daily newspaper that is the oldest Francophone publication in the Americas, ran under the headline: "We've had enough of cheaply produced books" (Chavenet n.p.; "Ça suffit, les livres mal faits"; my translation). Even if their success can be measured in part precisely by their availability as cheap paperbacks, classic books also come with an expectation of editorial attention and standards, the respect accorded to a literary achievement of a certain stature. This respect has been long awaited in Chauvet's case.

The reappearance of the trilogy in French was the prompt for the translations that soon followed, not just into English, but even before that into several European languages: "The German (Ullstein) and Italian (Bompiani) translations were published in 2007, the Serbian (Laguna) in 2008, and the Spanish (Acantilado) in 2012" (Spear 20). In the case of the English translation, published by Random House, we learn in the Translator's Note of another significant factor in the book's history, namely, the chosen translators' availability to undertake the work:

> Ten years ago, Régine Charlier, Marie Chauvet's eldest daughter, wrote to me and Val about her desire to publish a translation of *Amour, Colère et Folie* [...] We wrote back right away, explaining that we had to decline because we had just returned to our Ph.D. programs and needed to focus on passing exams and writing our dissertations. We are moved that we were given a second chance. (Réjouis xxi)

The making of a classic is a complex process that underlines the fact that all books are cultural artifacts dependent not just on a single person but rather an entire network of social and cultural agents. In this sense we might interrogate the title of our collection, "This Is a Classic," to ask, is this a descriptive or a performative declaration? How does translation contribute to the performative possibilities of such a claim? The conditions of production are forces that define material possibilities, avenues for creation, and, at a certain point, the consecration of the classic. In the instance of *Love, Anger, Madness* such an endorsement began with the false start of the prestigious Parisian publishing house followed by a stubborn unwillingness to disappear until receiving in 2016, the centenary of Chauvet's birth, full and due recognition at home. In that year, in his article "Marie Chauvet: The Fortress Still Stands," Spear celebrated the stature of *Love, Anger, Madness* by placing it in the proudest revolutionary tradition of the country's most famous monument of resistance:

> Chauvet's *oeuvre*, like the mighty Citadelle Laferrière, remains a stylistic and thematic benchmark—an epic fortress that overshadows a half-century of Haitian letters, steadfastly enduring it as it finally gains broader international recognition in the twenty-first century. (Spear 9)

The year 2016, the centenary of Chauvet's birth, represents what Jean-Charles characterizes as the "Chauvet turn" (Jean-Charles 51), during which a series of events took place that finally granted the author her status. To start with, in May 2016 the annual book fair in Port-au-Prince, Livres en folie, selected her as "guest of honor." At the Bibliothèque nationale, a day of study gathered international scholars to discuss her work and celebrate the republication of her entire oeuvre in Haiti, as well as the aforementioned collective tribute, *En Amour avec Marie*. The Haitian-based literary journal *Legs et littérature* also produced a special volume, *Marie Vieux-Chauvet* (ed. Pierre). Marie Chauvet was finally enjoying her due at home, with extensive newspaper coverage in *Le Nouvelliste*, discussions on local radio stations and a photo exhibit at the cultural center Fokal.

This cataloging of recognition in Haiti was paired with events in the diaspora, including a Centennial Celebration of Marie Vieux-Chauvet at the CUNY Graduate Center in New York on March 4 followed by a daylong conference, "Chauvet's Theaters of Revolt" on October 24. These gatherings brought together many Chauvet specialists including several of those whose work is cited here who published together in the 2015 *Yale French Studies* journal "Revisiting Marie Vieux Chauvet: Paradoxes of the Postcolonial Feminine" (Glover and Benedicty-Kokken). Clearly, now, Chauvet's voice was enjoying an amplification that addressed not only "Chauvet's 'silencing'" but also "the miraculous persistence of Chauvet's voice" (2). As I have suggested elsewhere, however, all this drama and noise in fact drowns out another essential, creative silence from which her voice emerges and from which she speaks, a silence without which a classic cannot be made (Shread, "Les silences de Marie Chauvet").

Who makes a classic? It starts with an author who lays down powerful words on the page and then whose voice ripples out, transformed and transported through the many lives of a text. As Jean-Charles argues, to question the reiteration of the publishing drama associated with Chauvet's work is a "feminist act intended to shed additional light on the author, and actively question the politics of her initial reception" (Jean-Charles 69). Intersectional analyses have demonstrated over and again that positionality is complex both in its manifestations and consequences. Joseph's careful reading of Chauvet's correspondence with de Beauvoir testifies to the way in which her status as an educated member of the bourgeoisie afforded her the privilege and self-confidence to conceive of herself as a "public, female intellectual from Haiti" (Joseph, "The Letters of Marie Chauvet and Simone de Beauvoir" 28). However, such self-fashioning depended on a chain of feminist solidarity that extends from the work to the many translations—published and unpublished—to the extensive work of scholars and critics, initially in the specialized field of Haitian or Caribbean studies, but now extending to world literatures. The story of making *Love, Anger, Madness* a classic exemplifies global feminism at work across the generations and across the globe, from the initial relation formed between Simone de Beauvoir and Marie Chauvet to all those feminist scholars cited in this account and many more who have contributed to her appreciation. If Chauvet makes the grade as a classic, it is due to this chain of transnational solidarity, a communal work of lifting up and amplifying voices. Just as Simone de Beauvoir wrote in her famous opening sentence, "One is not born, but rather becomes a woman" (De Beauvoir 301), the same can be said for classics: these are cultural formations that express the contest of powers and interests at work. This classic was made by the international community of Chauvet's fervent readers, publishers, and translators. If ever we needed proof that a book depends for its life and survival on the *Love, Anger, Madness* of its readers and translators in every language, this is it.

Works Cited

Berrou, Raphaël and Pradel Pompilus. *Histoire de la littérature haïtienne illustrée par les textes*, 3 Vols. Éditions Caraïbes/Éditions de l'École, Vol. 1 and Vol 2, 1975; Vol. 3, 1977.

Chauvet, Marie. *Amour, Colère et Folie*. Gallimard, 1968.

Chavenet, Anaïse. "Anaïse Chavenet: Ça suffit, les livres mal faits." *Le Nouvelliste*, June 24, 2015, lenouvelliste.com/article/146446/anaise-chavenet-ca-suffit-les-livres-mal-faits.

Danticat, Edwidge. "Introduction." *Love, Anger, Madness*, by Marie Vieux-Chauvet, Trans. Rose-Myriam Rejouis and Val Vinokur. Random House, 2009, pp. vii–xiii.

De Beauvoir, Simone. *The Second Sex*. Trans. Howard M. Parshley. Vintage Books, 1973.

Depestre, Renée. *Hadriana in All My Dreams*. Trans. Kaiama Glover. Akashic Books, 2017.

Frankétienne. "Marie Chauvet affirmait sa vie par l'écriture." *En Amour avec Marie*, Ed. Emmelie Prophète. Imprimeur, S.A. 2016, pp. 82–8.

Glover, Kaiama L. "'Black' Radicalism in Haiti and the Disorderly Feminine: The Case of Marie Vieux Chauvet." *Small Axe: A Caribbean Journal of Criticism*, vol. 40, March 2013, pp. 7–21.

Glover, Kaiama L. "Daughter of Haiti: Marie Vieux Chauvet." *Toward an Intellectual History of Black Women*, Ed. Mia Bay, Farah J. Griffin, Martha S. Jones, and Barbara D. Savage, 2015, pp. 145–59.

Glover, Kaiama L. "Marie Chauvet: théoricienne sociale." *Legs et littérature: Marie Vieux Chauvet*, special issue of *Revue de la littérature contemporaine*, vol. 8, July 2016, pp. 17–30.

Glover, Kaiama L and Alessandra Benedicty-Kokken, eds. "Editor's Preface: Marie Vieux Chauvet Untethered." *Revisiting Marie Vieux Chauvet: Paradoxes of the Postcolonial Feminine*, Special Issue of *Yale French Studies*, vol. 128, 2015, pp. 1–6.

Jacobson, Erik. "Critical Sociolinguistics in the Adult ESOL Classroom." *Radical Teacher*, vol. 68, Winter 2003, pp. 13–17.

Jean-Charles, Régine Michelle. "Naming, Claiming, and Framing Marie Chauvet." *Meridians: Feminism, Race, Transnationalism*, vol. 16, no. 1, 2018, pp. 50–76.

Jean-Charles, Régine Michelle. "They Never Call It Rape: Critical Reception and Representation of Sexual Violence in Marie Vieux-Chauvet's Amour, Colère et Folie." *The Journal of Haitian Studies*, vol. 12, no. 2, 2006, pp. 4–21.

Joseph, Régine Isabelle. Introduction. "Marie Chauvet—Lettre à Gaston Gallimard." *Île en île*, ile-en-ile.org/chauvet_gallimard/.

Joseph, Régine Isabelle. "The Letters of Marie Chauvet and Simone de Beauvoir: A Critical Introduction." *Revisiting Marie Vieux Chauvet: Paradoxes of the Postcolonial Feminine*, Special Issue of *Yale French Studies*, vol. 128, 2015, pp. 25–39.

Laferrière, Dany, "Marie Chauvet a bien écrit le grand roman des années noires de la dictature haïtienne." *Amour, Colère et Folie,* by Marie Vieux Chauvet. Éditions Zulma, 2015, pp. 493–9.

Lahens, Yanick. "Marie Chauvet ou la voix de la femme est nudité." *En Amour avec Marie*, Ed. Emmelie Prophète. L'Imprimeur, 2016, pp. 127–33.

Martelly, Stéphane. "Un cri sans ordre pour le tuer. Sens sous emprise/signe saturé." *En Amour avec Marie*, Ed. Emmelie Prophète. L'Imprimeur, 2016, pp. 141–50.

Marxsen, Patti M. "In Perpetual Revolt." *Women's Review of Books*, vol. 27, no. 2, 2010, pp. 5–7.

"Meanness of the Heart; Fiction from Haiti." *The Economist*, vol. 392, no. 8644, August 15, 2009, p. 66.

Meï, Siobhan Marie. "Haiti in Translation: General Sun, My Brother and in the Flicker of an Eyelid by Jacques Stephen Alexis, An Interview with Carrol F. Coates," *H-Net Haiti in Translation*, January 18, 2017, networks.hnet.org/node/116721/discussions/162063/haiti-translation-general-sun-my-brother-and-flicker-eyelid.

Meï, Siobhan Marie and Nathan Dize. "Vodou in Translation: A Roundtable on the English-Language Translation of Vodou." *H-Net*, February 17, 2018, networks.h-net.org/node/116721/discussions/1397315/vodou-translation-roundtable-english-language-translation-vodou.

Mukherjee, Ankhi. *What Is a Classic? Postcolonial Rewriting and Invention of the Canon*. Stanford University Press, 2013.

Nzengou Tayo, Marie-José. "La traduction des textes littéraires antillais: quels enjeux?" *Proceedings of the University of Liège Colloquium La Traduction, et après? Éthique et Professions*. April 27–28, 2007.

Pierre, Mirline, ed. *Legs et littérature: Marie Vieux Chauvet*, special issue of *Revue de la littérature contemporaine*, vol. 8, July 2016.

Prophète, Emmelie, ed. *En Amour avec Marie*. L'Imprimeur, 2016.

Réjouis, Rose-Myriam. "Translator's Note." *Love, Anger, Madness*, by Marie Vieux Chauvet, Trans. Rose-Myriam Rejouis and Val Vinokur. Random House, 2009, p. xxi.

Shread, Carolyn. "Éditorial: Les silences de Marie Chauvet." *Legs et littérature*. Ed. Mirline Pierre, special issue of *Revue de la littérature contemporaine*, vol. 8, 2016, pp. 5–8.

Shread, Carolyn. "La Traduction métramorphique: Entendre le kreyòl dans la traduction anglaise des *Rapaces* de Marie Vieux-Chauvet." *Palimpsestes*, vol. 22, 2009, pp. 225–43.

Smart Bell, Madison. "Permanent Exile." *The Nation*, February 1, 2010, pp. 30–3.

Smith, Matthew. *Red and Black in Haiti: Radicalism, Conflict, and Political Change, 1934–57*. University of North Carolina Press, 2009.

Spear, Thomas C. "Marie Chauvet: The Fortress Still Stands." *Revisiting Marie Vieux Chauvet: Paradoxes of the Postcolonial Feminine*, special issue of *Yale French Studies*, vol. 128, pp. 9–24.

Taleb-Khyar, Mohamed, (trans.) and Yanick Lahens. "Haitian Literature and Culture." *Callaloo*, vol. 15, no. 2, Spring 1992, pp. 441–4.

Vieux-Chauvet, Marie. *Amour, Colère et Folie*. Emina Soleil, 2005.

Vieux-Chauvet, Marie. *Love, Anger, Madness*. Trans. Rose-Myriam Rejouis and Val Vinokur. Random House, 2009.

Vieux, Marie. *Les Rapaces*. Henri Deschamps, 1986.

Wilson, Betty. "Literature and Activism, Literature as Activism: Case Studies from Caribbean Women's Writing in French: Marie Chauvet, Edwidge Danticat, Yanick Lahens, Gisèle Pinea." *Caribbean Quarterly*, vol. 66, no. 3, pp. 405–24.

Zimra, Clarisse. "Haitian Literature after Duvalier: An Interview with Yanick Lahens." *Callaloo*, vol. 16, no. 1, Winter 1993, pp. 77–93.

17

What Besides Words?

Translating Bilge Karasu's *A Long Day's Evening*

Aron Aji

> The emergence of a literary text means that, first, its language has been made to express that text. [...] Literature is... the memory of language. I am not saying, the memory of individuals; it's the memory of language.
>
> (Bilge Karasu 18; translation mine)

Bilge Karasu (1930–95) was one of the most inventive prose writers of Turkey. He was born in Istanbul and lived most of his life in Ankara. From 1974 onward, he taught semiotics and critical reading—the latter being a topic he pioneered—at Hacettepe University, in Ankara. Steeped in world literature, Karasu could read in eight languages and translated from at least five (including works by Eliot, Lorca, Simenon, Yourcenar, and Calvino). Richly cosmopolitan in upbringing and training and widely schooled in poststructuralism, Karasu achieved a deft synthesis between European genre play and local storytelling traditions, paving the way for an authentically Turkish fiction that optimizes the poetic possibilities of the language.

Karasu's *A Long Day's Evening* (*Uzun Sürmüş Bir Günün Akşamı*) was the undisputed modern classic that Karasu's literary executor and publisher Müge Gürsoy Sökmen had handed me in 1995, at the end of our first meeting in Istanbul, stating emphatically, "You must translate this." It would take me six years to brave this extraordinary book, a task for which I had to prepare myself by first translating two other books by Karasu—*Death in Troy*, which he wrote before *A Long Day's Evening*, and *The Garden of Departed Cats*, which he wrote after. I came to *A Long Day's Evening* as if swimming in a tempest, experiencing the inward thrust and the outward surf of Karasu's linguistic vortex. It took me another six years to complete the actual translation of the book. As these twelve years also included several other translation projects that involved different texts by different authors, the process of decoding

Karasu's language inevitably overlapped with and saturated the development of my own translation methods. When I was not translating Karasu, it often felt that I was translating for Karasu, an omnipresent reader.[1]

Key to my patient (prolonged?)[2] preparation were the two assertions by Karasu that I offer in the epigraph earlier. For the author, each new literary work engenders its own expressive idiom and, in doing so, adds to "the memory of language," in turn expanding the capacity of language to engender further creativity. The "memory of individuals," that is, that of the authors, is instrumentalized in the creative process because, for Karasu, meaning materializes in and through language. Things, ideas, emotions, while experienced in inchoate form in ordinary lives, germinate, ripen, and find their most authentic reality in and through language, which itself is consciously developed so it can express this reality. This regenerative relationship between literary production and language was what I strove to trace in Karasu's own literary evolution from his earlier writing to *A Long Day's Evening* and then beyond. The same relation is the reason why I continue to believe that the language of the source text, rather than the expressive conventions of the target language, inscribes its own expectations into the translation process.

The arrival of a future classic in its native literary environment is often an unforeseen event, a transgression. Whether for its style, its language, narrative structure, form, theme, and often for some combination thereof, the future classic presents a strange and new literary articulation when compared to what came before it. Initially, the new text is, in some yet undefined terms, "foreign" to its native readers. Its novelty lures them as much as it challenges their reading habits and expectations. Gaining the status of a classic involves a confrontation, a process of de-foreignization, if you will, of re-positioning within the continuum of the national literary tradition, effected through readings, re-readings, interpretations, scholarship, and so on. The classic also alters the native literary tradition; emerging as it does at the outer margin of tradition and marking a point of linguistic and aesthetic excess, the classic compels a rapprochement between itself and its literary tradition, disturbing the banks and the itinerary of the literary mainstream. Karasu's *A Long Day's Evening* was such an event.

---

[1] In retrospect, I see that I have been speaking about my Karasu translations incessantly. This chapter carries the echoes of several interviews and talks I have given over the years, including those published in *Eleven Eleven*, *M-Dash*, and *Words Without Borders*.

[2] By some delightful fortuity, the most literal translation of the book's title, *Uzun Sürmüş Bir Günün Akşamı*, would be "A Prolonged Day's Evening."

Originally published in 1970, A *Long Day's Evening* contains a two-part main narrative by the same title, accompanied by a short, fifteen-page autobiographical essay. The main narrative is about two eighth-century Byzantine monks, Andronikos and Ioakim, each of whom endures a wrenching crisis of faith during the period of iconoclasm, when their mode of worship is forbidden by Leo III. The meanings of the names that Karasu gives his monks, Andronikos (man victorious) and Ioakim (god's chosen), inevitably allude to the conflict between humanism and dogma, or individual will and conformity. The three narratives are held together by several thematic dualities—faith/creed, truth/dogma, freedom/loyalty, personal will/social acceptance, among others. The dynamic interplay of these themes makes the book a complex novel of ideas, not unlike the "polyphonic" *The Book of Laughter and Forgetting* that Milan Kundera would publish nine years later, in 1979. Karasu's book also works like a sonata: the first two parts developing contrapuntally while the third providing a provocative coda. Conspicuously far removed from the chronology of Andronikos's and Ioakim's stories, the coda is suggestively autobiographical: a very brief, fifteen-page essay set in the 1960s—a decade bracketed by military coups in Turkey (1960, 1971)—that lends a contemporary significance to the paradox of liberation by tyranny during the Byzantine emperor Leo III's reign. Across this sweeping chronology of the book, the narrative voice in each part exists in a dialogic relationship with the voices in the other parts. By the end of the book, we discover that the three voices might well belong to a single consciousness interrogating (deciphering) itself through invented others.

Appearing against the backdrop of contemporary social-realist literature that aimed at holding a critical and often diagnostic mirror to its immediate historical milieu, *A Long Day's Evening* comes bearing plenty of strange and unforeseen characteristics. The book's ostensibly Byzantine setting and subject matter, its relentlessly introspective monks, its examination of the lyric consciousness of individuals caught in the epic sweep of religious and political change, all combine to both widen and deepen the traditionally local and collectivist perspective of social realism. Most strikingly, *A Long Day's Evening* is an expansive novel of ideas enacted in the ever-deepening interiority of its characters—a psycho-philosophical treatment of a twelve-hundred-year history of totalitarian idealism (the dark underside of humanism) presented in the meditations of three characters in the timeframe of three excursions, that in "real-time" would have lasted less than two hours!

Walter Benjamin sees translation as granting the original work a new currency or, as he famously calls it, an afterlife; however, this afterlife of the classic begins, once again, as an unforeseen event replete with its own forms of confrontation. Once transplanted in the target language, a classic may not readily exhibit all the qualities that made it a classic in its native soil. It may also be further disadvantaged when its native literary tradition is inadequately represented in the target language—as is the case with Turkish literature, and, for that matter, with any of the myriad literatures from less commonly translated languages. Its status as a classic, now an abstract hearsay, an extenuating circumstance, must be somehow revalorized in the new context. This revalorization carries a significant risk of over-domestication, foregrounding those of its aspects (i.e., themes, plot, or characters) that are more readily recognizable to its new readership, "explicitating"[3] or, worse yet, occluding the radical originality of the classic, in turn, making the source text foreign to itself. In setting out to translate Karasu's *A Long Day's Evening*, it was, above all, its radical originality that I wanted to recreate, namely, its language.

The thematic and formal characteristics that I mention earlier—the Byzantine setting, Eastern Orthodoxy, the philosophical novel of ideas presented through psychological introspection, the thematic polyphony and sonata-like narrative form, while certainly innovative in the Turkish literary context—are relatively familiar to the Anglophone reader, and they are therefore readily translatable—especially in 2013, when my translation came out, forty years after the book's first publication date. *A Long Day's Evening* obtains its radical originality and its status as a classic primarily because it alters the trajectory of the language of Turkish literary modernism.[4] Any translation that did not foreground first and foremost Karasu's language would not do. As I discussed elsewhere, Karasu had been a master *artificer* of the new Turkish, also called "pure" Turkish,[5] a major element of the national project of creating a modern republic and its new cultural identity. The most distinctive characteristics of pure Turkish have been its rejection of borrowed vocabulary from Arabic and Farsi, and the invention and introduction of new words built on Turkic verb roots. Karasu is among the most celebrated proponents of this new vocabulary, which, in the works of many other authors, and especially in its early—perhaps overzealous—manifestations, often comes across as contrived, artificial, or outright alienating.[6] However, Karasu's innovation goes significantly beyond propagating a new vocabulary.

---

[3] The term is offered by Shoshana Blum-Kulka to describe translation's tendency to render meaning more explicitly than in the original.
[4] Historically, Karasu was part of a Second New Wave in Turkey, the second generation of writers since the founding of the Republic, who were instrumental in Turkish modernism. Karasu was at the same time trained in post-structuralist theory, and his writings certainly herald postmodernism in Turkish literature.
[5] See Aron Aji, "Artificer of Language: Translational Strategies in Bilge Karasu's Writing."
[6] For a comprehensive analysis of Karasu's use of pure Turkish, see Nurdan Gurbilek.

In his hands, and most conspicuously in *A Long Day's Evening*, pure Turkish develops into a *dynamic* language complete with deep structures—organic syntax, metaphoric resonance, inner rhythms, and acoustic effects—in order to engender a mode of expression that corresponds more naturally to one's mode of thinking and meaning-making. Karasu wants language to shape and take shape inside the literary artifice, in other words, to be both the medium and the very substance of invention. Indeed, *A Long Day's Evening* is an acutely self-conscious, studiously constructed and reconstructed artifice that renders its invention process both obvious and integral to its scope. Among Karasu's most persistent questions are: how language can be made authentic; how it can narrow the gap between experience and expression; and how it can embody the emotional and intellectual "matter" of experience with acute immediacy.

In translating *A Long Day's Evening*, I was therefore keenly aware that the language of the source text is the original and primary medium of invention that I needed to recreate. How this language is made, how the source text reinvents/reinvests its native language—lexically, sonically, formally— to express its meaning. My translation had to attempt the closest possible synergy between the linguistic codes of the source text and the expressive capacity of the target language. Accordingly, my translation engaged Karasu's language on three levels: lexical, syntactic, and acoustic.

What Besides Words?

The first rule I set for myself was to use a plain and contemporary vocabulary in English, stripped of archaisms, Latinate words, and so on, a vocabulary that, consistent with Karasu's intent, would obviate the historicity of the Byzantine content to foreground the contemporary (*or* extemporary) questions the book explores. My lexical choice was also a compensatory choice since, sadly, I would not be able to reenact fully the newness of Karasu's pure Turkish vocabulary— a radical intervention at the time with lasting effects that brought Turkish to a lexical level commensurate with contemporary English.

If Karasu's lexical innovations got lost in the translation, it was still crucial to recognize his logic and intent in the translated text. Compared to English, Turkish has a seemingly small vocabulary—about a fifth of the English—but, as an agglutinated language, it employs a large but set number of suffixes to modify root verbs or nouns and to indicate tense, case, relation, etc., widening the range of meanings a root word can convey. For instance, "bil," the root verb "know," can be made "bildik" to mean "we knew," "bilmeden" to mean "unknowingly," "bilinmez," to mean "unknowable," or "bilinç" to mean "consciousness," and "bilemediklerimdensin" to mean an entire sentence, "you are one of the people I don't know." These diverse meanings, wildly ranging in semantic density, are conveyed through words that bear phonetic similarities; in turn, the words implicitly evoke each other's meaning because they explicitly echo each other's sounds. Furthermore, the highly consistent sound structures of Turkish (each word containing either high or low vowels but only exceptionally both) often create a close phonic correspondence between the sense of a word and its emotional tenor, or in the case of a sentence, between the train of thought and its emotional cadence. These characteristics naturally exist in Turkish and are not easily approximated in English. What Karasu achieves by compounding suffixes in a single Turkish word has to inform the composition of phrases, clauses and even entire sentences in English.

An early passage in the second part of *A Long Day's Evening*[7] when the elderly Ioakim is thinking about his mortality and its postponement, serves as an apt illustration of my translation decisions concerning Karasu's lexicon in Turkish. This passage also reaches its climax with possibly the most memorable phrase in the entire corpus of Karasu's writing: YAKLAŞMANIN UZAKLAŞTIRICILIĞI.

> To see March again, to feel the warm sun in his joints, to watch the river gradually change from brown to green, to taste again the watermelon, the fig, the grape—these seem to him now as incredible, as improbable as fairytales from faraway times, faraway places, only vaguely remembered. Yet is it not also true that tasting the fig and the grape will once again bring him closer to another winter, sweep him into an altogether incredible, and all the more improbable adventure? Will he not experience all the more keenly in his heart that being ever near is also being never, ever there? (76)

Those inclined to follow visual or auditory cues will probably be hard pressed to determine where in the translation this famous phrase occurs. And they might be puzzled to find out that I translated "yaklaşmanın uzak laştırıcılığı" as "being ever near is also being never, ever there." This two-word assertion encapsulates Zeno's paradox, heightening especially the existential crisis it entails: getting progressively closer to a destination (*yaklaşmanın*) without ever arriving, and simultaneously feeling farther and farther away from it (*uzaklaştırıcılığı*). The elderly monk must endure

---

[7] All quotations hereafter are taken from Bilge Karasu, *A Long Day's Evening*, translated by Aron Aji.

life even as he is approaching his death for which he has long prepared. This two-word phrase in Turkish gains its singularity because Karasu conveys its complex meaning by ingeniously relying on the phonic and suffix rules regulating modern Turkish grammar. The phrase consists of two noun roots each modified by three and four suffixes respectively: *yak-laş-manın / uzak-laş-tır-ıcı-lığı*. The root words are strikingly commonplace and simple: *yakın* (near) and *uzak* (far), so are the suffixes, but what Karasu makes of them is decidedly, strikingly complex and elegant. While the first and shorter word comes to a firm stop with *–nın*, as if marking the desired destination, the second word, extending along the string of *-ı/ğ* sound, only leads to an open ending *-tır-ıcı-lığı*, evoking the sense of indefinite postponement. The two words in Turkish also evokes a tidal movement, the flow of the first countered by the ebb of the second. To this day, I am not sure if my decision, admittedly stewed in my obsessive thinking, is the right translation. However, "being ever near / being never, ever there," I hope, reflects the lexical dexterity characteristic of Karasu's innovative language.

Syntax as Individuation

Because Karasu wants language to approximate experience as *immediately* as possible, his unconventional syntax (fragments, extended run-ons, indented clauses, dispersed paragraphs, etc.) are intended to capture the moods, rhythms, and the pace of his characters' acute introspection as they seek self-understanding. I strove to remain faithful to his syntax as much as possible, but I also found it necessary to diverge from it in those instances when capturing the tone and mood seemed the more essential task of revealing characterization. Karasu's narrative emulates the inner monologues of two monks; the paragraphs and even discrete sentences often consist of extended streams of associations that interrupt each other or intermingle or stray. Ironically, I was helped by my own internal monologues while wrestling with Karasu's language. I realized how, for instance, when someone is thinking to oneself, thoughts tangle and dis-entangle more by instinct than by grammar, how the train of thought is associative and indexical. Consequently, to find correct English correspondences required not only decoding the logic or grammar of Karasu's language but also somehow *inhabiting* the intimate existential space created simultaneously by that language so that the reader can, in turn, inhabit this space just as intimately.

The opening paragraph describing Andronikos's arrival on the island is illustrative of Andronikos's narrative in the first part of the book:

> He turns to look ahead. He must be getting close to the island, since the dark imposing mass of its rocky peak has grown more distinct in the advancing dawn. His exhausted arms pull the oars with the numbed ease of a body that has grown indifferent to thought or will. He can hardly hear sounds. The oars plunge into the water, withdraw, plunge again; the sea tears open, yielding to the boat, mends itself in the morning calm. (17)

This brief seventy-nine-word paragraph contains five sentences, ranging in length from five to twenty mostly mono- or bi-syllabic words. The pattern of short-then-long sentences, compounded by the terse clauses in the longer sentences, evokes a quiet and tense mood; the punctuation, more in the last sentences than in the preceding four combined, is intended to mimic the rhythm of Andronikos's rowing as well as breathing at the end of his arduous escape. This opening also foreshadows Andronikos' mental clarity and the clarity of his convictions. He leaves Byzantium because he refuses to renounce his faith; he chooses exile over conformity. Karasu's syntax in this first section is consistently unlabored, mimicking the workings of an untroubled mind. Even the occasionally long paragraphs hint at no indecision or oscillation on the part of the young monk.

Ioakim presents a dramatic contrast to Andronikos. We meet him several decades after his friendship with Andronikos. Now an aging monk, he has retired to Ravenna, but even in his own exile, and perhaps because he had chosen to conform rather than rebel against the iconoclasm and Leo III's new creed, Ioakim is riddled with remorse, shame, guilt, self-doubt. Long accustomed to introspection, his thinking, even at its most logical, is claustrophobic, periphrastic, expressed in complex labyrinthine sentences:

> Just as no one knows exactly where the sun rises or where it sets, conversely, just as everyone knows with reasonable certainty the path the sun follows during the day, just as this sun hanging above you at the noon hour is among the few things you know with absolute certainty in the world, so do the farthest reaches of the walk vanish into the misty forgottenness of a certain fog-covered meadow, while near the midpoint, the summit, the noon hour, the brightest moment of the walk, memories gradually come into light, then, once at the summit—the walker caught in the acute brilliance of a piece of ice that refuses to thaw, beholding

the point where the arms of the sea converge—the walk attains a kind of eternity that defies all other memories. (87)

Or the thread of his thoughts, snarled into a startlingly beautiful knot of images and ideas, nevertheless comes loose and slips through his mind:

> This steadily emptying form, this walk that gradually became the shadow of something beautiful, this walk that resembled living, crowned by a moment of fullness, of completeness, experienced at the summit while gazing at one's surroundings, at the past, at the ordeal of the long ascent, the moment of rest before the descent, the soon-to-begin descent toward death, the moment of equilibrium that gained meaning because recognizing it demanded every ounce of one's strength, this walk that, in time, began to feel like a sorrowful recess, a heartrending remorse, a thorn in the side of one's commonplace life. (88)

Acoustics: The Gathering Force of Sounds or Making English Sing in Turkish

Finally, and predictably, I resisted domestication and favored foreignization as my overall strategy. Given that Karasu's innovations (linguistic, formal, aesthetic) are transformative and, in that sense, translational, I wanted the readers of my translation not to lose sight of the fact that they were reading a translation, and, like the Turkish readers of the original, to remain aware that the book they are reading is an invented artifice, its language taking shape within. However, my foreignizing translation did not involve such surface effects as retaining Turkish words or inventing neologisms and such in English. Rather, operating on the level of acoustics, I attempted to bond English as closely as possible to the acoustic and affective range of the source text and to make the tone and timbre of the Turkish text breathe through the language of my translation as much as possible.

Before offering an example, let me briefly explain how I understand acoustics. When translating for sound, our experience tends to be regulated by our critical training. We detect figures of sound, phonic patterns that we try to closely approximate. However, sounds in a text (assonance, rhythms, stresses, pauses, etc.) also communicate with our senses, prompt visual images, smells, tastes, tactile memories that we experience or intuit through simultaneous sensory associations. The acoustics of a text have to do with this inextricably composite experience, the mental imprint or notation of how the text wants to be read or, more holistically, experienced. Attention to acoustics in *A Long Day's Evening* was especially important, given Karasu's preference for the natural, organic (spoken) cadences of modern Turkish, to counteract the highly formal musicality of traditional literature.

As the themes interlace and the language mirrors the complexity of the characters' emotions, Karasu's language in *A Long Day's Evening* at times assumes an almost operatic quality. One of the most resonant examples of this occurs, unsurprisingly, at the book's climax, while Ioakim recollects the time when, as a young monk, he was made to watch Andronikos being tortured by imperial guards for his transgression and escape. The following passage comes at the end of a longer section that steadily gains emotional force and reaches here its crescendo before dying out. (Emphasis is mine to indicate the acoustic composition—with italics suggesting perhaps softer tones.)

> Andronikos had been forced to talk for *eight* straight *days*.
> For *eight* straight *days*, more than food or water, he had been forced to swallow air. For *eight* straight *days*.
> *Eight days, eight nights.*
> **First** he had spoken of God, **then** of his deeds, **then** of his beliefs, **then** of his disbeliefs, **then** of unbelief, **then** of the essential precepts in his heart, **then** of his essential worthlessness, **then** of his suffering, **then** of his fatigue, **then** of friendship, **then** of love, **then** of indifference, **then** of his childhood, **then** whatever came to his mind or his lips, **then**, finally, whatever could not even leave his heart or mind.
> He had not spoken.
> He had been forced to speak.
> **Then, fast**er, **fast**er, he had spun like the spinning wheels of a toppled cart. **Then** the spinning had slowed down, **then** down, **then** stopped until it was forced to resume, **then** it had stopped, **then** been forced to resume, **then** later
> The candle had burnt its wick. The wheel had gotten stuck. Later it had squeaked, **then**
> **Stopped.** Outright. While speaking—screaming—of the vanity of feeling pride for one's mistakes. (138–39)

Reading the passage in Turkish, I was caught in the repetition of unvoiced and voiced consonants, the former evoking for me Andronikos's labored breathing, while the latter Ioakim's throbbing body as he helplessly watched his friend being tortured. The sea of nasals (*m, n*) and elongated '*ı*'s in the Turkish also created a mournful tone, with plosives (*d, k, t, p*) periodically intruding, creating a harsh, pulsive effect. My modulated repetition of "then" is sonically different from the repetition of "sonra" (then) in the Turkish, but it is meant to echo the plosives in the Turkish. In both languages, the duration of the phrase units in between identical words follows the same pattern—from short to longer, then short to longer again. The two single-sentence paragraphs that follow are conspicuously quieter, marking perhaps a brief respite, before the onset of the most sonorous, almost percussive, paragraph where the acoustics complements the imagery; then, the sounds gradually dissipate, occurring farther apart until all falls quiet.

As we read this resonant passage, the sounds both carry us forward and deepen our understanding, our experience, of what is being described. The acoustics of this passage binds together not only representation and its emotional affect but also Ioakim's memory and the experience of Andronikos's torture; ultimately, it is again acoustics that intimates the possibility of a reconciliation between young Ioakim who passively witnessed the torture and the older, penitent Ioakim when he is able to witness it to himself.

Literature Is . . . the Memory of Language

Karasu, a prolific translator, was skeptical about translation's ability to transplant a text in foreign soil without turning it into what he called a "lonely" text. The danger cannot be overstated. In the translation boom of the last decade or so, major international works that have managed to lay sturdy roots in their new soil are far outnumbered by those that have had brief periods of bloom. The limited critical discourse about literary translation, one that engages the works themselves—how they are translated or how they might invite different forms of reading—inevitably leaves the works to fend for themselves.

At the same time, translating foreign classics might well alter the soil condition of their new environment. When Karasu says, "Literature is . . . the memory of language" (qtd. in Aji 11), I do not think he means that texts only carry the memory of their language, but they also expand this memory each time by altering and renewing it. Literature is a regenerative event not just in language but of language. So can be translation. Particularly, translation of a literary classic. As a consummate performance in and of its language, the literary classic can—and should, I happen to think—expect a similar performance from the language into which it is translated. To recreate the radical originality of *Uzun Sürmüş Bir Günün Akşamı* in the language of *A*

Long Day's Evening, I wanted the English language to perform on the outer peripheries of convention, to push its reserves so as to reach the expressive capacity that the consummate language of the original work deserved. Each foreign classic in translation thus inscribes itself in the evolving memory of the English language.

Works Cited

Aji, Aron. "Artificer of Language: Translational Strategies in Bilge Karasu's Writing." *Journal of Turkish Studies*, 2010, Harvard UP, pp. 1-7.

Aji, Aron. "By Way of a Preface." *A Long Day's Evening*. By Bilge Karasu. Trans. Aron Aji. City Lights Books, 2012, pp. 9-14.

Akatlı, Fusun and Müge Gürsoy Sökmen. *Bilge Karasu Aramızda*. Trans. Aron Aji. Metis Publishing, 1997.

Blum-Kulka, Shoshana. "Shifts of Cohesion and Coherence in Translation." *The Translation Studies Reader*, Ed. Lawrence Venuti. Routledge, 2000, pp. 298-313.

Gürbilek, Nurdan. "Yazı ve Arınma" (Writing and Distillation). *Bilge Karasu Aramızda*, Ed. Füsun Akatlı and Müge Gürsoy Sökmen. Metis Publishing, 1997, pp. 82-204.

Karasu, Bilge. *Uzun Sürmüş Bir Günün Akşamı* (A Long Day's Evening). Metis Publishing, 1970.

18

Nonsense in a Given Direction

Translating the Timelessness of Marguerite Duras

Emma Ramadan

How Is Translating Marguerite Duras Like Bobbing in the Ocean?

Marguerite Duras's *The Lover* (1984) is taught in classrooms around the world. Her screenplay *Hiroshima mon amour* (1959) has been hailed as a cinematic masterpiece. She is praised as a forerunner of autofiction, of psychologically complex female narrators, of blending the personal and the political, of writing about the pain and the ecstasy of simply being alive and in love. Her name is, in certain homes, a household name. Her legend has exceeded the bounds of her native country of France and the celebration of her literary work has rippled abroad through the act of translation. Duras's books do not encompass universal themes, nor are they written in a form that is accessible or easily comprehensible. Most of her books are wondrously opaque. Many are about love, but Duras writes about love in a way no one else does. Marguerite Duras (1914–96) has gained worldwide renown not only because of what she writes but because of *how* she writes, because of the very texture of her writing. The way her rhythm pulls you along as you bob in her wake. The way the speed and flow of her writing become integral to the story's telling.

Tempête et soleil. Yann est arrivé

Marguerite Duras has been translated by at least nineteen translators into at least thirty-five books in English, and many more worldwide. No two translators will make the same choices. Every translator will imagine a different version of the sea when they read Duras's sea. And yet Duras has managed to reach so many readers across the globe because her words and her spirit remain forcefully "Durassian" despite all these inevitable filters. Her voice and singularity burst through the page, and she is always utterly herself despite being spit out of countless mouths, despite being written and typed by several hands.

When Olivia Baes and I translated *Me & Other Writing*, selected nonfiction and hybrid texts by Marguerite Duras, for Dorothy, a publishing project, in 2019, we didn't read other translations of Duras in English. We knew what she sounded like in her own language. We had her musicality rolling through our heads. Longtime lovers of Duras's writing, we had been walking to her rhythm for years. Her writing had infected ours, her stories had affected our life stories, she was already within us. We practically reeked of her.

And so we had no idea how difficult it would be to translate Duras on the page.

L'Été 80, *Summer 80* in English, is a short text in ten chapters that was originally published in installments by the newspaper *Libération* over the course of the summer of 1980. Duras was commissioned to write about that summer's events in whatever form she chose. Duras blended commentary on the political happenings unfolding throughout the summer with real and fictional observations of the seaside town of Trouville, where she wrote from, as well as an imagined courtship between a camper and his counselor, as well as a story that counselor tells the camper about a boy named David and a shark, as well as Duras's own complicated relationship with a younger man named Yann Andréa, which would begin in earnest that very summer. There is a smashing together of the personal and the political, the I and the you, the real and the written. There are no paragraph breaks, and a sentence about a real-world event is separated only by a period from a glance at the sea, from something witnessed or merely imagined.

> Fog covers the entire sky, it's unfathomably thick, as vast as Europe, static. It's July 13th. The French athletes are going to participate in the Moscow Olympic Games. Until the last minute we had hoped that some would not go, but no, it's been confirmed. For a long time this morning sunlight slid between the storm and the wind. (Duras, *Me & Other Writing* 103)

No matter the subject in a given sentence, present throughout is Duras's characteristic aloof yet intensely personal tone, jumping from passion to detached voyeurism, all of it buoyed by the overpowering rhythm of her prose. She wrote exactly what she wanted, when she felt like it, with no care for separating out her most impulsive inner thoughts from her careful reconstruction of the world around her.

I can see that every crime reveals the essential stupidity of the world, that of force, weapons, and that most populations fear and revere this stupidity as if it were power itself. It's shameful. The child who keeps quiet is still looking all around him, at the high sea, the empty beaches. (*Me & Other Writing* 103–4)

When I came across *Summer 80* and discovered that it hadn't been translated into English, I asked myself why. It's a messy text, often referred to as a laboratory of writing for her works to come. It's a text that's difficult to enter into without previous experience with Marguerite Duras, not the first text of hers I would recommend someone read, but an important little text that allows Duras devotees to gain deeper insight into the way she thinks and how that overflows into her writing. It's a valuable addition to her works available in English precisely because it was the starting point for some of her later, more popular writing. Her earliest book to use the first person, it would herald a shift into autofiction that dominated her later works, and Duras would draw again from *Summer 80* to write *Agatha*, and then *Summer Rain*, and then *Yann Andréa Steiner*. Perhaps this book didn't have the necessary precursors and interest, the right foundation, to find an audience in English until now. Perhaps now that Duras is more of a household name in English, there is enough hunger for more, and for more complicated work.

The rhythms of French don't map themselves neatly onto English words, never mind the sounds. The tiniest cogs of language posed problems for us as translators. Should *l'enfant aux yeux gris* be the child with gray eyes, or the child with the gray eyes? In Duras's endless lists, the French article "de" was repeated over and over to incantatory effect, but in English a repeated "of" was clunky, distracting, not propulsive. The argument "but if Duras had wanted to say x, she could have used y French word, and instead she used z French word" was often foiled by the retort "yes, but listen to the sound of the word." We had to tweak the smallest increments of language, the articles, the conjunctions, and the word endings to make sure that when we read her aloud to ourselves, we heard Duras. Even adding a comma where Duras didn't have one risked disrupting her flow. Consider this sentence from *Summer 80*: "Up close, [the sea is] entirely white, profusely white, endlessly dispensing armfuls of whiteness, vaster and vaster embraces as if gathering and bringing into its reign a mysterious lifeblood of sand and light" (*Me & Other Writing* 100). Imagine adding a comma after "embraces"—it would slow down the sentence, dissolve the powerful buildup of the sea's vast gathering. Imagine inverting the last sentence to read "as if gathering a mysterious lifeblood of sand and light into its reign." It would unravel the mystery too early.

As a translator, your job is to render comprehensible something that is incomprehensible to a certain group of people. You are to serve as a conduit, so that an English speaker can read a French writer like Duras and understand her, partake in the enjoyment or criticism of a given work. But what if the author is simply not interested in being easily understood?

In another piece included in *Me & Other Writing*, a transcribed interview titled "Flaubert is . . .," Duras said:

> How you write something, why, how I wrote, I don't know, I don't know how it started. I can't explain it. Where do certain books come from? There is nothing on the page and then all of a sudden there are three hundred pages. Where does it come from? You have to let it happen when you write, you can't control yourself, you have to let go because you don't know everything about yourself. You don't know what you're capable of writing. (*Me & Other Writing* 6–7)

Duras wrote, simply wrote, from her intuition, according to her whims, just like that. There were seemingly nonsensical sentences in the book that even the Duras scholars and native French speakers we turned to simply could not decode. And then we decided, well, maybe these sentences are in fact "nonsense in a given direction," as Duras put it in that same essay (*Me & Other Writing* 5). Maybe we, too, needed to let go of the idea of uncovering a clear meaning. And so instead we let her sounds and rhythms carry us, we let our intuitive sense of her guide us. We had to lose ourselves in translation the way Duras lost herself in writing, let ourselves drift in her current, match her flow. We almost had to squint, glimpse Duras's words out of the corners of our eyes, not try overly hard to pin down meaning, to dissect her sentences. Let them wash over us and come up gasping with words.

Elisa Gabbert states in her book *The Word Pretty*:

> Perhaps most importantly, for fiction in translation to work, the interest can't be all in "perfect" or "beautiful" sentences, since the words and rhythm and syntax will all be different in the new language—lovely still, one hopes, but not in the same way. Instead, other elements—the ideas, the characters, the story—have to carry across. These other elements are constructed from language but are less subject to corruption or erosion through translation. (Gabbert, 89)

Authors like Marguerite Duras refute this otherwise convincing idea; many classic texts or authors become classics across the globe precisely because they defy this idea. It is Duras's signature way of writing that has been studied by scholars, students, and the average reader alike for decades; she is known for the texture and style of her sentences as much as for the other elements of her text. What has made Duras a classic name in both France and abroad is the way her sentences seem to circumvent the typical rules of syntax and structure, honoring rhythm and flow as much as plot or character.

> In *Summer 80*, often you don't know where you are. I don't know where I am, if I'm with the sea, or with God, a hypothetical or real God, or with Poland, with the children . . . I'm everywhere . . . I'm everywhere at once, but they don't see me and I can't be seen, I don't want to be seen. If they see me, I don't write. (Duras, Françoise Faucher interview n.p.)

How do you translate an author who doesn't want to be seen? You hear her. Each successive translator must contend with and channel Duras's marine rhythm, move through the waves of her inner thoughts, convey her sea. Breathe as she breathes. After all, Duras's writing was given the label "écriture courante"—literally current writing, flowing writing, swept-by-the-sea writing. An intuitive writing that gives us a glimpse at something else, something unspoken. It's the rhythm that is often precisely what is important, what evokes and allows for that glimpse, not those other elements, not the ideas, the characters, the story, but the current that sweeps the nonsense in a given direction. A rhythm so commanding as to find its way under the skin of readers from Trouville to Rhode Island.

The notion that the musicality of a text cannot be rendered in translation, that it is easily corrupted or eroded, rears its head all too often, because sounds and rhythms between languages seldom coincide. As demonstrated by the notorious quotation attributed to Robert Frost and everywhere (mis)quoted, "Poetry is what gets lost in translation." This idea is arguably misguided at best, and destructive at worst. Duras agreed. In one of the book's pieces titled "Translation," Duras posits:

> Everyone knows that translation is not a matter of the literal exactitude of a text, but perhaps we must go even further: and say that it is more of a musical approach, rigorously personal and even, if necessary, deviant. . . . A translated text has been translated by someone based on a first reading which is always just as personal as the writing, and which can never be erased. Is it possible to talk about a musical translation? We talk about musical interpretations. It's a shame that when we talk about translation, we stop at its literal meaning. As if meaning could only be found in texts,

and not in music. Doesn't the convention of respected meaning in fact propagate backwards ideas that work against the liberty of a text, against its breath, or its madness? (*Me & Other Writing* 38)

Translation is indeed inherently personal, because literary texts are translated by persons, and not machines. Our decision to adopt a musical approach was a rigorously personal (deviant?) choice. How can such a personal act lend itself to translating authors and texts considered classic, writing that transcends the time period and historical context in which it was written? How does the intervention of translators allow for an author to remain continuously relevant? Our answer was to translate not just the literal meaning, not just the ideas, characters, and story, but also the meaning found in Duras's music, to always honor the liberty, breath, and madness of her text. The day we turned in our translation, Olivia said she knew we were done because it sounded like Duras, and not like either of us.

Rhythms have to be re-invented with each new generation of translator. What might have once sounded smooth or hypnotic might not enchant readers anymore four decades later. Barbara Bray's recreation of Duras in her English translation of *The Lover* in 1986 might not resemble the work of translators hoping to achieve the same effect today. A translator must always find the most authentic way of translating someone in their given moment and context, to make them ring true for readers of their translation, to make Duras sound like Duras in 1986 or in 2019.

Despite her many, many translators over a number of decades, what is almost always agreed upon is that for Duras, *la mer* is the sea. *La mer.* The sea. It's obvious. The word ocean is two syllables—that's your first problem. Saying it makes your mouth pucker. The sea is simple, sweet, and easy, it topples out of your lips, was barely there to begin with, is gone as soon as it's uttered. I am scanning the pages of Duras translations by various translators; I see no ocean. Her rhythm and tone are commanding enough to compel agreement on this, and other, points. A voice expansive and cohesive enough to span generations of translators with different philosophies, different vocabularies, different literary propensities, different pay grades and backgrounds, different time periods and translation contexts, is a voice expansive and cohesive enough to assert itself in any language, to become a classic.

Tempête et soleil. Yann est arrivé. Storm and sun. Yann has come

When our translation was published in 2019, there had also been renewed interest in overlooked (in America) women authors, seemingly plucked from the depths to be celebrated in a new context—such as Leonora Carrington, Alejandra Pizarnik, Clarice Lispector, Eve Babitz, and Lucia Berlin—as well as interest in slim experimental novellas by women (in fact Dorothy, a publishing project specializes in exactly this), and in women in translation (there is even a Women in Translation Month, started in 2014 by Meytal Radzinski). Our translation came out with a small experimental publishing house with a focus on women writers, whereas Duras's previous English translations had been primarily published by large houses. This placed Duras in a different frame of reference and helped her reach new readers, new reviewers, and new bookstores. Her work was juxtaposed and placed in conversation with other writers published by Dorothy, a publishing project. Her words resounded with new echoes and were inserted into new conversations. Excerpts were published in *The Paris Review* and *The New Yorker*, appearing on the desktops or mailboxes of people who might not have read her before. I did a launch event for the book at the Center for Fiction in Brooklyn with established experimental writer Kate Zambreno, who drew in fans of her own books who might have been encouraged to pick up Duras for the first time upon hearing of Duras's influence on her work. Famous musician and poet Patti Smith posted about the translation on Instagram, as did poet and essayist Anne Boyer. The model and actress Kaia Gerber posed with the book in a bikini on her Instagram for her 5.7 million followers, many of whom asked what the book was in the comments, expanding Duras's exposure to an audience not usually targeted by publicity directors of publishing houses.

Dorothy, a publishing project, asked us to pair *Summer 80* with a collection of Duras's other newspaper writings to ground the novella, give it some context, and shed light on Duras as a "subjective journalist," adding another layer to both *Summer 80* and to Duras's oeuvre in English. These newspaper writings are a more accessible entry point to Duras's inner nature and to her writing, a sort of warm-up to *Summer 80*. In "Marguerite Duras: Internet Essayist?" reviewer Maddie Crum compares Duras's style to online writing. Duras's "true crime" pieces—"Horror at Choisy-le-Roi," an in-depth observation of the court case of a woman accused of murdering her lover's wife, and "Nadine from Orange," an interview with the wife of a man accused of kidnapping and engaging in inappropriate relations with a young girl—seemed to take on a new meaning in 2019's true crime-obsessed society. What might have seemed like an arbitrary off-shoot of Duras's work makes her highly relatable to many readers today.

The other articles included in the collection, including Duras's take on various political events of the time, can also be read in a new light today, when the average person is encouraged to post personal political messages to their social media pages and in other various public forums. How can Duras's subjective journalism speak to today's writers who bring a journalistic approach to the personal, or a personal approach to journalism?

And so as the ripples of our own efforts buoy Duras to new readers, what these readers will find is what readers of Duras have always found. Her repetitions and rewritings of her own stories, her unfiltered explorations of the female psyche and a woman's power. Her odd use of syntax, frequently shifting tenses and perspectives. Her fragments. Her tone often described simply as "Durassian" because it is so unlike anyone else's with its unaffected, pared-down language, flittering between extreme close-ups and unsettling detachment. Her approach to writing as coming from a place of genuine curiosity, of pure emotion and raw lived experience. What people might say if they said exactly what they wanted, how people might love if they loved without fear. How we might live if we lived without shame. And, above all, how people might write if they wrote from the current within, with no regard for the rules. As Dan Gunn states in the introduction to *Me & Other Writing*, Duras's work explores the "fundamental impossibility . . . to live honestly or meaningfully within the conventions dictated by society, with its religions, its laws, its tyrannies, its grammar, its syntax" (*Me & Other Writing* XI).

What does Duras have to offer readers, no matter when or where they are reading her? Proof that you can throw off the binds of language and write however you want, whatever you want, in a given direction. That you can carve out your own voice, your own syntax, musicality, and madness. No one writes like Duras. Except for her translators.

Works Cited

Brooks, Cleanth. *Conversations on the Craft of Poetry*. Holt, Rinehart and Winston, 1961.

Crum, Maddie. "Marguerite Duras: Internet Essayist?" Review of *Me & Other Writing*, by Marguerite Duras, Trans. Olivia Baes and Emma Ramadan. *Literary Hub*, October 21, 2019, lithub.com/marguerite-duras-internet-essayist/.

Duras, Marguerite. *Agatha*. Les Éditions de Minuit, 1981.

Duras, Marguerite. Interview between Marguerite Duras and Françoise Faucher for Radio-Canada, April 11, 1981.

Duras, Marguerite. *La Pluie d'été*. Éditions P.O.L, 1990.

Duras, Marguerite. *L'Été 80*. Les Éditions de Minuit, 1980.

Duras, Marguerite. *Me & Other Writing*. Trans. Olivia Baes and Emma Ramadan. Dorothy, a publishing project, 2019.

Duras, Marguerite. *Practicalities*. Trans. Barbara Bray. Grove Press, 1992.

Duras, Marguerite. *Yann Andréa Steiner*. Gallimard, 1992.

Gabbert, Elisa. *The Word Pretty*. Black Ocean, 2018.

19

"Sentence" as Lifeline

Translating David Albahari's Novels

Ellen Elias-Bursać

The opening sentences of the first David Albahari story I ever translated, "My Wife Has Light Eyes," revolve around the word "sentence":

"This will be a simple story," I think, "and it will have no compound sentences."
"Don't be silly," says my wife. "That sentence is already pretty compound."
I turn and look at her. I see her as I've never seen her before, but she doesn't know it. "What are you," I say, "a mind reader?"[1]

I'd written to him in 1988, at a time when he was living in Belgrade and I was living in Zagreb, to ask if I might try my hand at translating his stories. When he agreed, the first one I started with was "My Wife Has Light Eyes"—still one of my favorites. Since then I've translated two collections of his short stories and five of his fifteen novels,[2] the most recent being *Checkpoint*, which came

---

[1] Ovo je jednostavna priča, pomišljam, i u njoj neće biti složenih rečenica. Smešno, kaže moja žena, pa već ta rečenica je dovoljno složena. Okrećem se i gledam je. Gledam je onako kako je nikada do sad nisam gledao, ali ona to ne zna. Šta si ti, kažem, čitač misli? ("Moja žena ima svetle oči," *Jednostavnost* 7).

[2] Novels: *Snow Man* (*Snežni čovek* 1995, English translation: Douglas & McIntyre 2005); *Götz and Meyer* (*Gec i Majer* 1998, English translation: Harvill Press 2004, Harcourt Brace Jovanovich 2005, Dalkey Archive 2015); *Globetrotter* (*Svetski putnik* 2001, English translation: Yale University Press 2014); *Leeches* (*Pijavice* 2005, English translation: Houghton Mifflin Harcourt 2011, Harvill Secker 2011); *Checkpoint* (Kontrolni punkt 2011, English translation: Restless Books 2018). Short story collections: *Words Are Something Else*, Northwestern University Press 1996; *Learning Cyrillic*, Dalkey Archive 2014.

out thirty years after our collaboration began.[3] When Tess Lewis proposed a panel on translating sentences for the 2018 ALTA conference, I realized that what has held my attention in Albahari's writing is not the challenge of translating his often long sentences, but the role played by his meta-sentence as it crops up in novel after novel; it is this use of "sentence" that I trace here.

In an interview with *Words without Borders* in 2011, David Albahari defines himself as a postmodernist: "People keep telling me postmodernism is dead. I always tell them, 'But I am alive!' I really think of myself as a dead postmodern writer." In "My Wife Has Light Eyes," the exchanges between the first-person narrator, a writer, and his wife, through bickering banter, create parallel storylines, one about their failing marriage and the other about the nature of fiction, closing with their breakup, again through the prism of literature. She has just told a story in which her protagonist ends up standing at the front door to his empty apartment, ringing the doorbell. The writer asks his wife whether, if he were to ring the doorbell of their apartment, she would open the door for him.

> I'd repeat the question, but that technique has been so overworked in literature and the movies that I opt for silence.
> No amount of silence, however, can shield us from the truth, because we all know, and have long known, her reply.
> "No," says my wife, "I would not." (124)[4]

In 1990 I moved from Zagreb to Boston, where I'm from, while in 1994, in the middle of the war, David Albahari moved from Belgrade to Calgary, in Alberta, Canada. Not long after that, he inscribed my copy of *Snow Man*, as follows: "To Ellen: this story about words which do not succeed in replacing worlds that no longer exist. Sincerely, David Albahari, Calgary 1996."[5] This aptly captures the pain of displacement evoked by *Snow Man*. The first time I read it I was devastated by the novel's evocation of loss. The 1990s were the

---

[3] Three other novels of David Albahari's have been translated into English by other translators: *Tsing* (*Cink*, 1988, English translation by the author, 1997), *Bait* (*Mamac* 1996, English translation by Peter Agnone, 2001), and *Darkness* (*Mrak*, 1997, English translation by Amela Marin, 2020). Ammiel Alcalay and Christina Pribićević Zorić have also translated stories by David Albahari. The examples I use here are taken from my own translations.
[4] "Ponovio bih pitanje, ali taj postupak je toliko puta do sada korišćen u literaturi i na filmu, da se radije odlučujem za ćutanje.
Nikakva tišina, međutim, ne može da nas spasi od istine, jer svi već i to odavno, znamo njen odgovor:
Ne, kaže moja žena, ne bih" (*Jednostavnost* 12).
[5] "Za Ellen, Ova priča o rečima koje ne uspevaju da zamene svetove kojih više nema. Iskreno, David Albahari, Calgary, 1996."

years of the wars in what had been Yugoslavia, where I'd lived for eighteen years and where Albahari was born and spent most of his life. Furthermore, this was a novel about a war that the writer/narrator is grappling with while living abroad. Perhaps this is why I found it so painful—too close to the bone for me, as I had also been grappling with the war from afar. I told him I couldn't bear to translate it. At his urging, however, I reread it and began hearing the lilt of the narrator's manic humor. The humor was what gave me a way in.

In his afterword to *Snow Man*, David Albahari writes that until he wrote it, he'd always been against novels based on history, yet here he was, writing about history. These words mark the turning point when he pushed aside his musings about the nature of fiction as such and began writing about the tragedies unfolding around us. But in doing so he never jettisoned his metafictional toolkit. Indeed, his references to "sentence," his metafictional excursions, assume even greater importance. Albahari's use of references to language, words, and wordlessness has the effect of shunting the reader back and forth between sentence and story. As he began querying the impact of war in his novels, he used his metafictional tools to protect his prose from the cheap thrills of trauma porn.

Snow Man begins with the arrival of the (unnamed) protagonist from an (unnamed) wartorn country to an (unnamed) North American city, to spend a year there as a writer in residence at the local university. The first-person narrative is peppered with wry references to sentence and language as the writer's saving grace:

> The whole airport was no more than a cluster of sentences, but if it hadn't been for those sentences, I would have already keeled over. I was on my feet thanks to words, something I would never have believed if someone else had told me. I was kept in one piece by letters, words held me; I breathed thanks to punctuation. (3)[6]

"Sentence" serves as a measure of the protagonist's sanity:

> I had to get serious, I needed to pull myself together, I needed to find a rhythm. I had never learned to be patient, I thought, to allow sentences to find their end in the haystacks of language. (42)[7]

---

[6] "Ceo aerodrom je bio samo skup rečenica, ali da nije bilo svih tih rečenica, odavno bih se srušio. Stajao sam zahvaljujući rečima, što nikada ne bih poverovao da mi je neko drugi pričao. Držala su me slova, držale su me reči; disao sam zahvaljujući interpunkciji" (*Snežni čovek* 7).

[7] "Morao sam da se uozbiljim, trebalo je da dovedem sebe u red, morao sam da pronađem ritam. Nikad nisam naučio da budem strpljiv, pomislio sam, da dopuštam rečenicama da same nalaze svoj kraj u stogovima jezika" (*Snežni čovek*, 49–50).

And as the character unravels, so does the syntax:

> I couldn't remember a single sentence; I thought only in words, in the spaces between the words. (101)[8]

There are many ways that Albahari uses humor and a metafictional distance to approach his writing about trauma; his use of "sentence" has been, for me, perhaps one of the most memorable. I translated his novel *Leeches*, while I was working with a team of translators at the International Criminal Tribunal for the former Yugoslavia. Guided by instructions from Albahari, I visited Zemun and walked through the city where he'd grown up and where this murder mystery takes place. The narrator of *Leeches* is a writer, unnamed (again), who is writing the story while in hiding, at a great distance from Belgrade, having fled Serbian warmongers. While all Albahari's novels to come out after the fighting began in 1991 are unambiguously anti-war, in *Leeches* he speaks the most incisively about the bellicose Serbian mindset.

The writer-narrator's ruminations about and mentions of "sentence" also play a key role throughout *Leeches* as they do in *Snow Man*, but this narrator is angrier than was *Snow Man*'s frozen narrator:

> I yanked sentences out of myself as if I were extracting molars, then raged because I couldn't link them together; the piece wouldn't sound like a cohesive whole, but rather like a series of discordant, differing positions that often contradicted themselves. (7)[9]

Long sentences are a hallmark of *Leeches*, but even they are ironicized, as is the case in the following scene:

> All right, said Marko, he had come to show me something, or to take me to where he'd show me something, something he felt I had to see, as it was directly related, or at least that was how he perceived it, to stuff that had been going on with me recently, and even if he'd read it wrong, which was not impossible, anyone can make a mistake, I'd be interested in what he had to show me, and we should get going as soon as possible,

---

[8] "Nisam mogao da se setim nijedne rečenice; mislio sam samo u rečima, u razmacima između reči" (*Snežni čovek* 115).
[9] "Čupao sam rečenice iz sebe kao da kleštima vadim kutnjake; potom sam se ljutio što ne uspevam dovoljno da ih povežem, tako da tekst nije zvučao kao celina, već kao zbir raštimovanih, zasebnih stavova koji su često protivrečili jedni drugima" (*Pijavice* 10–11).

so he was getting up, which was a good thing because tangled sentences like this were terribly draining for him. (160)[10]

Soon after the previous sentence appears in the narrative, the narrator learns that his friend, Marko, has betrayed him. After "sentence" serving as a measure of the narrator's descent into madness in *Snow Man*, we see "sentence" in *Leeches*, serving not only as a barometer of the narrator's frame of mind but also as a lifeline for the reader, a wink, a nod to humor, for when the going gets rough.

Rage as manifested through "sentence" also comes up with the character Daniel Atijas (note the initials: D.A.), in the novel *Globetrotter*. The narrator is an (unnamed) painter from Saskatchewan who has an obsessive crush on Atijas, a writer who has come from Belgrade to Canada for a writer's residency. The two men meet at the Banff Centre for the Arts where they are both taking part in residencies[11] and spend their days there walking around Banff with a man of Croatian descent whose grandfather was a war criminal in the Second World War. The trio discusses art, and writing, and blame and guilt in war.

The painter muses in the abstract:

> Our works, I said to Daniel Atijas one evening, exist precisely because there always are those blank spaces between the words and between the visual forms, and when the day comes when the interspace is filled, writers will stop writing and painters will jettison their paintings and drawings. (45)[12]

Meanwhile, Daniel Atijas speaks of language as a gut-wrenching, violent experience:

> Last night, for instance, he said, we gorged ourselves on words, and if we had vomited later, if we could have, out of us would have gushed half-

---

[10] "Dobro, rekao je Marko, i objasnio da je došao da mi nešto pokaže, odnosno, da me odvede na jedno mesto gde bi mi nešto pokazao, nešto što, smatrao je, moram da vidim, jer je to, šta god to bilo, stajalo u direktnoj vezi, tako se bar njemu činilo, sa stvarima koje su mi se događale u poslednje vreme, a šta ću i sam moći da se uverim, a čak i ako se on prevario u svojoj proceni, što nije nemoguće, uostalom, ljudski je grešiti, ali čak i u tom slučaju, rekao je, zanimaće me to što hoće da mi pokaže, i što pre krenemo, ustao je, tim bolje, jer ga ovako zapetljane rečenice užasno iscrpljuju" (*Pijavice* 148).

[11] I should add that thanks to the generosity of the Banff Centre for the Arts, I was able to work on the translation of the novel *Globetrotter* while participating in the BILTC literary translation residency in June 2011, and David Albahari joined me there for five days.

[12] "Naša dela, rekao sam Danielu Atijasu jedne večeri, postoje upravo zbog toga što još uvek ima tih praznina između reči i vizuelnih formi, i kada se taj međuprostor jednom popuni, pisci će prestati da pišu a slikari će bataiti svoje slike i crteže" (*Svetski putnik* 55–6).

chewed, gnawed words, jumbled sentences, the occasional punctuation mark. (49)[13]

Again, a lifeline for the reader: the attention to language, words, and sentences pulls us back. The shift from story to metalanguage allows us to see his anger yet colors his fury with a lilt of strange amusement.

In 2011, David Albahari moved back to Belgrade from Calgary. Meanwhile his fiction had been shifting to postwar stories. Albahari has published six novels since *Leeches*, which bring us experimentation with narrative forms, but also sustain his already legendary ironic use of metafictional distance. These post-Canadian novels also explore deeply traumatic subjects, such as violence against trans people in Serbia in *Brother*, and a more direct treatment of wartime atrocity than we have seen in his previous novels in *Checkpoint*.

The protagonist of *Brother*, Filip, a writer, frequently thinks in terms of "sentence." In a passage echoing the opening lines of "My Wife Has Light Eyes," Filip, the novel's central character, receives a letter from someone purporting to be a brother he has never heard of.

> He then brought the letter to his eyes, he said, and gave himself over passionately to those first short sentences, relishing in advance the prospect of that final, compound, one, which he was already taking as proof of kinship, likeness, since the writing of a compound sentence implied at least some small talent for writing and disclosed readerly bents which, he said, are essential if that gift, no matter how limited, is to surface. (17, manuscript)[14]

The swirl of emotions to be expected at a moment when one learns of a brother one has never heard of before is instantly ironicized with the mention of "sentence," and this allows Albahari to evade the vast melodramatic potential such a scene implies.

Brother[15] is a masterpiece of indirect narration and shows the same interlacing of humor and pain that Albahari's writing is best known for.

---

[13] "Noćas smo se, na primer, rekao je, prejeli reči, i da smo povraćali, da smo mogli da povraćamo, iz nas bi izletele, rekao je, polusažvakane ili oglodane reči, ispreturane rečenice, poneki znak interpunkcije" (*Svetski putnik* 60).

[14] "Prineo je, dakle, pismo bliže očima, rekao je, i sladostrasno se prepustio njegovim početnim kratkim rečenicama, unapred se radujući završnoj složenoj rečenici, koju je već video kao dokaz srodstva, kao potvrdu sličnosti, budući da ispisivanje složene rečenice podrazumeva bar mali dar za pisanje i otkriva čitalačke sklonosti koje su, rekao je, neophodne da bi se taj dar, ma koliko mali, ipak poakazao" (*Brat* 31).

[15] To date, *Brother* has appeared in English translation only in a brief excerpt in the online journal *Words without Borders*.

A never-explained, effectively invisible first-person narrator retells for us how Filip and his long-lost brother, Robert, are reunited. Robert contacts Filip by letter and requests a meeting. When they meet at a Belgrade restaurant, Robert comes out to Filip and—before a crowd of belligerent, transphobic onlookers—appears in a dress and wig and explains that she'd requested this reunion with Filip to give him the opportunity first to meet, and then bid farewell, to his brother Robert, and then welcome her as his sister Alisa. The situation spirals out of control, and soon Alisa is lying on the floor, knocked unconscious by a bully from a neighboring table.

> Robert sighed. His was such a long and ponderous sigh, said Filip, that it sent him back to thoughts of death. Not his own, of course, but Robert's. He wasn't picturing Robert himself, he said, he was summoning no images. It was the sentence "Robert is dead" that he thought of and this is what he saw. He saw, he said, a sentence that was more final than an image ever could be, because after it, after the sentence, there was nothing left. The sentence notwithstanding, Robert was alive. (86, manuscript)[16]

So even in this devastating, violent scene, the flip to "sentence" throws us a lifeline, the peculiar lilt of humor.

Checkpoint is set apart from Albahari's other novels by its use of first-person plural narration—the protagonist being the entire military unit posted at a checkpoint between two (unnamed) countries in an (unnamed) war. Here, again, we find quintessential scenes of truly bizarre humor comingling with atrocities of massacre, rape, devastation, and refugees. In the passage that follows, Albahari sets out more explicitly than he has elsewhere the way his characters rely on language, words, and sentence as a lifeline to shield them from calamity:

> The amateur soldier, like all amateurs, generally speaks of things with pomposity, using long words and gnarly sentences. He might, for instance, say the "absorption of non-homogeneous phenomena, including the exploitation of the image of death as a universal, is a sufficiently grandiose conspiracy and, indeed, wellspring of alarm, which will most certainly amalgamate the negative charge of our every aspiration." And

---

[16] "Robert je uzdahnuo. Bio je to tako dug i težak uzdah, rekao je Filip, da je morao ponovo da pomisli na smrt. Ne na svoju, naravno, već na Robertovu. Nije zamišljao samog Roberta, rekao je, nije u sebi prizivao nikakve slike. Jednostavno je pomislio na rečenicu 'Robert je mrtav' i to je video. Video je, rekao je, rečenicu koja je bila konačnija od bilo koje slike, jer posle nje, poslije te rečenice, nije više bilo ničega. Robert je, ipak, usprkos toj rečenici, bio živ" (*Brat* 143–4).

while the professional soldier merely shrugs at such platitudes, amateur fighters devote to them their best hours and days. They spew nonsense as if these are the ultimate mantras to elevate them high above the fray where the less fortunate wretches litter their lives like caramel candy wrappers. (33)[17]

One of the upsides of spending a lifetime translating an author's writing is being able to follow the ebb and flow of themes and obsessions over time. Albahari's fiction has developed many such themes and obsessions, several of which I have written about elsewhere;[18] his attention to "sentence" is something of which I have been mindful ever since I translated the opening gambit of "My Wife Has Light Eyes" about the simple and/or compound sentence in 1988. To examine more closely the way his metafiction functions and how it comes across in translation, I counted how many times the word "sentence" appears in each of the novels I analyzed for this chapter. In *Snow Man*: 27 times in the 108 pages of the English translation. In *Leeches*: over 50 times (309 pages); 12 times in *Globetrotter* and 29 times in *Brother*.

Having had the privilege of watching David Albahari's opus take shape over several decades, I have come to appreciate the significance of identifying and sustaining the prevailing themes in his writing from book to book. This sort of decades-long relationship between a writer and translator, when it works, is a rare and precious thing. I was relieved to see, with the benefit of hindsight, that what I had hoped would be consistency in translating his fictional world has paid off, not only in the context of a single novel but across his opus.

I have spent most of my thirty years as a literary translator translating novels and stories about war. The wars of the 1990s have, after all, been the defining experience for most of the writers of recent generations who write in the language/s I translate from. And I have learned from David Albahari that his postmodernist approach to the painful subjects of war, illness, loss, and violence—his way of shunting between sentence and story and his

---

[17] "Vojnik amater, kao i svi amateri, misli da o stvarima treba govoriti pompezno, koristeći dugačke reči i zamršene rečenice. Stoga će on reći da je „apsorpcija nehomogenih fenomena, uključujući eksploataciju imidža smrti kao univerzalnog fenomena, dovoljno grandiozna konspiracija i, slobodno se može reći, konsternacija, što će definitivno akumulirati negativan naboj svih naših aspiracija." I dok profesionalni vojnik samo odmahne rukom na takve tvrdnje, vojnici amateri posvećuju tome najbolje sate i dane svog života. Ponavljaju takve besmislice kao da su vrhovne mantre koje će ih vertikalno podići iznad bojnog polja na kojem će manje srećni nesrećnici ostavljati svoje živote kao da su omoti od mlečnih karamela" (*Kontrolni punkt* 34–5).

[18] "Translating Dubravka Ugrešić and David Albahari" ; "Albahari's Amusing Leeches"; translator's note for "Trash Is Better"; and translator's afterword for *Globetrotter*.

lilting use of humor—allows us to look pain and trauma in the eyes and watch ourselves as we do it. It teaches the invaluable role of skepticism and irony in counterbalancing the all-consuming compulsions of blood and soil. Postmodernism may be dead, but the lessons learned from David Albahari's fiction are alive and well.

Works Cited

Albahari, David. *Brat*. Stubovi kulture, 2008.
Albahari, David. *Brother* (excerpt). Trans. Ellen Elias-Bursać. Words Without Borders, 2017.
Albahari, David. *Checkpoint*. Trans. Ellen Elias-Bursać. Restless Books, 2018.
Albahari, David. *Globetrotter*. Trans. Ellen Elias-Bursać. Yale University Press, 2014.
Albahari, David. *Jednostavnost*. Rad, 1989.
Albahari, David. *Kontrolni punkt*. Stubovi Kulture, 2010.
Albahari, David. *Leeches*. Trans. Ellen Elias-Bursać. Houghton Mifflin Harcourt, 2011.
Albahari, David. "My Wife Has Light Eyes." *Words Are Something Else*. Trans. Ellen Elias-Bursać. Northwestern University Press, 1996, pp. 119–24.
Albahari, David. *Pijavice*. Stubovi Kulture, 2005.
Albahari, David. *Snežni čovek*. Narodna knjiga, 1996: 7.
Albahari, David. *Snow Man*. Trans. Ellen Elias-Bursać. Douglas & McIntyre, 2005.
Albahari, David. *Svetski putnik*. Stubovi Kulture, 2001.
Elias-Bursać, Ellen. "Albahari's Amusing Leeches." April 2011. http://beatrice.com/wordpress/2011/04/29/ellen-elias-bursac-in-translation/.
Elias-Bursać, Ellen, trans. *Brother* (excerpt). By David Albahari. Words Without Borders, 2017.
Elias-Bursać, Ellen, trans. *Checkpoint*. By David Albahari. Restless Books, 2018.
Elias-Bursać, Ellen, trans. *Globetrotter*. By David Albahari. Yale University Press, 2014.
Elias-Bursać, Ellen. "Translating Dubravka Ugrešić and David Albahari." *Shoreless Bridges: Southeast European Writing in Diaspora after 1990*. Editions Rodopi B.V, 2010, pp. 133–47.
Elias-Bursać, Ellen. Translator's note. "Trash Is Better." By David Albahari. *Asymptote Journal*, October 2013.
Words Without Borders. Interview with David Albahari. wordswithoutborders.org/dispatches/article/beyond-the-physical-world-an-interview-with-david-albahari.

Epilogue

Matching Socks in the Dark; or How to Translate from Languages You Don't Know

Ilan Stavans

Fidelity to meaning alone in translation is a kind of betrayal.
—Paul Valéry

You love the trade but what are you accomplishing? Lazy thinkers believe that translators are, well, lazy thinkers, that they hide behind someone else's work. You, instead, are convinced translation is an exquisite mental exercise. How to convey in one tongue the silences of another? For a true translation isn't about what's visible on the page; it is about what is hidden, what might only be insinuated.

Needless to say, translation is the art of the impossible. What can be said well in one tongue might only be reinvented in another. It is thus a deception. Who cares? Every intellectual effort is a theft: we domesticate things, setting them free from their original context.

Still, translation is a bona fide business. It isn't for con artists. A translation might be better than the original if the translator is humble, for humility invariably comes across in every sentence. You're always at the risk of being exposed.

You dislike the automatic nature of the craft, though. At some point, between your eyes studying the original and reformulating them on the page, it's easy to feel anesthetized. Translation is mechanical: back and forth, back and forth. Your challenge, when in the middle of it, is to always be alert: awake, though not woke.

That state is essential; the success or failure of the enterprise depends on it. For an interesting translation depends on the nuanced relationship forged between author and translator (even if and when the author is dead).

You've reached these conclusions over time. Now that Covid-19 has injected the bizarre into the mundane, you are in for a surprise: you are interested not in what you know but in what you don't.

The most suitable comparison you are able to think of is matching socks in the dark. On the surface, it is—according to common knowledge—hopeless. With no light, all matches are decided at random. Darkness is seldom full darkness, meaning a state in which you don't see anything. Your eyes just need to be acclimated. After a while, you start figuring out patterns, colors, and silhouettes. While there is still a lot of guess work; the blind do see. Do you remember one of those seven lectures Borges delivered in Buenos Aires' Teatro Coliseo in 1977 about blindness? In it he describes how the blind like him, rather than being surrounded by blackness, actually see certain colors.

Those colors, he declares, are "loyal" to him. And in his sonnet "On His Blindness" (*Poetry Magazine*, May 1994), Borges writes:

Others have the world, for better or worse;
I have this half-dark, and the toil of verse.

In Spanish, he praises that darkness, calling them shadows.

You're fascinated by the challenges posed in translating from languages you don't know. It is like turning darkness into color. How often have you done it? Not infrequently. Predominantly you've translated poetry this way; you've done an occasional story or two as well. For instance, not long ago you rendered a short story—it could be called a soliloquy or perhaps a diatribe— by Anton Chekhov. You might recognize a few dozen words in Cyrillic.

Your volume *Selected Translations: Poems, 2000–2020* (2021) contains a number of pieces from unknown tongues: one in German by Paul Celan, one in Russian by Anna Akhmatova, one in Georgian by Besik Kharanauli, and a couple in Portuguese by Ferreira Gullar. Portuguese you know much more, capable as you are of reading Machado de Assis and Graciliano Ramos in the original. Arabic you're still pondering.

Are these worth the effort? It is up to the reader, just as everything else is in literature. I am far from the first to indulge in such treat. Samuel Beckett put together an anthology of Mexican poetry (Octavio Paz introduced it), yet his Spanish was minimal. The authors he chose aren't easy: Sor Juana Inés de la Cruz, Bernardo de Balbuena, Juan Ruíz de Alarcón, *modernistas* like Amado Nervo, Enrique González Martínez, and others. The result is astounding.

You called the preface to the volume "Translation and Hallucination." In it you describe translation as liberation:

Words caught in a single language jump out, becoming worlds in another. This is all the more noticeable in poetry, where each sound, each cadence is strategically placed.

I approach translation as hallucination. I let myself go as much as possible, attuned to every type of stimulation, happy to wander as I wonder, eventually coming to the realization that the universe I am in actually depends on *me* to perpetuate itself. Throughout the process, my mind isn't fully mine. The fact that I emerge in one piece at the end is nothing short of miraculous.

I'm an immigrant. This is my condition. Immigration is untenable without translation. Translation fosters a kind of immigration. To translate is to survive on a day-to-day basis.

I started my life in Yiddish and Spanish interchangeably, then changed to Hebrew, hoping for redemption, and eventually settled in English, with other companions like Ladino saving me along the way. I am ambivalent about the term "mother tongue" to describe my first language, for where are all subsequent ones left? Are they stepmothers? Mistresses? I also don't like describing them as "firsts" because it gives them an unsustainable location. Whatever tongue one is using at the moment is first. For those reasons, I prefer a leveling of fields: all languages—all *my* languages, for that matter—are equal; I love them just the same. All are engaged in giving birth to reality.

For me it is harder to think that I was born in Mexico than to say that I was born into Yiddish and Spanish. Languages are more than a lexicon; they contain the DNA of entire civilizations. The words we use aren't really ours; we borrow them, using them to communicate not only with our contemporaries but with those which preceded us and those who will follow us. It is our responsibility to safeguard them while we also push them onto new heights. And, obviously, while creating new words, for no living language is static.

As for poetry, I disliked it when I was young; I found it remote, pedantic. Age humbles us; it was I, of course, who was being snobbish. Poetry is tradition. In the short time we have on earth, it is up to us to unpack and extend it, to become full-fledged members of that tradition.

In short, I live in translation *without an original*. Yet originals are sacred to me, starting with the Bible. My duty as translator is to inject them with energy, to make them urgent.

You go on to suggest in the preface that your heroes are John Florio, who made Montaigne feel comfortable in English and, on the way, inspired Shakespeare; Richard Burton, whose *One Thousand and One Nights* is exquisite; and Adrienne Rich, who appreciated, perhaps disingenuously, that if language is power, silence is violence.

In translating from languages you don't know, you aren't talking about retellings, for example, recreations, the famous "after such and such." That's altogether different. In your case, it is more than clear that these are full-fledged renditions.

At this point, you should make a reference to the "informer." You don't always use one—not knowing pushes you to resort to all sorts of strategies—because the technique varies from case to case. In select cases you do. At times your informer is actually a co-translator, as when you translated Gullar with Tal Goldfajn or Kharanauli with Gvantsa Jobava.

This is how you explain it. In a number of instances, after you've made your choice about a poem you've fallen in love with, after you've studied it from top to bottom, you've found an "stoolpigeon," as you once called it. This is a person you trust, often a close friend, who is an insider in the language of the poem. You spend generous time—a day, a weekend, sometimes up to a month—discussing every detail, every twist and turn of the text, until you feel you know it as if it was in your own language.

It isn't an easy task. You might become intimate with the poem, but the language is still "*en chino*," as Mexicans say. Nevertheless, your foreignness with the original language, you acknowledge, will never cease. It is then a matter of turning your anxiety into art.

The informer is your spy. You want to know everything. You want to make the relationship between the two of you absolutely clear. Unless you've defined it that way (and you have on a few occasions), the translation you've embarked on isn't a joint venture. It is yours alone. You will take full credit for the good and the bad.

That's why the image of matching socks feels right. If you end up with an unmatched pair and put them on, it is you who is subjected to ridicule, no one else.

So what, you ask? Does anyone still care anymore about non-matching socks? The Age of Aquarium has come and gone. To be freaky means being normal.

Is that why you don't care if the translation misses the mark? Actually, you do care. To invoke Elizabeth Bishop's riposte, it isn't a disaster.

Anyway, after the informer informs, does the snitch look at your work? Come on, it's wrong to call it snitch. The insider isn't a censor; that is, very rarely will you show your versions for approval. You share them all the time with friends, not to mention editors. Nevertheless, this is done to help you see what you can't see. In fact, that spy—that's closer to it!—might not even know you ever finished the task. You're unapologetically thankful. And then you take leave.

You said before that translation is the art of the impossible. It is also, as you've stated elsewhere, the art of the inevitable. Without translation, we are trapped in our own solipsism. Translation brings us out; it builds bridges between the self and the world.

It also cures us from our unbearable individualism. In writing, writers foster national literatures; in translating, translators make those writers global.

You hate the Russian proverb that states that translation is like a woman: if she is faithful, she is not beautiful; if she is beautiful, she is not faithful. Gregory Rabassa, the translator of *One Hundred Years of Solitude*, taught it to you. Forget about it being egregiously misogynistic. Its problem is that it builds a vision of the world as an either/or. The world is seldom that way: someone might be good *and* bad.

The same goes for translation.

A Translation Experiment

Kleptomaniac Classic: *Ramona*

Esther Allen and Sean Cotter

El que roba una vez, robará mil.
Nadie se considere seguro bajo el gobierno de los americanos.
[He who steals once will steal a thousand times.
No one can consider himself safe under the government of the Americans.]

—Helen Hunt Jackson, *Ramona, novela americana*,
trans. José Martí (New York, 1888)

Once a thief, always a thief.
Nobody need feel himself safe under American rule.

Helen Hunt Jackson, *Ramona: A Story* (Boston, 1884)

The Ponca chief Standing Bear (in Ponca, Mantcunanjin) filed a lawsuit in Omaha, Nebraska, in 1879 to argue that Native Americans were "persons within the meaning of the law." The case soon became a landmark victory for Native American rights and that same year the chief embarked on a lecture tour to raise money for the Ponca people. His lectures were delivered in Ponca and interpreted into English by Susette LaFlesche (known as Bright Eyes), the mixed-race woman who interpreted during the trial. In Boston, the audience included the poet Henry Wadsworth Longfellow, the abolitionist Wendell Phillips, and a then—and perhaps still now—rather obscure writer named Helen Hunt Jackson, wife of a wealthy banker and railway executive, who had published a few poems and three anonymous novels (Mathes).

The influence of Standing Bear's lecture on Helen Hunt Jackson's life cannot be overstated. From that moment, she devoted herself to the cause of Native American rights, traveling extensively to investigate conditions and exposing government misconduct and corruption in a series of newspaper articles. In 1881, she published *A Century of Dishonor*, a history of the horrors endured by Native American peoples across the United States.

She sent a copy to every member of Congress, but the book didn't have the impact she'd hoped. Two years later, Jackson checked into a New York City hotel and in a breakneck three months wrote a novel, *Ramona*. Her aim was to raise the consciousness of white elites, awakening the sympathy of her peers to the plight of indigenous and Mexican inhabitants of the territory of California following the region's takeover by the United States. Her most pressing concern was for the indigenous peoples who were subjected to state-sponsored extermination campaigns from the mid-1840s through the early 1870s, which deliberately hunted down and killed thousands. The massacres were often carried out by organized militias, paid, sometimes on a per-scalp basis, by the governments of California and the United States.[1]

Jackson hoped her novel, unlike the nonfiction work that preceded it, would be widely read. And it was. *Ramona* was already a bestseller by the time of her early death from stomach cancer in 1885, only a year after it was published, only six years after she attended Standing Bear's lecture. Though it failed utterly to achieve Jackson's stated aim of improving the lot of California's Native Americans—in fact, it had quite the opposite effect[2]—*Ramona* had a tremendous and lasting impact on US tourism, real estate development, architecture, home décor, film, music, television, and theater. That impact extended beyond the United States. Jackson's dedication to the pre-Anglo peoples of California, as victims of theft, so stirred one contemporary translator that he appropriated the novel shortly after it was published, to put it into the language most of its characters are said to be speaking.

José Martí, a journalist, poet, diplomat, and revolutionary leader, living in New York City in exile from colonial Cuba, was a longtime admirer of Jackson's activism. He took note of her death in a *crónica* on "The Indian Problem in the United States," published in the Buenos Aires newspaper *La Nación*:

> It was a woman, Beecher Stowe, who awoke hearts to pity for the negroes in the United States, and no one helped free them more than she. . . . It was also a woman who, with greater tenderness and sensitivity, has worked year after year to alleviate the misfortune of the Indians: Helen Hunt Jackson, of strong mind and loving soul, who has just died. (321)

---

[1] For a detailed account of the atrocities committed against the California Indians, see Madley, *An American Genocide*.

[2] See DeLyser, *Ramona Memories*. For a comparison of Jackson's aims and impact with those of a more recent self-proclaimed social reform novel, Jeanine Cummins' 2020 *American Dirt*, see Allen, "Pies on the Windowsills of 'El Norte,'" online in the *Los Angeles Review of Books*.

Shortly thereafter, Martí resolved to translate *Ramona* into Spanish. He was already an accomplished translator and had been earning part of his living by rendering books into Spanish for D. Appleton & Co, a New York firm that distributed books across Latin America. This project was different; no one commissioned it. Martí—a man of infinite resources, few of them financial—self-published his translation, *Ramona, novela americana,* in New York in 1888, and paid out of his own pocket, as well, for its subsequent distribution in Mexico.

Martí's aims were as political as Jackson's had been, and he shared Jackson's concern for the plight of indigenous peoples. He'd lived and traveled in Mexico and Guatemala for four years and had written about the cultures, languages, and histories of indigenous communities he met. If the emotional appeal of *Ramona, novela americana* could affect the way the Mexican elites, who were Martí's intended readers, viewed and treated indigenous peoples, so much the better. But Martí's aims were also, in many respects, distinct from Jackson's.

Born to a Spanish soldier posted in colonial Cuba, Martí had decided, at a very young age, to reject the white colonial power that was his birthright and espouse the twinned causes of abolition and Cuban independence. The central aim of his life was to liberate Cuba from Spanish rule while, at the same time, ensuring the island's freedom from annexation, occupation, or domination by the United States. He translated *Ramona* because he admired it as a work of literature and because he saw its circulation in Mexico as a means of furthering this goal. Martí saw a potential doom for Cubans, Mexicans, and, ultimately, all Latin Americans in the fate of Native Americans and *californios Ramona* describes—invasion by violent, looting, English-speaking settlers who impose self-serving laws that rob all social classes of their rights and lands. The best way for this fate to be averted, he argued throughout his life, was for the nations of Latin America to present a solid and united front, a counterbalance to the growing might of the United States. And Mexico, with its geographic proximity to Cuba, could make a particularly strong ally for Martí's cause. He had lived in Mexico City for three years in the late 1870s and had every reason to believe that a novel about the US invasion and annexation of what was once half of Mexico's national territory would strike a powerful chord there.

Martí believed, with good reason, that if the rapidly expanding US empire were to succeed in its long-expressed ambition of annexing Cuba, it would then be more likely to "fall, with all the greater force," on Mexico and the rest of Latin America. On the last day of his life, in 1895, as he led an armed insurgency in the jungles of Eastern Cuba, Martí composed a famous letter which speaks of that danger to Manuel Mercado, the Mexican who had helped him with the distribution of his translation. *Ramona, novela americana*, too, functioned as a warning of that worst-case scenario. Though he was too astute to say so openly in his preface, Martí's translation offers its readers the story of the dismal fate of the *californios* as a clarion call for the nations of Latin America to protect themselves by forming an international alliance powerful enough to dissuade the United States from invasion or intervention. It was the same appeal he would make in his most famous essay "Nuestra América."

None of this would work if readers didn't pick up the book. Over the course of 1888, Martí's fervent prologue to *Ramona, novela americana* appeared in two Mexican papers, *El Lunes* and *El Partido Liberal*; in two New York City papers, *El Economista Americano* (of which Martí was then editor) and *El Avisador Cubano*; and in Buenos Aires's *La Nación*, a paper with which Martí had a long professional relationship.[3] The prologue harnesses the intellectual and cultural prestige of the United States among Latin American elites to sell readers on the novel, citing a rave review in the US press. It goes on to praise the gripping intrigue into which the novel plunges its mesmerized readers, and then, in a final twist, claims *Ramona, novela americana* for Latin American literature. Helen Hunt Jackson, the English-speaking lady from the North, has written, Martí asserts, *nuestra novela*—our novel.

The story of Jackson's *Ramona* and its translation by Martí involves dizzying cultural, political, and historical kleptomania. The subsequent history of relations between the United States and Latin America amply attests that *Ramona, novela americana* was no more successful at achieving Martí's aims for it than *Ramona* had been at achieving Jackson's. But the history of the reclamation and re-appropriation of the story *Ramona* tells did not end with them.

Against the background of the theft of their lands, first by Mexicans, and then by Anglos, Jackson's novel tries to convey systematic genocide by creating a nineteenth-century Romeo and Juliet, a pair of gloriously perfect star-crossed fantasy Native American lovers, minutely calculated to appeal to Anglo-American readers. As she wrote, she kept nearby an ethereal photograph, inspired by a painting by English Pre-Raphaelite Dante Gabriel Rossetti, of two heads, a man's and a woman's, surrounded by a halo of clouds. The image embodied her idea of Ramona and her lover, and she aspired to translate it into all *Ramona*'s descriptions of its central characters. She even went so far as to render some Spanish names into Italian—Alejandro into Alessandro, Padre Salvatierra into Father Salvierderra—perhaps as an

---

[3] Noted in the introduction by Jonathan Alcántar and Anne Fountain to their very useful critical edition of Martí's translation, *Ramona, novela americana, Traducida del inglés por José Martí*.

homage to Rossetti, or perhaps because Italian was a more familiar language to her intended readers in the Northeastern United States, and she wanted to suggest a tacit connection between the prevailing racial prejudice against Italian immigrants and the prejudice against Hispanics and Native Americans in the Southwest.[4]

Jackson's California isn't wholly imagined. She based *Ramona* on observations made and information gleaned over more than a year spent in Southern California in 1882 and 1883. She took considerable risks in order to witness at first hand the tragedy of its indigenous peoples and the plight of the "white Mexicans," who'd been promised special rights under early California law, some of whom became her intimate friends. She even managed to have herself appointed a Special Commissioner of Indian Affairs and sent a 56-page report to Congress on the condition of the Mission Indians. (As a woman, she did not have the right to vote, but she did not allow that to prevent her from making her views known to her nation's legislative body.) Nonetheless, Jackson did not speak the languages—Spanish, Luiseño—that the novel's characters are supposedly conversing in, and her knowledge of their cultures was based only on the experiences of one peripatetic journey.

Martí, for his part, straightforwardly appropriates Jackson's cultural appropriation. In the late 1880s, no copyright agreement existed between the United States and Mexico, so there was no need to pay Jackson's estate for rights to the work. Still, in keeping with his aim of connecting *Ramona* to the people it claims to depict—and perhaps also as a way of somehow connecting to Jackson herself, though she died before he embarked on the translation—Martí did reach out to one of Jackson's contacts in California. In their critical edition of Martí's translation, Jonathan Alcantar and Anne Fountain cite a 1913 letter by Mariana de Coronel, who, with her husband Antonio, hosted Jackson during her travels in California. Coronel served as Jackson's interpreter in conversations with "Indian chiefs" and with her husband and claims Jackson proposed making the Coronel's Los Angeles hacienda the setting for *Ramona*, a proposal the couple modestly declined. Coronel adds, "I have . . . the Spanish translation of *Ramona*, which was sent me by the translator."[5] To date, the only person to have created a Spanish

---

[4] Martí himself memorably chronicled the 1891 lynching of eleven Italians in New Orleans, in a piece that was published in *La Nación* (Buenos Aires) on May 20 of that year. See *José Martí: Selected Writings*, trans. Esther Allen 296–303.

[5] Mariana de Coronel's letter is reproduced in its entirety in Chapter XV of Carlyle Channing Davis and William A. Alderson's *The True Story of Ramona: Its Facts and Fictions, Inspiration and Purpose*.

translation of *Ramona* is Martí,[6] one of the most internationally renowned Latin Americans of his time, who has remained an object of intensive study and veneration ever since. But such is the status of a translator's work that Coronel's letter makes no mention of the name of the individual who sent her this Spanish *Ramona*.

Martí's *Ramona, novela americana* puts Jackson's novel into the language its characters speak and its author didn't. Is this theft or restoration? Though Martí never set foot in California, he sustained intimate, lifelong connections with friends he made during the years he lived in Mexico, and frequently published his *crónicas* in Mexican newspapers. Neither Martí nor Jackson was indigenous or Mexican, but Martí's cultural ties to Mexico and its people were far closer than Jackson's. Who, then, is the thief? Who has earned the right to tell the story? Whose claim to this classic is the more legitimate?

Martí and Jackson were both progressive activists, would-be allies, negotiating between cultures and languages, drawing on their own experiences and on the experiences of others, which they tried to imagine, empathize with, inhabit, and speak forth. They were both, in their original contexts, whites, who were concerned with seeing beyond white privilege and espousing the causes of those oppressed by the brutality of colonialism. Both were translators of those experiences. As powerful, authoritarian forces within the United States continue promoting racial animosity in general and fear of Latin Americans in particular—against whose menacing contamination, the US public has been told, the nation can only protect itself by building a giant wall—one way to read the English and Spanish *Ramonas* could be as evidence of cultural connection, alliance, joint resistance to oppression beyond national or linguistic boundaries. And that is part of the story.

The pages that follow attempt to complete this linkage by bringing it full circle. Inspired by the many layers of appropriation and repurposing in Martí's and Jackson's works, both of us have selected passages from Martí's *Ramona, novela americana* to translate anew into an English distinct from Jackson's, leaving out what seems extraneous, adding in what seems necessary, and claiming for our own purposes whatever in the excerpt has struck us as useful to the needs of the present moment.

---

[6] *Ramona, novela americana* was reprinted numerous times in Mexico for decades following its initial distribution there, and according to the translation history scholar Patricia Willson was published in Argentina around 1906, as volume 208 in a series titled "La Biblioteca de La Nación." That edition credited Martí as author of the volume's preface but not as its translator. Martí's translation was reprinted by Alfaguara in Madrid as recently as 2005, as part of a series of Clásicos modernos.

Our inspiration has come from another cross-cultural alliance: the Hungarian modernist Dezső Kosztolányi, whose novel *Kornél Esti* includes an account of its eponymous main character's friend Gallus, the kleptomaniac translator. Gallus has just served two years in jail for pickpocketing a Moravian businessman—the latest in a string of compulsive thefts. When Gallus comes to him, "hungry and in rags," Kornél lands him the job of translating a thriller from English, "the sort of rubbish we wouldn't soil our hands with. We wouldn't read it. The most we'd do is translate it, and even then we'd wear gloves" (Dezső Kosztolányi, *Kornél Esti: a Novel* 200–3).

When the publisher rejects the translation, Kornél discovers just how strong is Gallus's illness; he compares Gallus's text to the original and finds that objects of value are missing. If, for example, a character pays out 5,000 pounds in English, he only pays 150 in Hungarian:

> Wherever the translator's pen went it always plundered the characters, whom he had only just met, and spared property neither personal nor real, violating the scarcely debatable sanctity of private ownership. He worked in a variety of ways. Most often items simply disappeared entirely. In the Hungarian text I found looted wholesale the carpets, safes, and silverware which are called upon to raise the tone in English literature. At other times he had filched a part of them, half or two-thirds. If a character told his servant to put five suitcases into his railway compartment, there was mention of only two and a dishonest silence about the other three.

At first, the translatory theft seems like the punchline to a shaggy-dog story: Gallus is so confused he even steals imaginary things. At best it seems to deprecate translation—"the most we'd do is translate it"—yet Kostolányi (in Bernard Adams's translation) has scattered a series of remarks that make Gallus seem more like us and translation more like the world that Martí and Jackson inhabit. Why would protective equipment ("And even then we'd wear gloves") be necessary to translate the novel that "after all, existed only on paper"? Kornél registers his indignation at Gallus's treatment of "the characters, whom he had only just met," for example the "inexcusable frivolity" with which Gallus "robbed Count Vicislav . . . who was such a nice man." Becoming ever more heated, Kornél accuses Gallus of "violating the scarcely debatable sanctity of private ownership . . . . It definitely spoke of bad faith and unmanliness." If at first Kornél seems the figure of detached good taste, by the end of the story he is doing "detective work," obsessively tabulating the total loot. Even theft that occurs only on paper transforms Kornél. He resembles another detective, Auguste Dupin in "The Purloined

Letter," who coolly retrieves the Queen's letter, only to passionately replace it with one giving vent to his old enmity with the thief.

In Lacan's famous reading of that story, this transformation is one in a regular pattern of shifting subject positions created by the movement of the letter, which he presents as an allegory of the signifier. Just as, in Poe's story, we never learn the contents of the letter, so too does the signifier create positions for its subjects without recourse to a signified.[7] But as many readings of this argument have suggested, the signified returns with a stubborn persistence, if only, in Lacan's case, as the sign of a lack of signification. Even Dupin objects, on the grounds of a term's signified, to the mistranslation of Latin: "if a term is of any importance—if words derive any value from applicability—then 'analysis' conveys 'algebra' about as much as, in Latin '*ambitus*' implies 'ambition,' '*religio*' 'religion,' or '*homines honesti*,' a set of honorable men" (Muller and Richardson 18). What happens on paper, Gallus demonstrates, does not stay on paper. Kornél is upset precisely by the change in signifieds; the two suitcases are no equivalent for the original five. The signified inescapably returns, in order to provide the story its punchline and the translation its reason for being.

The case of Gallus turns on the point that his mental illness functions in similar ways in the world and in the text. Jackson's *Ramona* turns on the same principle: we should be as angry about the ongoing and violent theft suffered by California's Native American and Mexican inhabitants as we are about the fictional tragedies that represent it in the novel. Kostalyáni allows us to see Martí's translation as an act of alliance, a theft to amplify the account of a theft. In the old saying, it takes a thief to catch a thief. In this case, it takes a kleptomaniac translator to investigate and amplify literary accounts of human conflict.

---

[7] The weeds of many readings are collected in *The Purloined Poe: Lacan, Derrida, and Psychoanalytic Reading*, ed. John Muller and William Richardson.

MY MAJELA!

Sean Cotter

alejandro responded to this heartfelt cry by holding *raMona* in his arms, tighter and tighter, until the embrace was almost painful: she could hear his heart beating: he did not speak. *finallY*, alejandro released her, took one of *raMonA's* hands, brought it to his forehead with noble reverence, and said, in a voice so trembling and low that she could barely hear the words:

"my señorita knows my life is hers. if she tells me to throw myself into a fire or into the sea, i will throw myself happily into the fire or the sea, because she commands it: but i cannot take my señorita's life: she doesn't know what it's like to have nothing to eat. my señorita doesn't know what she is saying."

that same solemn tone; that way of talking as though he were speaking about her, not to her; as though he were not talking to her but to god himself, these calmed and strengthened ramona, rather than frightened her: "i am strong, i too can work, *aleJandro*: you don't *undErstand*: we can both work: i am not afraid to *sLeep* on the ground. god will give us food."

"*thAt's* what i used to think! when i left that *Morning*, that is what thought: 'if she is not afraid, *whY* should i be?': i've always had enough to eat, and i could keep you *froM* suffering! but the *sAints* have turned their backs, señorita. those americans will finish us. they will shoot or poison all of us. they will drive us out of the country, like rabbits and gophers. what more can they do? truly, señorita: wouldn't death be better that what i have now?"

every word *aleJandro spokE* made ramona more determined to share his fate: "*aLejAndro*," she broke in, "in your village, *ManY Men hAve* wives, don't they?"

"yes, señorita, they do," he answered, surprised.

"and have their wives left them, *aleJandro*, during all this *suffEring*?"

"no, señorita, no!" he said, even more surprised, "how *couLd* they?"

"they *stAy* with *theM*, don't *theY*, to help *theM*, *becAuse* they are happy. they stay, don't they?"

"they stay, they do," *aleJandro rEsponded*, now understanding these questions, no *Less* pointed *thAn* those he would ask the señora.

"and the *woMen* in your village, do *theY* love their husbands greatly?"

"greatly, señorita."

they were both silent for a *Moment*. it *wAs* very dark. *aleJandro* couldn't *sEe* how the *bLood* burned in *rAmona's* face; how even her neck was tinged with ruby when she asked her last question:

"and do you think that any of those *woMen* love their husbands more than i love *You*, alejandro?"

before the sentence was over, the indian's *arMs Already* held her again. don't words like these bring a dead man to life? they would bring a dead man to life, yes, but they did not make *aleJandro sElfish*. he did not respond.

"you know there is not one who *wouLd*!" *rAMona* said hotly.

"*aY*, this is too *Much*, too much!" he *exclAimed*, throwing up his hands. and then he pulled her again to his heart, speaking to her with broken and quick words, "my señorita, she takes me to the gates of heaven; but i dare not enter. i know it will kill me, i know, if i take her to live this kind of life: the life that i live will kill her. let me go, let me go, my señorita! i wish you had never seen me!"

"do you know, *aleJandro*, what i was going to do if you hadn't *comE*? i was going to run away, *aLone, Alejandro*, and i would have walked to santa barbara, to beg padre salvatierra to let *Me* enter the convent at san juan bautista. and i will do that now, alejandro, if you don't take me with *You*."

"oh, no, no, señorita, *My señoritA* cannot do that! my beautiful señorita in a convent! no, no!" he said, shaking.

"yes, if you won't let me come with you, that is what i will do. i will go tomorrow."

and she surely would: he knew it.

"but this would be better than living on the run like a wild animal, my señorita! this is better than coming with me!"

"when i thought you were dead, *aleJandro*, *thE* convent did not scare me: there they *wouLd hAve* let *Me* live in peace, teaching children. but if i know *You're* alive, what peace can i have? not one *Minute, AleJandro*! i would rather *diE* than be without you. take me with you, *aLejAndro*!"

alejandro was vanquished. "i will take her, *MY* señorita of my life," he said gravely, without a lover's joy in his low voice, "i will take her with *Me*. *mAy* the saints have mercy on the señorita, as they have not had mercy on me or my people!"

"my *aleJandro*, your *pEopLe Are MY* people. the saints are good to those who love *theM*. you'll see how *hAppy* we will be, you will," and in solemn silence she leaned her head against *aleJandro's chEst*, as though she had sworn a vow. no wonder *feLipe wAnted* to be loved by the *woMan* he loved, as ramona loved alejandro! when she raised her head, she said, *timidlY*, now that she was sure he would take her, "so, you will take your *raMonA*, *aleJandro*?"

"my ramona will *bE* beside me *untiL* i die!" he *exclAimed*, *eMbracing* her, tilting his head over hers. but the tears in his eyes were not *happY*, and in his beating heart he heard the same painful voice that had erupted from *hiM* when he *sAw* her the first time, "*JEsus* protect me!"

it wasn't easy to decide what to do. he *wouLd hAve* wanted to walk into the house, to talk with felipe, to confront the señora, if it had to be: but the idea made *raMona* tremble:

"*You* don't know the señora, alejandro: you don't know how she treats *Me*: she *hAtes* me so much that if she dared, she would kill me: she says she would let me leave if i wanted to, but i believe that, at the last moment, she would throw me down the well before she let me leave with you."

"and wouldn't i defend my señorita? and wouldn't señor felipe?"

"felipe! she plays with him like he was soft wax. she can make him change his mind a hundred times a minute. i think he's with the enemy, *aleJandro*! don't *lEave*. i *wiLl* come *bAck* here once everyone is asleep. we have to leave right away, we have to leave."

he, convinced by *raMona's* fears, agreed to wait for her. he would wait for her right there. twice she returned to embrace him again.

"promise me, promise me *You* will not *Move* from this spot until i come! i'll be *bAck* in two hours, three at the most. it has to be nine o'clock now. promise me!"

"i will be here when you come," he answered.

ramona didn't notice that *aleJandro* hadn't *promisEd* not to move, *onLy* to be there when she *cAme* back. he had *soMething* to do for this sudden flight: he thought of her, who in her innocence had forgotten the difficulties of that long *journeY*. when alejandro had left for *teMecula*, he *hAd* painted a picture in his mind of his return to the hacienda to get ramona. he would be riding benito, his strong and swift benito, and bringing antonio's beautiful brown mare, saddled for her to ride. it had been only eighteen days since, with this image in his mind, he had raised his head to see antonio coming toward him, galloping like mad on the brown mare, he saw the bleeding cuts from the spurs, used by the master who loved her, he saw the animal stop before him, panting and steaming like a worn out machine. antonio saw him and cried out, leaped from the saddle and landed beside him, and with broken words told him what had happened. *aleJandro* couldn't *rEmember* the words, but as he heard them he had *cLosed* his mouth, took the reins, put his *heAd* against benito's neck, he spoke to benito's ear, and benito didn't stop galloping, he didn't stop the whole day, until they arrived at *teMecula*. there alejandro saw the roofless houses, the wagons being loaded, the people running, the women and children *crYing*: they pointed to where his father was, stretched on the ground in the shadow of a tule plant: he leaped off his horse, he let benito go and he never saw *hiM Again*: only eighteen days since then. and now he was there, under the same willow trees where he had seen ramona for the first time: at night, a dark night, and ramona had been in his arms: ramona was his: ramona would return to leave with him . . . to go! but where? nowhere in the wide world did he have a house to give her shelter. and that poor animal he had brought, would it be strong enough to carry her? *aleJandro* didn't think so: to *sparE* the good beast, he had *waLked* more *thAn* half the way; but since it hadn't eaten, the horse was now *alMost* dead: in pachanga, the grass was burned *bY* the sun, and some of the horses they saved had died.

but alejandro, while he *eMbrAced* ramona, had silently developed a plan. if babá, ramona's horse, were in the corral, he could take it without making a sound. he wouldn't be guilty of anything: and even if he was, so what? ramona needed to go by horse, and babá was hers, had always been hers, ever since as a foal he had followed her like a dog wherever she went, and no one had tamed it more than she did, with bread and honey. he had fought off all the others: but ramona could lead him where she wanted, without using any more rein than a lock of his silky mane. *aleJandro* had almost *thE* same power, because during the summer he was used to taking care of babá when he *couLdn't* see *rAMona*, so soon, the animal loved him like he did his own master. "i hope he's still in the corral!" . . . as soon as ramona's footsteps faded, alejandro stepped *carefullY* and quickly, surrounded by the deepest and darkest parts of the artichoke planting and the corrals, and came back up the hill to sneak into the corral on the furthest end. there was no light in any of the sleeping *herdsMen's* houses, *And* well did *aleJandro* know how soundly *thE* herdsmen *sLept*, *becAuse* often, when he was living *aMong* them, he would jump over their bodies sleeping on their hides, without *anYone* hearing *hiM* come *And* go. "i hope babá doesn't make any noise!" leaning over the circle of the corral, *aleJandro* whistlEd so *Lowly thAt* he could barely hear it *hiMself*. the horses were all grouped together, at the other end of the circle: he saw a soft movement among them, and one took a few steps toward alejandro. "i think that's babá!" and he whistled again. the horse started to walk, but *suddenlY* stopped, as though scared of *soMe* danger. "*bAbá!*" murmured *aleJandro*. *thE* wise *animaL* knew his name *And* alejandro's voice. he *seeMed* to understand that something secret was happening, and that if alejandro told him to *staY*, he should respond: he whinnied as though they couldn't hear *hiM*, he trotted *Across* the circle and his lips recognized his friend, showing him his *Joy* with *carEsses* and soft whinnies.

"i wonder if i *shouLdn't tAke* a saddle, too . . ."

. . .

A Translation Experiment   285

at the start of that *suMmer*, alejandro had given her, as a *curiositY*, two large, webbed saddlebags, the kind that indian *woMen* use to *cArry* all kinds of things. there were made from a hemp-like fiber, strong as iron, with the weave as wide as the bags were light: they pulled shut at the top and were connected by a band of the same fiber, which the indian women wore across their foreheads: in this way they could carry weights on their backs that they could never carry otherwise. until she remembered the sacks, she didn't know how she was going to carry all she thought she had a right to take from the house: actually not very much: only what was needed: a dress and her shawls, the new lace cloth, and two changes of clothes. this wasn't too much, thinking of the señora, who had those *JEwels*: "i *wiLl* tell *pAdre* salvatierra what i take: he will tell *Me* if it was too much." she hated to think that the clothes she was forced to take had been paid for with señora moreno's *moneY*.

and alejandro's violin. she would have left anything else behind, but not the violin. what would *becoMe* of *AleJandro* without his music? and if *thEy* went to *Los Angeles*, they could *Make moneY* playing for dances. and *raMonA*, spinning in her thoughts, imagined various ways to make money in their new home: both of them, she and her husband.

and food for the *Journey*. and it *nEeded* to be *substantiaL, And* wine for alejandro. her heart stopped when she thought of his *alarMing* appearance. he said he was "*hungrY*": good lord, how hungry! and during all of this she had eaten at such full tables, and she had seen so *Much* good food thrown to the dogs.

the *señorA* didn't go to her room for a long time, felipe also took a while to fall completely asleep. finally, ramona dared to leave her room. all was dark.

with the nets hanging onto her back—"like the good indian i am," she said almost happily—she stole across the patio, turned toward the south-east side of the house, and walking along the garden to the willows, she deposited what she was carrying to go back to the house for more.

now came the difficult part. she had decided to take wine, bread, and fresh meat. she didn't know marta's part of the house as well as she did her own, and she didn't dare light a candle. she had to make several trips to the kitchen and pantry, to get all the provisions she needed. she happened to find two full bottles of wine in the dining room; and a little mill in a leather bag, hanging on a hook on the wall. now she was ready.

…

ramona rode babá, with the reins hanging over the horn of her saddle. *aleJandro walkEd* and *Led* the poor pony. it *wAs* a pitiful wedding *March*; but the heart ramona carried was full of happiness.

"i don't know *whY,*" she said, "but *i'M* not *Afraid*. i'm not afraid at all, *aleJandro*, isn't it *strangE*?"

"yes," he said *seriousLy*, putting his *hAnd*, without interrupting his stride, on *raMona's*, "it is strange. i am scared, scared for *mY* señorita. the saints will help her. but they won't help *Me* or my *villAge*!"

"but why do you never call me anything but 'señorita'? will you never call me 'tú'? the señora always called me that when she yelled at me: "señorita!"

"then i will never say it again! i'd rather lose my tongue than talk to you like she did."

"won't you call me 'tú,' call me ramona?"

aleJandro didn't know how to explain why it was so difficult for him to call *hEr* ramona. the "tú" he could say: the "tú" came from his heart.

"what was that name you said you were thinking of *caLling* me, the *indiAn naMe*, the name of the dove?"

"majel," he said. "i call you majel in *mY* mind, ever since the night we first kissed, when i was waiting in the garden, listening to the cooing of two lovebirds. 'the girl of *My* life is like *thAt* to me,' i said, 'like the dove: the dove's song was like the music of your voice, the sweetest song in the world: and the dove is faithful to its partner for its whole life,'" saying this, he stopped walking.

"as i am to you, *aleJandro*," said ramona, *lEaning* toward him, putting her hand on his *shouLder*.

bAbá stopped: he could always sense his *Mistress's* smallest desire: that *journeY* had surprised *hiM*: no one *hAd* ever dared walk beside him when he took ramona for a ride, nor had anyone ever played with his mane. if it had been anyone but *aleJandro*! . . . but if his *mistrEss* was happy, this is how it had to be. and now his mistress was putting her hand on *aLejAndro's* shoulder! was that supposed to *Mean* he should stop? so it seemed: he stopped and turned his head to see what would happen. alejandro embraced ramona, their heads touching, and their lips! what was all that? babá *impishlY* hopped to one side, separating the two lovers. they laughed, and trotted on: alejandro ran: the poor pony, following his *exaMple*, trotted with *An* energy that his fatigue had not permitted him for many days.

"*maJEL* is my *nAme*, then?" asked ramona, "*Majela* is better, alejandro, it's sweeter: call me majela."

"better, *Yes*, because there's never been anyone with that *naMe*. i will *cAll* you *maJELA*!" he then said, "i don't know why it is so hard for *Me* to *saY raMonA*."

"because you had to give me a new name. no more ramona. that is what the señora called me . . . and felipe! he won't recognize me under my new name. him i would like to always call me ramona. but now i am *maJELA* for everyone, alejandro's *Majel*!"

Who Speaks My Title?

Sean Cotter

Helen Hunt Jackson's chapter asks why the characters' theft of provisions and a horse should be connected to a revision of Ramona's name. Martí's translation answers: the new name creates the space the characters need to escape Señora Moreno. Martí's translation aids and abets their theft, in a clever reversal of the story of Gallus: rather than subtracting objects from the translation, Martí adds to the Spanish version of the chapter, taking the side of those who steal as they steal away. In particular, he adds to the presence of Ramona's new name. The chapter title, "Mi Majela," is Martí's addition, and he leaves the last words of the chapter as another genitive, "la Majel de Alejandro" (368). Only in this translation is the action of the chapter framed by this unusual word. Alejandro teaches us that "majel" is the Luiseño word for "dove," but that word does not have a final "a." Ramona invents her new name by Hispanicizing the ending, on the model of her own name. Just as the word is a collaboration between the two eloping lovers, her name exists only in the overlap of two languages, Spanish and Luiseño. The space of overlapping languages is a new space, which we may call the space of translation. Martí gives the lovers additional space through which they fly toward a new place, one called by a Spanish name in English, "loss an-juh-lace." It fits the themes of theft and translation for this city to be located in the overlap of words always signaled by the appearance of angels.

    Any theft in this chapter is a form of addition. Alejandro takes a horse and saddle, Ramona takes clothes, some lace, wine, food, a violin—even the dog, "Capitán," in a passage I elided—but since Señora Moreno's wealth seems infinite, they are not "guilty of anything." The chapter does not define theft as subtraction: infinity minus some clothes and wine still equals infinity. Theft adds as much to the characters' provisions as it reinforces their identities: Ramona hauls her loot in carefully described nets resting on her forehead, "like the good Indian I am." Where Martí removes details from his translation, he also does so for the sake of these characters. He refuses to have the noble Babá compared to a dog (Jackson II.4), and he refuses to attribute the lover's passion solely to sex. When Ramona dismisses the hardship involved in her journey, in Spanish she forgets "en su candor de las dificultades de aquel largo viaje" (360) ("in her innocence forgotten the difficulties of that long journey"). In English she does not make a slip, she makes plans: "in her innocence, *her absorption in her thoughts of Alessandro and of love*, she had never seemed to consider how she would make this long journey" (II.8). In a similar vein, Martí has Alejandro remember with less detail his first sight of Ramona: "aquella misma voz de alarma dolorosa en que prorrumpió al verla por primera vez: '¡Jesús me valga!'" (the same voice of painful excitement that had burst from him when he saw her the first time, "Jesus protect me!," 359). In English, Alessandro, apparently also forming a plan, prays more specifically, "as in his rapturous delight when he first saw Ramona *bending over the brook under the willows he had said aloud, 'My God! what shall I do!*'" (II.7). While these changes might seem like subtractive bowlderization, these elisions like the thefts themselves are better understood as additions. By not having Alejandro contemplate Ramona from behind, Martí adds gallantry to his text. By not having Ramona controlled by physical attraction, he adds to her complexity of character.

Beyond these additions to content, Martí constantly adds bits of language to the text: the plethora of colons is one example, the accent mark over "Babá" is another. These tiny type-marks glitter across the Spanish page, marking its difference from the English original. Each accent mark increases the space of the translation, as well as the space the lovers need within the translation. The most important example of this effect—one which combines accent marks, escape, and emotion—is Martí's addition of "tú." Before Ramona runs away with her lover, she makes sure he will address her correctly. The original refers only to using her first name:

> "Are you never going to call me by my name?" asked Ramona. "I hate your calling me Senorita. That was what the Senora always called me when she was displeased."
>
> "I will never speak the word again!" cried Alessandro. "The saints forbid I should speak to you in the words of that woman!"
>
> "Can't you say Ramona?" she asked.
>
> Alessandro hesitated. He could not have told why it seemed to him difficult to say Ramona. (Jackson II.24–5)

Martí adds:

> --Pero ¿que nunca me vas a decir más que "Señorita"? ¿nunca me vas a decir "tú"? Así es como me decía siempre la Señora cuando me regañaba: "¡Señorita!"
>
> --¡Pues nunca lo volveré a decir! ¡sin lengua me quiero quedar antes que decirle como le decía ella!
>
> --¿No me puedes decir "tú," decirme Ramona?
>
> No sabia Alejandro explicar por qué le parecía difícil llamarle Ramona. El "tú" no: el "tú" se le salía del alma. (367)

> "But why do you never call me anything but 'Señorita'? Will you never call me 'tú'? The Señora always called me that when she yelled at me: 'Señorita!'"

"Then I will never say it again! I'd rather lose my tongue than talk to you like she did."
"Won't you call me 'tú,' call me Ramona?"
Alejandro didn't know how to explain why it was so difficult for him to call her Ramona. The "tú" he could say: the "tú" came from his heart.

Jackson does not give Alejandro, in the literal sense, either "a heart" or "un alma." This depth does not exist in her passage. Martí provides an additional word for Alejandro, a "tú," which carries an accent like the one Martí places on "Babá." "Tú" is the only word that gives voice to Alejandro's innermost feelings. Martí adds concretely to the language of the chapter, both accents and souls.

My method of aligning myself with Ramona, Alejandro, and Martí is to also add to my translation. Inspired by the colons and accents Martí distributes, I have created an ostentatious pattern of accentuation throughout my translation of Martí's version of this chapter. The most visible and thematically important addition he makes to the text is the chapter title, "Mi Majela." Therefore, I have woven "MY MAJELA" into the text by capitalizing only the letters from these words, in the order they appear, and italicizing the words that include them. This technique is a version of John Cage's "writing through," in which he extracts words from a text (e.g., *Finnegans Wake*) when they can be used to spell a key term (e.g., J-A-M-E-S-J-O-Y-C-E [Cage 282]). In order to read "MY MAJELA" in my translation, we read only the capital letters. Since this selectiveness can be a little difficult, we end up reading the italicized words, as well. By switching between accented and unaccented text, we may experience an almost musical interference between the content and the typography. The text resounds with the name Ramona choses, a resonance that interferes with the text of the translation itself. I intend this effect to mark the space of overlap, in all its overdetermination: Martí's Spanish and my English, Jackson's English and Martí's Spanish, Jackson's English and Alejandro's Luiseño—in a miming of the "tú" that comes from the heart. In this sense, my translation can emphasize the space created in translation, and can give the lovers the room they need to run.

This procedure has an unexpected and thematically appropriate effect. In order to repeatedly spell "MY MAJELA," I needed words that contained the letter "J." The text has only a few: "journey," "Jesus," and fifty-one repetitions of "Alejandro." The repetitions of "Majela" thus cause me to repeatedly accent "Alejandro," conjoining their names through my kleptomaniac additions to my translation. Not only is "Majela," as I've argued, a name created by the overlap of languages, so is "Alejandro": that is Martí's spelling, Jackson calls him "Alessandro." Reading "MY MAJELA" through Jackson's original would not create a harmony of the lover's names. My procedure of writing "MY MAJELA" through my translation thus brings the lovers together in a way only possible through the space of translation. Taking this procedure one step further, I have created a paragraph consisting of only the words selected by "MY MAJELA." In this text, the procedure repeats "Ramona" and "Alejandro," over and over, churning through a strange text, one that seems to speak, most of all, to the emotions of the chapter. The emotions it registers are the closest my procedure comes to Martí's "tú."

ramona finally ramona's alejandro understand
from saints alejandro spoke
many men have alejandro suffering
because alejandro responded less than women
would ramona ay much exclaimed alejandro
come alone alejandro
you my señorita alejandro
you're minute alejandro die alejandro my me may alejandro
embracing happy him saw jesus
journey temecula had alejandro remember closed head temecula crying
women carry jewels will padre me money become alejandro
los angeles make money ramona journey needed
her calling indian name my my that alejandro
majel name majela yes name call majela me say ramona majela majel

Any of these might make a good title for my translation.[8]

---

[8] Here is the entire text created by "reading through": raMona finallY raMonA's aleJandro undErstand sLeep thAt's Morning whY froM sAints aleJandro spokE aLejAndro ManY Men hAve aleJandro suffEring couLd stAy theM theY theM, becAuse aleJandro rEsponded Less thAn woMen theY Moment wAs aleJandro sEe bLood rAmona's woMen You arMs Already aleJandro sElfish wouLd rAMona aY Much exclAimed aleJandro comE aLone Alejandro Me You My señoritA aleJandro, thE wouLd hAve Me You're Minute AleJandro diE aLejAndro MY Me mAy aleJandro pEopLe Are MY theM hAppy aleJandro's chEst feLipe wAnted woMan timidlY raMonA, aleJandro bE untiL exclAimed eMbracing happY hiM sAw JEsus wouLd hAve raMona You Me hAtes aleJandro lEave wiLl bAck raMona's You Move bAck aleJandro promisEd onLy cAme soMething journeY teMecula hAd aleJandro rEmember cLosed heAd teMecula crYing hiM Again aleJandro sparE waLked thAn alMost bY eMbrAced aleJandro thE couLdn't rAMona carefullY herdsMen's And aleJandro thE sLept, becAuse aMong anYone hiM And aleJandro whistlEd Lowly thAt hiMself suddenlY soMe bAbá aleJandro. thE animaL And seeMed staY hiM Across Joy carEsses shouLdn't tAke suMmer curiositY woMen cArry JEwels wiLl pAdre Me moneY becoMe AleJandro thEy Los Angeles Make moneY raMonA Journey nEeded substantiaL And alarMing hungrY Much señorA aleJandro walkEd Led wAs March whY i'M Afraid aleJandro strangE seriousLy hAnd raMona's mY Me villAge aleJandro hEr caLling indiAn naMe mY My thAt aleJandro lEaning shouLder bAbá Mistress's journeY hiM hAd aleJandro mistrEss aLejAndro's Mean impishlY exaMple maJEL nAme Majela Yes naMe cAll maJELA Me saY raMonA maJELA Majel.

Permission

Esther Allen

The snowfall was so dense they were soon lost in an opaque, menacing whiteness, darker and more suffocating than any night. The old truck had run off the road and was stuck.

"Estamos muertos si nos quedamos aquí." Alejandro got out and pushed with all his might, inching it back. Inside, Ramona was struggling to stay awake. Her arms had gone numb. Was she still holding the baby? The wind heaped the snow higher and higher, howling like the screeching metal and drumming pistons of a monstrous factory. Alejandro couldn't hear her cry out.

Nos vamos a morir, Ramona told herself: ¡mejor será! *Better that we die.* She lost all awareness of time. Until she heard a shout and felt hands grabbing and shaking her. "Sorry to be rough, ma'am, but we've got to get you inside by the fire." A stranger's voice.

Did fire and warmth exist? Without conscious thought, an automaton, she handed her baby to the stranger, tried to get out of the truck.

"Stay right there! Hold still!" said the voice. "You can't stand on your own. I'll take the baby in to my wife. Be right back." Snatched suddenly from warm sleep, the baby started bawling as the tall man disappeared into the whiteness, holding her in his arms.

"¡Dios bueno!" said Alejandro from behind the car. "Majela, ¡la niña está viva!" *Thank God she's alive!* Majela, Luiseño for wood dove, was his private name for Ramona.

"Sí, Alejandro," she answered weakly, her voice a distant echo in the screaming wind.

It was a miracle. They'd been closer to the cabin than Alejandro realized, but never would have found it if another vehicle hadn't driven through the snow ahead of them. At moments, Alejandro had felt himself letting go, told himself, in almost the same words as Ramona: *well, at least it's an end to our troubles.* Then he glimpsed a light over on the left and drove toward it. The road was steep and rutted and more than once the truck almost rolled, but Alejandro didn't panic, even as Ramona fell silent beside him and the fuel gauge crawled past empty. He kept moving slowly forward and rolled the window down just far enough to shout through it for help. Finally his cries were heard. Another light appeared and came bobbing toward them, a flashlight, carried by a man whose English greeting—"Looks like you're in some trouble!"—was as clear to Alejandro as if it had been delivered in the limpid Luiseño spoken by his grandparents. But the man with the flashlight understood little or nothing of Alejandro's grateful response.

"Boy oh boy, another idiot Mexican. If I'd lived my whole life in country like this I'd sure as hell know it ain't any kind of weather to be out driving around in." As the man handed the baby over to his wife inside the cabin, he said uneasily, "Why, if I'd known they was Mexicans, I'd never have gone out there, Ri. They know more'n I do 'bout this damn climate."

"That's a lie and you know it, Jeff. You couldn't leave an animal outside on a night like this." Feeling herself in a mother's arms, the baby quieted down.

"Well my goodness, you little sweetie, you blue-eyed sweetie," said the woman, drinking her in. "Jeff, how could you even think of leaving this precious darling out in the snow. I'm gonna give her some milk."

"See to the mother first, Ri," said Jeff, coming back through the door practically carrying Ramona. "Half frozen to death, poor woman."

But the sight of her daughter alive and smiling quickly revived Ramona and within a few minutes she felt like herself again. And found herself in rather strange company. Lying on a bare mattress in the corner was a man of about twenty-five with the glittering eyes and sharp cheekbones of serious illness. The woman wasn't much to look at either—tall and awkward, with a gaunt face and rough, wrinkled hands, her clothes in tatters and more hole than shoe on her feet. Her hair was the color and texture of straw, some of it fastened back in a ponytail, the rest flying around her face. Even so, there was a dignity about her, a compassion in her gaze that won people over. Her pale blue eyes were still sharp, and the moment she clapped them on Ramona, she saw signs of privilege and said to herself, *this ain't no poor Mexican woman, I'll bet*. What she said aloud was, "Where you and your husband headed?"

Ramona stared back at her. The words exceeded her grasp. "Ay, señora! Yo no sé hablar inglés: castellano sé no más."

"Castellano? That's Mexican, ain't it? Jos there speaks some Mexican. Though he can't do much talking—not good for 'im. That's why we brung him down here, the warm weather. Jus' look at 'im!" she said, half-laughing but with a mother's tenderness for her sick child in the sidelong glance she cast his way. "Ask her, Jos."

Jos propped himself on an elbow, turned his wild, bright eyes to Ramona, and asked whether she and her husband were traveling somewhere.

"Sí, venimos de San Diego," Ramona replied. "Somos indígenas. Indians."

"Indians!" the woman exclaimed. "Well, God save and protect us, Jos, we got us some Indians in the house! And oh my goodness, she loves her baby just like any white woman, I can see that for sure. Indian or not, she can stay right here. I wouldn't send a dog outside on a night like this, Jos. The baby's dad must be white, too: just look at those blue eyes."

Ramona heard all this without understanding a word. She wondered whether it was English, even. For better or worse, she'd learned a fair amount of that language in her life but had never heard anything like the Tennessee drawl these people spoke in.

"¡Siento tanto no hablar inglés!" Ramona apologized to Jos. "If you not tired, tell what la madre say?"

Jos had his mother's contrarian and benevolent mind, so with a quiet, inward laugh for all he was leaving out he told Ramona only that his mother said she could stay until the storm passed.

Faster than lightning, Ramona darted over, grabbed the woman's hand, and pressed it against her heart. "¡Gracias! ¡Gracias, señora!"

"What's that she calling me, Jos?" the mother asked.

"Señora."

"Aw heck, Jos, you tell her I ain't no señora. Back home ever'body calls me Aunt Ri or Miss Hyer. She should, too. My goodness, she talks fine."

With some difficulty, Josh explained that his mother didn't want to be called señora, and told Ramona to choose between Aunt Ri and Miss Hyer. Ramona listened with a smile so friendly it captivated their hearts. She repeated both names more than once, and though she had an especially hard time pronouncing it, the one she chose was Aunt Ri. "¡Me gusta más! Aunt Ri es tan buena. Like familia, para todo el mundo. For everybody."

"Ain't it strange, Jos? She says just what they used to say back in Tennessee. I don't know that I'm so good. I'm just like everbody else. It's just, if I see anyone lay down the law on poor folks, I won't stand for it. And I can't bear suffering neither. No one should be suffering if there's anything I can do about it. But what's so special 'bout that?"

"There ain't many like you, Ma. If you'd seen more of the world, you'd know that."

Sitting on the floor by the fire, arms around her knees, Ramona observed that what had seemed a paradise when she came inside was actually a rather fragile refuge against the storm. The cabin's plank walls had been carelessly nailed together long ago by a hunter or shepherd who didn't plan to spend much time there, and every gust blew more snow in through the cracks. Next to the hearth, only a few sticks of the wood Jeff Hyer had managed to gather before the storm hit were left. Aunt Ri's eyes measured the scantiness of their fuel against the long, cold night ahead.

"You warm enough, Jos?"

"Not really, Mom, but I'm not too cold, at least. That's something."

The virtue of resignation was so deeply rooted in the Hyers that it had become almost a vice. Few families in Tennessee lived in less comfort or with dimmer prospects, but they never complained. No matter how bad a hand they were dealt, they never lost their good humor or treated each other with anything less than affection. Many a rich family lived far less happily than the Hyers, whose only wealth was their natural goodness. When Jos started having trouble breathing and complained of constant pain, they took him to a doctor who couldn't diagnose the condition but prescribed painkillers. Soon enough Jos was addicted. They'd lost dozens of their neighbors to opioids. The only way to save him was a change of scene. They resolved to move someplace far away, where the climate would be easier on his lungs.

They chose California. "It's good luck Lizzy got married last year. Let's sell the house and go."

They sold the house for half what they'd paid for it and traded in their three cars on a used camper—which, they'd only realized earlier that day, had a busted heater. With almost nothing to live on but their strength of will, they'd driven away with their invalid son stretched out in back, all of them as delighted as a family setting off on a long vacation. For weeks they'd made their way from Tennessee to the San Jacinto valley, camping for long stretches here and there. Now that they'd reached their destination, Aunt Ri walked around with a look of "Who's smarter than me?" on her face. Wasn't Jos better? Hadn't they saved their boy?

His full name was Joshua, not Jos, and Maria, not Ri, was his mother's real name, but she'd been called Ri since she was a girl. After she grew up and had a house of her own where everyone could always count on finding something to eat and a word of comfort, the whole town back in Tennessee had thought of her as a close relative; there wasn't a child or grown man or woman who didn't call her Aunt Ri.

"Don't know what to do about that fire," she said. "If this wind keeps up, we ain't gonna have enough wood."

The door opened and Jeff came staggering in with Alejandro behind him. Both men were covered in snow and loaded down with logs. Alejandro had remembered a stand of cottonwood in a nearby gully and when Jeff saw him take an ax from the back of the truck, he went for his own. They chopped enough wood to keep everyone warm for the night. As soon as he set down his cargo, Alejandro knelt next to Ramona and peered anxiously at his daughter's face, then back at Ramona, then back at the baby. Then he exclaimed jubilantly, "¡Milagro, Majela, milagro! Los santos sean benditos."

Jos took note. "Catholics," he thought. Well, I'm not going to tell Ma. Doesn't matter to me what they are, that girl has the most beautiful eyes I ever saw.

With Jos interpreting, each family soon knew what the other was doing there and despite the strange circumstances a kind of friendship began to blossom.

"Seeing they don't speak our language, Jeff, it ain't rude for us to talk about 'em, even if I don't like sayin' things they can't understand. I just have to tell you, these Indians have changed my thinking. I never cared much for Indians, but my goodness that girl is the soul of loveliness, and she just lives for that little baby, just as much as any woman in the whole world. And the man? Why, he flat-out worships the ground she walks on. I've never known a white man to love his wife like that, have you, Jeff?"

Truth was, Aunt Ri didn't know any more about Indians or Mexicans than what she'd seen in Western movies or on the TV news, always trumpeting stories of mayhem and murder. She'd watched some groups from a distance on the reservations they passed through along the way from Tennessee. But here she was now, speaking face to face with an Indian couple whose beauty and noble bearing drew her heart to them.

"He's pure Indian," she told Jos, "but her dad was white. Just look at the way she looks at her Indian man, as if he were the whole, entire world. I can't see nothing wrong with that."

Jos had already noticed. No one who saw Ramona and Alejandro together could fail to see how the blue-eyed wife adored her husband. What Ramona alone knew was that her love was now charged with ceaseless vigilance and a terrible fear that Alejandro's mind was coming unhinged. Where would she find the strength to face that?

When the storm let up a few hours later, the whole valley was a vast sea of white and the stars overhead shone with Arctic glitter. Jos could hardly believe it when Alejandro said that within a single day the snow would all be gone. But it was.

Afterword

Esther Allen

Martí's 1888 Spanish translation gives *Ramona*'s chapter 22 a title, "Tempestad y amigos," that has been removed and replaced on this journey back into English. The more tellingly nineteenth-century elements of the passage presented here have also been taken away and replaced with contemporary details. Stories can be privately owned and zealously defended, but unlike land, they revert to the public domain after a certain number of years. This is an old story and no law requires its reteller to obtain permission from anyone, so we can now do with it as we please.

The stealing away of some of the nineteenth century to leave, in its place, the twentieth or twenty-first demands that the resulting work be read as a borderland chronotope: at once a rather implausible piece of contemporary short fiction and a passage from a classic nineteenth-century novel, a translation into English from Spanish and a work written originally in English. Beneath the palimpsest of past and present is *Ramona*'s subject: the unending brutalization of the communities its two lovers represent. That brutalization continues in the dire neglect of Puerto Rico during and after 2017's Hurricane Maria, which pushed the storm's death toll to 2,975;[9] the separation and incarceration of more than 2,600 children, torn from their parents at the US-Mexico border;[10] the stripping of US citizenship from those born along the US-Mexico border;[11] the disproportionate impact of Covid-19 among Latinos and Native Americans;[12] and the long-established and ongoing practice of forced deportation of US residents[13] which causes families across the nation to live in terror, as children say goodbye to their parents in the morning, wondering if they'll see them again that night.[14]

In the nineteenth-century classic, a pair of Spanish-speaking Native American lovers on a dangerous journey in search of a place to live find provisional safety from freezing to death in a cabin with a white family. In the twenty-first century, families, children, and, no doubt, pairs of lovers,

---

[9] Fink, "Nearly a Year After Hurricane Maria, Puerto Rico Revises Death Toll to 2975."
[10] Shapiro and Sharma, "How Many Migrant Children are Still Separated from Their Families?"
[11] Seiff, "U.S. is Denying Passports to Americans along the Border, Throwing Their Citizenship into Question."
[12] Healy, "Tribal Elders are Dying from the Pandemic, Causing a Cultural Crisis for American Indians."
[13] Woodward, "ICE Deports Hundreds of Immigrants Including El Paso Massacre Survivor after Judge Blocks Biden Freeze."
[14] Greenberg, "In the Valley of Fear."

Spanish-speaking, indigenous, and from all over the world, are dragged into rooms where freezing cold is a weapon deliberately wielded against helpless people on a dangerous journey in search of a place to live. The chilling acronym of the US Immigration Customs Enforcement agency—ICE—is believed by many to be a deliberate and menacing allusion to the dire *hieleras*, frigid cages, sometimes so overcrowded there's no space to lie down on the concrete floors, where individuals and families are detained.[15]

The concept of "mass media" didn't exist—the phrase was coined in 1923—but in composing *Ramona*, Helen Hunt Jackson set out to write a "mass novel" of social reform, modeled on works like *Uncle Tom's Cabin* (1852) and Victor Hugo's *Les Miserables* (1862). *Ramona* was intended to loom large in popular consciousness, to influence attitudes, create sympathies, break down barriers, and change minds and historical outcomes.

The word "genocide" didn't exist when it was published, either, but *Ramona* tells a tale of romance amid genocide. The fictional love story is between Ramona, brought up by the Morenos (a wealthy Mexican family who've never told her that her mother was indigenous and her father Scottish), and Alessandro—or, as we'll call him, following Martí, Alejandro—a man of the Luiseño people whose family does sheep-shearing on the vast Moreno estate in Southern California. The real genocide was perpetrated against California's indigenous peoples during the 1846 US invasion of Mexico and the 1849 Gold Rush, and in the decades after 1850, when California became the thirty-first state in the union.

After Ramona and Alejandro fall in love, the powerful matriarch of the Moreno clan forbids them to marry. Ramona has been raised a *blanca*, with many of the attendant privileges; the idea that she would voluntarily forego that to throw in her lot with a Native man is unthinkable. The lovers elope, and though their love is great, nothing but misery awaits. Waves of ruthless white settlers drive Alejandro's people from their village and drive Ramona and Alejandro from several successive homesteads. Eventually, genocide wreaks havoc on Alejandro's mind. In a distracted fugue, he rides the wrong horse home, and is pursued and shot dead by its white owner, who accuses Alejandro of intentional theft, though he knows full well it was only a moment of distraction. The killer faces no consequences. Finally, Ramona and her young daughter are rescued by Felipe Moreno, fraternal companion of her childhood. As Felipe's wife, Ramona's privilege is largely restored, but it cannot be conferred upon the visibly indigenous daughter she had with Alejandro. Meanwhile, even the once-powerful Morenos are losing their lands to Anglo settlers. As *Ramona* ends, Felipe, Ramona, and her daughter

---

[15] Cantor, "Hieleras (Iceboxes) in the Rio Grande Valley Sector: Lengthy Detention, Deplorable Conditions and Abuse in CBP Holding Cells."

leave California for good to begin life anew in Mexico City, where the little girl, also named Ramona, can grow up in safety. (Though Jackson doesn't allude to it, one reason little Ramona's parents might have felt she'd be safer there is that the man who was Mexico's president from 1858 to 1872, the period when *Ramona* takes place, was Benito Juárez, a full-blooded Zapotec who did not begin learning Spanish until the age of twelve.)

The final flight to safety in Mexico arises naturally out of the novel's vivid depiction of brutal Anglo racism against Native Americans and Mexicans. It also fit perfectly with a centuries-old stance that held white supremacism to be so endemic to the national character, so impossible to overcome, that racial coexistence in the United States was a pipedream. This stance led to the formation of the American Colonization Society in 1817 to send free African Americans to Liberia; it made Ulysses Grant propose the idea of annexing Santo Domingo in 1869, as a place for African Americans after the Civil War. In both cases, at least part of the intention was to protect people of color from the inexorable brutality of white supremacism.

Martí himself would come to adopt a version of this stance with regard to the Cuban community. During his many years in New York City, he often depicted Cubans in the United States as integral to the fabric of the cities and country they were living in. Then, a year before his death, in 1894, he wrote, in response to the harsh treatment of striking Cuban tobacco workers in Key West, Florida, a stirring manifesto that concluded by urging his people back to the island: "Once more, Cubans, with our homes at our backs, abandoning our dead, we must make our way across the sea! Cubans: to Cuba!" (Martí, *Selected Writings* 329).[16] The exhortation is foreshadowed in the 1891 essay "Nuestra América," which very specifically defines the geographical boundaries of the America Martí viewed as "ours": it stretches "From the Rio Bravo [known in the United States as the Rio Grande] to the Straits of Magellan."

Few have ever thought that *Ramona* was a literary masterpiece, and the passage adapted here—more soap opera than Great Work, with its cartoonish characters and cloying combination of sentimentality and racism—is unlikely to bring about any revision of that. One of the most frequently cited assessments is from Jackson's friend and schoolmate Emily Dickinson, who quipped, "She has the facts but not the phosphorescence." José Martí generally disliked novels but did not agree. He promises his readers, in the preface he wrote to *Ramona, novela americana*, that through her long and patient research Jackson took the full measure of their superiority, "the

---

[16] First published in both Spanish and English in the *Patria*, the New York newspaper, organ of the Cuban Revolutionary Party, that Martí founded and edited.

seductive poetry and nobility that lift our race above its born rivals." She has, the preface claims, written "nuestra novela"—"our novel," the novel of nuestra América.

A classic conjures up myths and manufactures desires of which it may, itself, be hardly aware, myths and desires that can vary a great deal according to context, and that can also change the very objects—the places, the people—that the classic work alludes to. That, indeed, was Jackson's and Martí's goal: to effect change. And change did happen. Few works of fiction in the history of literature can have impacted the places they describe as massively as *Ramona*. Jackson meant for her social reform novel to inspire her white peers with a desire for dignity, equality, and justice for Native Americans and *californios*. Instead, it inspired her white peers with desire for orange groves, crystalline skies, picturesque adobe houses with red-tiled roofs, and fertile valleys with distant shimmering vistas of snow-capped mountains. Emily Dickinson had it all wrong: what readers took from *Ramona* was not fact but pure phosphorescence, the exotic bedazzlement of a tourist brochure or a real estate prospectus. In 1846, Thomas Gordon Bennett, editor of the *New York Herald,* boasted that "imbecile" Mexicans were "sure to melt away at the approach of Anglo-Saxon energy and enterprise, as snow before a southern sun" (qtd. in Grandin 91). *Ramona*, perhaps unwittingly, describes much the same phenomenon but ascribes it to white brutality rather than Mexican inferiority. Packaging it up in great sympathy for Natives and Mexicans made the message far more effective. The compassion *Ramona* seeks to generate offered white Anglophone readers comforting reassurance of their personal goodness as it imbued the California landscape with a poignant and enticing nostalgia for the Native American and *Californio* past whose "melting away" it portrays. The Morenos' final departure for Mexico served both Jackson's and Martí's political aims but also those of the massive land speculation and development interests that seized on the affective landscape *Ramona* created—a bedazzling Ramonaland, conveniently emptied out—and used it to sell California. Martí derived no financial gain from his version and Jackson died before the novel's earning power really kicked in, but for a number of decades after *Ramona's* publication, it generated great wealth for many people, almost none of whom shared the ethnic and racial heritage of its main characters.

In Jackson's story, indigenous and Hispanic characters, even the imperious Señora Moreno, are almost always good, at heart, while white Anglo-Americans, particularly men, are ignorant louts, when not brutal murderers. During her years of researching first her 1881 catalogue of horrors *A Century of Dishonor*, and then *Ramona*, Jackson repeatedly came face to face with genocide, and though it was not directed against her, it shaped her views. After writing more than half the novel, she must have realized that a story wholly devoid of sympathetic white characters might have trouble winning over the white mass audience she envisaged. It's the perennial dilemma of the social reform narrative: how to attract and retain the mass audience without gratifying its preconceptions and expectations. Cordelia Chávez Candelaria puts it more sharply in *The Encyclopedia of Latino Popular Culture*, "As a literary work, [*Ramona*] is challenged by the author's failure to seamlessly braid its social reform message with the literary conventions of the romance genre" (Chávez Candelaria, pg 663).In the novel's latter half, Jackson briefly includes a white trading post owner named Hartsel who is "by no means a bad fellow"—except when he's drunk. Later, she devises a chapter out of a terrifying experience during her research in California, when a sudden blizzard trapped her and several companions in a remote cabin in the San Jacinto Mountains for three days. She introduces the Hyers, a family whose very name suggests a better sort of white. (Aunt Ri, the Hyer matriarch, is based, exegetes of *Ramona* insist, on a Mrs. C. C. Jordan, originally from Tennessee, who ran a California boarding house where Jackson stayed [Davis and Alderson 159]).

Everything about the Hyers—their poverty, their invalid son, the wealth of spirit with which they stoically withstand their misfortunes—is calculated to inspire sympathy and encourage white readers to identify with them. Yet the Hyers's remarkable goodness is so pointedly commented upon, by the Hyers themselves and by the novel's omniscient narrator, that a certain skepticism also seems to be suggested.

Jackson pushes forward the Hyers as an instance of racism overcome, while also tacitly underscoring the intractability of their racism and unconsciously revealing the intractability of her own. The sharp double edge of the terms in which she describes them becomes more apparent in Martí's Spanish. This has less to do with any reworking by Martí—though he does rework—than with the fact that a Spanish-language text has a different implied reader than an English one does. In a preface to the 2005 Modern Library edition of *Ramona* (an edition that includes my translation of Martí's preface), New Mexican novelist and playwright Denise Chávez confesses that Jackson's *Ramona* was at first difficult for her to read because of descriptions that struck her as racial slurs (Chávez xiv). Martí does nothing to attenuate that disagreeable impression, translating Jackson's characterization of the matriarchal Señora Moreno—"indolent"—into the cognate "indolente," and her description of the Moreno household—"half barbaric, half elegant"—as "medio elegante y medio bárbara." Such pejoratives served his purpose.

While Jackson wanted to induce sympathy for Native Americans, Martí wanted to warn Mexican readers of the fate of those left behind when Mexico's former territory was annexed by the United States. The story was all the more effective, from Martí's perspective, for having originally been written by a concerned white Anglophone who, for all her sympathy and sentiment, describes Mexican places and characters in clichéd racist terms. If the readers of Martí's Spanish text felt lost and endangered within the opaque and menacing whiteness of Jackson's story, so much the better.

Even pre-translation, *Ramona* uses movement between languages to underscore a distinction between Native and white humanity. When Alejandro, lost in a blizzard, hears a voice responding to his distress call, the words are, in Jackson's line, "as intelligible . . . as if they had been spoken in the purest San Luiseno dialect"—Alejandro's first language. In a moment of dire need, the sound of human language, any language, holds out the promise of a shared and compassionate humanity—what Frederick Jackson Turner described in *The Frontier in American History* (1920) as "the old pioneer conceptions of the obligations and opportunities of neighborliness." By contrast, Jeff Hyer, a man decent enough to go out in a blizzard to rescue a stranger, explicitly regrets his action, while holding the stranger's baby in his arms, simply because the response to his call is in Spanish.

Jeff's wife, Aunt Ri, epicenter of the Hyer family goodness, reproaches Jeff for that reaction, and here Martí's translation heightens the impact. In Jackson's text, Aunt Ri says "Naow, Jeff, yer know yer wouldn't let ennythin' in shape ev a human creetur go perishin' past aour fire sech weather's this." In Martí's, she says "¡Mentira, Jeff!: tú no eres capaz de dejar al animal más infeliz puertas afuera con un tiempo como este."[17]) "[H]uman creetur" becomes "animal," further baring the hypocrisy in Ri's hyperbole.

Next Ri notices and begins cooing over the baby's blue eyes—the same color as her own. Jackson underscores that whiteness's compassion is only for itself. The evidence of at least some genetic whiteness (and, later, the hint of privilege) in Ramona's background is what first makes the imperiled family less unacceptable. What ultimately makes Ramona and Alejandro acceptable and sympathetic—both to the Hyers and, throughout the novel, to Jackson's anticipated readers, and, in the end, to Jackson herself—is the absurdly idealized exceptionalism that characterizes both her and her lover: their "beauty and noble bearing," the perfect adoration between them. Were Alejandro and Romana somewhat less than perfect, as the Hyers are allowed to be, what would be their fate?

The possibility of coexistence, *convivencia*, frontier neighborliness, that the budding friendship between the Hyers and Ramona's family proposes is largely predicated on Aunt Ri's goodness. But the cabin where the two families have taken refuge belongs to neither; the Hyers simply got there first. And they stumbled on it by accident, while Alejandro knows the place

---

[17] Wisely, Martí makes no attempt to come up with a Spanish equivalent of the "Tennessee drawl" that Jackson is at such pains to portray.

from previous visits, knows that there are cottonwood trees nearby. Even as it advances a possibility of white goodness, the passage puts the entitlements of whiteness on brazen display. Aunt Ri unhesitatingly asserts her right to *allow* Ramona and Alejandro to stay where they are—*giving them permission to stay alive*—and congratulates herself on that. Perhaps, somewhere in nineteenth-century Ri's mind, however she tries to repress it, lurks the thought of the money Alejandro's scalp might fetch, were they to present it for a bounty. Nineteenth-century Ri knows that the whole legal system of the state of California is there to defend her and her family's rights, over and against those of the Native American family, who are now fugitives on territory that their people have freely inhabited for tens of thousands of years. Ramona, though raised in privileged circumstances, as Ri recognizes, fully grasps her current racial status, knows she can't respond to Ri as a Moreno would: by calmly stating that she and Alejandro have as much right to the cabin as the Hyers do. Instead, she deliberately performs her inferior status, making a display of effusive, tearful gratitude, to join in the general celebration of Ri's goodness. Her family's life depends on it.

Both in New York City, where she completed the writing of *Ramona,* and in Los Angeles, where she made her initial notes on the story, Jackson had ample opportunity to observe communities we would now describe as Latino around her. In New York, she could have picked up any of a number of Spanish-language publications, several of them edited by Martí, that circulated in the city during the early 1880s; the many advertisements within them attest to the restaurants, hotels, schools, lawyers, and doctors that served the city's growing Latino population. In Los Angeles, as an honored guest in the home of Mariana de Coronel and her husband Don Antonio, Jackson became intimate friends with people she described in an article for *The Century Magazine* as both "Spanish" and "Mexican." Was it the dissociative power of whiteness itself or the fearsome terror of the white supremacist brutality she had witnessed that made Jackson, for all her sentimental attachment to them, unable to perceive the Coronels as anything but rare hold-outs of a rapidly vanishing past? She could not see that they were also harbingers of a powerful future. The bilingual Mariana de Coronel—to whom Martí sent a copy of his translation—was born in San Antonio, Texas, in 1851, six years after its annexation to the United States. Mariana's father, as California historian D. J. Waldie notes, was Nels Williamson, of Augusta, Maine; her Mexican-born *tejana* mother was—really—named Gertrudes Ramona. After her family moved to Los Angeles, Mariana was educated in the LA public school system. Her much-older husband, Antonio Coronel, "was a key figure in the political transition from Mexican to American Los Angeles in the 1850s and 1860s." He became mayor of Los Angeles in 1853, served nine terms on the City Council between 1854 and 1867, and in 1883 was a founder of the Historical Society of Southern California.[18]

Jackson's desire to save and preserve the *californio* culture the Coronels represented made her want to protect them from invasive whiteness by maintaining their separate national identity, whatever it was. This attitude did not trouble the Coronels, who seem even to have encouraged it. In the case of Native Americans, however, Jackson's white savoir mentality could have had very dire consequences. In her 1913 letter about their friendship, Mariana de Coronel mentions the final project of Jackson's life, a planned school that would ensure safety for Indian women and girls by adapting them into Ramonas: genetically indigenous, culturally white. Jackson, ever the would-be protector and benefactress, saw Native American culture itself— Native American families and their traditions—as a major barrier to the achievement of this goal. Coronel's letter cites Jackson's words: "I am counting upon meeting with numerous obstacles in getting the Indians to give up their tribal relations. To them it will be an immense problem" (Davis and Alderson 186). Jackson's death put an end to the plan, but countless schools like the one she envisaged were built, and added cultural eradication to genocide.

The most improbable element in Jackson's chapter 22 is Jos Hyer's ability to speak Spanish. How this skill might have been acquired by an untutored invalid who grew up in Tennessee in the 1840s in a family with deep prejudice against Spanish speakers is a mystery *Ramona* never tries to explain. Without Jos's Spanish no friendship could develop, and Jackson's purposes require friendship. The elimination of this linguistic improbability is a primary effect of transposing the scene to the present. Twenty-first century recovering opioid addict Jos might have picked up Spanish from the internet, from watching telenovelas or TV news on Univisión, from listening to music by Shakira or Luis Fonsi, Pitbull or Gloria Estefan, from required Spanish classes in high school, from friends, classmates, or co-workers, from a combination of the above. As of 2014, 5 percent of Tennessee's population was Hispanic.[19]

Biographer Kate Phillips astutely observes that although Jackson was a great transcriber of regional English dialect such as the Hyers' Tennessee drawl, the Native American and Latino characters in *Ramona* "speak a heightened, formal English, one perhaps modeled after the English of Susette LaFlesche" (262)— the mixed-race woman who interpreted the Boston lecture by Standing Bear

---

[18] Waldie, "The Mythmakers Fandango: H.H. Jackson, Antonio Coronel, and *Ramona* Memories," a series by Los Angeles PBS station KCET, www.kcet.org/shows/lost-la/the-mythmakers-fandango-h-h-jackson-antonio-coronel-and-ramona-memories.

[19] See "Demographic Profile of Hispanics in Tennessee, 2014," Pew Research Center Hispanic Trends, www.pewhispanic.org/states/state/tn/.

that first engaged Jackson with the cause of Native rights. (Jackson claimed LaFlesche had learned English from a small volume of Shakespeare she won as a prize at school.) *Ramona* contains only a small sprinkling of anglicized words like "senora" and "senorita," while Martí's translation barely nods to the source language with an occasional "Miss" or "Mister." Neither he nor Jackson goes so far as to include whole phrases in their texts' other languages, even in passages where the characters are explicitly confronting a language barrier. Like its character Jos, the passage adapted here has linguistic opportunities unavailable to its nineteenth-century predecessors.

The far greater bilingualism this new adaptation can engage in is a possibility it inherits from a literary lineage of brilliant Latino and Native American writers such as María Ruiz de Burton, Luis Valdéz, Miguel Méndez, Gloria Anzaldúa, Richard Rodriguez, Luis Humberto Crosthwaite, Francisco Goldman, Natalie Diaz, Roberto Tejada, Achy Obejas, Valeria Luiselli, Roberto Lovato, Javier Zamora, and Karla Cornejo Villavicencio, to name only a very few of them. Jackson's novel and Martí's translation of it are problematic forebearers and might not be identified as such by the Latino and Native writers who have, over the course of a century and a half, created a literary space of overlapping languages that has transformed the expectations of readers and changed US literature. The continuity between *Ramona* and their work consists primarily in the shared subject matter—that "applicability" from which, Poe's Auguste Dupin suggests, words derive their value. The brutality that *Ramona* protested has not ended.

By the mid-twentieth century, *Ramona* had a well-established reputation as a lowbrow exercise in gauzy sentimentality for mass consumption, a book that serious people wouldn't touch with gloves on. In 1961, Theodora Kroeber, also a white woman, published *Ishi in Two Worlds*, another attempt to engage white sentiment with the history of California's indigenous people and the genocide perpetrated against them by telling the story of an exceptional individual. Kroeber's sober, nonfiction biography, rooted in historical fact and the scientific field of anthropology, in which her husband Alfred was a pioneer, makes no allusion to Jackson or *Ramona*, which probably represented everything Kroeber wanted to avoid. But for all her conscientiousness, sensitivity, and narrative brilliance, Kroeber was still more like Jackson than she wanted to be. Even as it defends indigenous rights, *Ishi*, subtitled *A Biography of the Last Wild Indian in North America*, trades in the myth of the vanished race that has melted away.

A classic is, in the end, a work that continues to be read and told and evolves in the telling as history adapts it to shifting contexts and purposes. Simple persistence in time may be the classic's one defining characteristic. And *Ramona* has persisted. Over the years, it has been four Hollywood movies

(1910, 1916, 1928, and 1936), a 1928 song that became hugely popular across the world, a Mexican movie (1946), a Screen Guild Theater radio broadcast (1945), a 69-episode Mexican telenovela (2000), and many stage plays. The role of Ramona has been played by actresses from Mary Pickford and Loretta Young to Dolores del Río, Raquel Welch, Kate del Castillo, and countless others. Among the people (primarily in Mexico, Cuba, and the Southwestern United States) who remain aware of it today, *Ramona* has become an archetype of the nineteenth-century conflict between white settlers and Mexicans in California—and of the genocide perpetrated there against Natives.

The story's most studied retelling is the annual Ramona Pageant which celebrates its centennial in 2023, and is held in the Ramona Bowl, in Hemet, California. In its early years, whites were usually cast in the central roles now played by Latinos and Native Americans; Hemet's current population is 40 percent Latino, and Pageant performers are often locals. In a recent study, anthropologist Julia Sizek describes how, over the years, the Pageant increasingly came to advocate a message of harmonious multiculturalism, first by the inclusion of Spanish dialog, then by making itself a showcase for performance of Native American cultural traditions such as Bird Singing and Hoop Dancing, which are now featured prominently. A scene where Native elders pronounce a blessing has been carefully revised by its Native American Advisory Council. In 2015, the Pageant, increasingly dissatisfied with the version it had been using for more than eighty years, commissioned an entirely new adaptation from local playwright Steven Savage, who transformed Jackson's ending so that Ramona and her family remain in California. The Pageant's final line, spoken by Ramona, is now: "My home, California, where everyone can receive justice."

Helen Hunt Jackson intended for *Ramona* to help save Native Americans, but more recently, as interest in the Pageant has waned, Native Americans have been helping to save *Ramona*. Since 2000, the Pageant has received financial support from several local tribal governments. "We want to preserve the story," Rose Salgado, a council member of the Soboba Band of Luiseño Indians, one of the tribes that funds the Pageant, has explained, adding, in a statement that fulfills some of Jackson's deepest ambitions, "[*Ramona*] depicts all of the injustices, and it makes people realize what has happened" (Reynolds). The feelings of a tribe member and former Pageant performer interviewed by Sizek were decidedly more mixed: "[He] told me that he still hasn't decided whether the Pageant can bring awareness to Native issues or be a viable social critique, even after a lifetime of attending the event and seven years of participating as a Bird Singer."

In 2002, another of the tribes that helps fund the Pageant, the Pechanga Band of Luiseño Indians, founded the Chámmakilawish School, where the Luiseño language, cham'teela, is taught to new generations of children. Perhaps one day, a cham'teela speaker will find something in *Ramona* that makes them want to create a cham'teela version.

While Aunt Ri has an important role, the Pageant leaves out the part of the novel where Ramona and Alejandro are stranded in a blizzard. But it is often re-enacted. In January of 2018, three men, two Central Americans and a United States citizen, found fragile refuge together in an isolated and decrepit building in the Sonoran Desert. After US federal agents entered and placed them all under arrest, the Central Americans were taken into custody, and the citizen was charged with violating federal law by "harboring illegal migrants."[20] In the spring of 2019, a Texas woman pulled over to help three teenaged siblings, one of whom appeared very ill. She helped them into the warmth of her car and was making phone calls to see what could be done for them when the Border Patrol arrived and placed her under arrest, charged with "transporting illegal aliens."[21] The three siblings—one of whom would almost certainly have died if not for the medical care she received as a result of the woman's neighborly kindness—were handed over to ICE. Volunteers who leave out food and water along the US-Mexico border to help save the lives of those who come across the hostile desert terrain have faced an array of similar charges, as the US government, in keeping with an immigration policy of deterrence by cruelty it has pursued since the 1990s, sends the message that "Humanitarian aid to migrants is a crime."[22]

Imagined within our own time, Aunt Ri's permission, her decision to harbor the strangers, involves significant risk to herself and her family. The US government no longer offers a bounty on scalps, but today the Hyers could be brought up on criminal charges for helping out a family in trouble.

And Ramona and Alejandro—the people they are today? We know what happens to them, again and again, after day dawns and all the snow melts away from the landscape where they have no permission from the government to be. The federal agents arrive. The baby is wrenched from their arms and taken away, they don't know where. The lovers are shackled and shoved into a vehicle, and from there into a freezing cell.

---

[20] Lucas, "Deep in the Desert, A Case Pits Immigration Crackdown Against Religious Freedom." In November of 2019, following a two-year ordeal, and after an initial jury deadlocked, the second jury before which Scott Warren was tried unanimously declared him not guilty. "The government failed in its attempt to criminalize basic human kindness," Warren said. Allyn, "Jury Acquits Aid Worker Accused of Helping Border Crossing Migrants in Arizona."

[21] Fernandez, "She Stopped to Help Migrants on a Texas Highway. Moments Later, She Was Arrested."

[22] See, for example, Orlovsky-Schnitzler, "When the Desert Becomes a Weapon."

Works Cited

Allen, Esther. "Pies on the Windowsills of 'El Norte.'" *Los Angeles Review of Books*, February 5, 2020.

Allyn, Bobby. "Jury Acquits Aid Worker Accused of Helping Border Crossing Migrants in Arizona." *NPR*, November 21, 2019, www.npr.org/2019/11/21/781658800/jury-acquits-aid-worker-accused-of-helping-border-crossing-migrants-in-arizona.

Cantor, Guillermo. "Hieleras (Iceboxes) in the Rio Grande Valley Sector: Lengthy Detention, Deplorable Conditions and Abuse in CBP Holding Cells." *American Immigration Council*, December 17, 2015, www.immigrationpolicy.org/research/hieleras-iceboxes-rio-grande-valley-sector.

Chávez, Denise. *My Long Hot Ramona Summer*. Ramona: Penguin Random House, 2005.

Chávez Candelaria, Cordelia. "Ramona." *Encyclopedia of Latino Popular Culture*. Greenwood, vol. 2, 2004, pp. 663–5.

Cummins, Jeanine. *American Dirt*. Flatiron Books, 2020.

Davis, Carlyle Channing and William A. Alderson. *The True Story of Ramona: Its Facts and Fictions, Inspiration and Purpose*. Dodge Pub. Co., 1914. Chapters XIII and XV.

DeLyser, Dydia. *Ramona Memories: Tourism and the Shaping of Southern California*. University of Minnesota Press, 2005.

Fernandez, Manny. "She Stopped to Help Migrants on a Texas Highway. Moments Later, She Was Arrested." *New York Times,* May 10, 2019, www.nytimes.com/2019/05/10/us/texas-border-good-samaritan.html.

Fink, Sheri. "Nearly a Year After Hurricane Maria, Puerto Rico Revises Death Toll to 2975." *New York Times,* August 28, 2018, www.nytimes.com/2018/08/28/us/puerto-rico-hurricane-maria-deaths.html.

Grandin, Greg. *The End of the Myth*. Henry Holt, 2019.

Greenberg, Michael. "In the Valley of Fear." *The New York Review of Books,* December 20, 2018, www.nybooks.com/articles/2018/12/20/in-the-valley-of-fear/.

Healy, Jack. "Tribal Elders are Dying from the Pandemic, Causing a Cultural Crisis for American Indians." *New York Times,* January 12, 2021, www.nytimes.com/2021/01/12/us/tribal-elders-native-americans-coronavirus.html.

Kosztolányi, Dezső. *Kornél Esti: a Novel*. Trans. Bernard Adams. New Directions, 2011, pp. 200–3.

Lucas, Ryan. "Deep in the Desert, A Case Pits Immigration Crackdown Against Religious Freedom." *NPR*, October 18, 2018, www.npr.org/2018/10/18/658255488/deep-in-the-desert-a-case-pits-immigration-crackdown-against-religious-freedom.

Madley, Benjamin. *An American Genocide: The United States and the California Indian Catastrophe*. Yale University Press, 2016.

Martí, José. "The Indian Problem in the United States." *Obras Completas* (La Habana: Editorial de Ciencias Sociales), Vol. 10.

Martí, José. *José Martí: Selected Writings*. Trans. Esther Allen. Penguin Classics, 2002, pp. 296–303.

Martí, José. *Ramona, novela americana, Traducida del inglés por José Martí*. Ed. Jonathan Alcántar and Anne Fountain. Ediciones Stockcero, 2018.

Mathes, Valerie Sherer. "Boston, the Boston Indian Citizenship Committee, and the Poncas." *Massachusetts Historical Review*, vol. 14, 2012, pp. 119–48.

Muller, John and William Richardson, eds. *The Purloined Poe: Lacan, Derrida, and Psychoanalytic Reading*. Johns Hopkins UP, 1988.

Orlovsky-Schnitzler, Justine. "When the Desert Becomes a Weapon." *New York Times*, December 19, 2018, www.nytimes.com/2018/12/18/opinion/migrants-border-death.html.

Phillips, Kate. *Helen Hunt Jackson: A Literary Life*. University of California, 2003, p. 262.

Seiff, Kevin. "U.S. is Denying Passports to Americans along the Border, Throwing Their Citizenship into Question." *Washington Post*, September 13, 2018, www.washingtonpost.com/world/the_americas/us-is-denying-passports-to-americans-along-the-border-throwing-their-citizenship-into-question/2018/08/29/1d630e84-a0da-11e8-a3dd-2a1991f075d5_story.html?utm_term=.6a71bb40ce03.

Shapiro, Leslie and Sharma, Manas. "How Many Migrant Children are Still Separated from Their Families?" *Washington Post,* last updated August 30, 2018, https://www.washingtonpost.com/graphics/2018/local/tracking-migrant-family-separation/?utm_term=.d464ad6243c3.

Reynolds, Christopher. "On the Trail of *Ramona* in California." *Los Angeles Times*, January 11, 2009, www.latimes.com/travel/la-trw-ramona11-2009jan11-story.html.

Sizek, Julia. "Our Ramona: Multicultural Dreams and Legacies of the Great California Outdoor Play." *Boom California*, April 29, 2019, https://boomcalifornia.org/2019/04/29/our-ramona/.

Waldie, D.J.. "The Mythmakers Fandango: H.H. Jackson, Antonio Coronel, and *Ramona* Memories." *Lost L.A.*, October 10, 2017.

Woodward, Alex. "ICE Deports Hundreds of Immigrants Including El Paso Massacre Survivor after Judge Blocks Biden Freeze." *The Independent*, February 2, 2021, www.independent.co.uk/news/world/americas/us-politics/biden-immigration-ice-deported-el-paso-b1796657.html.

Contributors

Aron Aji is the director of MFA in literary translation at the University of Iowa. Originally from Turkey, he has translated poetry, fiction, and drama from Turkish, including Bilge Karasu's *Death in Troy*, *The Garden of Departed Cats* and *A Long Day's Evening*. His forthcoming translations include Ferit Edgu's *The Wounded Age & Eastern Tales* and Murathan Mungan's *Tales of Valor* (co-translated with David Gramling).

Esther Allen is professor in the PhD Programs in French and in Latin American, Iberian, and Latino Cultures at City University of New York Graduate Center, and director of the Sidney Harman Writer-in-Residence Program at Baruch College, CUNY. She edited, annotated, and translated *José Martí: Selected Writings* (2002). In 2017, her translation of *Zama*, a 1956 novel by Antonio Di Benedetto, won the National Translation Award, and she was a 2018 Guggenheim Fellow. Her essays, articles, interviews, and translations have appeared in the *New York Review of Books*, *Paris Review*, *Los Angeles Review of Books*, *Words without Borders*, *LitHub*, *Bomb*, and other publications.

Mary Jo Bang is the author of eight books of poems, including *Louise in Love*, *The Eye Like a Strange Balloon*, *Elegy* (winner of the 2007 National Book Critics Circle Award), *The Bride of E*, *The Last Two Seconds*, and *A Doll for Throwing*. Her translation of Dante's *Inferno*, with illustrations by Henrik Drescher, was published in 2012 and her translation of *Purgatorio* in 2021. She's received a Hodder Fellowship from Princeton University, a Guggenheim Foundation Fellowship, and a fellowship from the American Academy in Berlin. She is a professor in the English Department at Washington University in St. Louis.

Susan Bernofsky is the director of literary translation in the Columbia University School of the Arts MFA Writing Program. Her many prizewinning translations include works by Robert Walser, Yoko Tawada, Franz Kafka, Hermann Hesse, Jenny Erpenbeck, and Uljana Wolf. A Guggenheim, Cullman, and Berlin Prize fellow, she is currently working on a new translation of Thomas Mann's *The Magic Mountain* and has just published a biography of Robert Walser, *Clairvoyant of the Small*, that appeared in spring 2021.

Peter Bush's first literary translation was Juan Goytisolo's *Forbidden Territory*, and he has translated eleven other books by this writer, including *The Marx Family Saga*. He has translated a number of classics: from Spanish, Fernando de Roja's *Celestina* and Pedro de Alarcón's *The Three-Cornered Hat*; from Catalan, Mercè Rodoreda's *In Diamond Square*, Joan Sales's *Uncertain Glory*, and Josep Pla's *The Gray Notebook*, *Life Embitters*, and *Salt Water*; and from French, Balzac's *The Lily in the Valley*. His translation of Proust's *The Guermantes Way* is forthcoming. He is a former director of the British Centre for Literary Translation.

Sean Cotter is professor of literature and translation studies at the University of Texas at Dallas. His study of Romanian translators, *Literary Translation and the Idea of a Minor Romania*, was awarded the biennial book prize of the Society for Romanian Studies. Recipient of a PEN/Heim grant and two fellowships from the National Endowment for the Arts, Cotter is the translator of many works of Romanian literature, including an award-winning edition of Nichita Stănescu's poetry *Wheel with a Single Spoke* and the first volume of Mircea Cărtărescu's *Blinding*. His translation of Magda Cârneci's *FEM* is forthcoming with Deep Vellum Books.

Ellen Elias-Bursać has been translating novels and nonfiction by Bosnian, Croatian, and Serbian writers since the 1980s, including writings by David Albahari, Ivana Bodrožić, Miljenko Jergović, Kristian Novak, Dubravka Ugrešić, and Karim Zaimović. ALTA's National Translation Award was given to her translation of Albahari's novel *Götz and Meyer* in 2006. She was awarded the Mary Zirin Prize by the Association of Women in Slavic Studies in 2015 for her work as a scholar and translator. She is president of the American Literary Translators Association.

Regina Galasso is associate professor in the Spanish and Portuguese Studies Program and director of the Translation Center at the University of Massachusetts Amherst. She is the author of *Translating New York: The City's Languages in Iberian Literatures* (2018) and recipient of the 2017 NeMLA Book Award. She is the co-editor of two edited volumes, *Avenues of Translation: The City in Iberian and Latin American Writing* (2019), recipient of the 2020 SAMLA Book Award, with Evelyn Scaramella, and a special Nueva York issue of *Translation Review* 81 (2012) with Carmen Boullosa. She is the translator of Alicia Borinsky's *Lost Cities Go to Paradise* (2015) and Miguel Barnet's *A True Story: A Cuban in New York* (2010).

Michelle Hartman is professor of Arabic literature at the Institute of Islamic Studies, McGill University. She is also a literary translator of Arab women's fiction, from Arabic into English. Some of her most recent translations include Radwa Ashour's *The Journey*, Shahla Ujayli's *Summer with the Enemy*, and Jana Elhassan's *The 99th Floor*. Her scholarly monograph, *Breaking Broken English: Black-Arab Literary Solidarity and the Politics of Language*, won the College Language Association book award for creative scholarship in 2019.

Sabina Knight is author of *The Heart of Time: Moral Agency in Twentieth-Century Chinese Fiction* (2006) and *Chinese Literature: A Very Short Introduction* (2012, *Die chinesische Literatur* 2016 and 中國文學 2018), as well as essays in *The National Interest*, 翻「家的「「, and journals of Chinese studies, literary studies, and the medical humanities. Since 1998 Knight has taught Chinese and comparative literature at Smith College. She is also a translator, a speaker on Chinese-English literary and cultural translation, and a fellow in the Public Intellectuals Program of the National Committee on US-China Relations.

Lynn Kozak is an associate professor at McGill University, with research focusing on serial poetics across media. Theoretical work on translation includes the 2019 co-edited volume *The Classics in Modernist Translation* and co-written articles on H.D.'s translations of Greek tragic choruses—all with Miranda Hickman. Recent translations include literal translations of Aristophanes's *Birds*, Hroswitha's *Sapientia*, and Sophocles's *Oedipus Tyrannnus* for Scapegoat Carnivale Theatre, and serially performing/translating the *Iliad* in a 2018 FQRSC-funded project entitled "Previously on the Iliad." They also performed/translated the *Odyssey's Apologoi* at the 2019 Festival Interculturel du Conte.

Arvind Krishna Mehrotra is the author of many books. His most recently published books include *Translating the Indian Past and Other Essays in Literary History* (2019), *Selected Poems and Translations* (2020), and, as editor, *The Book of Indian Essays: Two Hundred Years of English Prose* (2020). He lives in Dehra Dun, India.

Johnny Lorenz, son of Brazilian immigrants to the United States, received his PhD in English from the University of Texas at Austin in 2000. He has received a Fulbright grant for his translations of Mario Quintana, a PEN/Heim Translation Fund grant for his translation of *Notebook of Return* by Edimilson de Almeida Pereira, and an NEA grant to support his translation of *Crooked Plow* by Itamar Vieira Junior. He has written numerous articles on Brazilian literature and translation. His volume of original poetry is entitled *Education by Windows*. He is a professor of English at Montclair State University.

Adalberto Müller is an associate professor for literary theory at the University Federal Fluminense in Rio de Janeiro. He was a visiting scholar at the University at Buffalo in 2018 and at Yale University in 2013. Besides publishing two collections of essays, he translated the complete poems of Emily Dickinson into Portuguese (*Poesia Completa*, 2020/2021, 2 vols.), as well as works by Walter Benjamin, e. e. cummings, Paul Celan, and Francis Ponge. His recent works are a collection of texts on plants—*Transplantations (from My Mother's Garden)*, 2019—and a book of short stories—*O Traço do calígrafo*, 2020.

Emma Ramadan is a literary translator based in Providence, Rhode Island, where she also co-owns Riffraff bookstore and bar. She is the recipient of the Albertine Prize, an NEA Translation Grant, and a Fulbright for her work. Her translations include Anne Garréta's *Sphinx* and *Not One Day*, Virginie Despentes's *Pretty Things*, Abdellah Taïa's *A Country for Dying*, and Marguerite Duras's *Me & Other Writing*.

Chantal Ringuet is a Canadian award-winning author, scholar, and translator. She is the author of a historical essay on Yiddish culture and of Montreal, and she edited the first anthology of Yiddish literature in Canada in French translation. With Pierre Anctil, she has translated Marc Chagall's original biography *Eygens* (*Mon univers. Autobiographie*, 2017). She has been a fellow of the YIVO Institute for Jewish Research in New York, scholar-in-residence at the Hadassah-Brandeis Institute (Brandeis University), and translator in residence at the Banff International Literary Translation Center (BILTC). She is a member of the Literary Translation Association of Canada (LTAC).

Marian Schwartz translates Russian classic and contemporary fiction and nonfiction. She is the recipient of numerous honors, including two NEA Translation Fellowships, the 2014 Read Russia Prize for Contemporary Literature, and the 2018 Linda Gaboriau Award for Translation awarded by the Banff Centre for Arts and Creativity and is a past president of the American Literary Translators Association. Her translation of Aleksandr Solzhenitsyn's *March 1917: The Red Wheel, Node III, Book 2* was named the 2019 Foreword INDIES 2019 Silver Winner for History. Her most recent translation is of Nina Berberova's first novel *The Last and the First* (2021).

Carolyn Shread is senior lecturer in French at Mount Holyoke College in Massachusetts and also teaches translation at Smith College. She has translated ten books, including five by French philosopher Catherine Malabou. Her entry on "Translating Feminist Philosophers" appeared in *The Routledge Handbook of Translation Studies and Philosophy* (2019). Recent translations include Véronique Tadjo's *Aimer: Fields of Battle, Fields of Love* (2019) and Achille Mbembe's "The Universal Right to Breath" in *Critical Inquiry* (2020). Shread has a long-standing interest in theorizing translation and has done so through Malabou's signature concept of plasticity. As translator, she signs herself *plasticienne textuelle*.

Kidder Smith was graced to study with Y. K. Kao at Princeton and Peter Boodberg at Berkeley. For many years he taught Chinese history at Bowdoin College, where he also directed the Asian Studies Program. He is senior author of *Sung Dynasty Uses of the I Ching* (1990), *Sun Tzu's The Art of War* (with Denma, 2001), *Having Once Paused: Poems of Zen Master Ikkyū* (2015), *Li Bo Unkempt* (2020), and *Abruptly Dogen* (2022).

Lytton Smith is the translator of over a dozen books from the Icelandic, including Andri Snær Magnason's *On Time and Water* (2021). His translations of *Tómas Jónsson, Bestseller* by Guðbergur Bergsson and *Öræfi* by Ófeigur Sigurðsson were finalists for the US Best Translated Book Award in 2018 and 2019 respectively. He is a 2019 National Endowment for the Arts Literature Translation Fellowship recipient. His most recent poetry collection is *The Square* (2021). He lives in western upstate New York where he teaches creative writing at SUNY Geneseo and serves as the director of the Center for Integrative Learning.

Mark Statman has written ten books. These include the poetry collections *Exile Home* (2019), *That Train Again* (2015), *A Map of the Winds* (2013), and *Tourist at a Miracle* (2010) and the translations *Never Made in America: Selected Poetry of Martín Barea Mattos* (2017), *Black Tulips: The Selected Poems of José María Hinojosa* (2012), and, with Pablo Medina, a translation of Federico García Lorca's *Poet in New York* (2008). Statman is emeritus professor of Literary Studies at Eugene Lang College of Liberal Arts, the New School, and lives in San Pedro Ixtlahuaca and Oaxaca de Juárez, Mexico.

Ilan Stavans is Lewis-Sebring professor of humanities, Latin American and Latino studies at Amherst College and the publisher of Restless Books. His most recent books include *The Seventh Heaven: Travels through Jewish Latin America* (2019), *How Yiddish Changed America and How America Changed Yiddish* (2020), *Popol Vuh: A Retelling* (2020), and *Selected Translations:*

Poems 2000–2020 (2021). His work, translated into twenty languages, has been adapted into film, theater, TV, and radio.

Humphrey Tonkin is university professor of humanities emeritus and president emeritus at the University of Hartford. His publications include two books on the poetry of Edmund Spenser, books on international education and service-learning, and numerous publications in and on Esperanto, most recently *Memoru ĉi praulojn*, essays on Esperanto literature (2020). Translations from Esperanto include Tivadar Soros's *Masquerade: Dancing around Death in Nazi-Occupied Budapest* (2001). Educated at Cambridge and Harvard, he has served as board chair of the Center for Applied Linguistics, the Center for the International Exchange of Scholars, and the Canadian Fulbright Commission.

Anna Zielinska-Elliott is a translator of modern Japanese literature into Polish. Educated in Poland and Japan, she is best known for her translations of Haruki Murakami and has also translated Mishima Yukio, Yoshimoto Banana, and Junichiro Tanizaki. She is the author of a Polish-language monograph on gender in Murakami, a literary guidebook to Murakami's Tokyo, and several articles on European translation practices relating to contemporary Japanese fiction. Zielinska-Elliott teaches Japanese language, literature, and translation studies at Boston University and is director of the MFA Program in Literary Translation.

Index

Abramovitsch, Sholem Yankev 113.
 See also Sforim, Mendele
 Moyher
abstract words 33
Academia Cațavencu 189
Académie française 218
Achilles 52
acoustical innovations 245–7
activism 278, 298, 305
Adamson, Ginette Plummer 230
Adorno, Theodor 164 n.4
aesthetics 90, 164, 164 n.4
African Americans 298
Aji, Aron 19, 237–48
Akhmatova, Anna 268
Albahari, David 19–20, 257–65
 Brother 262–4
 Checkpoint 20, 257–8, 263–4
 Globetrotter 264
 Leeches 260–2, 264
 "My Wife Has Light Eyes"
  257–8, 262, 264
 Snow Man 258–61, 264
Albert, Caterina 17, 127. *See also*
 Català, Víctor
Alcantar, Jonathan 277
Alevato do Amaral, Vitor 11, 59–68
Alexander II, Tsar 83
Alexis, Jacques Stéphen 222, 229
Allen, Esther 7, 20, 296–308
 "Permission" 291–5
Alliance Française 85
al-Qays, Imru 199
ALTA conference 258
Alvarez, Julia 15
American Colonization Society 298
American University in Cairo
 Press 197
Amerindian perspectivism 36

Amherst, Massachusetts 28, 29
Amyot, Jacques 80
anachronism 72, 73
Anderson, Benedict 90, 184
Anderson, Hans 94
anthropology 36–7
anthropophagy 35
anti-*noucestisme* 127
anti-Semitism 83, 91–2
Anzaldúa, Glora 304
Arab Book Prize (International Prize
 for Arab Fiction [IPAF]) 196
Arab feminist classics 197–8
Arabian Nights (*Alf layla wa
 layla*, also known as the
 1001 Nights) 11, 194–5
Arabic 14, 18–19, 193–201
Arabic literature 193–201
Arabic novels 199–200. *See also
 specific writers*
Arabic poetry 199–200
Archipelago Books 189
Arnold, Matthew 87
Arquimbau, Rosa Maria 134,
 134 n.5
 Forty Lost Years 132
Ashkenazi Jews 111–23
Astier, Pierre 231
Atwood, Margaret, *The Handmaid's
 Tale* 57
Auden, W. H. 66
Auld, William 95
Australian 95
authenticity 241
autobiography 181
El Avisador Cubano 276

Baalbaki, Layla 198
 I Am Alive! (*Ana Ahya!*) 198

Babington, Thomas, Lord Macaulay, Minute on Education 87
Babitz, Eve 255
Bacon, Francis 84
Baer, Brian James 7
Baes, Olivia 19, 250, 254
Balbuena, Bernardo de 268
Balzac, Honoré de, *The Lily in the Valley* 125
Bang, Mary Jo 16
Baptist Mission Press 70
Barnes, Julian 72
Barthes, Roland 179–80
  A Lover's Discourse 75
Bauman, Zygmunt 184
Bayard-Sakai, Anne 173, 174
Beauvoir, Simone de 227–9, 234
Beecher Stowe, Harriet, *Uncle Tom's Cabin* 274, 297
Bein, Kazimierz 95
Belgian 95
Belich, James 88
Belitt, Ben 1, 2, 8
Benjamin, Walter 239–40
  "The Task of the Translator" 63–4
Bennett, Thomas Gordon 299
Beowulf 9, 181
Bergsson, Guðbergur 19
  Tómas Jónsson Metsölubók 204
  translations by 203, 208, 212
Bergvall, Caroline, "Via" 59–61
Berk Albachten, Özlem 11
Berlin, Lucia 255
Berman, Antoine 11
Bernofsky, Susan 7, 17, 137–45
Berrou, Raphaël 222
Beyoncé, *Lemonade* 54
The Bhagavad Gita 8
Bharatiya Vidya Bhavan 70
Biblioteca Selecta 125
Biblioteko de la lingvo internacia Esperanto 93
Bibliothèque nationale 233
bilingual ediitons 72

bilingualism 304
Bingen, Hildegard 84
Birk, Sandow 62
Bishop, Elizabeth 270
Bjarnadóttir, Birna 205
Black radicalism 222–3
Blandiana, Ana 185
Bloom, Harold 203
Blum-Kulka, Shoshana 240 n.4
Bly, Robert 72
Bohigas, Maria 128
Boia, Lucian 185
Booth, Marilyn 197
Border Patrol 306. *See also* US Immigration Customs Enforcement (ICE)
Borges, Jorge Luis 268
  "On Blindness" 268
Bouton, Marjorie 79–82, 95–7
Bray, Barbara 254
Brazilian literature 157–65
Brazilian Portuguese 25–37
Bréal, Michel 87
Bridgman, Raymond 88, 92
Briggs, Kate 137
British and Foreign Bible Society 94
Bucci, Julia 13
Bulgakov, Mikhail, *White Guard* 103
Bulgarian 95
Burton, Richard, *One Thousand and One Nights* 269
Bush, Peter 125–36

Cadera, Susanne M. 9
California 274, 277, 280, 297, 304
californios 299, 302–3
Calvino, Italo 20–1
Calvo, Javier 9
Canada, Jewish immigration to 114
cannibalism 36–7
canon
  more? 191
  power structures and 181
  canonical, *vs.* classic 18, 179–80

capitalism 195-6
CARAF Books 231
Caribbean studies 234
Carne-Ross, D. S. 71
Carrington, Leonora 255
Carroll, Lewis, *Alice's Adventures in Wonderland* 13
Carson, Anne 181
Cary, Henry Francis 62
Cass 173
Cassedy, Ellen 120
Cassing, Katja 173
Català, Victor
  A Film (3,000 meters) 17, 125-36
  La Infanticida 127
  Solitude 125, 127-8
Catalan 2-3, 14, 95, 125-36, 173, 174
Catalana 128
Catalan literature 125-36
Catalonia 126
Cawnpore 70
Ceaușescu, Nicolae 183, 185, 188
Celan, Paul 268
censorship 169, 169 n.1, 171, 174
Center for Fiction, Brooklyn, New York 255
The Century Magazine 302
Cervantes, Miguel de 208
  Don Quijote 4, 8, 9, 12-13, 60, 203, 204, 211
Chámmakilawish School 305-6
Charles II, King 84
Charlier, Régine 232
Chauvet, Marie. *See* Vieux-Chavet, Marie
Chauvet, Pierre 216
Chavenet, Anaïse 232
Chávez Candelaria, Cordelia 300
Chekhov, Anton 101, 268
  "The Lady with a Dog" 102
Chevreal, Yves 12
Chinese 14, 95, 174
Chinese characters 172-3

Chinese classics 15, 39-49
Chinese novels 39-49
Chūo Kōron 168
Chronicle Books 62
Citadelle Laferrière 218, 230, 233
Civil War 298
Cixous, Hélène 162 n.2
classic(s) 1-23, 181. *See also specific literatures*
  vs. canonical 18, 179-80
  definitions of 20, 180, 193-201, 304-5
  macro-classic 191
  micro-classic 191
  notion of a 112
  produced in peripheries 198-9
  reading through lens of translation 2-4
  retranslations of 7-12
Club Editor 128
Coates, Carrol F. 225
Cohen, Madeleine 118
Colibri 216. *See also* Vieux-Chavet, Marie
Columbia University
  Creative Writing Program 60
  García Lorca at 149-50
Comanegra 134 n.5
Communication Plus 232
community, language and 91
concrete words 33
"Confucian canon" 38
connotations 56
constructed languages 79-100
contextual analysis, translation and 187
copyright, expiration of 8
Corneille, Pierre 85
Cornejo Villavicencio, Karla 304
Coronel, Antonio 302-3
Coronel, Mariana de 277, 302-3
co-translators 270
Cotter, Sean 10, 18, 20, 179-92, 287-90
  "My Majela!" 281-6

Covid-19 pandemic   1, 147, 153–5, 267, 296
Crosthwaite, Luis Humberto   304
Crum, Maddie   255
Cuba   149
Cubans   298
cultural appropriation   277–8
cultural connotations   56
culture, shared   66
Cunliffe, Richard John   54
CUNY Graduate Center, Centennial Celebration of Marie Vieux-Chauvet   233

Daðason, Sigfús   205–6
Daily Beast   51
Dalí, Salvador   13, 135
Damrosch, David   6, 179, 180
Danilov, Nichita   186
Danish   170
Dante Alighieri   59–67
  Catholicism and   65–6
  Convivio (*The Banquet*)   60
  The Divine Comedy (*La Commedia*)   59, 60, 62–7
  Inferno   16, 59, 62–6
  Paradiso   59
  Purgatorio   16, 59, 65
Danticat, Edwidge   218
D. Appleton & Co   275
Darwish, Mahmoud   198, 200
Davis, Lydia   3
Del Castillo, Kate   305
Delos: A Magazine on and of Translation   71, 72
Del Río, Dolores   305
Depestre, René   222
Derrida, Jacques   226
Descartes, René   84, 85
Dharwadker, Vinay   72
diaspora   226. *See also specific diasporas*
Diaz, Natalie   304
Dickinson, Emily   15, 25–38, 66, 159, 298
  "Forbidden Fruit a Flavor Has"   31
  "A Little Madness in the Spring"   29
  "The Mind Lives on the Heart"   32–3
  Poems as She Preserved Them   29 n.1
  "A Weight with Needles on the Pounds–"   33–4
  "Yesterday Is History"   29–30
Diderot, Denis   85
Di Forvets   114
Di Inzikhistin (The Introspectivists)   114
Di Yunge (The Young Ones)   114
Dorothy   250, 255
d'Ors, Eugeni   126
Dostoevsky, Fyodor   101, 121
  Crime and Punishment   102
draumaheima   206, 209, 212
Dream of the Red Chamber   39
Dropkin, Celia   115, 118
Dryden, John   66
duende   147
Dulichenko, Aleksandr   89
Dunbar-Nelson, Alice   66
Duras, Marguerite   19, 249–56
  Hiroshima mon amour   249
  journalism and   255–6
  L'Été 80 (*Summer 80*)   250–1, 253, 255
  The Lover   249, 254
  Me & Other Writing   19, 250
  "Translation"   253–4
Dutch   170
Duvalier, "Baby Doc" Claude   218, 230
Duvalier, "Papa Doc" François   218, 230

East India Company   87
East-West Series of literature translations   95
The Economist   222
El Economista Americano   276

Egyptian literature 196–8
Elhassan, Jana, *The 99th Floor* 193
Elias-Bursać, Ellen 19–20, 257–65
ellipsis 32, 33, 162, 173–5, 181
Emily Dickinson Museum 15, 25
Emina Soleil 231–2
Eminescu, Mihai 183–5, 189–91
"Şi dacă ..." ("And If...")
184
"A Dacian's Prayer" 186
in Romanian language
classrooms 186
Emmerich, Karen 7
Encyclopedia of Esperanto 95
Engle, Paul 72
English 3, 85, 95, 140, 163, 170,
172, 174, 175, 189, 190,
193–201
drive for world dominance 87–8
English-language teaching 184
power of English-language
translators 195–6
English Education Act of 1835 87
Enlightenment 85
Ephemer-illz 51
Episcolpal Church 188
epithets 53, 55
erotica. *See* sexuality
La Esperantisto 91, 93
Esperanto 12, 16, 79–100
anthologies translated into 95
literature and 93
roots in French and Latin 92–6
translated culture and 96
translation and 93–6
Esperanto movement 91
Esperanto poets and poetry 95–6
Estonian 95
Eternal Kool Project, *The Inferno
Rap* 62
Ethos Traductora 13
etymology 32
European literature, translated into
Yiddish 114–15. *See also
specific literatures*

exile 112
*The Exile Book of Yiddish Women
Writers* 121
explicitating 240, 240 n.4
Eysteinsson, Ástráður 208

Fagles, Robert 55, 180
fascism 126
Faulkner, William 15
feminism 57, 227, 234
Fichte, Johann Gottlieb, *Fourth
Discourse to the German
Nation* 87
Finnish 170
first person perspective, significance
of 219–20
Fitzgerald, F. Scott 15
The Great Gatsby 9–10
Flaubert, Gustave, *Madame
Bovary* 3
Florio, John 269
Fokal 233
Forman, Frieda Johles 121
*Found Treasures: Stories by Yiddish
Women Writers* 121
Fountain, Anne 277
Franco, Francisco 125, 126
Francophone literature 215–36
Frankétienne 226 n.10
Dézafi 223
Frankfurt Book Fair 126
Franks 85
French 14, 19, 85, 87–90, 92, 94,
113, 143, 170, 173–5, 251
French colonialism 220, 225
French literature 19, 249–56.
See also Francophone
literature
French republicanism 85
French Revolution 85
Frost, Robert 253

Gabbert, Elisa 5, 203–5, 208, 209,
251
Galasso, Regina 1–23

Gallimard 173, 216, 226 n.10, 227–8, 230, 231
Gallimard, Gaston 226
Gangadhara 75–6
Garcés, Tomàs 127
García Márquez, Gabriel
 Chronicle of a Death Foretold (*Crónica de una muerte anunciada*) 4
 One Hundred Years of Solitude 208, 210, 211, 271
Garrett, Constance Clara 16, 101–2
gatha form 75
Gaudí, Antoni 135
Geneva Convention 88
genocide 276–7, 297, 303. See also Holocaust
genres
 Arabic literature and 199–200
 Yiddish classics and 115
Gentzler, Edwin 12
Geoghegan, Richard 82
Georgian 268
Gerber, Kaia 255
German 14, 83, 85–9, 113, 140, 173, 175, 232, 268
Germanic languages 87, 93, 111. See also specific languages
German literature 137–45
German Romanticism 184
Ginsberg, Allen 66
Glatshteyn, Jacob 114–15
Glenny, Michael 103
globalization 195–6
Glover, Kaiama L. 222, 223, 225, 228–9
Goethe, Johann Wolfgang von 6, 86, 93
 Die Geschwister 91
 Iphigenie auf Tauris 94
Goldfajn, Tal 270
Goldman, Francisco 304
Gold Rush 297

Goncharov, Ivan 101
 Oblomov 104–5
González Martínez, Enrique 268
Google Translate 2
Grabowski, Antoni, *La Neĝa Blovado* 91
Grant, Ulysses 298
Great Depression 147, 149, 150
Greece 86–7
Greek 14, 51–8
Greek literature 51–8
Grimm, Brothers (Jacob and Wilhelm), "Allerleirauh" (All Kinds of Fur) 143
Grossman, Edith 6, 8, 9, 203
 Why Translation Matters 3–4
Grove Press 176
Gullar, Ferreira 268

Habitat for Humanity 188
Hachette 93
Haiti, US occupation of 218
Haitian Creole 19, 223–4, 224 n.8
Haitian diaspora 218–19, 225–6
Haitian literature 19, 215–36, 224 n.8
Haitian studies 234
Hala, Satavahana
 The Absent Traveller: Prakrit Love Poetry from the Gathasaptasati *of Satavahana Hala* 75
 Gathasaptasati (*Seven Centuries*) 75, 76
Hall, Edith 7
Harlem 149, 150
Harshav, Benjamin 117
al-Harthi, Jokha, *Celestial Bodies* (*Sayyidat al-qamar*) 199
Hartman, Michelle 10, 11, 18–19, 193–201
Haskalah 111
Hausa 84
Headley, Maria Dahvana 9
Heaney, Seamus 180

Hebraists, *vs.* Yiddishists   113, 113 n.4
Hebrew   83, 269
Hebrew alphabet   113
Heian period   73
Hellerstein, Kathryn   118–19
  A Question of Tradition   118
Herder, Johann   184
Herzen, Alexander   102
Hess, Linda   72
Hesse, Hermann, *Siddhartha*   17, 137–8, 140
Hibbett, Howard   168, 170–3, 175
Hindi   14, 69–73
hiragana script   172–3
Hirsch, Marianne   116
Hispanics   274, 277
historical consciousness, translation and   115–16
history, memory and   115–16
Hobsbawm, Eric   90
Hohendahl, Peter Uwe   164 n.4
Hollander, Jean   61
Hollander, Robert   61
Holocaust   111, 112
"homaranismo"   92
Homer
  Iliad   15, 51–8, 95, 181
  misogyny and   57
  Odyssey   53, 55, 142
Horowitz, Rosemary   121
Hugo, Victor, *Les Miserables*   297
Humboldt, Wilhelm Von   86
humor   260
Humphries, Rolfe   8
Hungarian   95
Hurricane Maria   296

iambic pentameter   52
Icelandic   14
Icelandic literature   203–13
I Ching   46–7
Ikkyū   41–4
Illustrated Modern Library   13

Imperial Moscow University   83
India   87
Indian literature   69–73
indigenous peoples   273–4, 297, 304. See also Native Americans
Indo-European languages   86, 87, 113. See also specific languages
Industrial Revolution   88
innovation, translation and   12–13
instability   30–1
Institut Ramon Llull   126, 128
intellectual exchange, language and   86
International Criminal Tribunal for the former Yugoslavia   260
internationalism   87, 88, 92
international languages   79–100
International Red Cross   88
intertextuality   49
Italian   14, 95, 170, 173, 174, 232
Italian literature   59–67

Jackson, Helen Hunt   271
  A Century of Dishonor   273–4, 299–300
  Ramona: A Story   20, 273–80
Jacobi, Derek   180, 181
Japanese   14, 18, 95, 172–3
Japanese literature   167–77
Japenese literature, golden age of   168
Japenese phonetic systems of writing, gendered nature of   172–3
Jean-Charles, Régine Michelle   221, 229–34
Jewish culture, translation and   112 n.2
Jewish diaspora   111–23
Jewish humor   121
Jobava, Gvantsa   270
Johnson, Samuel   89
Jones, William   86
Jónsson, Ólafur   205–6
Jónsson, Tómas   203–13

Joseph, Régine Isabelle 221, 226–9
Juana Inés de la Cruz 268

Kabir 16, 69–72
   The Fish in the Sea Is Not Thirsty 72
Kafka, Franz 14, 113
   The Metamorphisis 17
   The Metamorphosis 137, 139–40
Kahf, Mohja 198
Kaindl, Klaus 7
Kaloscay, Kálmán 81, 95
Karashima, David 13–14
Karasu, Bilge 19
   Death in Troy 237
   The Garden of Departed Cats 237
   A Long Day's Evening (Uzun Sürmü? Bir Günün Ak?am?) 237–48
   translations by 247–8
Karpilove, Miriam, *Diary of a Lonely Girl, or The Battle against Free Love* 120
al-Karrat, Edward 196, 198
katakana script 172–3
Kawabata, Yasunari 168
Keats, John 80, 89
Keene, Donald 170, 171
Kellerman, Ivy 81
Kelter, Chaim 82
Der Keneder Adler 114
Khalifeh, Sahar 198
   Passage to the Plaza (Bab al-Saha) 198
al-Khansa' 199
Kharanauli, Besik 268, 270
Khuri, Colette 198
   Days with Him (Ayyam ma'hu) 198
Kirzane, Jessica 120
Klerk, Carina de 51
Knauss, Gerard 173

Knight, Sabina 15, 39–50
Knopf 18, 170, 175
Kofman, Abram 95
Kolatkar, Arun 76
   "The Doorstep" 76
   Jejuri 76
Korman, Ezra, "Yiddishe dikhterins" (*Yiddish poetesses*) 118
Korn, Rokhl 115, 118
Koskinen, Kaisa 10
Kosztolányi, Dezső 279–80
   Kornél Esti 279–80
Kozak, Lynn 15, 51–8
Kroeber, Theodora, *Ishi in Two Worlds* 304
Kübler, Gunhild 29 n.1
Kundera, Milan, *The Book of Laughter and Forgetting* 239
Kyzer, Larissa 11

Lacan, Jacques 31 n.7, 280
Ladino 269
LaFlesche, Susette 273, 303
Lahens, Yanick 219–20
Lambert, Joshua 116
language ideology 184–5
language invention 89–93
language pedagogy 3, 184, 186.
   See also translation pedagogy
language(s). *See also specific languages*
   aesthetics of 90
   community and 91
   history of 87
   intellectual exchange and 86
   "learned" *vs.* "popular" 116
   literature and 93
   of power 184
   revival of 116
   revived 116
   transactional 84
   translating from languages not known 267–71

universal 79–100
  vernacularization of 184
Lao Tzu/Laozi 47–9
Larsen, Nella 15
Latin 60, 84, 85, 89, 90, 92–4
Latino writers 304. *See also specific writers*
Lattimore, Richard 52–7
Lawrence, D. H., *Lady Chatterley's lover* 176
Laxness, Halldór 209–10
League of Nations 85
Legs et littérature 233
Leib, Mani 114–15
Leibniz, Gottfried Wilhelm 84
Lempel, Blume, *Oedipus in Brooklyn ad Other Stories* 120
Leo III 239, 244
Lermontov, Mikhail 101
  A Hero of Our Time 102–3
Le Serpent à Plumes 231
Lewis, Tess 258
lexical innovations 241–3
Lianeri, Alexandra 7
Libération 250
Liberia 298
Li Bo 44–6
Lillabulero Press 72
Lingua Franca 84
lingua ignota 84
linguistic internationalism 87
Lispector, Clarice 157–65, 255
  The Besieged City 18, 157–60
  A Breath of Life 18, 161–4
  The Passion According to G.H. 160-1, 164
  syntax of 160
literary history, translation roots of 20
literary pedagogy 4–5, 196
Literary Translator Studies 7
literature. *See also specific literatures*
  Barthes's definition of 179–80
  language and 93
  memory and 247–8
Literatures, Cultures, Translation series 7
Lithuanian 95
"little mag" circuit 71
Livres en folie 233
Longfellow, Henry Wadsworth 273
Lorca, Federico García
  "Back from a Walk" 149–50
  "Blind Panorama of New York" 151
  at Columbia University 149–50
  "Crucifixion" 153
  "Cry toward Rome (From the Tower of the Chrysler Building)" 153–4
  "Dance of Death" 150
  Diwan of the Tamarit 154
  "Jewish Cemetery" 153
  "The King of Harlem" 150
  Lament for Ignacio Sánchez Mejías 154
  "Landscape of the Urinating Crowd [Nocturne of Battery Place]" 151
  "Landscape of the Vomiting Crowd [Twilight at Coney Island]" 147–8
  "New York: Office and Denunciation" 152–3
  "Ode to Walt Whitman" 153–4
  plays of 154
  "Poems of Solitude at Columbia University" 149
  Poet in New York 17
  Poet in New York (*Poeta en Nueva York*) 1–2, 8, 147–55
  "Small Infinite Poem" 153
  Sonnets of Dark Love 154
  "Two Odes" 152
  "Vuelta de paseo" 1–2
Lorenz, Johnny 18, 157–65
Louwagie, Frasiska 7
Lovato, Roberto 304

Lowe-Porter, Helen 137, 142–4
Loyola University 188
Luiselli, Valeria 304
El Lunes 276

Macedonian 95
Machado de Assis, Joachim 268
the macro-canonical 191
magical realism 208–9
Mahadevan, T. M. P. 197
  Ten Saints of India 70
Mahfouz, Naguib 196, 198
al-Mala'ika, Nazik, *Revolt against the Sun* (*Thawra 'ala al-shams*) 200
Malay 84
Malkjær, Kirsten 7
Malroux, Claire 29 n.1
Mann, Thomas, *The Magic Mountain* (*Der Zauberberg*) 17, 137, 141–4
Maragall, Joan 127
Marathi 76
Margolin, Anna 115, 118
Martelly, Stéphane 219
Martí, José 274
  Ramona, novela americana 20, 273–80, 278 n.6
Marx-Aveling, Eleanor 3
Matisoff, James 117
Maze, Ida 115
McLaughlin, Martin 20–1
McLellan, Edwin 171
McNerney, Kathleen 125
meaning 31
Medina, Pedro 1, 8, 17, 147–55
Mehrotra, Arvind Krishna 16, 69–70
  Songs of Kabir 72–3
Melville, Hermann, *Moby-Dick* 28–9, 210, 212
Mémoire d'encrier 231
memory
  emotional 25

history and 115–16
literature and 247–8
Méndez, Miguel 304
Mercado, Manuel 275–6
meshing ("remaillage") 116
metafictional distance 260
metaphor 161
Mexicans 280, 298–301, 305
Mexico, US invasion of 297
Micle, Veronica 185, 186
MicPwr 62
the micro-personal 191
Middle East 86
migration 112, 115. *See also* diaspora
Mill, John Stuart 87
Miller, Cristanne 29 n.1
Miller, Henry, *Tropic of Cancer* 176
Miró, Joan 135
Mishima, Yukio 168
misogyny 57
Mission Indians 277
mnemonics 51–2
modernism 126
  Icelandic literature and 208
  Turkish 240 n.5
  Yiddish literature and 114
modernity 17, 120
Modern Langauge Association 196
Molière (Jean-Baptiste Poquelin) 114
Molodowsky, Kadya 16–17, 112, 115, 118–19
  "Froyen-lider" ("Women-Poems") 17, 119–20
  A Jewish Refugee in New York: Rivke Zilberg's Journal 120
  Kheshvandike nekht 119
Montaigne, Michel de 80, 85, 269
  "Des Cannibales" 36
Morgenthaler, Goldie 120
Morrill Act of 1862 87
Morrison, Toni 15
Morson, Gary Saul 106–7

Moser, Benjamin   158–9
Motteux, Peter   13
Mr. Moe   62
Muʾallaqat   200
Mukherjee Ankhi   219, 225
Müller, Adalberto   15, 25–38
multilateralism   88
multilingual education   87
multinaturalism   36
Murakami, Haruki   4, 9–10, 13–14
musicality   251, 253, 254
al-Mutanabbi   199

Nabokov, Dmitri   103
Nabokov, Vladimir   102–3
La Nación   276
Nagari script   73
#NametheTranslator campaign   6
Narayanan, Vivek   11
national poets   186–7
national self-consciousness   88
national symbols   184–5
Native Americans   273–4, 277, 280, 296–7, 299, 300, 303, 305
Nervo, Amado   268
New Directions   74
Newell, Alex   81 n.1
Newton, Isaac   84
New York, New York   147–55, 190
New Yorker   255
New York Herald   299
New York Review of Books   125
New York Times   171, 193, 195
Nietzsche, Friedrich, *The Gay Science*   159–60
Niger, Shmuel   111
Nobel Prize   196, 209–10
Nopca, Jordi   128
Norich, Anita   117, 120
North, Thomas   80–1
North America, Yiddish literature in   114
noucentisme   126, 128
Le Nouvelliste   232, 233

novels. See *specific literatures; specific writers*
Novey, Idra   160
Nuwas, Abu   199
Nzengou-Tayo, Marie-José   225

Obejas, Achy   304
Old Testament   94, 154
Olesha, Yuri   103
Oller, Narcís   127
Open Letter   128
Oppen, George   74
Orientalism   195
Orzeszkowa, Eliza, *Marta*   94
Ostrovsky, Alexander   101–2
Oudart, Jean-Pierre   31 n.7
Ozick, Cynthia   111, 112 n.2

Pale of Settlement   84, 111, 113
Paloposki, Outi   10
Panter, Gary, *Jimbo's Inferno*   62
Paravisini-Gebert, Lizabeth   231
Paris Review   5, 203, 255
El Partido Liberal   276
Paterson, Mike   56, 57
Patton, Laurie   8, 11
Paz, Octavio   268
Peace Corps   182–4, 187, 188, 191
Pearl   79
Pechanga Band, Luiseño Indians   305–6
Penguin Classics   8
Peretz, I. L.   114, 115
performance   15
peripheries, classics produced in   198–9
Perrault, Charles, "Peau d'Âne" (Donkey Skin)   142–3
Persian   86
the personal   191
   in translation   179–92
personification   97
perspectivism   35
Peyser, Thomas   88

Phillips, Henry, Jr. 83
Phillips, Kate 303–4
Pickford, Mary 305
Pizarnik, Alejandra 255
Pla, Josep 126, 135
Plath, Sylvia 15
Plutarch, *Parallel Lives* 80
Poe, Edgar Allen 15, 280, 304
poetry. *See also specific literatures; specific poets; specific writers*
  Arabic 199–200
  Esperanto 199–200
  high status of in Romania 183–4, 186
Poets House 190
Poland 175
Polish 18, 83, 167–77
Polish literature 95
Pompilus, Pradel 222
Ponca people 273
Portuguese 3, 14, 18, 25–37, 268
Portuguese literature 157–64
Post, Chad 128
"postmemory" 116
postmodernism 240 n.5, 258, 264–5
postmodernity 62, 67
Pound, Ezra 69, 74, 77, 190
Prakrit 73–6
Protestantism 31
Prus, Boleslaw, *Faraon* 95
Puerto Rico 296
puritanism 31
Pushkin, Alexander 91, 101
Putnam, Samuel 8

Qabbani, Nizar 198, 200
Quddous, Ihsan Abdel 196, 198
Quint, Alyssa 114

Rabassa, Gregory 4, 271
Racine, Jean 85
racism 150, 195, 298, 300
Radzinski, Meytal 255
Ragnarsson, Baldur 95

Raicus, Ethel 121
Rakosi, Carl 74
Ramadan, Emma 19, 249–56
Ramanjuan, A. K. 73
Ramona, Gertrudes 302
Ramona Pageant 305–6
Ramos, Graciliano 268
Random House 232
rap music 62
readability 171
Real Academia Española 12–13
Rebón, Marta 9
recontextualizaiton 179
redondilhas 32
register 65, 72
Réjouis, Rose-Myriam 215
Renaixença movement 126
Renondeau 173
retranslation 8–12, 101–8, 179, 180
Rexroth, Kenneth 74
Reznikoff, Charles 74
rhythm 251, 254
Rich, Adrienne 269
Ringuet, Chantal 16–17, 111–23
Rock, Chris 54
Rodoreda, Mercè 135
  In Diamond Square 132
Rodriguez, Richard 304
Rodway, Stella 111 n.1
Roenthal, David 125
Rolland, Romain 114
Romania, high status of poetry in 183–4, 186
Romanian 14, 179–92
Romanian Cultural Institute 190
Romanian identity 185–6
Romanian language ideology 184–5
Romanian literature 179–92
Romanian national symbols 184–5
Rome 85–7
Rosenfarb, Chava 115, 118
  Confessions of a Yiddish Writer and Other Essays 120
Rosenwald, Larry 118

Rossetti, Dante Gabriel 277
Rossetti, Reto 81
Roumain, Jacques 222, 229
Rowohlt 173
Ruíz de Alarcón, Juan 268
Ruiz de Burton, María 304
Russian 14, 83, 88, 172, 268
Russian canon 101–8
Russian Empire 83–4
Russian literature 114
   retranslation of 101–8
   Russian classics 16, 101–8
Russian Revolution 114

El Saadawi, Nawal 197, 198
Sainte-Beuve, Charles Augustin 85
Saint-Éloi, Rodney 231
Saint-Exupéry, Antoine de, *The Little Prince* 13
Salgado, Rose 305
Salih, Tayeb, *Season of Migration to the North* (*Mawsim al-hijra ila al-shamal*) 198–9
Salted Feathers 71
Sanders, Marcus 62
The San Fancisco Keeper's Voice 71
Sanger, Margaret, "The Use of the Pessary" 144
Sanskrit 14, 75, 86
Santo Domingo 298
Sappho 181
Satterfield, Jay 13
Saussure, Ferdinand de 91
Scarry, Elaine 162 n.2
Schiller, Friedrich 184
   Die Räuber 94
Schlegel, August Wilhelm 94
Schleyer, Johann Martin 89
Schoolman, Jill 189, 190
Schuyler, Eugene 102
Schwartz, Marian 16, 101–8
Scottish 95
Seciu, Valeria 186
Second New Wave (Turkey) 240 n.5
Segal, Jacob-Isaac 115

Segal, J.-I. 115
Seidensticker, edward 168
self-fashioning 234
Sells, Michael, *Desert Tracings* 200
Serban, Adriana 7
Serbian 14
Serbian literature 19–20, 257–65
"settler revolution" 88
sexuality 151, 168, 169, 174–6, 221
Sforim, Mendele Moyher 114, 115
   Dos kleyne mentshele ("The Little Person") 113
Shah, Ahmad 70
Shakespeare, William 3, 12, 16, 66, 88, 114, 269
   Antony and Cleopatra 80
   Coriolanus 79–82, 96–8
   Hamlet 81 n.1, 93–4
   Henry V 79, 81
   Julius Caesar 80
   Lear 81
   Othello 81
   The Winter's Tale 79, 81
   As You Like It 81
shamanism 35–6
Shimanaka, Hōji 169
Shishkin, Mikhail 104–5
Sholem Aleichem 114, 115
Shragge, Joseph 55
Shread, Carolyn 19, 215–36
Shūkan Asahi 169
Sidney, Philip 89
Silbernik, Klara 82
Simon, Greg 1, 8
Singer, I B. 115
Singer, I. J. 115
Singer, Isaac Bachevis 115, 121
Singleton, Charles s. 61
Sizek, Julia 305–6
slavery 220
Slavic languages 89, 93
small literatures 179–92
Smith, Dinitia 1
Smith, Kidder 15
   Li Bo Unkempt 44–6

Smith, Lytton 19, 203–13
Smith, Matthew 222
Songs of Kabir 16
Sorescu, Marin 185
Spain 149
Spanglish 12–13
Spanish 3, 14, 134, 173, 174, 269, 303
Spanish civil war 125–6
Spanish literature 147–55
Spear, Thomas C. 215 n.1, 216 n.2, 230–3
Springfield, Massachusetts 28
Stalph, Jürgen 173
standardization, Yiddish literature and 116, 117
Standing Bear 273, 274, 303–4
Stănescu, Nichita 18, 179–92
  "The Land" 186
  Peace Corps 189
  "Poem" 18, 181–2, 184, 189–91
  in Romanian language classrooms 186
  Wheel with a Single Spoke 189, 190
Stanislavski, Konstantin 25
Statman, Mark 1, 8, 17, 147–55
Stavans, Ilan 12–13, 20, 116
Stead, Henry 7
Stein, Gertrude 66
Stevenson, Robert Louis, *The Strange Case of Dr. Jekyll and Mr. Hyde* 204, 209
Stojan, Petr E. 89
storytelling, translation as 137–45
Strakhov, N. N. 105 n.6
Straumanis, Kaija 128
Strauss, Harold 18, 170–1
style, retranslation and 104
Sukhu, Gopal 11
Sun Tzu, *The Art of War* 39–41
Suteu, Corina 190
Sutzever, Avrom 115
Swahili 84
Swartz, Sarah Silberstein 121
Swedish 170

symbols 184–5
syntactical innovations 243–5

Tagore, Rabindranath 95
  One Hundred Poems of Kabir 72
Tahir Gürçaglar, Sehnaz 11
Taiwanese 174
The Tale of Genji 169
Tanizaki, Jun'ichirŌ 18
  Censor (Ken'etsukan) 169 n.1
  La clef 173
  La confession impudique 173
  Diary of a Mad Old Man 168
  The Key (Kagi) 18, 167–77
  The Makioka Sisters 168, 169
  Der Schlüssel 173
  Seven Japanese Tales 168
  Some Prefer Nettles 168
Tărîţă, Dora, ED: diacritic neeede 186
Taub, Yermiyahu Ahron 120
Tejada, Roberto 304
terrorist attacks of September 11, 2001 17, 148, 153–5
textual engagement, degree of 161
textual production, historical circumstances of 176
A Thousand and One Nights 11. See also *Arabian Nights* (*Alf layla wa layla*, also known as the *1001 Nights*)
Tolstoy, Leo 101, 105 n.6, 106–7
  Anna Karenina 16, 101, 105–8
  War and Peace 102, 105–6
Tonkin, Humphrey 12, 16, 79–100
tonton macoutes 218
tourism 143, 188, 274
tradition 120
  modernity and 17
translation. See also *specific languages; specific literatures; specific writers*
  acknowledgment of 5–6
  as activism 278, 298
  as a business 267–71

contextual analysis and 187
as hallucination 269
historical consciousness and 115–16
as inherently personal 254
innovation and 12–13
as liberation 268–9
as map of the world 78
as part of a classic's future 203–13
reading through lens of 2–4
retranslation 8–12, 101–8, 179, 180
role in creating classics 195–6
as storytelling 137–45
survival of works and 225–6
without knowing the original 20, 69
translation experiments 20, 273–80
translation pedagogy 1–3
Translation Review 1–23
translators. *See also specific translators*
acknowledgment of 5–6
power of 195–6
translator-centered approach 7–8
trauma 112, 116, 161, 193, 260, 262
travel 188. *See also* tourism
Tsvetaeva, Marina 121
Tucci, Maria 180, 181
Tupinambá 36–7
Turgenev, Ivan 101
Fathers and Children 102
Turkish 14, 19, 173, 174
Turkish literature 19, 237–48, 240 n.5
Turkish modernism 240 n.5
Turner, Andrew 52
Turner, Frederick Jackson 301
Tussman, Malka Heifetz 115
typography 172–6

undecidability 31
Universal Esperanto Association 95
Universal Postal Union 88
University of Iowa, International Writing Program 72, 74
University of London 87
University of Rochester 128
University of Texas Press 71
University of Virginia Press 231
Urquhart, Thoma, *Logopandecteision* 84
US Immigration Customs Enforcement (ICE) 297, 306
US imperialism 195–6, 218, 225, 275–6, 297
US-Mexico border 296, 306

Valdéz, Luis 304
Valéry, Paul 267
Vallienne, Henri 95
La vanguardia 12–13
Vaudeville, Charlotte 72
Venuti, Lawrence 4, 7, 10
Verdery, Katherine 185
vernacularization 184
Vieux, Marie. *See* Vieux-Chavet, Marie
Vieux-Chavet, Marie 19, 216 nn.1–2
Amour, Colère et Folie (*Love, Anger, Madness*) 19, 215–36
Les Rapaces 216, 224, 224 n.8, 226, 230
Vinokur 215
Virgil 64, 65
Aeneid 95
Vivieros de Castro, Eduardo 35–6
vocabulary 241–3
Volapük 89
the *Volk* 87
Voltaire (François-Marie Arouet) 85
Vuillard, Edward 72

Waldie, D. J. 302
Walser, Robert 143
Walsh, Andrew Samuel 9

Wang, Helen 6
Warhol, Andy 157
Weaver, William 60
Weil, Roberto 13
Weinreich, Max 113
Weinreich, Uriel 117
Welch, Raquel 305
Welles, Orson 28, 29
Weltliteratur 6, 86, 93
Wevill, David 71
White, Steven F. 1, 8
white supremacism 298
Whitman, Walt 15, 152
Wiesel, Elie 111
  Night 111 n.1
Wilkins, John 84
  Essay Towards a Real Character and a Philosophical Language 84
Williams, William Carlos 73–5, 77
  Autobiography 75–6
  "The Red Wheelbarrow" 73–6
Williamson, Nels 302
Wilson, A. N. 106
Wilson, Betty 220
Wilson, Emily 52, 53, 55, 57, 142
Wishaw, Frederick 102
women writers 254–5. See also specific writers
  Arabic 197–8
  excluded from "canon" 115
  in Yiddish 118–19 (*see also specific writers*)
  Women Writers of Yiddish Literature 121
Wood, Michelle 7
Woods, John E. 137, 143
Woods, Michelle 14
Words without Borders 258
world literature 6, 86, 93
"world self-consciousness" 88, 92
World War I 85
World War II 111

Yale French Studies 233
Yale University Press 106–7
Yatsushiro, Sachiko 173
Yiddish 14, 16–17, 83, 269
  classics of European literature and 114–15
  decline of 112
  golden age of 120, 121
  history of 113
  as "language of fusion" 116
  as language of the diaspora 121
  recent emergency as "literary" language 113–14
  vocabulary of 117
  as "wandering language" 121
Yiddish classics 111–23
  feminist view on 118–19
  literary genres and 115
  migration and 115
Yiddish culture, plurilingualism and 114
Yiddishists, *vs.* Hebraists 113, 113 n.4
Yiddishland 112
Yiddish literature 111–23
  anthologies of 118, 120–1
  feminist view on 118–19
  issues and challenges in translating 116–18
  literary genres and 115
  migration and 115
  modernism and 114
  in North America 114
  standardization and 116, 117
Yiddish women writers 118–19. *See also specific writers*
Yip, Wai Lim 190
YIVO 113
Young, Loretta 305

Zajko, Vanda 7
Zambreno, Kate 255
Zamenhof, L. L. 81–4, 81 n.1, 90–3
  anti-Semitism and 83, 91–2

Dua Libro (Second Book)   83–4
importance of literature to his
   project   93
Lingvaj Respondoj   93
move away from Zionism   92
translation and   93–5
translation of Shakespeare's
   Hamlet   93–4
Unua Libro (First Book)   83–4,
   91

Zamora, Javier   304
al-Zayyat, Latifa   197, 198
   The Open Door (*Al-Bab
   al-maftuh*)   197
   The Owner of the House (*Sahib
   al-bayt*)   197
   The Search (Awraq Shakhsiyyah:
   Hamlat taftish*)   197
Zielinska-Elliott, Anna   18,
   167–77